WAR AND GOLD

WAR AND GOLD

A FIVE-HUNDRED-YEAR HISTORY OF EMPIRES, ADVENTURES AND DEBT

KWASI KWARTENG

BLOOMSBURY

LONDON · NEW DELHI · NEW YORK · SYDNEY

First published in Great Britain 2014

Copyright © 2014 by Kwasi Kwarteng

The moral right of the author has been asserted

No part of this book may be used or reproduced in any manner
whatsoever without written permission from the publisher except in the
case of brief quotations embedded in critical articles or reviews

Every reasonable effort has been made to trace copyright holders of
material reproduced in this book, but if any have been inadvertently
overlooked the publisher would be glad to hear from them

Bloomsbury Publishing Plc
50 Bedford Square
London
WC1B 3DP

www.bloomsbury.com

Bloomsbury is a trademark of Bloomsbury Publishing Plc

Bloomsbury Publishing, London, New Delhi, New York and Sydney

A CIP catalogue record for this book is available from the British Library

ISBN 978 1 4088 4815 9 (hardback edition)
ISBN 978 1 4088 4816 6 (trade paperback edition)

10 9 8 7 6 5 4 3 2 1

Typeset by Hewer Text UK Ltd, Edinburgh
Printed and bound in Great Britain by CPI Group (UK) Ltd, Croydon CR0 4YY

MIX
Paper from
responsible sources
FSC® C020471

Contents

Introduction

The financial crisis of 2008 spawned an enormous amount of literature, in journalism and in books. Many of these works dealt with the fine details of the conferences, the highly dramatic meetings which took place surrounding the fall of Lehman's, that weekend in September 2008, when global finance itself seemed to be on the verge of the abyss. Many treatments of the crisis have described the aggressive culture of the banks themselves. They have depicted the fabulous wealth of the hedge-fund owners who made, or lost, millions as a result of the credit bubble and bust. Other writers have concentrated on the high level of government indebtedness which existed after the crisis began, as governments poured billions into supporting the financial system. Some observers have even questioned the nature of paper money and credit itself, suggesting that the adoption of paper money led inevitably to the collapse of 2008.

This book adopts a longer view of the events surrounding the financial crisis and its consequences. The financial crisis naturally elicited many reflections on the nature of money and credit, on the nature of the banking system, and even on the future of capitalism. To anybody interested in a wider context, the events of 2008 also prompted some consideration of how such a fragile system had developed. It was partly motivated by a desire to understand this background that I began research for this book. *War and Gold* attempts to tell a narrative story about the history of money from the time of the Spanish conquistadors and their discovery of the New World.

Of course, anyone so bold as to attempt a history of money needs to decide where to start. Accounts of money and currencies have sometimes started with the Old Testament, with the Greeks; some have even found the origins of money in prehistoric times. This book is less ambitious. The starting point of the Spanish conquistadors was chosen mainly because I share the view of John Maynard Keynes when he wrote that 'the modern age opened . . . with the accumulation of capital which began in the sixteenth century'. This, according to Keynes's assessment, was a result of the stimulus provided by the 'treasure of gold and silver which Spain brought from the New World into the Old'.[1] This influx of gold and silver which led to higher prices is consequently the subject of the first chapter of this book.

The Spanish conquest of parts of the New World is often cited as the most extreme example of the West's colonial expansion. The ruthless single-mindedness with which the Spanish sought gold and silver led to tragic scenes of devastation, both social and physical, in Central and Southern America. From the point of view of the historian of finance, the scene is more prosaic. Inca gold and silver were used to support the spending of the Habsburg monarchs of Spain. It was in this respect that the conquistadors' efforts were both significant for the history of money and paradoxical, since the Spanish monarchy, despite the wealth it had acquired in the New World, was almost always indebted and often was compelled to declare bankruptcy.

It is a premise of this book that government finance, the need to accumulate treasure, whether by conquest, by borrowing or by taxation, provides a powerful impetus behind developments in society. This idea was expressed by the great Austrian economist Joseph Schumpeter in his article 'The Crisis of the Tax State', published in 1919.[2] More specifically, this book argues that the needs of government spending, in particular relating to war finance, are responsible for the development of what is often thought of as a narrow and specialist field, that of monetary history. Currency arrangements – the gold standard, which tied the value of a currency to a fixed amount of gold, Bretton Woods, the Smithsonian Agreement of 1971 – have been brokered in the aftermath, or have collapsed under the pressure, of war. It is fiscal policy – the character of a government's spending and taxation – that provides the context for monetary policy. Fiscal policies clearly have an additional significance in times of war, but in the modern welfare state government spending plays just as central a role in the lives of most citizens. This fact establishes what may be termed the 'primacy of fiscal policy' and is a reason why much of the political debate in Western democracies is centred on the nature of public spending: how much should be spent? How much should the government borrow? What should the government spend this money on? What tax levels are best suited to maximizing government income?

By contrast, monetary debates, regarding levels of interest rates and, even more technically, quantities of money which should be injected into the economy, tend to be the preserve of a specialist cadre of central bankers and, occasionally, politicians who have arrogated to themselves the responsibility in such matters. The historic record on what I call the 'primacy of fiscal policy' is clear. It was under pressure to defend militarily their vast dominions that the Habsburgs of Spain promoted gold and silver exploration in the New World. It was under pressure to finance the Nine Years' War, which lasted from 1688 to 1697, that William III's government established the Bank of England. John Law's fantastic scheme of paper money was a failed attempt to convert French government debt into equity. Law was attempting to restore France's public finances after two decades of war.

Similarly, the pressures of revolutionary wars forced both the Americans and the French to issue paper money in unprecedented amounts. The British suspended gold payments in 1797, under pressure of war. It is often forgotten that it was only after these experiments in paper money during the eighteenth century that the famous stability of the gold standard was reached. The gold standard, itself a symbol of permanence and immutability, was developed after the relative chaos generated by the paper currencies of the American and French Revolutions, and the suspension of gold payments by the Bank of England. The gold standard seemed, to contemporaries and supporters, a simple, almost natural idea, an expression of the 'spontaneous order' of the free-market system. Yet the almost universal adoption of the gold standard at the end of the nineteenth century is an excellent example of the dictum uttered by the great British legal historian F. W. Maitland: 'Simplicity is the outcome of technical subtlety; it is the goal not the starting point.'[3] The apparent ease and simplicity with which the gold standard was believed to operate marked the end, and not the beginning, of a process which had evolved over 200 years.

It was a world war which first overturned the certainties of the nineteenth-century gold standard. Governments, under the immense pressure of unprecedented industrialized warfare, were forced to spend colossal quantities of money. These sums of money were found by borrowing and printing money. Gold payments were suspended. The gold standard was put to one side, as governments borrowed ever greater sums and issued paper money. A partial result of all this paper money was a hyperinflation in Germany in the 1920s which even today symbolizes the chaos of runaway inflation and continues to influence German politicians and the German people. The people and politicians were, however, so attached to the memory of the gold standard that many attempted to bring it back. Winston Churchill, as Britain's Chancellor of the Exchequer, famously went back to gold in 1925 at the same rate of $4.86 to £1 which had prevailed before 1914.

The Depression of the 1930s and the exigencies of another world war seemed finally to resolve any lingering doubts about the efficacy of a gold standard. The Second World War was financed by borrowing, unbacked by any form of commodity standard. At the end of the war, all the belligerents faced an enormous burden of public debt. Yet, rather to the surprise of many politicians at the time, the monetary arrangements established by the Bretton Woods Agreement of 1944 still put gold at the centre of the system. This time it would be the dollar, and not the pound sterling, which would be the anchor of the new monetary order. But it was significant that a role was still envisaged for gold. After the stresses of two world wars and the trauma of the Depression, it was remarkable that any role for gold was found in the new international currency arrangements.

This shows the extent to which gold was seen as a symbol of stability. Gold itself was inextricably bound up with notions of what a currency should be. It is amusing and also significant to notice that in Ian Fleming's *Goldfinger*, published in 1959, the object of Auric Goldfinger's ambition is the sabotage of the US gold supply in Fort Knox.[4] The move back to some form of 'gold exchange standard' was an attempt to restore a degree of order to a world still devastated by world war and depression. This development reveals a theme and dynamic in the book. My original working title for *War and Gold* was 'Order and Chaos', since it seemed to me that the history of money could be understood as an oscillation between these two conditions. Periods of monetary chaos, such as followed the introduction of the French revolutionary assignat or the American 'continental' paper money, were followed by periods of relative order, exemplified by the gold standard. In much the same way, the relative order of the Bretton Woods arrangements, which lasted almost three decades, followed the disorder of the 1920s and 1930s. It could be argued that the post-1971 settlement, in which currencies were allowed to float freely against one another without any reference to gold, was a period of relative chaos.

Many writers, as a consequence of the 2008 crisis, have suggested that the abandonment of dollar convertibility into gold in 1971 marked the beginning of a process which resulted in the almost limitless extension of credit, upon the basis of paper money. In a moderate and lucidly written account of our modern monetary arrangements, entitled appropriately *Paper Promises*, Philip Coggan, a British financial journalist, has written that the world 'now operates with a system where money can be created at will or by decree' ('fiat money' as it is known in the jargon). He added that paper money is always a claim on someone else, whether a bank or a government. This was also the same with gold-backed money. The difference with paper money is that it can be 'issued', to use the quasi-technical term, at will. Paper money led, in Coggan's view, to a sharp increase in debt. 'It is no coincidence that debt levels have exploded in the last forty years, culminating in the credit crisis of 2007 and 2008.'[5]

Debt, particularly government debt, has now been the focus of dozens of studies. It is a theme of this book that the link between paper currencies and excessive debts was well established by the beginning of the eighteenth century. Certainly by the end of that century, as a consequence of the highly conspicuous examples of French and American revolutionary finance, paper money was associated principally with indebtedness. Such eighteenth-century luminaries as Edmund Burke, Thomas Jefferson and David Hume were all fervent in their denunciations of paper money.

Today government debt and deficits are arguably the greatest challenge facing the developed economies of the world. In a widely cited book, *This Time is Different: Eight Centuries of Financial Folly*, Carmen Reinhart and Kenneth Rogoff analysed the nature of government indebtedness over 800 years of 'financial folly'. Debt crises have been punctuating world history for centuries, as governments continued to spend beyond their resources. This is the theme of Reinhart and Rogoff's work.[6] My book implicitly argues a rather different case. Britain during the nineteenth century and the United States for much of the twentieth century sustained a remarkable degree of fiscal equilibrium, largely backed by a commitment to 'hard money', to the gold standard.

War and Gold does not advocate a return to the gold standard of the pre-1914 era. It simply tries to tell the story of some of the monetary developments which have shaped government in the last 500 years. It would be wrong, though, at this point not to mention that the conduct of British public finance in the century between the defeat of Napoleon in 1815 and the outbreak of the First World War in 1914 was one of the most remarkable fiscal performances of any government. This, of course, was the era of the gold standard. What was remarkable was that in 1818 Britain's nominal debt stood at £843 million and in 1914 the nominal figure was actually lower at £706 million.[7] The 1818 figure represented approximately 250 per cent of GDP, whereas the 1914 figure was barely 25 per cent. This was a substantial achievement, perhaps unequalled in the history of public finance over so long a stretch of time. It is striking that this achievement was built upon the basis of a gold currency and balanced budgets. 'Between 1816 and 1899 the UK government ran a deficit in excess of 1 per cent of GNP in only four years,' wrote Niall Ferguson in *The Cash Nexus*.[8] As A. J. P. Taylor remarked in *The Origins of the Second World War*, people 'reared in the stable economic world of the later nineteenth century' simply assumed that 'a country could not flourish without a balanced budget and a gold currency'.[9] Together with the Bank of England, the British Treasury, situated in Whitehall, was the physical embodiment of the doctrine of sound money and balanced budgets.

When speaking of 'doctrine' in terms of public policy, we are inevitably confronted with the notion of theory, in particular economic theory. The extent to which theories inform the decisions of practical bankers and politicians is sometimes the subject of debate. As so often, Keynes pronounced with quasi-Messianic authority on this subject towards the very end of his great work *The General Theory of Employment, Interest and Money*. Many have subsequently accepted these eloquent words as the gospel truth: 'Practical men, who believe themselves to be quite exempt from any intellectual influences, are usually the slaves of some defunct economist.'[10] It is unclear how far the practices of the British Treasury in the nineteenth century, that is the balanced budgets espoused successively by Peel and Gladstone, can be attributed to any particular 'defunct economist'. Keynes himself was an economist and it was natural for him to hold a high opinion of the influence of his fellow professionals. Those practical men of Victorian London would simply have described what they did in terms of common sense, or 'prudence'.

It is true that both Adam Smith and David Ricardo had promoted the notion of the balanced budget, but it does not automatically follow that their theories actually affected British government policy in so direct a manner. Indeed, it had been the practice of the British Treasury to run small surpluses in peacetime from the very beginning of the eighteenth century, well before the publication of Adam Smith's *Wealth of Nations* in 1776. The concept of a 'sinking fund' whereby budget surpluses could be used to pay off debt had been established by Robert Walpole as early as 1716. It 'worked quite effectively in the 1720s and early 1730s'.[11] Anyone who has spoken about taxation and public spending to a finance minister ahead of an actual budget will be aware of how often intensely political considerations outweigh the finer points of theory.

This book is a work of history. It is not a tract of economic theory. It uses fairly basic economic concepts as one might find them in newspapers and financial journalism. As John Kenneth Galbraith wrote, at the start of his entertaining history of money, *Money: Whence It Came, Where It Went*, 'The reader should proceed in these pages in the knowledge that money is nothing more or less than what he or she always thought it was – what is commonly offered or received for the purchase or sale of goods, services or other things.'[12] Attempts to give more theoretically robust definitions of money have tended to be incoherent or too abstruse to be useful. Some will, of course, be disappointed that their favourite anecdotes or episodes of financial history have been omitted. Any attempt to write about the history of money, within a single volume, will be found equally at fault. To construct such a narrative is, of its nature, an exercise in simplification, omission and condensation. The book simply attempts to tell a story in a linear, narrative way. *War and Gold* has been conceived under the conviction that an understanding of basic chronology is essential to the historian's craft. Without some chronological framework, history too often mutates into economics, sociology or even political theory. It is in this sense that *War and Gold* aspires to give an account of the history of money in the modern age.

PART I

Gold: The Establishment of Order, c.1500–1914

I

Sweat of the Sun

The gout-ridden old man sat still throughout the ceremony, with his ill-fitting spectacles, in the pomp of the Great Hall of the Palace in Brussels. The Hall itself was adorned with rich tapestries, including one which depicted scenes from the life of Gideon, the great slayer of the Midianites. Charles V, Holy Roman Emperor, had decided to abdicate his throne and this ceremony, on Tuesday 25 October 1555, was the culminating point in a series of acts by which he relinquished his power. As hereditary ruler of the Netherlands, Charles had summoned the Estates General, a kind of parliament, to appear before him, as witnesses of this ultimate act of self-abnegation.[1]

The Emperor then proceeded to give a justification of his life. From the moment of his election as Holy Roman Emperor in 1519, Charles had been burdened by extraordinary commitments. His life as emperor had been marked by a seemingly endless succession of military campaigns against rival European monarchs, particularly the French King, Francis, against the Ottoman Turks and, latterly, against heresy and revolt in Germany. As head of the Habsburg imperial family, as the inheritor, through his mother, of the Spanish crown, Charles had undertaken military commitments that had caused a financial crisis. In the course of his reign, he had managed to raise unprecedented loans from the financial centres of Western Europe. Between 1520 and 1532, he had borrowed 5.4 million ducats. By the end of his tenure of the imperial crown, between 1552 and 1556, the amount borrowed had risen to 9.6 million ducats. (In today's values that is about US$600 million and US$1 billion respectively, taking gold at $1,000 an ounce.) The ducat was a Venetian coin introduced in 1284 which, alongside the Florentine florin, was the most widely used coin in Europe throughout the medieval and early modern period.[2] This increase in costs had been accompanied by a rise in the interest rate which Charles had to pay his bankers. Having paid about 18 per cent annual interest on loans taken in the 1520s, he was required to pay almost 50 per cent in the 1550s.[3]

Charles's son Philip, a slight man in his late twenties, with blond hair and the famous protruding jaw of the Habsburgs, faced enormous financial difficulties. He resorted to a drastic expedient. On his full accession in July 1556, the young monarch discovered that all the Spanish revenues had been pledged to repay loans and interest. Faced with this prospect, he simply suspended all payments to his bankers in January 1557.[4] The device of declaring bankruptcy was a trick Philip played several times. On 1 September 1575, Philip announced the second bankruptcy of his reign. The suspension of payments to the bankers for a second time led to unrest among the Spanish troops in the Netherlands, their frustration stemming from their lack of pay. As the months went by, the soldiers grew increasingly wild. On 4 and 5 November they sacked the city of Antwerp. This event has been long remembered as the 'Spanish fury' at Antwerp of 1576.[5]

The humiliating declarations of bankruptcy, the constant need for more money, had not been anticipated when the great discovery of New World treasure had been made. The windfall of the gold and silver from the Indies was a subject which the historians and court writers of the Spanish court celebrated in fulsome prose. Referring to Charles V, Pedro Mexía wrote in his *Historia del emperador Carlos V* (1545) that 'God kept for this prince the great favor and good fortune of discovering the provinces of Peru, where such a great treasure of gold and silver was hidden, the like of which past centuries have never seen, nor do I think that the coming ones will believe.'[6]

The circumstances under which the gold and silver of the Americas had poured into Spain had been extraordinary. A handful of Spanish adventurers, in the first decades after the discovery of America by Christopher Columbus in 1492, had conquered and practically enslaved an entire continent, unknown to Europeans in previous centuries. The Spanish discovery of the New World has been called the 'greatest event in history'.[7] Its protagonists, men such as Hernando Cortés and Francisco Pizarro, became celebrated in their own lifetimes. Among the native populations, the Spanish were regarded as supermen, endowed with magical powers and equally superhuman greed. 'Even if the snows of the Andes turned to gold still they would not be satisfied,' observed Manco, the Inca noble who encountered Pizarro in the 1530s. In Mexico, Cortés told the Aztecs that he and his men 'suffered from a disease of the heart which is only cured by gold'.[8] The initial impetus behind the voyages of discovery had been to find gold, coupled with the sheer lust for adventure which young men in many different cultures have felt. The minds of young Spaniards, in the years after 1492, were roused, in the words of W. H. Prescott, the great American historian of the Spanish conquest of Peru, by 'flaming pictures of an El Dorado where the sands sparkled with gems and golden pebbles as large as birds' eggs'.[9] The young conquistador and contemporary historian Pedro Cieza de León was inspired to sail to Peru after seeing large heaps of Inca gold being unloaded in Seville: 'As long as I live I cannot get it out of my mind.'[10]

Hernan Cortés himself was the archetypal conquistador. Born in about 1480 to a family of the lesser nobility, he received a literary education at the University of Salamanca, where he is said to have learned Latin, but was unsuited to the sedentary life of a state official or a priest. He had first gone to the Indies in 1506. He combined several contradictory elements in his character; cautious and serene, he boasted an outward disdain for material comforts and yet had a notorious appetite for women, and the list of his sexual conquests during his military campaign in Mexico is long. Despite the ambivalences of his nature, no one has disputed the scale, even if accomplished at a high price in human lives, of what was achieved in the conquest of Mexico. Cortés always showed himself to be an excellent commander, with an outstandingly even temperament, who could always improvise creatively in adversity. He spoke to his men in a steady, unruffled tone which often proved inspirational.[11]

Cortés's exploits in Mexico were rivalled by those of Francisco Pizarro in Peru. Both men, like the other conquistadors, endured uncommon hardships in the pursuit of their calling, but they were often cruel. The 'physical toughness' and 'sheer determination' of the conquistadors have 'certainly never been surpassed . . . Nor can we readily call to mind their equals in duplicity, greed, and utterly callous and unbridled cruelty.'[12] The success Pizarro enjoyed in Peru was even more spectacular than Cortés's triumphs in Mexico, though Pizarro had far fewer soldiers. But, regardless of the relative merits of the military campaigns in Peru and Mexico, the result was a considerable flow of gold and particularly of silver into Spain which, over the coming decades, would transform the economy of Western Europe.

Francisco Pizarro had been born in Trujillo, a town in Extremadura in Castile, in the late 1470s. He was in fact a distant cousin of Hernan Cortés, whose grandmother, Leonor, had been a Pizarro. As he was the illegitimate son of a soldier, Francisco Pizarro's prospects were unfavourable, and reports that he had been a swineherd in his youth are plausible, since pigs were important in the local economy.[13] Despite being illiterate and poor, he was bold and determined. As early as 1502, he had left Spain to travel to the New World and had, over the years, made a fortune in the new Spanish colony of Panama. In 1532, accompanied by a mere 168 men, he arrived in Peru. These men were mostly in their mid-twenties to early thirties; they constituted more of a gang than a regular battalion of soldiers, and there was 'the spirit of a gold rush' about the expedition, combined with the 'conviction of a crusade'. They came to the New World to better themselves, to 'be worth more [*valer más*]', in the language of their time, which meant the acquisition not only of wealth but also of honour and social status.[14] These men were generally drawn from the dispossessed, the poor and aspiring. Only about a quarter of the 168 men who followed Pizarro could claim any trace of lineage from the gentry, and none was entitled to be addressed as 'don', which was at the time reserved for those in Castile who had close family ties to the nobility.[15]

Pizarro himself has been described as a man with a 'reputation for leadership', coupled with extraordinary stamina which enabled him to endure the most arduous conditions. Like many good leaders, he had an easy manner and was popular with his men. To his own men, or to those of the Inca who had won his favour, he was modest and gentle. His clothing was austere, even old-fashioned, since he never abandoned the black cassock he had worn in his youth. Later, in a more expansive mood, he would often wear the fur coat which Cortés, his cousin and fellow conquistador, had sent him from Mexico. Yet, in contrast to the generally affable manner he showed to his countrymen, he could be ruthless when he needed to be, and would kill Indians sometimes just to gain a psychological advantage.[16]

It was fortunate for Pizarro and his gang of ambitious men, eager for gold and treasure, that the Inca empire was riven by civil war at the very moment of the Spaniards' arrival. The last independent ruler of Peru, Huayna Capac, reigned over his empire from 1498 till 1527; he was inactive and ill, perhaps from syphilis. On his death, he left two sons, Huascar, a son by his first wife, and Atahualpa, a son by his second wife, a princess from a northern tribe conquered by the Inca. Huayna had apparently considered giving both of his sons a portion of the kingdom, with Atahualpa ruling the northern part and Huascar, the elder brother, the southern. On the old Emperor's death, each of his sons, unwilling to compromise, wanted the entire inheritance for himself.[17] There was launched a fierce civil war in which Atahualpa triumphed. It was the context of the civil war which allowed Pizarro and his small band to achieve their dramatic successes.

The contest between Pizarro and Atahualpa, the encounter of two different cultures and mentalities, has fascinated historians and dramatists ever since. In *The Royal Hunt of the Sun*, the playwright Peter Shaffer portrays Atahualpa and Pizarro as representatives of two opposed civilizations. In Act II of the play, Atahualpa tells Pizarro, 'You want gold. I know. Speak,' to which Pizarro simply responds with the direct question, 'You have gold?' Atahualpa replies: 'It is the sweat of the sun. It belongs to me.'[18] The process by which Atahualpa fell into Pizarro's hands seems almost miraculous. The Spanish accomplished what they had done in Mexico, effectively seizing the head of the empire and taking control by this means. It was the ultimate 'decapitation' strategy. Cortés had done this successfully by imprisoning Montezuma; Pizarro did the same to Atahualpa. It is easy to portray the Spanish as cruel, pitiless warriors who showed no mercy or compassion to their Indian subjects, but one should remember the sanguinary nature of the Inca empire. Atahualpa himself made no attempt to conceal his intentions towards the Spanish. He had intended to capture Pizarro and to take and breed the Spanish horses, which were what he admired most about the invaders. He would then have sacrificed some of the Spanish soldiers to the sun, the god from whom the Inca emperors claimed descent; others he would have castrated to serve as eunuchs in his household and guard his women.[19] The Inca Emperor was surprised by the sheer audacity and nerve of the Spanish. Armed with guns and artillery they set a brilliant trap for him. Having invited him for talks at dinner in Cajamarca, a town situated in the Andes mountains at an altitude of 9,500 feet, they prepared an ambush in which 7,000 Incas were killed. Atahualpa himself was captured. It was at this point that the Inca leader offered his notorious ransom.

Pizarro asked Atahualpa how much treasure he would give the Spanish to buy his liberty. Atahualpa, seemingly nonchalant, answered that he would give a room full of gold. The room measured 22 feet long by 17 feet wide and would be filled, according to the Inca leader, up to 8 feet high in various objects of gold – 'jars, pots, tiles and other pieces'.[20] Atahualpa also promised to give an even greater quantity of silver – the 'tears of the moon', as the Incas called it. All of this, he promised, would be delivered in two months. During their stay in Cajamarca, the Spanish observed that Atahualpa was about 'thirty years of age, of good appearance and manner, although somewhat thick-set'. He had a 'large face, handsome and fierce, his eyes were reddened with blood'. He spoke, they observed, 'with much gravity, as a great ruler'.[21]

After months of captivity, and after he had provided ample gold and silver to his captors, Atahualpa was tried on trumped-up charges of betraying the Spanish. Pizarro accused him of seeking to escape and ordering an army to set him at liberty. The conclusion of this episode was perhaps inevitable, given the conquistadors' single-minded search for gold, and their vulnerability in a strange land, thousands of miles from Spain. On 26 July 1533, trumpets greeted Atahualpa as he was led into the main plaza of Cajamarca. He was placed by Pizarro on a wooden plank. Almost by way of mockery, the unfortunate Inca monarch, a former ruler of one of the largest empires in the world, was ministered to by the priest the Spanish had brought, Father Valverde. Atahualpa was briefly instructed in the articles of a faith he barely understood. The Inca bizarrely requested the rite of baptism which was carried out. He received the name 'Francisco', perhaps in honour of his captor. After the formal ceremonies, Atahualpa was garrotted.[22]

The background to the conquest of the Incas is important because Peru was the most significant source of the gold and silver that flooded into Europe. The term 'Peru' applied in the sixteenth century 'to the whole of South America, not just to the territories which bear this name today'.[23] The empire of Atahualpa, the last Sapa Inca, or emperor, had abounded in gold and silver. It was in Peru that the largest mining discovery in the New World was made. In April 1545, a minor Indian nobleman, called Diego Gualpa by the Spanish, climbed a hill in search of a shrine and was thrown to the ground by a strong gust of wind. He found himself gripping silver ore with his hands and reported the discovery to some sceptical Spanish adventurers near by. On further investigation, five rich veins of silver were discovered at Potosí, where a silver rush quickly followed.[24] It was silver and not gold which in the eyes of the world 'became the symbol of quickly made fortunes'. To the French of the sixteenth century the term 'Peru' simply became a synonym for fabulous wealth.[25]

The Potosí deposits in Peru, situated in modern Bolivia, were described as 'a "silver mountain" of six miles around its base on a remote and desolate plateau, 12,000 feet above sea level'. The city built after this discovery rapidly grew in size, peopled entirely by immigrants. In 1555, only ten years after that discovery, the population of Potosí had risen from nothing to 45,000. It climbed to a peak of 160,000 just fifty-five years later in 1610.[26] The voluntary labour of many immigrants was supplemented by conscripted teams of miners, employed under the *mita* system, which prescribed that a number of Indian villages within a certain radius of Potosí should provide a quota of their population to work in the mines. This system itself was abolished only in 1812. Each year the Indians of the prescribed region had to send 'roughly a seventh of all adult males to work in the mines and refining mills of Potosí' – about 13,500 men, it has been estimated. The furthest village or town that the *mitayos* were expected to come from was Cuzco, the historic capital of the Inca empire, from which recruits would travel for two months across the Andes to complete the 600-mile journey. Once in Potosí, the *mitayos* were obliged to work only one week in three, and their chiefs accordingly divided the indentured men into three shifts when they arrived. The working conditions in the mines themselves became a byword for hardship and cruelty. The indentured *mitayo* had to work twelve hours a day, with only an hour's break at noon, in a mine up to 500 feet deep, where the air was 'thick and evil-smelling, trapped in the bowels of the earth', and where tough physical work would be undertaken in near-darkness, with only candlelight as a source of illumination.[27]

The Spanish Crown did not own, or manage, mines directly. The Habsburgs' share of the profits from the mineral wealth of the New World took the form of a tax, the *quinto real*, or royal fifth. As its name implied, this was a 20 per cent royalty fee imposed on every ounce of gold and silver extracted from the New World which came into Seville, the only permissible entry port into Europe for the Spanish treasures from further west. In a period just short of 160 years, from 1503 to 1660, it has been estimated that 16,000 metric tonnes of silver arrived at Seville, enough to triple the existing silver resources of Europe, while only 185 metric tonnes of gold entered Seville from the New World during the same period, which increased Europe's gold supplies by only a fifth.[28] Silver was the key element of the imaginary wealth of Spain. The wealth was imaginary because its effects on the Spanish monarchy were unexpected and would lead, in the long run, to bankruptcy and a diminution in the power of Spain in world affairs.

To understand the rather unexpected effect of the influx of gold and silver, we have to consider the general strategic context of the sixteenth century. Spain did not use its new-found wealth to build any infrastructure, or to increase its long-term productive potential. Rather, it 'dissipated its New World-based wealth on the first global war'.[29] New World silver was used to pay for troops to wage war successively against the French, the Turks, the German Protestant princes and the Dutch. Habsburg Spain was perpetually at war, and the resources of the New World were expended lavishly to pay for these campaigns. According to Earl Hamilton, the great American scholar of the Imperial Spanish New World economy, 'historians have generally agreed that American gold and silver fanned the flames of Habsburg imperialism'. This gold and silver 'furnished sinews of war' and 'constituted an important factor in Spain's aggressive foreign policy'.[30] Within Spain itself, it was the port of Seville which gained from the trade in gold and silver from the New World. It was in Seville that the House of Trade, a government bureau for the regulation and development of New World commerce, was established. Seville was also the location for the Council of the Indies, and it is in Seville that the extraordinary archives, documenting five centuries of the Spanish American empire, are housed in the Archivo General de Indias. It is no accident that four of the most widely performed operas in the modern era – Mozart's *The Marriage of Figaro* and *Don Giovanni*, Rossini's *Barber of Seville* and Bizet's *Carmen* – are set in this city, which in 2011 had a population of only 700,000. Seville in the sixteenth and seventeenth centuries was one of the greatest financial centres of the world. As if to entrench its position, in 1572 Philip II declared the town the only legal terminus of the American trade, a status which was kept in law until 1717.[31] In Seville, the flow of bullion offered an unrivalled opportunity to 'acquire great wealth in trading' which 'lured both the local nobility and businessmen from abroad and from other regions of Spain'.[32]

The Habsburgs were unfortunate in so far as their bid for European hegemony coincided with a revolution in military technology which led to a 'massive increase in the scale, costs and organization of war'.[33] Charles V managed to raise loans on the basis of the steady stream of gold and silver coming into Spain. Lacking a central bank, the Spanish Crown relied on private bankers, particularly from Genoa but most notably from the Fuggers of Augsburg, to whom the Habsburgs were close in the first quarter of the sixteenth century. In 1519, Jakob Fugger had famously contributed the largest proportion of Charles V's electoral expenses in his successful campaign to become the Holy Roman Emperor. Fugger contributed 530,000 florins out of the 850,000 which were spent in bribing the electors. (In terms of modern gold prices, this contribution was roughly US$60 million, assuming a gold price of $1,000 an ounce.)

Fugger openly boasted of his influence, declaring in a letter to Charles in April 1523 that '[it] is publicly notorious and clear as the day that, had it not been for me, you would not have been able to obtain the Roman crown'.[34] Unlike modern government bonds, which are open to the public to buy, the loans which the Fuggers gave Charles derived largely from their own personal fortunes. The sale of Spanish government debt (*juros*) to a wider public did not begin until the 1540s when officials discovered that merchants trading at the great fairs of Antwerp and Lyons were eager to buy shares in government loans.[35] A further problem of financial engineering arose from the desire of the Spanish soldiers on campaign to be paid in gold coins. As already remarked, the influx of silver from the New World was far more significant than that of gold, and consequently it was an important task of the bankers to convert the silver into gold. This was done efficiently, and it is likely that the Genoese bankers, in the service of the Spanish Crown, used American silver to purchase existing stocks of European gold coin.[36] American silver would find its way to the Spanish Netherlands which acted as a 'distribution centre from which . . . [it] passed to Germany, Northern Europe and the British Isles'.[37]

The biggest economic effect of the discovery of the New World was the inflation which occurred as a result of the greater supply of precious metals. Prices in Spain in the first quarter of the seventeenth century were more than three times as high as a hundred years previously, and though this does not seem to be a huge increase in the level of prices compared to modern developments, for contemporaries it marked a significant change.[38] One Spanish commentator remarked in 1551 that in Spain 'in times when money was scarcer, sellable goods and labor were given for very much less than after the discovery of the Indies, which flooded the country with gold and silver'. Most importantly, it was noticed that the reason behind this development was that 'money is worth more where and when it is scarce than where and when it is abundant'. A year earlier, in 1550, Diego de Covarrubias had lamented that in the recent past 'staple goods, food, and all other human necessities were so inexpensive and the prices so low that with one *real* of the same weight as those of today, once could buy what nowadays one cannot buy with ten, or fifteen, or twenty *reales*'.[39]

Yet, despite these Spanish observations, it was a contemporary Frenchman who has, perhaps unfairly, earned praise for being the first to identify the phenomenon of inflation caused by an increase in the supply of gold and silver. A lawyer, diplomat and political philosopher, Jean Bodin was born in 1530 near Angers in Maine, north-west France. Earl

Hamilton, the American economic historian, commented that 'so far as I know Jean Bodin . . . was the first to demonstrate by careful analysis that the American mines were the principal cause of the Price Revolution'.[40] The doctrine which would later be enshrined in economics as the 'quantity theory of money' is a fundamental one. According to a modern scholar, Bodin 'did indeed formulate a recognisable version of the quantity theory of money' in his *La Response de Jean Bodin à M. de Malestroit*, published in 1568.[41] The quantity theory of money simply states that 'the price level is proportional to the quantity of money'.[42] In Milton Friedman's more rhetorically flamboyant phrasing four centuries later, 'inflation is always and everywhere a monetary phenomenon'.[43] Four centuries earlier, Bodin had been equally forthright in ascribing the causes of price increases: 'The main and almost the only cause (which no one has mentioned until now) is the abundance of gold and silver, which is greater in this kingdom than it has been during the past 400 years.' Bodin was in no doubt that the Spanish were to blame for this increase in prices, since when 'the Spaniard made himself lord of the New World, axes and knives were sold there for more than pearls and precious stones'. As a consequence, 'everything is more expensive in Spain and Italy than in France, and more so in Spain than in Italy'.[44]

Bodin's insight into the monetary significance of the Spanish discovery of the New World was shared by other great economists. In Book I of *The Wealth of Nations*, Adam Smith asserted that the 'discovery of the mines of America diminished the value of gold and silver in Europe'. Smith made the further point that, after the discovery of Potosí, 'the silver mines of Europe were, the greater part of them, abandoned', since the value of silver 'was so much reduced that their produce [of the European silver mines] could no longer pay the expence of working them . . . with a profit'. Turning to England, Smith observed that American silver did not seem 'to have had any very sensible effect upon the price of things in England till after 1570; though even the mines of Potosi had been discovered more than twenty years before'.[45]

Yet, of the modern economists, it was John Maynard Keynes who most frequently returned to the theme of the discovery of the Americas and their effect on the modern world. In 1930 he wrote: 'The modern age opened . . . with the accumulation of capital which began in the sixteenth century. I believe . . . that this was initially due to the rise of prices, and the profits to which that led, which resulted from the treasure of gold and silver which Spain brought from the New World into the Old.'[46]

The possibilities thrown up by the expansion of Spain into the Americas, with the flow of bullion and treasure which accompanied the discovery of new mines, fascinated Keynes. In his *Treatise on Money* (1930), he spoke of the 'profit inflation' which 'commenced in 1519 when the Aztec spoils arrived, and terminated as early as 1588, the year of the Armada'; in a characteristically bold statement, he declared that this profit inflation had 'created the modern world'.[47] He described the initial influx from the booty of Pizarro's Incan conquests and the 'Aztec spoils from Mexico' as 'trifling in amount', recognizing that it was the 'new output of the mines of Potosi and elsewhere which came into being with the aid of improved methods of extraction'.

Like Adam Smith, Keynes noticed that in England inflation set in at a later date. He observed that there 'the sensational rise of prices did not really begin until after 1550, perhaps not until 1560'. According to Keynes, the years 'from (say) 1550 to 1600 were the period of revolutionary price changes, and by 1630 this particular phase of monetary history was at an end'. He linked the period of 'profit inflation' with 'a period of national rise', remarking that, as a consequence of the increase in prices, the English were 'just in a financial position to afford Shakespeare at the moment he presented himself'.[48]

Imperial Spain had developed a market in government debt, the *juros*, known to the financial traders of Antwerp. Yet no central bank had been established to organize government debt. This new institution would be the invention of the Dutch, later adapted by the English. Spain had discovered the New World and brought it into the structure of European power politics; yet other powers, employing more sophisticated instruments of finance, would soon eclipse the Habsburgs. The rise in prices was extremely important because of the boost it gave to the merchant class. As Keynes noted, 'a period of rising prices acts as a stimulus to enterprise and is beneficial to businessmen'. While prices increase, the merchant or manufacturer 'will generally buy before he sells . . . If, therefore, month after month his stock appreciates on his hands [if the prices of his goods increase], he is always selling at a better price than expected . . . In such a period the business of trade becomes unduly easy. Any one [*sic*] who can borrow money and is not exceptionally unlucky must make a profit, which he may have done little to deserve.'[49] It was the stimulus to enterprise given by this general inflation which, in Keynes's view, created the modern world. Meanwhile Spain with its extensive commitments and reckless government spending failed utterly to derive any lasting strategic benefit from the achievements of the conquistadors.

2

Rival Nations – England and France

The need to pay for wars was the principal engine of modern finance. In England, the year 1688 brought about a new settlement, in which King James II was deposed, largely for trying to introduce Roman Catholicism, and a new king, William III, Stadtholder of the Dutch Republic, was invited to take the throne. The first priority of William's government was to engage Britain in a continental war against the power of France, under the reign of its vainglorious king, Louis XIV. The financial innovations introduced, particularly in the City of London, as a consequence of this development have been called collectively 'the Financial Revolution'. More generally, 'England was at war for twenty-nine of the sixty-six years between 1688 . . . and 1756.' This prolonged state of war was waged on an unprecedented scale, involving enormous sums of money, unimaginable to earlier generations. As one historian has written, 'the real cause of conflict was that both England and France were growing in wealth and ambition' and there was 'bitter rivalry' between the two countries 'for influence in Europe and for colonial markets'.[1]

The nature of the Nine Years' War, which took place at the beginning of the period of intermittent warfare I have described, was such that England embarked on new forms of finance. The most significant development was probably the establishment of the Bank of England in 1694. The creation of the Bank, which for the following 200 years was perhaps the most prestigious institution of international finance, arose out of the government's lack of credibility as a borrower. It had been little more than twenty years before, in 1672, that England had experienced its last default, known as the Stop of the Exchequer. During the Stop, Charles II's government simply refused to pay interest on the loans it had been given by several goldsmiths, who were the bankers of the time.

The setting up of the Bank of England allowed the government to borrow more cheaply. The initial amount raised was £1.2 million, at a time when total government spending in any given year was not much more than this sum. This money was raised by individuals pledging or 'subscribing' to lend certain amounts. This involved writing your name and the amount of money pledged in a subscription book. The annual revenue settled on the King by Parliament in 1660 had been £1.2 million.[2] Against this background, the Bank of England was a resounding success. There was an initial cap of £20,000 for each individual subscription. The subscription books were opened in the Mercers' Chapel on 21 June 1694. A total of £300,000, a quarter of the initial sum, was subscribed on the first day. By noon on 2 July, in less than eleven days, the whole of the amount had been raised. There were over 1,200 subscribers and the very first names on the list were those of the King and Queen, who subscribed £10,000 jointly.[3] The Bank of England's first purpose was to act as a 'money-raising machine', its function being to draw on the immense 'fund of credit' which was already perceived to exist within the confines of the City of London.[4] The money raised was given to the government in December 1694 and in return it paid 8 per cent a year, a relatively high rate even at the time, but a sign of how desperately the government needed the funds.[5]

The City of London had already acquired many of the attributes which would mark its future character. It was an exciting place, where men from many different countries could be found, earnestly trying to make their fortune. Alongside such Englishmen as Sir Henry Furnese were others such as Solomon de Medina, of Portuguese Jewish origin, who had been born in Bordeaux around 1650. In a typically cosmopolitan fashion, Medina had learned his trade as a merchant, a trader of goods, in Amsterdam before moving to London in 1670, where he worked in the City. By 1696, he had switched his location to Pall Mall, only a few minutes' walk from the Court of St James's and close to Parliament. Remarkably, in November 1699 William III himself dined at Medina's house in Richmond, and the climax of Medina's career occurred only seven months later, in June 1700, when he was knighted at Hampton Court. To his modern biographer, Medina was the 'the most prominent British Jew in the world of politics and business affairs up to the nineteenth century and [who] in his own day held a position perhaps unparalleled in all Europe'.[6] This may be an exaggeration, but there is no denying the considerable influence Medina enjoyed. This was demonstrated even more strongly when he left England in 1702 to be based once more in Holland, where he could get closer to the war front, whose supplies he so expertly provided.[7]

Medina's role as a government fixer did not involve arranging finance so much as organizing supplies and provisions for armies fighting on the continent. In particular men like Medina and Sir Henry Furnese were involved in the actual organization of payments to the army. They were agents, or middlemen, who supplied clothing, gold coin and other essentials to the military. Furnese himself was something of a prodigy in finance. He was born in Kent in 1658 and was apprenticed aged only fourteen to a London hosier, a tailor specializing in making legwear. After setting up on his own, he used the opportunities offered by the outbreak of the Nine Years' War in 1689 to become rich. He personally clothed several regiments, and loaned his surplus capital to the government. He was knighted in 1691, aged only thirty-three. Being a native-born Englishman, he took advantage of the openings for social advancement. In 1701 he was elected to Parliament. He was a consistent Whig, a man who firmly supported the 1688 Revolution settlement and the principles of finance it had introduced.

As with many financiers since, Furnese's great strength lay in his wide network of contacts and the information he gathered from it. 'Throughout Holland, Flanders, France, and Germany, he maintained a complete and perfect train of intelligence.' So great was his advantage in this respect that, in many instances, the 'temptation to deceive was too great . . . He fabricated news; he insinuated false intelligence.' According to the same account, written in 1850, Furnese 'was the originator of some of those plans which at a later period were managed to much effect by [Nathan] Rothschild' in the early nineteenth century. If Furnese 'wished to buy, his brokers were ordered to look gloomy and mysterious, hint at important news, and after a time sell'. All the eyes of the exchange would be on

Furnese's movements and prices would be lowered if he and his brokers looked in any way downhearted. At this point, Furnese 'would reap the benefit by employing different brokers to purchase as much as possible at the reduced price'.[8]

When he died in 1712, his pride in his career was openly declared in a memorial he had ordered to be erected at his country seat in Waldershare, near Dover in Kent. In the inscription, Furnese expressed his gratitude for 'God's great goodness to me in advancing me to a considerable estate from a very small beginning'.[9] Even in the late seventeenth century, the City of London was known as a place where fortunes could be made from trade and finance. Some might even point to the fifteenth-century story of Dick Whittington and his journey to a London reputed to have streets 'paved with gold' as evidence of the widely held idea that the City was the place to go to if you wanted to become rich from modest beginnings.

London itself, even at this early date, was an established hub of international finance, an open market place where traders from many nations did business. Until 1698 the Royal Exchange was the site of the Stock Exchange. Here, according to an account written in the nineteenth century but relating to a time 150 years previously, were congregated representatives of firms from every civilized nation, including 'the Frenchman with his vivacious tones, the Spaniard with his dignified bearing, the Italian with his melodious tongue', all of whom were to be seen in their national dress – the 'flowing garb of the Turk, the fur-trimmed coat of the Fleming; the long robe of the Venetian . . . the short cloak of the Englishman'.[10]

While London in the 1690s was a thriving commercial centre, in which merchants like Henry Furnese and Solomon de Medina made their fortune, the city also harboured some shadier characters. It was a notorious scene for duelling young men, rakes who indulged in the night life, prostitutes and general debauchery London had to offer. One such energetic dueller of the period was Charles, 4th Baron Mohun, who as a seventeen-year-old peer was acquitted by the House of Lords in 1693 for his part in the murder of William Mountford, a rival of Mohun's friend Captain Richard Hill for the affections of Anne Bracegirdle, a much admired actress. Mohun would die in 1712, at the age of only thirty-seven, in a celebrated duel with the Duke of Hamilton, who was also killed.

Another dueller of this kind, only four years older than Mohun, was John Law, a young Scottish adventurer who had come to England from Scotland in the early 1690s.

Law's background was affluent, and banking was in his blood. Born in 1671 in Scotland, he was the son of a goldsmith and banker who purchased the Lauriston estate near Edinburgh. His father died when Law was only twelve years old, but the young Scotsman had already shown himself a gifted student of algebra and arithmetic. Law was a natural charmer, a handsome man, known as 'Beau Law' in his youth, and addicted to 'all games of chance, skill and dexterity'. Besides his abilities as a card player he was a 'capital player at tennis'. When he came to London, aged about twenty, he immediately distinguished himself by his 'superior personal beauty, ready wit, and engaging manners'. The event which, perhaps more than any other, defined his life was a duel that he fought in 1694, in which he killed Edward Wilson, a rival for the affections of a woman whose identity is unknown. The duel took place in the heart of London's fashionable West End, in Bloomsbury Square, which was then a new development, where the usual excitements of the city could be found. Law was arrested, tried, convicted and sentenced to death within the space of a month.[11]

There remains something of a mystery about John Law's next steps. His sentence evidently was never carried out, but how he managed to escape England is uncertain. He absconded from prison and ended up in Amsterdam. As an itinerant fugitive, he was compelled to live by his wits. He used his arithmetical skills in cards and gambling, eking out a precarious existence. The comparative freedom which his lifestyle afforded him gave time for more general speculation about the nature of money, risk and finance. In Amsterdam, Law's natural curiosity led him to investigate the operations of the 'mysterious bank of Amsterdam', founded in 1609 and the ultimate model and inspiration for the Bank of England.

Despite Law's abilities as a practical gambler and his appetite for the life of a man about town, he also had a strong theoretical bent, and it was this inclination to thinking hard about money which, despite his subsequent notoriety, is his enduring legacy. Very few professional gamblers have written as clearly about finance as he did in his short pamphlet *Money and*

Trade Considered, with a Proposal for Supplying the Nation with Money, which was published in Edinburgh in 1705. To most contemporaries, money meant gold and silver and nothing else. The Spanish had plundered the New World in their search for these precious commodities, which they regarded as the ultimate symbol of wealth. Against these principles, Law advanced the novel idea that paper was 'more qualified for the use of money, than silver'.[12]

The benefit of paper money, according to Law, was that it could stimulate trade. His pamphlet was published in Edinburgh because it had been written to persuade the Scottish Parliament of the potential advantage to be derived from paper credit or paper money. Scotland, in Law's opinion, had a 'very inconsiderable Trade, because she has but a very small part of the money'. Naturally enough, if the stock of money was increased, trade would increase with it. Law attributed the paucity of trade to the scarcity of money. In his own words, very simply put, 'A greater Quantity [of money] employs more People than a lesser Quantity.'[13] Another central component of Law's thinking was that more economic activity would lead to an export surplus. This latter conclusion has not been endorsed by modern economists, but Law's suggestion that the level of output, or 'trade' in his terminology, was related to the quantity of money is an idea which has been persistently espoused by later economists. Indeed, the modern advocates of 'quantitative easing', whereby a central bank prints more money to sustain economic activity, are the intellectual descendants of John Law.

Unlike most gamblers, and even most monetary theorists, Law, by a series of improbable circumstances, managed to put his theories into practice on a national stage. He spent much of his late thirties and early forties travelling around the 'principal cities of Italy', where he continued 'his speculations, playing at all sorts of games, betting, and engaging in the public funds and banks'. Venice and Turin have been verified as, at various times, the scenes of his gambling adventures.[14] As a nomadic gambler and man of the world, Law proposed to Victor Amadeus II, the Duke of Savoy, the establishment of a bank and a commercial company. The Duke, perhaps fortunately, allegedly remarked that he was not rich enough to take such risks. Rebuffed by Savoy, Law went to France where he was soon mixing in the highest circles of the nobility and the royal court.

Law lived in France from December 1713 until the end of 1720, and these seven years are the best-documented period of his eventful life. Initially, he tried to win over the ailing old King, Louis XIV, to his scheme for a royal bank. Of all the countries in Europe, France was probably the most likely to adopt innovative and daring financial policies. The long and expensive wars Louis had waged had left an 'enormous weight of debt'. The death of Louis himself in September 1715 gave Law even more cause to hope his plans might actually be adopted. The state of affairs in the kingdom at this point was one in which 'all industry [was] checked; trade . . . annihilated', while 'manufactures, commerce, and navigation had almost ceased; the merchant and the trader were reduced to beggary'.[15] The new Regent of France, Philippe, Duc d'Orléans, was a rake who had befriended Law. Orléans was an unconventional figure who was open to new ideas, particularly if they offered a solution to the most pressing problem the country faced, its enormous burden of debt.

Law's scheme was excellent in its simplicity. According to his own theory, outlined in his 1705 tract *Money and Trade Considered*, a scheme of 'paper credit', or what we would call paper money, could provide a remedy for the poor French state finances. In trying to convince the French, Law praised the benefits to England and Holland of the banks of London and Amsterdam. He believed he could show that setting up 'an establishment of a similar nature, but upon an improved plan in Paris', would produce 'the like good effects' in France.[16] The bank Law proposed would be secured on two types of assets. First, it would be a land bank, secured on the landed property of the whole kingdom. It would also be backed by the entire royal revenue. Law's Banque Générale was duly established in May 1716. But the creation of the bank which would issue paper credit to the French monarchy was only one aspect of John Law's financial plan. Soon afterwards, he began to 'lay open the plan of the great and stupendous project he had long meditated'. This plan was known by the name of the Mississippi System.

There were many different twists and turns in the story that ensued, but the main outline of Law's bold plan is easy enough to describe. Under the system, the Compagnie d'Occident (or Company of the West) was set up, and was then granted the whole of the province of Louisiana. This grant was responsible for the scheme being called the 'Mississippi System', since the French colony of Louisiana was an enormous tract of land which comprised most of the Mississippi river valley. It bordered the Great Lakes to the north, and its southern border was formed by the Gulf of Mexico. The Company was then expanded and relaunched in 1719 as the Company of the Indies. The principle behind the two companies was simple, and, as we shall see, the idea had in fact been borrowed from England. The Mississippi scheme, in modern terms, was a straight debt-for-equity swap.[17] In other words, the debts of France would be consolidated in shares in the Company. The scheme has been described as the 'vesting of the whole privileges, effects, and possessions of all the trading companies . . . the receipt of the king's revenues and the management and property of the bank in one great company'. This Company, in possession of all these sources of revenue, would then be able to issue shares.

In August 1719, the revenues of the French state were leased to the Company by the Regent, for which the Company agreed to pay 3.5 million livres. After receiving all these grants, the Company then promised an annual dividend of 200 livres on every share. The price per share rose in the market to 5,000 livres. The 200 livres, at this price, gave an attractive 4 per cent dividend. Law, as the mastermind of the Company, now became the most socially desirable man in Paris. The 'first quality' people in France appeared 'on foot in hundreds' before his house in the Place Vendôme.[18] The Company now began to lend money to the government. A sum of 1,500 million livres was loaned to the government at an interest rate of 3 per cent a year. To raise this sum, 300,000 new shares were created costing 5,000 livres each. The revenues were estimated to be around 80 million livres. Other writers made even more ambitious calculations, computing the annual revenue of the Company at about 130 millions. Either way, the dividend of 200 livres a share was deemed to be easily affordable. These 'prospects of immense profit . . . excited all ranks' to an extent that 'no nation had ever before witnessed'. 'A universal infatuation for the acquisition of shares in the India Company now seemed to occupy the whole kingdom, from the lowest of the people up to . . . princes.'

Of the 300,000 shares in circulation, the Regent, Philippe, Duc d'Orléans, had managed to acquire 100,000, leaving no more than 200,000 in the hands of the public. By November 1719, the shares were trading at 10,000 livres each, more than sixty times their original price. The rise in the price of the shares allowed 'several obscure and low' individuals to acquire 'princely fortunes'. By the end of the year, Law had 'arrived at a pitch of power and consequence that required a strength of intellect almost supernatural to be . . . undazzled'. He was in constant demand. In the mornings, rather like Louis XIV, he held a levée which was 'crowded with Princes, Dukes, and Peers, Marshals and Prelates'. They were often treated with 'consummate haughtiness' by the Scotsman. Law was 'so much plagued with suitors for [shares], that he could hardly get a moment of rest either by day or night'. Women pestered him 'incessantly', abandoning 'all ideas of decency and delicacy'. Avarice was king.

At this point, foreigners from all over Europe 'flocked in great numbers to Paris'. The climax of Law's career occurred perhaps in December 1719, when he converted to Roman Catholicism 'with great pomp'.[19] As a consequence of this timely conversion, Law was declared Comptroller General of the Finances of France in January 1720, and in April of the same year he received the still more honorific title of Superintendent, a title not used since 1661 in France, and never used again.[20] The spectacle of the foreigner and former fugitive rising to the head of affairs in France was rightly seen by contemporaries as extraordinary. Law was in effect Prime Minister of France. He was conspicuous for the plainness and simplicity of his dress, while epigrams and poems were written in Latin in his honour. A French translation of his *Money and Trade Considered* was published at The Hague in 1720, and underneath his portrait, in the frontispiece of the book, the legend read, 'Law, skilled in the art of regulating the finance, discovers the way to enrich subjects and the king.' The British Ambassador to Paris, the Earl of Stair, was now writing to James Craggs, one of the Secretaries of State, in London with concern. Law, according to the Ambassador, boasted that he would 'set France much higher than ever she was before'. France would be in a condition to dominate 'all Europe', while Law asserted that he could personally ruin 'the trade and credit of England and Holland whenever he pleases'. Law claimed that he could, so Lord Stair affirmed, 'break our bank whenever he has a mind; and our East India Company'.[21]

From January 1720, however, the fortunes of Law and his Mississippi company began to turn. An increasing number of speculators were turning the shares into gold at the Banque Générale. Several edicts between January and March 1720 restricted the conversion of shares to specie (actual gold and silver coins) to small amounts. Law now began to consider abolishing specie payments altogether. Imperiously, he issued an edict on 27 February prohibiting individuals, religious communities and colleges from having in their possession more than 500 livres in gold specie. People ran to the bank to change their gold into paper, a novel spectacle. From this moment, Law began to lose the confidence of his erstwhile supporters, the Duc d'Orléans and other courtiers.

There then occurred one of those moments of madness, of which the history of money is full. The Regent's other ministers in Council 'ordered that the shares of the Company should be reduced'. They even published a schedule by which the price of the shares should be lowered, completely contrary to any market principles. It was decreed that the value of the shares should decrease by 500 livres a month, starting with a value of 8,000 livres per share on 21 May, proceeding to 7,500 on 1 July and so on until a price of 5,000 livres should be reached on 1 December 1720.

The effects of this edict were profound. From the moment it was announced, 'the whole paper fabric fell to the ground'; the notes 'lost all credit', and nobody would 'meddle with them'. According to one of Law's early biographers, the fatal edict of 21 May was an act of folly 'hardly to be equalled in the annals of any nation'.[22] The edict precipitated a quick sale of the shares in the Company. As his system collapsed, John Law resigned on 9 December 1720. He then went into exile, first to Brussels, and then to Venice, and landed in England in October 1721, having secured a pardon for his original crime. The death of Philippe, Duc d'Orléans in December 1723 ended Law's hopes of any return to office in France. He continued to live in England but moved back to Venice, which it seems was his favourite city, and there he contracted pneumonia and died in relative poverty in March 1729. Despite his shortage of ready money, he left, by modern standards, an invaluable collection of art; the inventory of twenty-two paintings he bequeathed as a legacy included a Titian, a Raphael, four Tintorettos and three of Rubens's works.[23] At his death, he was about fifty-eight years old. He had lived a life of adventure and excitement such as few of his contemporaries could match.[24]

As we have seen, Law's innovations attracted the attention of the English, but, in many ways, his scheme had been modelled on an English example. The story of the South Sea Company, and its denouement in the South Sea Bubble, has been told countless times. Both bubbles had a common origin in the need to find new ways to finance government spending, aggravated by lengthy military campaigns in the struggle between Britain and France. Both the South Sea Company and Law's Compagnie d'Occident owed their immediate origin to the 'accumulated debts created during the War of the Spanish Succession which was waged from 1701 to 1713'. In England, an Act was passed in Parliament in 1711 under which £9.5 million of the government debt would be converted into the stock of a new company, the South Sea Company.[25] When Robert Harley, the head of the government, unfolded his plan to incorporate the holders of the British national debt into one company in May 1711, the House of Commons was 'ecstatic'.[26] Harley was made Earl of Oxford before the end of the month.

The outstanding national debt was to be exchanged compulsorily for shares at par in a company whose purpose was 'the sole trade and traffic from 1st August 1711, unto and from the Kingdoms, Lands etc.' of South America. In addition to this monopoly, the Company was guaranteed an annual payment from the exchequer of £568,279 and 10 shillings, which was 6 per cent on the debt of £9 million, including a management fee. The scheme was attractive to the government because it reduced the interest charge paid on its debt from 9 per cent to 6. The shareholders were happy too because, even though they received a reduction of 3 per cent in the interest payment, they now enjoyed the prospect of capital gains, if the Company's share price rose. There was, in modern market slang, more of an upside in owning shares, or equity, than in debt. This was not the first time that government debt had been converted into corporate stock. The Bank of England had converted government debt into its own shares in 1697.[27]

The problem with the South Sea Company began in 1719. As we have seen, officials at the British Embassy became hysterical about Law and about the pressing need to do something similar in England. 'I wish to God', wrote Thomas Crawford, the secretary to the British Ambassador in Paris, to a government minister at the end of September 1719, that the 'great men of Britain would think of something else than merely tripping up one another's heels'. The Ambassador, the Earl of Stair, was equally alarmed, complaining that 'by the success of Mr Law's project the public debts of France are paid off at a stroke, and the French king remains master of an immense revenue and credit without bounds'.[28] Stair believed that Britain should mount a scheme for discharging the national debt at once, if Law was not to 'raise the trade of France on the ruins' of British trade. On 23 November, the King of Great Britain, George I, arrived in London from a sojourn in his native Hanover and opened the new session of Parliament. There was rapidly introduced a proposal for the 'further reduction in the cost of the Debt'.[29]

By 1719, the British national debt was in the region of £30 million. The holders of this debt could not simply be forced into taking stock in the South Sea Company, but would have to be given an attractive offer. The basis on which the shares would be offered was complicated. The Company was allowed to issue shares with a nominal value of £31.5 million; there would be an issue of a maximum 315,000 new shares with a nominal value of £100 each. Against the background of the South Sea Company's bid to take over the government debt, there lurked other rivals. The Bank of England itself had offered £5 million to handle the national debt on the same basis as the South Sea Company was now offering. The Company agreed to pay £7.5 million, out of the money it raised from the issue of new shares, to the government for the privilege of taking on the national debt.

Robert Walpole, a former Chancellor of the Exchequer and the ablest financier in the House of Commons, spoke against the South Sea scheme in Parliament, but the spirit of speculation was all-pervasive. As soon as John Aislabie, the Chancellor of the Exchequer, announced the scheme on 21 January 1720, the price of South Sea shares began to rise. At Christmas 1719, the price of each share had been £126. By the middle of February, only three weeks after Aislabie's announcement in the House of Commons, the shares had reached £187; by March, shares were trading at £300.[30] The rise in the price of the shares of the South Sea Company was not the only manifestation of an almost universal mania for speculation in London that summer; there were a whole host of 'bubble' companies launched, often very simply by a notice in a newspaper advertising a company and offering to take subscriptions at one of the many coffeehouses in the City of London. These bubble companies mostly did not survive, although two insurance companies which later flourished, the Royal Exchange and London Assurance, owed their origin to this flurry of market activity. In the midsummer of 1720, the directors of the South Sea Company even began to fear that competition from the bubble companies would attract investors away from the South Sea Company, and thus depress its share price. The directors actually obtained writs against the bubble companies, to put an end to them.[31]

The bubble in the price of South Sea shares continued through the summer. The Company issued tranches of shares, as the stock price increased, and the third and final subscription was launched on 15 June 1720. The price for each share was £1,000, which was a third greater than the market price of £750. More and more people wanted to buy the shares. During June and July, foreign investors started to sell their shares in the South Sea Company to reinvest their gains in new bubble companies which had emerged in the Hamburg and Amsterdam stock markets. Yet, despite these sales, the share price was still hovering around £800 at the beginning of September, though it was starting to fall. By the middle of September, the share price fell through what market traders call a support level of £600. This means that the shares had been trading above that level for some months. At this point, the directors of the Company started selling shares to buy them back at a lower price. By the end of September the share price was below £200. This represented a fall of around 75 per cent in four weeks.[32]

This is a very bald account of the speculation which haunted London for decades, and which seriously damaged the reputation of the joint-stock company. There were, of course, human stories of tragedy and triumph during those fevered summer months of 1720. Thomas Guy, the philanthropist who founded Guy's Hospital on his gains, started selling his shares on 22 April, and was out of the stock in six weeks. He had converted a

£54,000 holding into £234,428. The already phenomenally rich Duke of Marlborough, the greatest general of the age, had, on the urging of his canny wife Sarah, sold his £27,000 holding for £100,000.[33] The Duchess of Portland shrewdly instructed her broker to buy as much as he could with the money she gave him and to 'sell it out again next week'.[34]

Many were ruined, however. The Duke of Chandos lost a paper fortune of £700,000, while, more grievously still, Sir Justus Beck, a director of the Bank of England, went bankrupt owing £347,000; Sir Isaac Newton, the great scientist, lost £20,000 by selling too early and then buying back into the shares at their peak.[35] There were political casualties, as many of the leading political figures such as Aislabie, the Chancellor, and Craggs, the Secretary of State, had been suspected of taking shares in the company and then using their parliamentary position to talk up the share price. Walpole emerged at the head of the government.

The failure of the South Sea Company was based on the inability of the Company to generate any income from actual trade with South America. It has been calculated that the inherent, or 'fair', value of the shares, based simply on the fixed income the government gave the Company, was around £150.[36] The idea behind the Company taking on the national debt was that the revenue from the trade would meet the burden of the interest on the national debt, and so, inevitably, if such trade failed to materialize, the worth of the Company's shares would be considerably lower.

Both the South Sea Bubble and John Law's Mississippi system can be easily categorized. Behind all the drama and fascination of the bubbles, both companies represented an early attempt to solve the problem of government indebtedness. By substituting equity, or shares, in a company for government debt, it was hoped that a lower interest rate could be achieved on the debt, while giving the equity investor a prospect of capital appreciation. The value of the shares in both companies would go up, as their profits from their exclusive concessions came rolling in. Both companies, unfortunately, were trading on delusive hopes. The vast riches of South America and what are now the Southern and Mid-Western United States just did not materialize. Shareholders were left with equity in companies whose prospects had been grossly exaggerated. Holding government debt was a much more profitable undertaking. It involved fewer risks, and, certainly for a Briton of the first half of the eighteenth century, there was still ample scope to invest in government debt, as the total bank debt of Great Britain increased from £16.5 million in 1697 to £30 million in 1713 and to £60 million by the end of 1748. It was also true, contrary to what some exponents of free enterprise might surmise, that the City of London's complex structures of services could not have been built up by the mid-eighteenth century without the government's extensive borrowing needs. There was simply 'no industrial sector whose bonds could be used for the same purpose'.[37]

3

Revolutions

The expansion of British government finance occurred at the same time as the impressive growth of British colonies in what we now know as the United States of America. The currency arrangements of the colonies in America, unlike those in the mother country, were unorthodox. The story has many times been told of how the tobacco-growing states of North America – Virginia, Maryland and North Carolina – long used tobacco as local currency.[1] The Seven Years' War, which lasted from 1756 to 1763, added a further £60 million to the existing British national debt, which was already an impressive £75 million. The war pursued its own course in the North American colonies, where Canada was eventually captured for the British Crown, but where large debts were incurred in the existing colonies. It became expedient for those colonies to issue bills of credit and, in the last resort, paper money for the continuation of trade.[2]

Of course, the economic effects of the Seven Years' War would be felt by the colonies in a more indirect, though eventually more consequential, manner. The indebtedness which Britain had incurred provoked genuine concern among the British political elite, and it was this concern that led in turn to the adoption of novel forms of taxation with which to pay for the burgeoning debt. The drive to secure more tax revenue to fund the debt was what gave rise to the British government's attempt to raise taxation from the American colonies which, as everyone knows, prompted the colonies' refusal to be taxed without representation in the Parliament in London. The details behind this episode are instructive. George Grenville, the British Prime Minister, announced plans to impose stamp duties on the colonies. Objection was naturally made that the colonies should be consulted, and Grenville obligingly postponed the tax for a

year. He meant the period of postponement to encourage other sugges-
tions from the colonies themselves as to how they should be taxed.
Perhaps unsurprisingly, not a single colony suggested another way of
being taxed by Parliament; instead they all greeted the proposal with
howls of protest. Grenville took a tough approach to the protests – he just
passed a Stamp Act, in which he demonstrated in the House of Commons
the right of Parliament to impose the tax, which was payable on newspapers, legal documents and shipping cargo lists among other items. Britain
itself had paid the duty for nearly a century, and it was widely assumed
that, despite some opposition, the Americans would acquiesce in doing
so. Grenville was an effective minister who showed an admirable talent
for economy and restraint in the administration of public finance:
cartoonists of the time often depicted him as saving candle ends.[3] He
avoided foreign wars, and the foreign alliances that resulted in those wars,
but his colonial policy, with regard to the American colonies, can only be
described as a failure.

The attempt to tax the colonies inevitably led to war. The American War
of Independence, from a fiscal point of view, occurred largely as the result
of too much government spending, on the part of the British, during the
Seven Years' War, and an inability to raise funds to pay for the debts
incurred in the course of the military engagements. British indebtedness
led directly to the attempt to tax Americans, which resulted in the famous
cry of 'no taxation without representation'. The North American British
colonies demanded representation in Parliament, though it is more likely
that this was merely an excuse. When the War of Independence eventually
broke out in 1775, the ten-year crisis which had begun with Grenville's
Stamp Act of 1765 finally reached explosion point.

Financially, the colonies were badly off. They had only just 'liquidated
the debts contracted in the French war' – that is, the Seven Years' War. The
colonies had 'only a few thousand pounds' in their treasury.[4] Their shortage of funds was further exacerbated by the reluctance of the colonies to
pay for the war through taxation. It was, after all, unwillingness to be taxed
by the British which had caused the conflict in the first place. This being
the case, it was most unlikely that any independent government would
dare attempt to raise taxes. In any case, the young country lacked the

administrative means, the bureaucracy, to enable it to raise significant sums in this way. So the colonies resorted to an expedient which would be used very often in the waging of war. They began to print money.

Of course, paper money was not something which eighteenth-century politicians or the public more generally particularly esteemed. One popular work of what became known as political economy, translated from French by none other than Thomas Jefferson, and recommended by John Adams, referred to paper money as a 'theft' which was 'ruinous' since 'in this money there is absolutely no real value'.[5] The commitment to paper money, though unorthodox, had occurred even before the Declaration of Independence in 1776. By the close of 1775, the continental Congress and the individual states had already issued $6 million of paper money; by the end of 1779, Congress had issued $241 million in continental bills of credit. It was the 'unwillingness of the states either to levy taxes themselves, or to allow Congress to do so' which led to the inevitable resort to the printing press and the issue of paper money.[6]

Paper money was immediately controversial. The Quakers of Pennsylvania refused to accept it on religious grounds. They were fined and imprisoned, and their property was confiscated. Many believed that the Quakers' opposition was inspired by avarice as much as by religious principle.[7] As a consequence of the introduction of paper money, there followed all those expedients which desperate governments employ to preserve the value of the paper. An Act passed in March 1780 declared that forty dollars in paper was equivalent to one in specie, but this Act had the effect of undermining further any confidence people still had in the paper currency. The usual effects of inflation fuelled by the printing press were soon felt. The cost of commodities began to rise; attempts to fix prices were unsuccessful.

Yet, despite the inflation, the stimulative powers of increased money supply were also felt. Paper money was 'at all times the poor man's friend'. Indeed, while 'it was current, all kinds of labor very readily found their reward'. It was also noted that in the 'first years of the war, none were idle from want of employment . . . To that class of people, whose daily labor was their support, the depreciation was no disadvantage to expending their money as fast as they received it, they always got its full value.'[8] The notes which the continental Congress issued held their value until 1777, yet by 1779 they were worth only two or three cents in specie. 'Not worth a continental' became a phrase in common parlance for 150 years after the War of Independence concluded.[9] After 1780, however, despite attempts to fix the value of the paper money, the depreciation continued. The continental dollar ceased to circulate as currency after May 1781 and was soon forgotten. Congress, recognizing that the main cause of the depreciation was the excessive amount issued, stopped printing continental dollars in 1779. In 1790, Congress finally redeemed such notes as were left at a hundred paper dollars to one in US government debt. Few of these notes were turned in as most had been destroyed earlier for being utterly worthless.[10]

The experience with paper money was not remembered fondly by earlier writers on monetary history. To the oddly named Pelatiah Webster, who lived through the American Revolution, paper money 'polluted the equity of our laws, turned them into engines of oppression, corrupted the justice of our public administration, destroyed the fortunes of thousands who had confidence in it . . . and went far to destroy the morality of our people'. To Albert Bolles, one of the first professors at the Wharton School of Business, writing in 1879, the 'principles of finance which long and intelligent experience has declared to be sound have been more frequently disregarded by the United States than by any contemporary nation'.[11]

It was this painful experience which led to the adoption in the United States Constitution of the clause that gold and silver were to be the only lawful currencies of the new republic. The Constitution gives Congress the power 'to coin money, regulate the value thereof, and of foreign coin'. Congress was particularly influenced by the Treasury Secretary, Alexander Hamilton, and passed the Coinage Act of April 1792. This Act designated the dollar as the currency unit of the United States and defined smaller denominations on a decimal basis, with cents, nickels (originally, half-dismes) and dimes (originally dismes) providing the currency in everyday transactions. More particularly, the dollar was defined as equal to 371.25 grains of pure silver or 24.75 grains of pure gold, which specified a ratio of 15 to 1 for the value of silver as compared to that of gold.[12] It was striking that the new country quickly affirmed the principles of a metallic standard for money, basing the new dollar's value on gold and silver. This was an implicit recognition of the fact that, while paper money might serve a purpose in revolutionary times, gold and silver, in respectable nations, constituted the sole measures of value.

The eighteenth century associated paper money with uncertainty, turmoil and desperate fiscal times. No more arresting example of this can be given than the period of the French Revolution. The events of July 1789 were, as is widely known, the consequence of the bankruptcy of the French state. Successive ministers of Louis XVI struggled in vain to pay the interest on a debt which had increased rapidly. Large fiscal deficits, the enormous gap between spending and revenues, were the prelude to upheaval and revolution.

The immediate prelude to the crisis which brought a thousand years of French monarchy to an end started in August 1786. Charles-Alexandre Calonne, the Comptroller General of the royal finances, first came to Louis XVI and told his master that France was on the brink of financial collapse. The French budget was 112 million livres in deficit: revenue was 475 million livres, while expenditure was 587 million. To put it another way, the deficit was a quarter of the actual revenue. This form of indebtedness was nothing new. As we have seen, the wars of Louis XIV at the beginning of the eighteenth century had imposed a crippling burden of debt on French finances. John Law's experiment had been designed to deal with this problem. From that time on, four major European and overseas wars had made the situation worse. During the American War of Independence, the French had sided with the Americans. Jacques Necker, the Swiss financier who had been brought in to save the French monarchy, had raised 520 million livres between 1777 and 1781. The French were offering to pay up to 10 per cent a year on their debt. Although Necker's loans offered a healthy return for investors, they were 'ruinously expensive' to France. Yet Necker, like many wartime ministers before and since, was committed to financing France's contribution to the American War 'without any new taxation'.[13] Calonne assumed his post in November 1783, only a couple of years after Necker had been dismissed. He was an aristocrat, a born optimist and an admirer of Great Britain.[14] A brilliant student who had been educated by Jesuits in Paris, he had a clear-headed notion of what France needed. Yet the French monarchy had very little of the will or administrative power needed to enact reforms.

In its broadest terms, the French state could not pay for itself. While it is true that the immediate cause of the French Revolution was the fiscal crisis of 1788, for seventy years France had confronted similar crises, largely because it had failed to adopt British fiscal policies. Unlike in Britain, French taxation was patchy and arbitrary across different regions and classes. Many groups were able to pay to become exempt from taxation. By 1789, for instance, the clergy's tax bill was 10 million livres, less than 2 per cent of the state's revenues, despite the Church owning between 10 and 15 per cent of all property in France. More alarmingly, the extent to which cities, whole provinces and the royal princes could be exempt from taxation surprised even the revolutionaries. They were astonished by the thousands of names on the pension lists, when these were found.[15] When, on that fateful day in 1786, Calonne announced to the King that the state was bankrupt, he proposed a major tax reform, but, on failing to bring this about, he was dismissed and forced to flee to England. As the summer of 1788 began, the French government was faced with a stark choice; it could either, as a temporary solution, increase taxes and default on part of the debt, or it could try to forge a new national consensus to introduce reform.

Ironically, given later depictions of the excessive aloofness and arrogance of the *ancien régime*, the Estates General were recalled in the summer of 1789 in a spirit of compromise. Interestingly, the ratio of the debt to the gross national product (GNP) in France in 1789, that is the size of the national debt as a proportion of the entire economy, was only 63 per cent, which would compare favourably to the ratios of advanced countries in the early twenty-first century. Yet, in a spirit of conciliation, Louis XVI agreed to the meeting of the Estates General, because according to Necker, now reinstated as Finance Minister, the King wanted to solve his financial difficulties 'hallowing all the commitments made by the rulers of a nation true to its honour and its word'. Necker's speech to the Estates General, in May 1789, went on to refer in broad terms to the need for a 'return of order and trust', and to the King's desire to put the 'order of finances under the whole nation's supervision'.[16] Having summoned the Estates General, the royal court quickly realized that it had set free forces which could prove difficult to manage. In July 1789, the Estates were transformed into a National Assembly, whose mission was to 'regenerate' France. The Assembly embarked on a radical programme, the most striking element of which was the plan to launch a new currency.

The Assembly devised a scheme to confiscate the Church's assets, sell the confiscated lands and then issue paper notes which would be secured on, or backed by, the proceeds of the land sales. Records of the debates show that members of the Assembly quoted David Hume, Adam Smith and the history of John Law's system, as well as the precedent of the American Revolutionary War, as examples of the dangers of paper money. The new notes were given the name assignats, and to many foreigners they represented everything that was wrong with the French Revolution. To Edmund Burke, the assignats were turning France into a 'nation of gamesters', and although 'all are forced to play, few can understand the game'. In his eloquent and forceful tirade against the French Revolution, written only a year after the tumultuous events of 1789, Burke denounced the Assembly's 'fanatical confidence in the omnipotence of church plunder'. He mocked the resort to assignats to solve every problem of public finance in France. Whatever the financing need, the French revolutionaries would perform their favourite trick of issuing assignats. 'Is there a debt which presses them – Issue assignats . . . Is a fleet to be fitted out . . . Assignats . . . The only difference among their financial factions is on the greater or lesser quantity of assignats to be imposed on the public sufferance.'[17] For Burke, a traditional conservative, the use of Church lands as security 'for any debts or any service whatsoever' was an 'abominable fraud'.[18] For Calonne, the old Finance Minister now in exile, the recourse to paper money was to be regarded as a 'sign of distress, a fatal extremity, ever to be viewed with dread, and scarcely to be excused by the most disastrous emergencies'. These words may have been written in the bitterness of defeat, but no one could deny Calonne's passion. He spoke of this 'tyrannical paper' which would 'put to flight the specie'. He alluded to the 'terrible catastrophe occasioned . . . by the abuse of the system of Law', and he naturally referred unfavourably to the recent example of the 'paper money created by the United States of America'.[19]

The reasons given for issuing the paper currency are familiar: the currency would help liquidity and alleviate a shortage of money. This would stimulate trade. It would also allow the state to finance its most immediate needs. It was even argued that the paper currency would bind citizens to the public good, as everyone had an interest in selling the Church's property. There were some distinguished opponents of the assignats closer to home. The great chemist Antoine Lavoisier, quoting Hume, argued that doubling the money supply would cause an increase in the price of all goods. French manufactures, as a consequence, would be even less competitive with foreign manufacturers.[20]

The story of the assignat, the paper currency, which for many people was the most potent economic symbol of the Revolution, was one of triumph followed by collapse and inflation. At first, the assignat kept its value. The turning point occurred in April 1792, when war was declared on the German empire and Austria. The war was broadly supported by the population, though some politicians, notably Robespierre, voiced their opposition. Debt payments were suspended and the assignat was converted from its initial purpose to become an instrument of war finance. By the beginning of the war the paper currency had already depreciated 40 per cent against gold. Seventeen-ninety-two was the great year of the French Revolution, with the monarchy abolished in September; and it was the year in which the stirring battle hymn of republican France, 'La Marseillaise', was written.

Seventeen-ninety-three, by contrast, was a year of defeat. The King's execution in January marked the beginning of a renewed period of pressure on the republic. That spring, defeats followed in quick succession, and a full civil war broke out in the summer of that year. The fiscal resources of the French state were now at a low ebb. This was the prelude to the intense period of bloodshed and repression known as the Terror. Contrary to what one might expect, the Terror stopped the incipient runaway inflation, which the chaos of the summer months had set in train. The government imposed severe legal restrictions, closing the stock market, abolishing joint-stock companies and imposing very harsh measures on those who refused to take the assignat at par. The Jacobins, which was the name given to the French revolutionary extremists, resorted to authoritarian methods, perhaps the most efficient way of preserving the value of a paper currency. Grain prices, consumer prices and wages were all controlled by the so-called laws of the Maximum. These controls were a massive bureaucratic undertaking, but were rigorously enforced. A law of March 1794, called the Second General Maximum, was published in three volumes running to 1,100 pages. In this immense publication were outlined the prices and wages set for each of the 550 or so districts of France. The Terror represented the ultimate control by the state of the free market, which was essentially abolished.

Under the Terror, citizens who were suspected of infringing any of these harsh laws could expect tough treatment. The law which attempted to guard the value of the assignat demanded arraignment and trial within forty-eight hours of the offence being committed. It encouraged denunciations from informants, and in some cases the death penalty was imposed. This authoritarian, repressive regime managed to secure some stability, at the cost of an appalling disregard for the rights of the individual; but when military successes were achieved in the summer of 1794 and enemies were expelled from all French territory, the Jacobins could no longer justify their Terror. Robespierre was executed in July, and on his way to the guillotine the fallen dictator was mocked by an outraged populace: 'Foutu Maximum!' was the cry. 'Fuck the Maximum!'

The purge of the Jacobins and military success led to a loosening of the currency constraints. In June 1795, the government ceased to value the assignat at par for tax receipts. As soon as the apparatus of legal restrictions disappeared, the demand for the currency fell. The assignat became known as 'Parisian money', yet even Parisians at this point were abandoning the currency and hoarding commodities. A modern historian has described the period immediately after the Terror as one 'of spectacular depreciation', during which the fall of the assignat was virtually uninterrupted from August 1794 to March 1796, at which later date the currency was replaced by the mandat.[21] In terms of actual value, if January 1791 was a base figure of the price of assignats to louis d'or (the French coin in circulation at the time of the Revolution) of 100, the index had moved to 167 by January 1793, and to 226 by January 1794. This represented a loss of value of more than 50 per cent in three years. But the index figure in January 1795 was 496, and in January 1796 it was 20,012.[22] To put it another way, the assignat's price was, by the end of 1795, only 0.5 per cent of its face value, but it continued to fall still further.[23]

It was easy to pour scorn on the assignat. Its story, bound up as it was in the drama of revolutionary France, was mocked by those who preferred tighter monetary arrangements, and, to contemporaries on both sides of the Atlantic, there remained a strong residual conservative bias in favour of a metallic basis for money, that is a belief in the merits of gold and silver. Yet to a certain French revolutionary, to Dominique-Vincent Ramel-Nogaret, Finance Minister in the years 1796–9 under the Directory, the assignats had 'made the Revolution'; they had 'brought about the destruction of orders and privileges'; they had 'overturned the throne and founded the Republic'. The assignats had, in this fulsome eulogy, 'carried the tricolor flag beyond the Alps and the Pyrenees'. They had brought 'freedom' to the French people.[24]

Meanwhile, in Britain, Burke's sceptical tone was widely shared among the political class. Distrust of paper money was rife, but so pragmatic was the British government that gold payments were actually suspended in 1797, chiefly as a result of the pressures of war. The irony of this development was that France had just experienced the horrors of hyperinflation induced by paper money, and was now committed to financing the war along more conservative lines. France, indeed, especially after the establishment of the Banque de France, would embark on a love affair with gold, or 'real money', retaining an intense scepticism about paper money which would last till well into the twentieth century. The French Revolution's financing techniques, which included heavy doses of inflation and confiscation, forced Napoleon's France to rely on taxation and metallic currencies.[25]

In London, on 26 February 1797, the government allowed the Bank of England to suspend specie payments. This meant that it would no longer be possible to present notes to the Bank and receive gold coins in payment. In the period immediately preceding the suspension, large quantities of gold had been shipped out of the country, to pay for loans to foreign governments and to meet the costs of war. It was also noted that, after France had begun to restore its own metallic standard in August 1795, the general revival in confidence meant that much of the savings of the émigrés, the French aristocrats who had fled to London from France in the wake of the Revolution and the Terror of 1793–4, were transferred from London to Paris. 'Metal from France which had helped the Bank to replenish its stock . . . was now drained away from it.'[26] The suspension of gold payments led to the introduction of what has been described as the 'world's first successful paper money regime'. A confused British public expected the suspension to last only a few weeks, but, in the end, it lasted twenty-four years until 1821.

The move to a paper currency stirred a debate. One of the participants, Sir Francis Baring, appeared relaxed about the prospect of paper money: 'Any thing [sic] may become a circulating medium; paper is as good a representative sign as gold, and in many instances it is better . . . because it is more easy to manage and transfer.'[27] Francis Baring was the son of a German immigrant who had settled in Exeter in 1720. He had a lifelong interest (and an unusual facility) in algebra and mental arithmetic and was a voluble commentator on financial affairs. His name would later be associated with Barings Bank, which he founded with his two brothers, John and Charles, in 1762.[28] Barings would eventually, in the course of the nineteenth century, become one of the greatest banking concerns in the City of London. Baring's views regarding a paper currency were more advanced than those of Edmund Burke, and Baring actually knew what he was talking about. He spoke of these 'enlightened times' in which paper, as a 'circulating medium', was 'necessary, and even indispensable'.[29] The paper money that he envisaged was, however, tightly controlled. Unlike some of his contemporaries, he believed that 'all convulsions in the circulation and commerce of every country must originate in the operations of government'. In this respect, 'the plans of ministers' were important, yet he believed also in the operation of the truth uttered by merchants to a minister of Louis XIV: 'let us alone'.[30] Again, it was Baring who was among the first writers to refer to the Bank of England as a 'dernier ressort', or 'last resort' in the lending market.

The notion of the lender of 'last resort' would occur many times in the future. It essentially means that the central bank would always provide credit to the banking system, even if all other banks were in difficulty. Baring used the term in recounting the banking crisis that had started in England in 1793, which he felt had been caused by the 'unexpected declaration of war' against France; as a result of the declaration 'foreigners withheld remittances' and the 'want of money became general . . . alarm in the country continued to increase', while confidence in the banks 'vanished'.[31] It was to guard against such a situation arising again that Baring argued that the 'Notes of the Bank of England should be made legal tender during the war.'[32] He was arguing for the general acceptance of paper notes, the 'Notes of the Bank of England', to provide what we would call 'liquidity'.

The suspension of gold payments in 1797 can be regarded as a success, since the paper money of Britain managed to hold about 70 per cent of its value, an impressive record by comparison with the assignats or the continental currency of the Americans. A *New York Times* leader of 1862, near the beginning of the American Civil War, referred to the fact that 'financial history records, so far as we are aware, but one example of paper currency which was kept for any considerable time at par'. The American newspaper went on, admiringly, to suggest that depreciation of the paper currency in Britain, 'for more than twelve years', was less than 3 per cent.[33] By the end of the Napoleonic Wars in 1815, the paper currency had depreciated 30 per cent. This achievement was all the greater given the enormous increase in the national debt between 1785 and 1815. The national debt had grown from £225 million in 1785 to over £880 million in 1821, six years after the Battle of Waterloo.[34] Despite this steep increase in borrowing, the fact that the paper pound essentially held its value was an extraordinary piece of financial management on the part of any central bank. The Bank of England had organized government borrowing, but it had not put money into circulation. In modern parlance, the Bank maintained a tight control of the money supply, in stark contrast to the French and American revolutionary regimes. By 1821, when a resumption of gold payments was being considered, many groups, including private bankers, Birmingham manufactures and Members of Parliament, recommended that the paper standard should become permanent. Yet it was the decision to resume gold payments in 1821 which would define British finance for a century and would construct a pillar of order which, even today, is looked upon as a crowning achievement of nineteenth-century civilization.

4

Pillars of Order

The establishment of British sound finance, the creation of the gold standard and the extraordinarily stable prices which followed have been widely celebrated. The image of high Victorian finance is one of gentlemen in frock coats wearing gold watch chains, reading crisply folded newspapers in darkened, oak-panelled rooms in the City of London. This picture of certainty and time-honoured tradition is largely a caricature. The foundations of Victorian finance were a lot shakier than historians have often suggested. Ensuring order and instituting the gold standard, with the impression of solidity that these developments conveyed, were achieved by an intense effort of will and by steady, consistent policies.

The debate surrounding the resumption of gold payments for pound notes was vigorous and finely balanced. None other than Nathan Rothschild, the greatest banker in the City, warned that he did not believe that a return to gold 'can be done without very great distress to this country'. Rothschild, the founder of the London branch of the banking family, thought that going back to gold would do a 'great deal of mischief'. It would ensure, he argued, that 'Money will be so very scarce' that the price of 'every article in this country will fall to such an enormous extent, that many persons will be ruined'.[1] The radical journalist William Cobbett painted a picture of rural distress and poverty in his book *Rural Rides*, which described a countryside struggling to pay off in gold, after the resumption of 1821, debts which it had contracted in paper money. For people who had lent the government money, the bondholders, gold payments were particularly generous.

A key political figure in the resumption of gold payments was the Victorian statesman Sir Robert Peel. As Chairman of the House of

Commons committee 'considering the expediency of requiring the Bank of England to resume paying gold on demand', Peel was an impartial and highly diligent judge of evidence. In 1811, as a young MP, he had voted against resumption while the war against Napoleon was still being fought, but by 1821 his thoughts were turning to the need to protect bondholders, the public creditors, who had financed Britain's military campaigns. In Peel's rather strict view, the public creditor was entitled to be repaid in the coin which he had lent. This made sense with regard to lenders who had bought bonds before the suspension of payments. It did not apply to those who had lent their money after February 1797. Yet of course the resumption would mean that, in future, interest payments could be convertible to gold. The committee recommended a resumption on the basis of the 'ancient and permanent standard of value'. This would later be known as the 'gold standard'. That an ounce of gold was worth £3 17s 10½d became another totem of British high finance.[2] This in fact had been the value which Sir Isaac Newton, the great physicist, had established more than a century before in 1717, when he was Master of the Mint.

Peel's diligence as Chairman of the committee would shame many modern parliamentarians. The committee began taking evidence on 11 February 1819 and continued until 1 May. After sifting through all the matter with 'the same attention, as he said, that he would give to the proof of a proposition in mathematics', Peel, writing to an old Oxford tutor, was convinced that the 'system of paper money had resulted in a depreciation of the currency, an increase in the price of bullion, and an unfavourable rate of exchange in the foreign markets'. This was in fact a slightly different view from that espoused by the Bank of England, which took a softer line.[3] While the committee was still sitting, Peel gave a clear indication of his opinion in a letter to another Oxford don, Charles Lloyd. The question, as Peel framed it, was simply a matter of how much risk would be involved in a 'return to that state in which we were twenty-two years ago'. This was Peel's preferred outcome, since the system before 1797 was 'confessedly the correct one', even though Britain had now 'become habituated to one that is pernicious', namely the institution of paper money.[4]

Peel's status as a guardian of high finance derived perhaps from his background as the son of a cotton-mill owner from Lancashire, also called

Robert Peel. The younger Robert Peel was the son of what we might call a capitalist, but he was educated at Harrow and Oxford, where he acquired many of the assumptions of the ruling class of Britain at that time. As we have seen, a presumption in favour of gold and a suspicion of paper money was an attitude widely shared among the political elite in Britain during those decades after the French Revolution. In the words of a recent biographer, Peel's 'economic thinking was throughout underpinned by a strong belief in a strong currency linked to gold'.[5]

The resumption of gold payments, while it established the good faith of the British government in its concern for the fate of those who had lent it money, created problems of its own. The years following the defeat of Napoleon at Waterloo in 1815 were a time of stress and economic pressure in Britain. The resumption of gold payments had the effect of sharpening the deflation which occurred after the Napoleonic Wars. Going back to gold meant that there would be a tighter money supply. Between 1818 and 1822, according to one calculation, consumer prices fell nearly 50 per cent.[6] The mood of repression and financial distress felt in Britain at this time was captured by Shelley, the radical poet, in his 1819 poem *The Mask of Anarchy*, written after the Peterloo Massacre, in which he denounces the harsh economic conditions of the age and the 'slavery' the government's deflationary policies had inflicted on the British people. Britain's rulers had:

> Let the Ghost of Gold
> Take from Toil a thousandfold
> More than e'er its substance could
> In the tyrannies of old.[7]

Shelley's poem, written in 1819 but not published until 1832, would probably not have made much impression on the merchants of London's great cities, but they too were rapidly affected by the downturn. The Birmingham-based economist and banker Thomas Attwood complained with a rhetorical turn of phrase that Peel's resumption of gold had caused 'more misery, more poverty, more discord than Attila caused in the Roman Empire'.[8] Yet the depressed conditions were followed by a bubble and an ensuing bust which, for many people who experienced it, would leave lifelong unhappy memories. Many of the characteristics of the bubble of 1825 would be repeated in 2008. The deflationary environment was accompanied by low interest rates, which prompted a desire for better-yielding assets. Gilts (British government bonds) were yielding low rates, so investors bought more speculative assets, such as foreign bonds (loans to foreign governments), to get a higher return. John B. Richards, Deputy Governor of the Bank of England from 1824 to 1826, and then Governor until 1828, put the matter in straightforward terms to a committee hearing in the House of Commons in 1832: 'There was at that time a reduction of interest by the Government, which did not assist the trading community inasmuch as the little interest to be made out of Government securities . . . drove individuals to fresh channels of employment of their money.'[9]

Low interest rates had caused what modern market commentators call a 'search for yield', which had in turn resulted in investors buying riskier assets. According to John Horsley Palmer, Governor of the Bank of England from 1830 to 1833, the 'reduction of interest . . . created that feverish feeling in the minds of the public at large, which prompted almost everybody to entertain any proposition for investment, however absurd'.[10] Nathaniel Rothschild, giving evidence to the same committee, remembered the period immediately preceding the panic of 1825 as a time when there 'was a great speculation in wool . . . and in different articles'.[11] The foreign investments of the time were dominated by loans to newly independent countries in South America. All kinds of schemes were promoted by enterprising projectors selling assets such as shares in South American mining companies. The complacency, which is a feature of most bubbles, had been, at the beginning of 1825, conspicuous among the members of the political elite. 'There was never a period in the history of this country, when all the great interests of the nation were at the same time in so thriving a condition,' intoned the Lord Chancellor at the opening of Parliament in February 1825.[12]

To one contemporary commentator the 'Mississippi scheme' was a 'rational project compared with the extravagance of the expectations held by whole armies of speculators' that summer. More alarmingly, in the 'universal mania' people 'hazarded the savings of a long life industry; they gazed only on the bright side of the future' and they simply 'shut their eyes to the reverse'.[13] The panic occurred at the end of 1825. Richards, the Deputy Governor of the Bank, remembered that 'on Monday morning [12 December] the storm began, and till Saturday night it raged with an intensity that it is impossible for me to describe'.[14] During that month, sixty county banks failed, more than half of them collapsing as a consequence of the failures of the London bank Pole & Co. and of Wentworth & Co., a leading Yorkshire bank. On 14 December, Pole & Co. stopped payment, which put forty of its correspondent county banks out of business.[15] Pole & Co. had been put under pressure by an old-fashioned bank run, when depositors simply withdrew their money from the bank.

The bank failures were only the last development of what had been a tumultuous year. The South American mining stocks also collapsed in dramatic fashion. One man caught up in the excitement of the stock market bubble was the young Benjamin Disraeli, a twenty-year-old Jewish adventurer, determined to make a name for himself in literature. The young Disraeli was a mere solicitor's clerk who eagerly and cynically speculated in South American shares. After the South American republics, which were fighting wars of independence from Spain, had been recognized as sovereign states just after Christmas 1824, there was a huge boom in the shares. The Anglo-Mexican Mining Association's shares rose from £33 on 10 December 1824 to £158 on 11 January the following year. This was a 479 per cent increase in a month. The Colombian Mining Association's shares went up from £19 to £82 in the same period. Both of these shares were promoted by J. & A. Powles, a leading firm of South American merchants. Mid-January saw the high point of the share prices of these firms, and it was, unfortunately, at this very point that Disraeli and a couple of young friends started buying into these companies. Disraeli, a young man of romantic sensibility, was then engaged by Powles as a writer on mining stocks. In March 1825 there appeared Disraeli's first published work, an anonymous pamphlet, nearly a hundred pages in length, entitled *An Enquiry into the Plans, Progress, and Policy of the American Mining Companies*. Disraeli wrote a further two pamphlets, the last of which was entitled *The Present State of Mexico*. These works were largely fictional accounts of the immense resources which were said to underpin the mining securities. Disraeli fatally borrowed money 'on margin' to acquire the stocks, and was £7,000 in debt by June 1825 when the stock-market bubble burst. These debts would hang over his finances for decades.[16]

Despite the outward show of respectability, it must be remembered that Victorian finance was often a highly speculative affair. The era of the gold standard was also an era when prominent financiers could go bankrupt and, metaphorically at least, lose their shirts. The British government may have 'virtually balanced' its budget in every year from 1815 to 1914, but at least four out of eight Governors of the Bank of England between 1833 and 1847 (Governors held the post for two years before handing over to the Deputy Governor) suffered the humiliation of personal bankruptcy.[17] One of these six Governors was the unfortunate William Robinson, a corn dealer, who became bankrupt during his governorship. Writing about this event, Samuel Jones Loyd, later Lord Overstone, attributed the failure to 'extensive corn speculations, entered into and very foolishly conducted by his son and partner'. These speculations, needless to say, were not 'properly controlled by himself'. The failure of Robinson's business meant that he gave up his governorship after only four months in post. The Chancellor of the Exchequer, Charles Wood, to whom Loyd's remarks were directed, merely retorted that it was an 'unfortunate business' and that he was sorry for Mr Robinson 'who seemed an excellent and honourable man'.[18]

Another bankruptcy of the autumn of 1847 was that of Reid, Irving & Co., a company of East India merchants, in which Sir John Rae Reid, a former Governor of the Bank between 1839 and 1841, was a partner.[19] Richard Mee Raikes, Governor between 1833 and 1834, could not serve his full two-year term as a consequence of his personal bankruptcy. Timothy Abraham Curtis, who served as Governor between 1837 and 1839, was even mentioned by Karl Marx in his book *Das Kapital*. Marx referred to details in Curtis's 'private balance sheet' of his income of between £800 and £900 a year from directorships, which was presented to the Court of Bankruptcy after his failure. Marx inevitably cited the case of Curtis as evidence of a 'swindle' in which directors without any real responsibility earned wealth from passive shareholders.[20] It was an age of rectitude in public finance and institutions – a balanced budget and a gold currency – but of relatively free-wheeling capitalism, where risks were taken, and fortunes were gained and lost.

The fact that Lord Overstone and Charles Wood, men who in their own way epitomized mid-Victorian restraint and respectability, could react in such a cool way to the bankruptcy of a serving Governor of the Bank of England showed how much these financial reversals were accepted as a fact of life. Wood, the Chancellor of the Exchequer, was one of those politicians who come and go but are representative party men. As a progressive Whig, Wood 'personified a cautiously progressive liberalism'. Overstone was a Whig too, a liberal who had also been a Member of Parliament but had not enjoyed the experience. His career in public life was significant and, although he left the House of Commons when still only thirty, after an eight-year stint, his influence over his contemporaries as an oracle of finance was immense.

The now largely forgotten Lord Overstone – he was elevated to the peerage in 1850 – was the embodiment of high Victorian finance. Born in 1796, the son of a Unitarian minister, who also happened to run his wife's bank, Samuel Jones Loyd received a gentleman's education at Eton and Cambridge. Like that of the Peels, the Loyd family fortune was based on the newly prosperous midlands and industrial north, but, unlike the Peels, the Loyds were not industrialists. They were bankers who supplied capital to businessmen. They made money cautiously but surely. Overstone's father, Lewis, was a Welshman who in 1793 had married a rather plain woman, Sarah Jones, the daughter of John Jones, a Manchester banker and manufacturer. The couple had met at the Unitarian chapel at Blackley in Manchester, where Lewis was a preacher.[21] After leaving Cambridge in 1818, Samuel devoted himself fully to the family bank. It has been estimated that between 1817 and 1848 the bank returned profits of £2.2 million, of which he collected £568,000, or an average of over £18,000 per annum.[22] As a practising banker, he was cautious and methodical, always weighing the risks and, over his thirty-year direct involvement with the bank, his business never made a loss in any year. By the end of his life, he was earning over £100,000 a year, and spending only half his income. In this way he acquired considerable capital over a long life and, in the words of his *Times* obituarist, built up 'an enormous fortune'.[23] At his death in November 1883, Overstone left securities valued at over £2 million, while his landed estates were valued at over £3 million.[24] He was one of the wealthiest men in Britain.

Despite being a full-time banker, the young Loyd began to make himself known as a currency expert and thinker. He was interested in the theoretical underpinnings of his trade and, in the 1830s, started to write papers on such abstruse topics as the 'causes and consequences of the pressure on the money markets', in which he recognized the importance of psychological factors in the trade cycle. On the question of the gold standard, he was characteristically orthodox. He strongly defended convertibility into gold in a pamphlet, *Remarks on the Management of the Currency*, in 1840. The pamphlets kept flowing in the 1840s and established him as the chief spokesmen of the orthodox financiers, the hard-money, 'gold-is-the-only-true-money' men. In 1844, Loyd's *Thoughts on the Separation of the Departments of the Bank of England* made its first appearance.[25] It was at this point that his life intersected directly with that of Sir Robert Peel, now the British Prime Minister. In this lucid work, Loyd argued in favour of a single bank being allowed to issue paper money. Up to that point, various banks had issued paper money, backed by gold. Yet it was up to the individual bank how much gold should be held in reserve to back the paper notes. It was Loyd's opinion that the proper function of the Bank of England was to regulate the amount and secure the foundations of the paper notes. It was hardly surprising that Sir Robert Peel's Bank Charter Act of 1844, better known as the Bank Act, closely reflected Loyd's views.

The Bank Charter Bill passed its Second Reading in the House of Commons with only thirty opponents.[26] Peel, in opening the debate, started from first principles. 'My first question, therefore, is what constitutes this measure of value? What is the signification of that word "a pound" with which we are all familiar?' Ever the fluent rhetorician, Peel answered his own questions in emphatic terms: the pound was 'a certain definite quantity of gold with a mark upon it to determine its weight and fineness'. To make no mistake about the connection between gold and value, Peel went on to suggest that 'to pay a pound means nothing [else], and can mean nothing else, than the promise to pay to the holder when he demands it, that definite quantity of gold'. Peel said what the overwhelming majority of Members of Parliament on both sides of the House believed. He wound up his speech affirming that he trusted that 'this House will adhere to the present standard, – will resolve on the maintenance of a single standard, and of gold as that standard'. Again, he repeated the same message: 'the gold coin is now the principal measure of property'. The dangers of not ensuring convertibility of paper money into gold on demand were obvious to the Victorian statesman. Peel showed an admirable knowledge of economic writers and contemporary history. He claimed that both Adam Smith and Ricardo had assumed that 'immediate convertibility into coin' is all that would be needed to prevent the 'excessive issue of paper'. Britain, according to Peel, did not 'want an abundant supply of cheap promissory paper'. Referring to contemporary events in the United States, he also made the case for a strong central bank which would enjoy a monopoly of note issue. An 'unlimited competition in respect to issue' would not 'afford a security for the paper currency'. 'What has been the result of unlimited competition in the United States? In the United States the paper circulation was supplied, not by private bankers, but by Joint Stock Banks . . .' This arrangement had 'utterly failed'. 'While there existed a Central Bank (the United States Bank) . . . there was some degree (imperfect it is true) of control over the general issues of paper.' When the 'principle of free competition' in note issue was left unchecked, then came 'immoderate issues of paper, extravagant speculation, and . . . complete insolvency'.[27] To Peel, central banking was simple. A central bank was an entity that had the sole right to issue paper notes which were backed by, and fully convertible into, gold.

The obsession with gold was something which later economists, notably of course John Maynard Keynes, would ridicule. In 1930, Keynes spoke of the 'garment of respectability' which surrounded gold, a garment 'as densely respectable as was ever met with, even in the realms of sex or religion'. Yet he recognized the power of gold. He acknowledged that, in the eyes of supporters of the gold standard, gold was the 'sole prophylactic against the plague of fiat moneys'.[28] In simple terms, Keynes knew that to its supporters gold was the only safeguard against the vagaries of paper money. This was precisely the reason gold became such a symbol in the nineteenth century. To Lord Overstone, gold was a true guardian of value. Writing to *The Times* in November 1855, during the Crimean War, he urged the preservation of convertibility of paper money by which 'we protect ourselves from the gigantic evils of depreciation'. In an earlier letter, he had written, in almost hysterical tones, about the suspension of cash payments (suspension of convertibility) and the 'depreciated currency, and the general fraud and confusion that must ensue'. Looking back at the period before Peel's Bank Act of 1844, he painted a picture of chaos caused by the 'excessive issues of paper money' which in his view had caused the panic of 1825, among other 'convulsions'. This period had been closed by the Bank Act, of which he had been an important proponent. For a conservative (he would have called himself a liberal) monetary expert like Overstone, war was 'the great destroyer of capital'. He was prescient in linking the needs of war with the pressures on maintaining a steadfast standard of value. The paradox of war, for him, was that not only was it a great destroyer of wealth but at the same time it created 'new competitors for it upon a gigantic scale'.[29]

Overstone's writings enjoyed immense prestige in the middle of the nineteenth century. To the American historian and Boston aristocrat Brooks Adams, writing at the end of the century, Overstone was a 'leader of the monied interest . . . who conceived the Bank Act of 1844 and who moulded the policy of Sir Robert Peel'. In Adams's view, Overstone was the 'great banker . . . who, perhaps more perfectly than any man who ever lived, represented Lombard Street and who was destined to dominate the financial policy of the kingdom for nearly a generation'.[30] To his lifelong friend the banker George Norman, Overstone was simply 'the most acute men I ever met with – The readiness, and logical power, with which he can decompose, as it were, the most complicated question . . . have often excited my wonder and delight.'[31] A modern historian asserts that in 'Overstone and his associates' we see 'the strength and limitations of upper-class Victorians'. They showed a 'faith in tradition; a high sense of personal integrity and of family loyalty; a distrust of speculative finance . . . a concern for the welfare of the poor, but not too much concern about the causes of poverty'.[32]

The gold standard was something which had grown organically and became an article of faith for mid-Victorian England. Reliance on a gold standard did not, however, prevent speculation and financial incompetence. The collapse of Overend, Gurney in 1866 shook the City of London. Walter Bagehot, the great Victorian journalist, described the partners of Overend, Gurney as men who had 'great estates, which had mostly been made in the business', from which they still derived 'an immense income'. Yet, despite their prosperity, in six years 'they lost all their own wealth'. In Bagehot's memorable metaphor, the losses were 'made in a manner so reckless and so foolish, that one would think a child who had lent money in the City of London would have lent it better'.[33]

The problem of Overend, Gurney was a familiar one to businesses in all periods. The old members of the firm had withdrawn from an active management of the bank, although they maintained their capital in it. Once they had left, new managers 'embarked in a new line of business, entirely foreign from their proper business'. The bank had been bill brokers and money dealers, essentially operators in the financial markets. (They are called 'interdealer brokers' in London today.) The new managers decided to start making loans backed by property assets, a completely different line of business. These loans, in modern parlance, were illiquid. In the words of a contemporary report of the case they were 'not capable of ready realisation, and [were] subject to rapid and disastrous depreciation'. This was a precise way of saying that the prices could fall, and the goods were difficult to sell, a circumstance which often accompanies a sudden panic in any market. Overend, Gurney had lent, over some years, money to 'steamship companies on the security of the shares, or to railway contractors on the security of shares, or to merchants on the security of goods'. They had lent £4 million, 'out of which not more than a million was estimated to be good'. In the language of modern financial analysis, 75 per cent of the loan book should have been written off. As the report put it, '£3,000,000 were bad assets.' Their traditional businesses, the bill-broking and money-dealing, continued to be profitable and were making between £180,000 and £200,000 a year. Unfortunately, the partners lost the £3 million. This, of course, was one of the risks of a partnership, which involved unlimited liability, in which capitalists could lose all, and more than all, of their stake in a business, since they were liable for any debts.[34]

Walter Bagehot, who had compared the actions of the partners of Overend, Gurney unfavourably to those of a child, was perhaps the most articulate writer on the subject of mid-Victorian finance. His book *Lombard Street: A Description of the Money Market*, published in 1873 and presenting a clear account of how the City worked, has justly been considered a classic. Unlike Sir Robert Peel and Lord Overstone, Bagehot was not from the plutocratic upper-middle classes. He was born in Somerset in 1826, the son of a provincial banker. Like the wealthy Overstone, Bagehot had Unitarian parents, but, unlike the more socially ambitious peer, he remained affiliated to his religion throughout his life. He was educated at the new, secular University College London, rather than at Oxford or Cambridge, which were still closed to those who did not adhere to the Church of England. In finance, however, Bagehot would prove to be as orthodox as either Peel or Overstone. Coming from the generation immediately following these public figures, Bagehot elucidated the system they had worked so hard to build. He described the edifice in terms which attributed a permanent solidity to something which, as we have suggested, was not as imposing or secure as it seemed.

To Bagehot, Lombard Street, a thoroughfare whose origins lie in medieval London and where Italian bankers had resided in the fourteenth century, symbolized the power of England. 'The briefest and truest way of describing Lombard Street is to say that it is by far the greatest combination of economical power . . . that the world has ever seen.' England was evidently 'the greatest moneyed country in the world' and money was 'economical power'. According to Bagehot, 'everyone admits that it [England] has much more immediately disposable and ready cash than any other country'. The easy complacency of his remarks hides an acute and perceptive understanding of the nature of England's 'moneyed power'. He compared the known deposits of banks in London, that is of the banks which published their accounts, and worked out that while London held £120 million worth of accounts, New York had only £40 million, while Paris had an inconsiderable total of £13 million. The chief advantage of Lombard Street was that 'in all but the rarest times money can be always obtained upon good security'.

More significantly, the culture of borrowing was more pervasive in England than elsewhere. 'English trade is carried on upon borrowed capital to an extent of which foreigners have no idea.' The disaster of Overend,

Gurney was, in Bagehot's conception, very much an exception. The great advantage of England's financial system was that a 'new man, with a small capital of his own and large borrowed capital, can undersell a rich man who depends on his own capital only'. In other countries where there 'was little money to lend . . . enterprising traders are long kept back'. The 'efficient and instantly-ready organisation gives us an enormous advantage in competition with less advanced countries, less advanced . . . in this particular respect of credit'.

Bagehot's remarks need to be reflected upon. It is commonly assumed that the gold standard was unduly restrictive, and that it could lead to a harsh environment for debtors. Yet, to Bagehot, a gold standard was compatible with a decent supply of credit to fund profitable enterprise. 'No country . . . was so little "sleepy", to use the only fit word, as England; no other was ever so prompt at once to seize new advantages.'[35] Bagehot accepted Peel's Act of 1844, while recognizing that 'since 1844, Lombard Street is so changed'. And he acquiesced in the victory of the 'Currency School', essentially the position of Overstone and Peel, as against those of the 'Banking School', whose advocates warned of the dangers of limiting note issues by gold and of the hardship that could ensue from such a limitation.

Bagehot's philosophy can broadly be described as classical liberal. He believed in free trade, open markets and minimal government intervention. The best thing, he argued, that 'a Government can do with the money market is to let it take care of itself'.[36] Yet despite being a classical liberal, Bagehot accepted the doctrine of central banking. He believed that 'all our credit system depends on the Bank of England' and he recognized that as a matter of great convenience since 1797 'the public have always expected the Government to help the Bank if necessary'. He described the origins of the Bank of England as 'a Whig finance company' which had been founded by 'a Whig Government because it was in desperate want of money'.[37] In spite of its origins in party politics, however, Bagehot believed that the Bank had transcended those beginnings. He outlined the process of electing directors to the board of the Bank. Since it would take 'about twenty years from the time of a man's first election that he arrives, as it is called, at the chair', and since 'the offices of Governor and

Deputy-Governor are very important', a man 'who fills them should still be in the vigour of life'. It followed that 'Bank directors, when first chosen by the board, are always young men.'[38]

This kind of reasoning showed a strong strategic sense. It implied a world which was unchanging but flexible, in which the new and old were seamlessly fused. A currency fully convertible into gold, a central bank which controlled the note issue, based on that gold, an extensive and highly developed market for credit – these were all features of the high Victorian Age. Bagehot himself published his work, as one critic has observed, 'in the great bulge of Victorian prosperity'.[39] It was a confident world and perhaps a little too self-satisfied. The bankruptcy of a serving Governor of the Bank of England, William Robinson, in 1847 and the collapse of Overend, Gurney in 1866 could be seen as indications of the latent fragility of much of Victorian finance. In the last third of the century, British industrial and financial strength would also be challenged by competition from abroad, particularly from across the Atlantic, in the form of the United States of America.

Great Republic

While Britain's position as the dominant economic power seemed unassailable during the nineteenth century, across the Atlantic there was vigorous development. The new republic had been conceived not so much in 'liberty', as Abraham Lincoln had claimed in his Gettysburg Address of 1863, as in debt, hyperinflation and worthless paper money. By 1789, however, a new government had been created, in which the first Treasury Secretary was Alexander Hamilton.

Hamilton's primary concern was to establish the young country on a firm commercial basis, and although he had opposed the British in the War of Independence he was an admirer of Britain's financial strength. Like many of the founding, revolutionary generation, he was a fluent writer, an educated man whose energies were directed as much towards rhetorical persuasion by his pen as towards the more practical affairs of politics. As the first Treasury Secretary, he was committed to gold and silver as legal currencies. Nearly all contemporaries favoured the US Constitution's ban on paper money.[1] For him, as for many of the leading political economists and politicians of the age, the metallic basis of currency was unquestioned. The more controversial part of Hamilton's programme was his desire to establish an American bank similar to the Bank of England. On 13 December 1790, he submitted to Congress his plan for a national bank. This Bank Report (he presented five reports altogether on the public finances) advocated the establishment of a national bank on the basis that banks were 'nurseries of national wealth'.[2] The Bill embodying this proposal was passed by the Senate, but ominously the vote by which the House of Representatives approved it was split along geographical lines: thirty-three of the thirty-nine votes in favour came from New England, New York, New Jersey and Pennsylvania; fifteen of the twenty negative votes were cast by representatives from Virginia, the Carolinas and Georgia. The Southern states, which were more agrarian, already entertained different ideas about the value of a central bank. Hamilton argued in his 1790 report that such a bank 'would be of the greatest utility in the operations connected with the support of the Public Credit'.[3]

The central bank itself, known as the First Bank, was opened at Philadelphia on 12 December 1791. It was followed by the establishment of eight branches in cities around the country, including Boston, New York, Washington and New Orleans.[4] The bank Hamilton established, however, lasted only twenty years, since its charter was not renewed when it expired in 1811. The Second Bank was created in 1816 and proved to be even more politically divisive than the first. It was set up, once more, in response to the 'extreme fiscal needs of the federal government' and the 'disorder of an unregulated currency'.[5] The Bank, though independent, was strongly tied to the federal government and five of its twenty-five Governors were appointed by the President. The Second Bank was undoubtedly a 'federal institution'. Its political opponents felt that it represented powerful, elite East Coast interests, the 'money power' of the Eastern seaboard against the agrarian interests of the South, and the indebted farmers who, in Thomas Jefferson's vision, represented the virtue of the young United States of America.

Yet, far from being a tool of the 'money power', the Second Bank fell victim to political pressure and hostility. It was the unashamedly populist and Southern President Andrew Jackson who was bent on its destruction. The Bank was, unsurprisingly, averse to making extravagant loans, and 'stood too much in the way of credit expansion to suit popular interests', as one historian of nineteenth-century American finance has put it. The Bank's adversaries were 'not farmers, but business men'.[6] Jackson himself was the last American President to have had direct experience of the War of Independence. He had been a thirteen-year-old recruit to the colonies' Continental Army and was a reactionary figure who believed in the Jeffersonian idyll of the agrarian republic. He hated banks and commercialism. He was a romantic Southerner, having been born in the Carolinas in 1767. Jackson saw himself as representing the common man who often, in a popular view of American history, stands against the powerful vested interests of wealth and elitism. The Second Bank of the United States was elitist, a characteristic reflected most vividly in its president, the precocious Nicholas Biddle, who had graduated, at the head of his class, from Princeton at the age of fifteen. Now aged only thirty-seven, Biddle had become the Bank's President, in which office he fought Jackson over the institution's future. The President vetoed renewal of its charter, when it came before Congress in July 1832. His objection to the Bank was that it was unconstitutional and that it represented too great a 'concentration of power' under private control.[7] As a consequence, there remained no central banking in the United States. The country's banking structure therefore consisted, as it would for another eighty years, of 'a multitude of small independent banks, each with its business confined to a narrow area'.[8]

There has been a suspicion that the crash in New York which occurred in 1837 had been a natural consequence of the demise of the Second Bank. The crash was a typical credit bubble. The state banks which had taken the place of the national Bank had been, naturally enough, much more liberal and open-handed in their extension of credit. As Philip Hone, a former Mayor of New York, reported in his diary in April 1837, 'the immense fortunes which we heard so much about in the days of speculation have melted like the snows before an April sun'. The only person who could escape ruin was 'he who owes no money'. In sentiments which would resonate down the decades, Hone observed, 'happy is he who has a little and is free from debt'.[9]

The controversy surrounding the Second Bank was not the only economic issue which divided the United States on sectional, geographical lines. Slavery, of course, did so too, but less well known is how much the debate about the tariff defined the politics of the age. The question of the tariff had emerged immediately in the aftermath of yet another war, the War of 1812, which the United States had fought with Great Britain. The conflict had created a demand for machine goods on the British side. Britain's industry was, at this time, expanding and taking its position at the top of global trade. When the war was over, British goods were dumped on the United States, as demand, which had been sustained by the war, fell away. 'Dumping' goods simply means selling exports at very cheap prices in order to unload them on a foreign market. This was bad for American manufacturers who had to compete with British goods.

Soon after the war finished, the cry arose from the American manufacturers, based primarily in the North-East of the country, for protection. Hamilton had originally used an 'infant industry' argument to defend protection. He contended that young countries, contrary to the free-trade doctrines of Adam Smith, could use tariffs to develop their nascent industries. Indeed the last of his reports to Congress, the Report on Manufactures in 1791, was often cited as a pro-protectionist tract. Modern scholars may dispute how much Hamilton was a protectionist, and may argue that his 'proposed tariffs were quite modest'.[10] Yet the argument he made in favour of protection, however modest, has been repeated over the course of two centuries and has been used to justify high degrees of trade protection that he may or may not have supported. But his language is as clear as one would expect from such a pellucid writer. He defended protection on grounds of national security. On this basis, manufacturing, what we might term 'an industrial base', was a fundamental prerequisite: 'Not only the wealth, but the independence and security of a country appear to be materially connected to the prosperity of manufactures. Every nation, with a view to those great objects, ought to endeavour to possess within itself all the essentials of national supply. These comprise the means of subsistence, habitation, clothing, and defence.'[11]

Hamilton thus saw the goal of national supply, or self-sufficiency, as justification for 'protecting duties' or 'duties on those foreign articles which are the rivals of the domestic ones intended to be encouraged'. This, in the language of eighteenth-century political economists, is unambiguous. As if to remove any doubts about his meaning, Hamilton mentioned emphatically that 'duties of this nature . . . by enhancing the charges on foreign articles . . . enable the national manufacturers to undersell all their foreign competitors'. Duties were not the only weapon in the arsenal of a statesman wishing to promote manufactures. Hamilton also called for the introduction of 'pecuniary bounties' as being 'one of the most efficacious means of encouraging manufactures'. We would call such 'pecuniary bounties' subsidies, which, Hamilton argued, were a 'species of encouragement more positive and direct than any other'.[12]

Not only was Hamilton held up as a patriot by federalists, he was celebrated as the father of American industrial might. His ideas were systematized and formed the basis of a large portion of the economic policy of the United States during the nineteenth and early twentieth centuries. Henry Clay, a national politician, developed the 'American System', which owed much of its inspiration to Hamilton's words of 1791. Clay was an ardent nationalist who believed in the 'manifest destiny' of the United States. This notion of 'manifest destiny' was a commonly held nineteenth-century conviction that the US was destined to expand across the entire continent of North America. To the countries of Europe which moaned about protection he declared, 'I too am a friend to free trade, but it must be free trade of perfect reciprocity.' In other words, other countries would have to open their markets to American goods. In reality, this free trade didn't exist: 'The maxim of free trade is truth in the books of European political economy. It is error in the practical code of every European state.'[13]

The sectional nature of the support for protection, the fact that the industries of the United States were located on the North-Eastern seaboard, while the South pursued a more agrarian commerce, had been remarked even by Hamilton in 1791. He observed that it was not uncommon to hear the view expressed that 'though the promoting of manufactures may be the interest of a part of the union, it is contrary to that of another part'. He noticed that the 'northern and southern regions are sometimes represented as having adverse interests in this respect', and that 'those are called manufacturing, these agricultural states'.[14] The sectional nature of the tariff dispute would sour relations between the North and South right up to the outbreak of the Civil War in 1861. The first real instance of such a fracture occurred in 1828 when a 45 per cent duty was placed by Congress on all woollen goods imports.[15]

Of course, as everyone appreciated at the time, slavery was the principal issue which divided North and South. The tariff was a subsidiary issue, but it defined the subsequent politics of the Union, and was enshrined in the programme established by the dominant party of the period, the

Republican Party. The degree to which financial and economic politics had underpinned Abraham Lincoln's earlier career has often been overlooked. Lincoln described himself, a year before his election in 1860, as an 'old Henry-Clay-Tariff Whig'. In 'old times', he observed, 'I made more speeches on that subject than any other.'[16] As a young local politician, he had, in the 1830s, opposed the populism of President Jackson, and had defended the Second Bank of the United States, seven years after the President had vetoed its charter.[17]

The economic impact of the American Civil War was perhaps most felt in the area of currency. The United States had, after its experience with the worthless paper continental currency, remained committed to gold convertibility, but the financing of the Civil War offered a fresh challenge to convertibility. Gold convertibility was suspended in the winter of 1861–2, after which the price of Union currency began to float against gold.[18] The Union started issuing greenbacks at the beginning of 1862, a paper currency which would sustain its war effort. Like the French in the Revolutionary Wars, like the British against Napoleon, and following their own example against the British in the 1770s, the Union government issued paper money to defeat an enemy in war. It is perhaps timely to reflect that paper money was almost always a wartime expedient, introduced as a means of extraordinary financing in extraordinary times.

The greenback did not manage to hold its value against gold, but it did allow the federal government to incur an unprecedented level of debt. It also helped the government issue bonds with which to defeat the Southern states. In a novel development, the Treasury Secretary, Salmon Chase, appointed Jay Cooke, a sharp Wall Street operative, as the 'General Subscription Agent' for the whole country. Cooke's task was to sell $1 million worth of bonds every day, and the Treasury Secretary allowed him to hire his own agents and granted him a liberal budget for advertising purposes. Cooke mounted an aggressive sales campaign to carry the public, a campaign which was so effective that every 'newspaper in the country' was effectively made 'his assistant', as one newspaper editor commented. This was one of the first instances in which bonds, or war finance, were marketed to a wider public. It had been a general assumption during the European wars of the eighteenth century that bondholders were part of an elite 'moneyed interest', whose interests were often at variance with those of the public. Yet during the American Civil War the wider public, however loosely defined, were large subscribers to Union debt. Later in the war, in an address delivered to a crowd of Western farmers and labourers, Chase boasted that, as a war financier, he had spurned England and turned to American investors for money.[19]

In terms of financial management, the Civil War, as in so many arenas, was the defining period of United States history. Before the war, 'America had neither a national currency nor, after the dissolution of the Second Bank of the United States, a national banking system'.[20] With regard to the currency, this was not strictly true, but the introduction of the greenback allowed a far greater measure of central control to the currency than had existed before. In the words of one writer, 'the Legal Tender and Revenue Acts of February and June 1862 and the National Currency Act of February, 1863 . . . pushed the exercise of federal power beyond precedent in any field. In these acts the 37th Congress had advanced federal power over the Northern States no less than over the Southern.'[21]

Meanwhile, the favoured economic tool of the Republican Party, the tariff, played an important role in the raising of finance for the central government. The 'high duties' which the war had imposed were, at first, regarded as temporary, but they were retained and even increased. The first of these tariff hikes was implemented by the once famous Morrill Tariff Act of 1861, which had been adopted even before the Civil War broke out. Yet the war helped the cause of the tariff, because, while it raged, 'all feeling of opposition to high import duties almost entirely disappeared'.[22] Not only was the tariff brought into play as a source of war revenue, the Civil War itself 'revolutionized the financial methods of the United States', by 'a series of extraordinary internal taxes': 'Every thing was taxed, and taxed heavily.' An income tax of 5 per cent was even raised on moderate incomes, and was applied at the rate of 10 per cent on incomes of more than US$10,000 a year.[23] This novel imposition, as far as federal taxes were concerned, was greeted with 'cordial acceptance', given the demands of wartime.[24]

Despite finding stringent and innovative ways to finance its war effort, the federal government resorted to borrowing on a heroic scale. As early as

February 1862, the Loan Act had authorized the issue of US$500 million worth of bonds. These bonds were payable after twenty years, but were redeemable after five years (they could be bought back by the government), and they paid 6 per cent interest per annum.[25] The issuance of federal debt, in an era when the federal government had been a great deal weaker than it would subsequently become, changed the United States. The national debt of the United States had stood at a paltry US$65 million in 1860. By 1866, after five bloody years of civil war, it had reached US$2,678 million.[26] Yet the issuance of so much debt had given a rather somnolent Wall Street the boost that it needed. 'The decade immediately following the Civil War, because of its extraordinary happenings in speculative finance and in legislative and judicial corruption, has been called the fantastic era,' wrote one observer in 1929.[27]

For all those who argue for a dynamic role to be adopted by government in stimulating economic growth, the history of money can afford some corroboration. We have seen how government borrowing stimulated such financial innovations as central banking in England in the last decade of the seventeenth century, and the conversion of debt into equity in both Paris and London in the early eighteenth century. In New York, the influence of government could be seen in the Wall Street of the 1860s. The issuance of government debt in the 1860s provided a platform which launched the careers of a 'distinctively American class of financiers'. In 1860, the US Secretary of the Treasury had estimated that foreign investment in the United States was about US$400 million. Between 1860 and 1863, the Civil War had 'dried up' European interest in new securities and had also witnessed the repatriation of half (about US$200 million) of the previous total. It was American capital which filled the void thus created. Symbolically, the New York Stock Exchange constructed its own building in 1863 and more than tripled its membership fees, from US$3,000 to US$10,000 between 1862 and 1866. This, however, did not deter the investment community, and it has been estimated that the number of bankers and brokers increased more than tenfold between 1864 and 1870.[28]

The conditions were now set for an extraordinary expansion of the United States economy. Interestingly, contrary to what is commonly

believed today about the efficacy of free markets and trade as an instrument of development, the United States continued throughout the second
half of the nineteenth century to be a strongly protectionist country. 'The
extreme protective system, which had been at the first a temporary
expedient for aiding in the struggle for the Union . . . gradually became
accepted as a permanent institution.' High protection became a 'dogma'.
Indeed, 'The restraint of trade with foreign countries, by means of import
duties of forty, fifty, sixty, even a hundred percent, came to be advocated
as a good thing in itself . . .' Ideas of this kind 'were no longer the exploded
errors of a small school of economists; they became the foundation of the
policy of a great people'.[29]

The Republican Party, the victorious party of the Civil War, the party of
the great quasi-martyr Abraham Lincoln, won election after general election in the forty-eight-year period from 1864 to 1912. In thirteen elections, the Democrats managed only three victories, the last of which
occurred in 1912. The only other years in which the Democrats won were
1884 and 1892, both of which were (uniquely in US history) won by the
same candidate, Grover Cleveland, who is known as both the twenty-
second and the twenty-fourth President of the United States. The
Republicans established themselves as a party of national economic might.
Their programme 'threw the entire weight of the federal government
behind the expansion of northern industry'. Republican policy naturally
supported a 'protective tariff for industry', and it was in these years that the
tariff became 'exclusively and distinctively a protective measure', shorn of
any idea that it was needed for revenue-raising purposes on the part of the
federal government.[30]

During the 1860s, the currency continued to be the soft greenback. It
was 'soft' because the currency was not backed by gold, as calls to resume
specie payments, the gold standard in short, were for a period rebuffed. In
his book *Outliers: The Story of Success*, the popular journalist Malcolm
Gladwell observed that in the 1860s and 1870s the 'American economy
went through perhaps the greatest transformation of its history'. Gladwell
added that this was the period when the 'railroads were being built and
when Wall Street emerged'. He was explaining why, of the seventy-five
richest people in human history, an impressive fourteen, or just under

20 per cent, were Americans born in one decade, the 1830s. The names he cites are an all-star team of capitalists and financial wizards. John Davidson Rockefeller (b. 1839) and Andrew Carnegie (b. 1835), perhaps unsurprisingly, come first and second in this list of the possessors of vast wealth. Other names include Cleopatra, the Roman general Marcus Licinius Crassus and Basil the Bulgar Slayer, a bloodthirsty Byzantine emperor of the eleventh century. For our purposes it is interesting to note that the banker J. P. Morgan (b. 1837), the Chicago retailer Marshall Field (b. 1834) and the Wall Street speculator Jay Gould (b. 1836) are others who were born in the same decade as Carnegie and Rockefeller.[31]

While such lists are hardly rigorous in their scientific method, it is significant that a considerable number of people who were in their late twenties to mid-thirties when the American Civil War ended in 1865 made enormous fortunes. It is a fact that the era in which much of this expansion took place was characterized by high levels of protection, paper money and very low levels of income tax. Much of the tax income raised in the Civil War by the federal government had been derived from sales taxes, which were not progressive (that is, the well off did not pay more as a proportion of their income than the less well off). The Republicans were identified quickly in the popular mind as the party of the New England bankers who bankrolled their industrialist friends and backed a gold currency. These type of people were the nearest the great republic ever came to an aristocracy. The kind of capitalism favoured by Rockefeller and Carnegie, shielded as they were by protection from foreign competition, was equally hostile to domestic competition. Rockefeller, the basis of whose fortune can be found in the industrial boom which followed the Civil War, conspired with others to 'kill competitive capitalism'. He was a monopolist who never hid his aversion to competition. 'The day of combination is here to stay. Individualism has gone never to return' was his rather terse and contemptuous dismissal of the notion of competition in business.[32]

If Rockefeller's practices were anti-competitive and monopolistic, the activities of his Wall Street contemporaries were even more dubious from a moral point of view. Men like Daniel Drew, a cattle trader turned Wall Street speculator, and Jay Gould were not particularly scrupulous in their

business activities. More conservative observers had noted the depreciation of the greenback. In 1866, this paper currency had sunk to a value of
only 37 cents to the old dollar, which had been backed by gold. The depreciation of the greenback dollar, after the conclusion of the Civil War,
formed the backdrop to a 'speculative mania such as the United States . . .
had never before known'. The whole nation, it seemed, 'flung itself into
the Stock Exchange . . . Everyone speculated, and for a time everyone
speculated successfully.'[33] Most characteristic of this bustling, hustling age
was James Fisk Jr, a native of Vermont known as 'Big Jim'. Fisk was 'coarse,
noisy, boastful', a 'young butcher in appearance', being large, florid and
gross, but he had considerable personal charm and his 'redeeming point
was his humour, which had a strong flavour of American nationality'. In
1865 he had just turned thirty. Fisk's business associate, Jay Gould, by
contrast, was 'dark, sallow . . . [and] reticent'.[34] It was their attempt to
corner the gold market on 24 September 1869 which gave the market the
term 'Black Friday', an epithet which has been appropriated for other days
of the week in subsequent financial history.

   The key feature of the American currency system between 1865, the end
of the Civil War, and 1879 was that there was no convertibility to gold.
The country used the paper greenback, since gold had been 'demonetized'.
In this environment, gold traded as a commodity, like wheat or copper,
and had no special status as legal tender. Gould and Fisk attempted to buy
up gold, because many believed that the government would need gold in
order to repurchase greenbacks. Gould started buying gold in the late
summer of 1869. On Monday 20 September, gold rose in price, and
continued to do so on the Tuesday and Wednesday. On Friday the 24th,
the government intervened, starting to sell a portion of its gold holdings.
The price in a few days had gone from 130 dollars an ounce to 162; it fell
back to 135 on that Friday, after the intervention from the government.[35]
The day was said to have been 'Black' from the perspective of speculative
buyers of gold. The attempt to corner the market had failed, leaving the
buyers with heavy losses.

   No move was made towards resumption of specie payments until 1879.
As an interim measure, Congress had passed the Coinage Act of 1873,
which prohibited the free coinage of silver. The United States Constitution

had given Congress the right 'to coin money, regulate the value thereof and of foreign coin'. It had also prohibited the states from making 'anything but gold and silver coin a tender in payment of debts'.[36] But from 1873 silver had no legal status in the United States as a currency. In the eyes of the proponents of silver, the Coinage Act was the 'crime of 1873'.[37] There followed a dispute about the status of silver, or about bimetallism (that is, using both gold and silver), which bubbled behind the scenes of American politics for a quarter of a century. In 1896, the presidential candidate of the Democratic Party, William Jennings Bryan, electrified his audience with his famous 'cross of gold' speech in which he denounced the gold standard favoured by the bankers and big businessmen of America's East Coast.[38] Bryan ran on a 'free silver' ticket, supported by farmers in the Mid-West, representatives of the old agrarian tradition of Thomas Jefferson. They favoured cheap money and easy loans, against the advocates of the gold standard, who were seen to represent the interests of the people lending the money, the bankers and Wall Street.

When specie payments were resumed in 1879, the US economy was at the beginning of a period of rapid growth. The identification of the Republican Party with the Union no doubt contributed to its extraordinary electoral success, but the great strides which had been made in the economy also helped to make the party appealing. From the point of view of the big industrialists, the Republican Party's adhesion to the tariff continued to be particularly attractive. A recent biographer has claimed that Carnegie, the steel magnate, was 'energized by the Harrison presidency'. Benjamin Harrison was a rather faceless Republican who held office from 1889 to 1893. Carnegie had contributed lavishly to Harrison's presidential campaign and felt his voice should be heard. During this presidency, the controversial McKinley Tariff of 1890 was introduced by the man who would defeat Bryan for the presidency in 1896. This tariff raised import duties to an average of 49.5 per cent. William McKinley himself, as well as being considered a stalwart of the gold standard, was also believed to be the 'high priest of high protection'. In his view the tariff created jobs and generated revenue for the government, while preserving the United States' industrial power.[39] It would seem fair to suggest that, for a steel manufacturer like Carnegie, the tariff was a helpful instrument of economic policy. It was appropriate that McKinley was the President who signed the Gold Standard Act of 1900. Although the US had 'followed the Gold Standard since 1879', the commitment to gold was only officially enshrined in the Act of 1900.[40]

Fortified by a gold currency, by a government which balanced its budget and by a protecting tariff, the industrial capitalists of the United States thrived during the late nineteenth century. The 1890s in particular were a decade of dramatic expansion. By 1907, the year of a major panic in the markets, the American economy had enjoyed an average annual growth rate of 7.3 per cent for more than a decade.[41] These growth rates were unprecedented in American history, and have only been equalled, in large countries, by the similarly impressive expansion of Japan in the 1950s and by China at the end of the twentieth century and beginning of the twenty-first. Such growth meant that all industrial production had doubled in absolute size in just ten years.

The one thing which the young, energetic United States lacked was, of course, a central bank. The events of 1907 hurried the United States towards such an institution. From June through September that year, the stock market in New York dropped another 8.1 per cent, and this was part of a decline of 24.4 per cent for first three quarters of the year. The fall in the market had occurred partly as a result of the San Francisco earthquake of 1906, after which gold reserves from New York had migrated to the stricken city to pay for much needed reconstruction. British insurers who were expected to pay for the damage in San Francisco sold their holdings of American shares, forcing prices downward. The Bank of England, fearful of the effect of declining liquidity in London, raised interest rates from 3.5 to 4 per cent, and then to 6 per cent in October 1906, the highest rate for seven years. On 18 December 1906, Jack Morgan, the son of J. P. Morgan, told his partners in London, 'things here are very uncomfortable owing to the tightness of money'.[42]

While the summer of 1907 had seen a tightness of money and a decline in the stock market, the financial panic on Wall Street itself occurred in late October.[43] 'The initial episode of the crisis on 16th October was, as has often happened in previous crises, insignificant enough.' An unsuccessful attempt to corner the stock of a minor copper company led to the failure

of certain brokerage firms. The crisis of 1907 reached its culminating point
in the collapse of the Knickerbocker Trust Company, a quasi-bank, which
had deposits of US$62 million, a collapse that began on Monday 21
October 1907. This occurred when the National Bank of Commerce
announced that it would no longer accept the cheques of the Knickerbocker
Trust.[44] On Thursday 24 October, the New York Stock Exchange President,
Ransom H. Thomas, went to J. P. Morgan's office and told him bluntly
that unless US$25 million were raised immediately, at least twenty-five
brokerage firms might fail. Thomas wanted to shut the Exchange. 'At what
time do you usually close it?' asked Morgan. This was an extraordinary
question from the man who was the leading banker on Wall Street, but he
considered stock trading vulgar and would not have been embarrassed to
be ignorant of the Exchange's trading hours. Thomas replied that trading
stopped at three o'clock. 'It must not close one minute before that today,'
replied Morgan.[45]

Morgan then summoned presidents of various New York banks and
relayed the news that dozens of brokerage firms would collapse unless the
required funds were forthcoming. The US$25 million was pledged in a
few minutes.[46] A subsequent meeting to arrange further finance took place
in J. P. Morgan's famous library, where there hung 'lofty, magnificent
tapestries' on the walls, amid a setting adorned by 'rare Bibles and illumi-
nated manuscripts of the Middle Ages', as Thomas Lamont, a future partner in the firm, remembered.[47] Through force of personality and a measure
of decisiveness, Morgan had provided the liquidity which prevented a
collapse of the financial system in New York. It was remarked at the time
that the Americans lacked a 'lender of last resort', along the lines described
nearly forty years previously by the Englishman Walter Bagehot, who in
turn had echoed Francis Baring's phrase of 1797. A direct consequence of
the 1907 panic was near-universal clamour for banking reform, and an
openness towards introducing a system of central banking comparable to
that which operated in Great Britain.

In 1907, J. P. Morgan was seventy years old, and had been a financier of
many of the great consolidations which had occurred in the 1880s and
1890s. His most famous achievement in finance had been the consolidation of US Steel in 1902, the first US$1 billion deal in the history of

corporate finance. He was an old-school Yankee, in the sense that he came from a banking family with ties to England, and had been born in Connecticut, New England, in 1837, which meant that the Civil War was very much a formative experience in his twenties.

Morgan represented old-world luxury, with his frequent holidays in Europe and his conservatism in finance. It is not surprising that he would be denounced as an elitist towards the end of his life. Perhaps more than any other individual, more than Carnegie and Rockefeller, Morgan typified the economic system of the United States before 1914. He had benefited from the opportunities for expansion which the Civil War and its aftermath created. He had been an eloquent and trenchant supporter of the gold standard in the debates of the 1890s. He had played a major role in the financing of deals which consolidated American industry, an industry which had been built behind a high tariff wall. Lastly, he had acted, in 1907, as an unofficial head of the central bank, organizing pools of capital to maintain confidence and liquidity during the crisis. Across the Atlantic, however, there would blow a gale which put the events of 1907 in Wall Street into their proper perspective. The war which broke out in 1914 would change the financial world for ever and would afford even greater opportunities for the financial power of the United States.

6

London 1914

London, at the beginning of 1914, was a civilized and self-contented city. John Maynard Keynes, a thirty-year-old Cambridge academic, remembered the time well when the inhabitant of London 'could order by telephone, sipping his morning tea in bed, the various products of the whole earth, in such quantity as he might see fit, and reasonably expect their early delivery upon his doorstep'. This fortunate gentleman 'could at the same time adventure his wealth in the natural resources and new enterprises of any quarter of the world, and share . . . in their prospective fruits and advantages'.[1]

In this justly famous passage from his *Economic Consequences of the Peace*, published in 1919, Keynes remarked on the apparent solidity of this state of affairs, which seemed 'normal', 'certain' and 'permanent'. The 'projects and politics of militarism and imperialism, of racial and cultural rivalries . . . which were to play the serpent to this paradise, were little more than the amusements of his [the London professional man's] daily newspaper'.[2] The world which Keynes referred to had never seemed more secure than at the beginning of 1914. This was the age in which British government bonds, known as gilts, represented the surest form of investment. By historic standards, and certainly by the standards of the inflationary 1970s, interest rates were relatively low. James Forsyte, in the 1880s, the eponymous patriarch of John Galsworthy's novel sequence *The Forsyte Saga*, felt it his right 'to invest his money at five per cent'.[3] Indeed, 5 per cent had been the historic maximum interest rate as decreed by British law. As Keynes himself observed, for 'seventy-six years – from 1st May 1746 to 20th June 1822, the Bank-rate stood unchanged at 5 per cent'.[4] In the period immediately after the legal maximum was repealed, the bank rate had actually fluctuated between 4 and 5 per cent. Keynes meticulously observed that the 'rate of 5½ per cent established on 20th June 1839' was the 'first occasion on which the official rate of the Bank of England had ever exceeded 5 per cent'.[5] Gilts paid a little less than that, and 3 per cent was considered a reasonable return.

For Forsyte, who had been engaged for 'fifty-four years . . . in arranging mortgages, preserving investments at a dead level of high and safe interest', the world of late Victorian capitalism was simply part of the natural order of things. In terms of currency, the gold standard reigned as an unquestioned fact of life. Keynes's description of the London upper-middle-class man buying international shares by telephone in bed, while sipping his morning tea, relied upon a gold currency. The mysterious investor, whom one of his biographers takes to be a description of Keynes himself, could 'despatch his servant to the neighbouring office of a bank for such supply of the precious metals as might seem convenient'. Once in possession of these metals, he 'could then proceed abroad to foreign quarters, without knowledge of their religion, language or customs, bearing coined wealth upon his person'.[6] This 'coined wealth' would have been gold currency. Keynes himself had started speculating on his own account with the help of an overdraft facility of £1,000 from Barclays Bank and a loan of another £1,000 from his friend the artist Roger Fry, a member of the wealthy Quaker Fry family who had made a fortune in chocolate.[7]

The ease and tranquillity with which the City of London conducted Britain's financial affairs gave rise to a certain complacency about the country's place in the world. This was a world in which half of global trade was financed by British capital.[8] More fundamentally, there was an appetite among the British investing public for foreign investment. 'The taste of the British public for investment abroad has grown rapidly with the increasing overflow of our surplus capital,' wrote Francis Hirst in his widely respected book *The Stock Exchange*, published in 1911. Hirst was a quintessentially Edwardian figure: a man with a double first in classics at Oxford, who had turned his well-trained mind to financial journalism and became editor of the *Economist* in 1907, at the precocious age of thirty-four. His creed, as had always been the case with the publication he edited, was one of undiluted classical liberalism. He was a believer in free markets,

and opposed conscription during the war, while railing against protectionism and irresponsible borrowing during the war itself, and writing trench-
antly in support of civil liberties.[9] His book on the Stock Exchange presents
an interesting insight into the City of London at the apex of its power. The
statements in the book have an air of oracular authority. 'For British
Consols [the standard British gilts] to yield more than 3 per cent in time
of peace and prosperous trade is certainly abnormal,' he declared.

The City of London that Hirst described was the centre of an intricate
network of international finance. In the words of the American journalist
and historian Herbert Feis, London was 'the centre of a financial empire',
in which 'distance lost all its meaning', and it was the international nature
of the City's business before 1914 which has often surprised modern economists.[10] While Paris was described by Hirst as the 'financier-in-chief' to
Russia, Spain and Turkey, London was the world's principal market in
foreign securities. Paris had its 'specialties', but foreign governments generally looked to London first to secure capital for their countries' development. In the case of Japan, Hirst observed, London held 'a great part of the
external debt'. This being the case, the price of Japanese bonds depended
'mainly upon London's judgement of financial strength at any given time'.
The rise of Japan had been 'of course . . . coincident with the creation of a
very heavy debt and a deplorably heavy system of taxation'. While Japan
had turned successfully to London as a source of finance, China had been
less receptive to this form of development finance. 'The awakening of
China has been very slow, but the pace has been marvellously quickened
in the last decade,' wrote Hirst in his 1911 work. His observations about
the Chinese are not without the casual racial stereotyping of the times:
'The Chinaman is not only a shrewd and competent businessman: he is
also a confirmed and incurable gambler.' Hirst noticed that 'From time to
time the Shanghai Stock Exchange becomes a scene of the wildest speculation' and that it was safe to predict that 'when a new China is evolved,
Stock Exchanges will spring up in all the large towns, and China will
become subject to vicissitudes and crises as violent as those which convulse
the United States'.[11]

London banking houses such as Barings and Rothschilds were key
participants in this international financing. Rothschilds of London was

the 'agent and guardian of Brazilian finance'. Hirst airily dismissed Central America, observing that it 'is hardly possible to speak of "investment" in Central America', since 'bankruptcy and repudiation are the rule, payment of interest the exception'.[12] The country which, of course, was seared on the consciousness of everybody in the City was Argentina, which had been the cause of the crisis in 1890, in which Barings had been laid low. The years preceding the actual failure of Barings were years of 'extensive speculation'. This may have been due to the same low-interest-rate environment which had prevailed in 1825, when low interest rates on government debt had prompted investors to seek riskier assets to order to obtain a better return, the 'search for yield' often referred to by modern market analysts.

Eighteen-eighty-eight was the year of the sensational crimes associated with the name 'Jack the Ripper'. In financial circles, it would be remembered as a year of significance, because it witnessed the 'conversion' of Britain's national debt. George Goschen, the Conservative Chancellor of the Exchequer between 1887 and 1892, simplified the nation's financial obligations by reducing the three different types of government debt which each paid 3 per cent into one new stock which would pay 2.75 per cent for fifteen years and then be reduced to 2.5 per cent for twenty years. This new 2.75 per cent rate would save the exchequer nearly £1.5 million a year, since the national debt was now £600 million. More relevantly from the point of view of the stock market, the lower interest rate, it has been argued, tempted investors to 'adventure their money', in Keynes's phrase, in higher-yielding, riskier stocks.

Whatever the actual cause of the speculative activity, a rush to Argentinian bonds occurred directly after Goschen's conversion of 1888. In the eyes of one early twentieth-century historian of the Bank of England, both '1888 and 1889 had been years of extensive speculation . . . probably due to the recent conversion of consols, which made the public look for investments with higher profits than 2¾ per cent'. A great many companies of a more or less speculative character were formed, such as American mining companies and brewery companies. In this context, a large proportion of the newly raised capital found its way to the Argentine Republic, and at the end of 1889 people in London began to become suspicious about the financial situation in Argentina.[13] Barings had been exposed to the fledgling capital markets in Argentina, helping to arrange loans and bonds to the government, as well as underwriting stock issues for companies. It was the attempt to underwrite the shares of one particular company, the Buenos Ayres Water Works Company, which pushed Barings to the brink of the abyss in November 1890. In this failed transaction, Barings had been obliged to keep the shares which they had 'underwritten'. Barings were also exposed to Argentinian sovereign debt, having been the main underwriter of the country's debt since independence.[14]

On Saturday 8 November, two or three 'prominent persons', of whom we can assume the Governor of the Bank of England was one, were informed of Barings' predicament. The following Friday it was agreed that the Bank of England should raise a fund which, at first, amounted to '5 or 6 millions' but rose to £10 million. The Governor of the Bank of England, William Lidderdale, was widely praised for showing so much 'resolution and courage'.[15] Having been informed of the situation on Saturday, Lidderdale is reported to have kept a cool head and spent the next day with his son at London Zoo.[16] During the following week, he arranged a loan of £3 million in gold from the Bank of France and a purchase of £1.5 million in gold from the Russian government to strengthen the Bank's reserve. These sums constituted the capital which, in an extreme situation, might be called upon. These loans and purchases might seem surprising, but it must be remembered that the Bank of England always operated with a very small amount of bullion held in reserve. As Goschen, the Chancellor of the Exchequer, observed in a speech in Leeds Town Hall in January 1891, 'the stock of bullion at the centre of this country is 24 millions, compared with 95 millions of gold and silver in the Bank of France', while there were '142 millions in the United States'.[17]

On Friday 14 November, the day on which the fund was arranged, Lidderdale saw the Prime Minister, Lord Salisbury, to inform him of the solution and of the reserve fund which he had organized for Barings. The conclusion of the drama was that Barings ceased to be a partnership and was reconstituted as a joint-stock company, in which there would be limited liability. The whole transaction was conducted with admirable swiftness, and banks outside London were 'hardly sensible of the crisis'. Remarkably, there were no failures among the county banks, either in the towns or in the countryside.[18] On Monday 17 November, the City was beginning 'to breathe again a little more freely'.[19]

Lidderdale, despite being widely praised, was asked to be Governor for only an extra year, but it meant a third year in office which was almost unprecedented in the history of the Bank of England up to that point. The manner in which this situation had been addressed was not that different from the way in which J. P. Morgan dealt with the panic in New York in 1907. The difference was that Lidderdale acted in an official capacity as the Governor of the Bank of England, while J. P. Morgan acted in an unofficial way, and used his high personal prestige to fulfil a similar role. This informality, the relatively ad hoc nature of the manner in which crises were dealt with, was a marked characteristic of financial arrangements of the time, in both London and New York. The rather leisurely and informal approach to financial supervision was matched by senior officials at the Treasury in Britain, where the Permanent Secretary from 1903 to 1911, Sir George Murray, was reported to have an 'old-fashioned three-course breakfast before coming to the office'. He would then 'work at his desk till one o'clock, when the messenger would bring him a large Havana cigar on a silver tray'. After half an hour or so, smoking and reading newspapers, Murray would resume work at 1.45 p.m. and work till 6 p.m., after which he left the office and went to his club, where, it was said, he 'did himself very well at dinner'.[20]

Both cities had a social structure dominated by a thin crust of plutocrats who, perhaps more in London than in New York, were by the early twentieth century very much in a class of their own. London had always welcomed talented foreign immigrants into the City. The City editor of *The Times* would complain in 1910 of the City being full of 'Hebrew millionaires and plodding Germans', but overwhelmingly the City stockbroker and banker was now of a certain type.[21] Between 1890 and 1914, the City was dominated by an 'aristocracy composed of the most prominent merchants, merchant bankers and private bankers'. These 'aristocrats', men of financial acumen and power, were now almost on equal terms with the landed aristocracy.[22] The City aristocracy were now much more uniform in terms of their social and educational provenance than had been the case half a century before. Education at a major public school, generally Eton or Harrow, membership of a distinguished London club and marriage into the 'aristocracy or the gentry' were very common characteristics of many of the leading City financiers.[23] The Edwardian age in Britain, at least for those at the top of society, has been most evocatively described by that great observer of British mores, the journalist George Orwell. In an essay 'Such, Such were the Joys', admittedly published only in 1952, Orwell remembered the opulent days of the British upper classes before 1914.

> There never was, I suppose, in the history of the world a time when the sheer vulgar fatness of wealth, without any kind of aristocratic elegance to redeem it, was so obtrusive as in those years before 1914 ... From the whole decade before 1914, there seems to breathe forth a smell of the more vulgar, un-grown-up kinds of luxury, a smell of brilliantine and crème de menthe and soft-centred chocolates – an atmosphere, as it were, of eating everlasting strawberry ices on green lawns to the tune of the Eton Boating Song.

Orwell spoke, decades later, of the 'oozing, bulging wealth of the English Upper and Upper-Middle classes'. Yet this picture of insouciant luxury hides some of the hard, professional work undertaken in the City of London at that time. The late nineteenth century was, after all, the period when professions such as accountancy received their first official recognition. The Institute of Chartered Accountants in England and Wales (ICAEW) was inaugurated in 1880. The Companies Act of 1862 was known as the 'accountants' friend', in that it gave them a profession.[24] Newly built railways, like the Metropolitan Line, brought thousands of commuters from the suburbs of London into the City every day to pursue relatively modern careers as actuaries or insurers. According to a census undertaken in 1891, there were 701 accountancy firms operating in the City, as well as over 2,000 firms of solicitors.[25] Accounting offered a route to prosperity, even affluence, for the lower-middle classes. One such person who did spectacularly well was John Ellerman, the son of a small-time corn merchant of a German Lutheran background. Born in 1862, Ellerman qualified as a chartered accountant in Birmingham. He opened his own firm of accountants in London at 10 Moorgate, and used his professional skill to acquire interests in a number of enterprises. By 1900, he had abandoned professional accountancy for a career as a shipping magnate. He also acquired significant interests in breweries and collieries and, by 1910, was considered the richest man in Britain.[26]

Contrary to the image portrayed by Orwell, the City's working week was actually longer than would be the case in subsequent decades. Saturday was generally a working day, right up to the end of the nineteenth century. City workers, as they always had been, were eager and ambitious. As Walter de Zoete, a member of the Stock Exchange from 1867 to 1909, advised his son, in 'the city as a young man you never walk but always run'.[27] The naturalist Richard Meinertzhagen remembered the misery of his job in the City, when he entered his father's bank in January 1896 and was allocated a 'small windowless room' and sat in this 'airless cell from 9am to 6pm'. He was given all sorts and conditions of 'Bills of lading, Accounts, Letters of Credit, Acceptances and Cheques which I did not understand and did not want to understand'. He 'loathed' the 'whole business and was miserable'. The business itself seemed to be 'making huge loans of cash on coffee crops in Brazil and Costa Rica, on furs from Russia, on wool from Australia and the Argentine'. It all seemed alien and dull to the eighteen-year-old. Moreover, he hated having to 'wear a black coat, London trousers and a top hat every day'. After a few months of this hellish experience, Meinertzhagen joined the army, where he was much happier.

While the City of London continued to suffer its share of hucksters and confidence tricksters, it also attracted talented foreigners who made considerable fortunes. Men like the German-born Sir Felix Schuster, 'a financier and economist of conspicuous ability', were able to make their way in a City which was often open and meritocratic, while paradoxically being conservative and retaining its clubby feel. Arguably, the most significant and successful of these immigrants was Sir Ernest Cassel, a German Jew who had been born in Cologne in 1852. In later life, Cassel gave such conflicting accounts of his youth that the full truth has been difficult to establish. He was reported to have emigrated to Liverpool in 1869, where he arrived with nothing more than a 'bag of clothes and a violin'. He then started working for a firm of German grain merchants in Liverpool. After a number of jobs in finance houses, including a short spell in Paris as a clerk in the Anglo-Egyptian Bank, he was taken on by a London merchant bank, Bischoffsheim and Goldschmidt, a firm whose origins lay in the 1820s in Belgium.

Cassel had a natural flair for business and deal making. His key strength was his ability to 'think on the massive scale demanded by a world developing more rapidly than ever before'.[28] In 1884, he struck out on his own, but his employers were good enough to allow him space in their offices until 1898. Cassel had a range of contacts and a sharpness in his deal making which aroused a great deal of suspicion. His financial interests were, by any standards, extensive. He arranged loans for Japan, Egypt, Turkey and Russia. He was a key financier of Swedish development and enterprise. He possessed in the words of Saemy Japhet, a business partner and banker, a 'unique power of concentration'.[29] Yet much of his prodigious energies were consumed not in the making of money but in the advancing of his social position and prestige. A member of the Carlton and Garrick clubs, he yearned for social recognition and accumulated a steady succession of honours and distinctions. He became a KCMG (Knight Commander of the Order of St Michael and St George) in 1899, and was sworn of the Privy Council in 1902, after the accession of his friend King Edward VII, whose patronage eased his entry into circles which would otherwise have been closed to a self-made German Jew. There also followed a string of pompous-sounding foreign titles and honours, including the Légion d'honneur (France) in 1906, the Grand Cross of the Polar Star (Sweden) in 1909 and the Order of the Rising Sun (Japan) in 1911. Cassel lived in splendour. He had numerous homes, including Brook House in Park Lane, with its six marble-lined kitchens and oak-panelled dining room designed to seat a hundred people. Its entrance hall was described by his granddaughter's friends as the 'giant's lavatory'. His other properties included a flat in Paris, villas in Switzerland, the South of France and Bournemouth, and a stud farm at Moulton Paddocks in Newmarket.[30]

Yet despite the enormous worldly success of people like Cassel, and despite its cosmopolitan charm, the City of London was, by 1914, a reflection of fading grandeur, of a country whose industrial position had been overtaken by the United States and Germany. The City's halcyon days occurred, perhaps ironically, after the meridian of Great Britain's industrial dominance of the world had already passed. Britain was falling dramatically behind its competitors in new industries such as electricity and chemistry. It had lost its pre-eminence in steel manufacturing as early as the late 1880s.[31] Yet, in matters of finance, London's dominance was more assured in the years immediately preceding 1914 than at any time before or since.

The first half of 1914 seemed no different from any other year. Historians have only recently begun to appreciate how quickly and unexpectedly the cataclysm of the First World War broke. The distinguished economic historian Niall Ferguson has reminded modern scholars that 'bond prices did not fall in the run-up to war in 1914 because the war was unexpected'. He has also reminded us that the UK 'accounted for just 3.6% per cent of all gold held by banks and treasuries in 1913'. This would not have surprised contemporaries in any way. The paucity of the Bank of England's gold reserves was notorious. Ferguson has also pointed out that it was not until 22 July 1914 – more than 'three weeks after the Sarajevo assassinations – that the possibility of a European crisis was first mentioned as a potential source of financial instability'.[32] Yet an American historian, writing in 1925, could confidently assert that the 'suddenness with which the European War broke out in the middle of 1914, the total absence of popular belief in the possibility of any such event, up to the very week in which it came, are *familiar history* [my italics]'.[33]

The assassination of the Archduke Ferdinand and of his wife, Sophie, had occurred on 28 June 1914. Despite this, financial markets failed 'so completely to foreshadow coming events that on July 4th, a week after the Archduke was assassinated . . . it was reported from the London Stock Exchange that the tragedy in the House of Habsburg "has had no effect"'.[34] On 9 July, observers in Berlin simply noted that the 'Norway visit of the Kaiser marks the beginning of the dead season in German politics'. In 1915, a financial writer remembered that 'not one' of the political and diplomatic experts 'on the morrow of Sarajevo' showed 'the slightest apprehension of the terrible sequel which deluged Europe with blood'. The

Times report covering the assassination spoke complacently of the 'new heir-presumptive', a more conservative figure than the Archduke, being 'unlikely to tread in his uncle's footsteps'. As a consequence, the 'constitutional development of the Hapsburg realms' seemed likely to 'proceed on steadier lines'.[35]

Contemporary accounts all bear witness to the unforeseen suddenness with which events took a violent turn. The general optimism of the era was something which all those who experienced it would never forget. Clive Bell, the Bloomsbury art critic, wrote in his 1917 essay 'Before the War': 'Not I suppose, since 1789 have days seemed more full of promise than those spring days of 1914.'[36] The war itself, wrote the financial journalist Hartley Withers in 1915, 'came upon us like a thunderbolt from a clear sky'.[37] When the markets' mood turned, it changed suddenly. On the morning of Friday 31 July 1914, there occurred what the *Economist* called the 'final thunderclap', the closure of the London Stock Exchange. As was observed at the time, the Exchange in London had never, 'even in the Napoleonic Wars', been suspended.[38] The market remained closed for the rest of the year. Despite the United States not yet being a belligerent in the conflict, the New York Stock Exchange closed too, as it would have been 'disastrous' for it to have remained open, given that foreign investors would have wanted to raise cash by selling their shares in American companies listed in New York.

Patrick Shaw Stewart, a young managing director of Barings Bank, wrote to his friends about what was happening. Shaw Stewart would turn twenty-six in August 1914. He had enjoyed a highly successful career at Oxford, where he was elected a Fellow of All Souls College in 1910, after winning a double first in classics at Balliol, as well as an impressive list of scholarships and prizes. His observations at the very beginning of August 1914 were sharp and perceptive. He commented firstly on the 'inevitable suspension of specie payments' and the need to 'stop the flow of gold out of the country somehow'. He noticed that the 'Americans [had] shipped vast quantities of gold' and had closed the New York Exchange, precisely to stop the liquidation of their stocks. Shaw Stewart declared that there was 'no panic in London', but he ominously noted that the 'entire existing machinery of credit is unequal to the international situation'.

To Shaw Stewart, a young banker who had combined a gilded social life with great academic success, the new world was full of promise. He noticed on 5 August how exciting it was in the City 'with the whole world going on a paper currency, and everyone owing everyone else money . . . at a bank rate of ten per cent'.[39] The bank rate had been raised to 10 per cent on 1 August, principally to stop the outflow of gold which was haemorrhaging from the Bank of England. Keynes, contrary to the stance he adopted later, was in favour of maintaining the gold standard. He believed that the future position of the City would be jeopardized if specie payments were suspended at the first sign of crisis.[40] Already an informal adviser at the Treasury, he wished to retain gold payments for international transactions, but restrict them internally. The panic had seen banks, fearful for their own solvency, cashing in their banknotes for gold at the Bank of England and then, notoriously, refusing to supply their own customers with gold. This double standard aroused the ire of the young Cambridge economist. 'Our system', he wrote, 'was endangered, not by the public running on the banks, but by the banks running on the Bank of England.' As a result of this 'internal run', the central bank's gold reserves had fallen from £17.5 million to £11 million in three days.[41]

The predicament of the banks, as described by Patrick Shaw Stewart, was acute. The 'main difficulty in two words', as this clever young banker saw it, was 'to prop up those big houses who have debts owing from Germany which will never be paid, and, if they go under, to prevent the whole City coming down like a pack of cards'.[42] The public, once the banks had suspended gold payments for customers, received paper money, notes issued by the British Treasury for everyday purposes, with denominations of £1 and 10 shillings (50p in modern terms). These notes were known as 'Bradburies', after Sir John Bradbury, the Joint Permanent Secretary of the Treasury. Gold payments for external trade and debts were preserved. By 8 August, after the suspension of gold payments internally, the bank rate was back to its more traditional level of 5 per cent. The immediate banking crisis had passed. The public may have thought, according to Shaw Stewart, that 'all is well now', after receiving the paper notes, but 'if you saw the length of the faces of those who know, you would realise this is one of the most terrific things London has been up against since finance existed'. Shaw Stewart wisely observed that the remedy would 'undoubtedly take the form of the Government shoulder-ing the whole thing'.

This casual Edwardian idiom about the government 'shouldering the whole thing' went to the core of the issue. The British government, in its fiscal policies, had been impressively consistent for a hundred years. Remarkably, the century from 1815 to 1914 had seen British nominal national debt actually fall. The debt in 1818 stood at £843 million. After a century of balanced budgets, that figure stood at just under £706 million in 1914.[43] This fact was a great testament to prudence and financial restraint, a legacy of the attitude towards public finance of such statesmen as Sir Robert Peel and his protégé William Gladstone. By 1921, after four years of carnage and three more of financial upheaval, the gold standard was still suspended and the national debt had soared to £7.8 billion, a nominal increase of 1,154 per cent in just seven years.

War inevitably put an end to the balanced rectitude of Victorian public finance. Yet there were also wider political currents which, astute contem-poraries remarked, had changed the government's attitude to public spending. Bernard Mallet, a career civil servant, had observed in 1913 that the previous twenty-five years had, in the 'political sphere', witnessed 'the final though long delayed triumph of the democratic elements in the constitution; and [they had] . . . also witnessed, whether as a consequence or not, a continuous decline in the power to control expenditure' which politicians like Gladstone had been 'accustomed to exercise'.[44] Although no causality is implied, there is a strong hint in this observation that demo-cratic electorates would place more demands on the exchequer through their desire for greater public spending. But, for the time being, it was once again the need to finance war, more than democracy, which proved to be a powerful agent of radical change in the sphere of money and public finance.

PART II

War: The Consequences of Armageddon, 1914–1945

Guns and Shells

Although unexpected, the outbreak of war in 1914 did not initially change the behaviour of the belligerents in many ways. Despite the suspension of gold payments internally, very few people in Europe anticipated that the war would last as long as it did. Few foresaw that a consequence of the war would, in fact, be the eclipse of London as a financial centre by New York. During the late summer of 1914, the immediate requirement was to finance the war. The atmosphere of uncertainty prevailed throughout August. It was in 1914 that John Maynard Keynes, the British economist, first properly emerged as a practical man of affairs

Keynes plays such a prominent role partly as a result of an accident of birth and his social background. Born in 1883 in Cambridge, the son of a university academic, Keynes was thirty-one at the outbreak of the First World War and, because of his connections, rapidly found himself involved in seeking innovative ways to finance Britain's war effort. A Cambridge don in economics, he was already the editor of the leading economics academic publication, the *Economic Journal*. As a journalist and academic theorist, as a polemicist and bureaucrat, his influence on events was significant, and from 1914 to his somewhat premature death in 1946 he participated, directly as an actor and adviser, in every development of international monetary affairs. Looking back in 1923 over his role in the war, he observed that he 'was in the Treasury throughout . . . and all the money we either lent or borrowed passed through my hands'.[1] This may have been an exaggeration, but it was not that far from the truth. He officially joined the Treasury in January 1915, but had been widely consulted in the highest circles of government since the summer of 1914.

Moreover, not only was Keynes a practical man of affairs, working in high bureaucratic circles, he was also a writer of great ability, who, by the written word, could galvanize opinion and dramatize situations, making the issues clear to intelligences less sharp and lucid than his own. Mention has already been made of his 1919 classic *The Economic Consequences of the Peace*, which became an instant success and is almost certainly the best-known work of popular economics – indeed among the best-known pieces of literature of any kind – to have emerged from the war itself.

Luckily for modern historians, Keynes did not only leave books as a memorial to the conflict, but in articles for newspapers he set out with his inimitable lucidity many of the key financial issues which the war had raised. In an article in the *Morning Post* entitled 'Currency Measures Abroad', he remarked rather boastfully, as early as 11 August 1914, that France, Russia and Germany had not followed England's example in maintaining the obligation for conversion of the notes into gold.[2] As we have seen, Britain's commitment to gold convertibility extended only to foreign transactions. For the people of Britain it was the first time since 1821 that their paper notes were not backed by gold currency which they could convert on demand. Keynes's articles for the *Morning Post* were revealing for the light they shed on war finance, not only of the British government but of other belligerent powers. He noticed very quickly in October 1914 that the German government was issuing 'large quantities of inconvertible paper money'. Keynes's particular strength was in the diverse range of skills he brought to bear. He was an excellent mathematician, but there had been better students in mathematics at Cambridge. He was a very good writer, but perhaps lacked the imagination of his friends E. M. Forster and Virginia Woolf. He was a highly capable philosopher, but did not aspire to contribute to the subject in the way that his friends Bertrand Russell and, later, Ludwig Wittgenstein did.

Keynes, however, brought all these various skills to bear as an economist. With his statistical bent he quickly noticed that the German government was spending about £2 million a day, and he referred to this fact in an article for the *Morning Post* published on 16 October. He would have been among the first people to comment on this, as the Reichsbank's figures were published only on 7 October.[3] Keynes's knowledge and his impregnable self-assurance are revealed in his memoranda on the subject of war finance. His sense of superiority, shared by many members of the British ruling class, was also on display, especially when he discussed the financing capabilities of other countries. In his 'Notes on French Finance', finished on 6 January 1915, he wrote that by 'the end of August the economic condition of France had become exceedingly serious'. The 'disorganisation of industry' in France was 'appalling'. The 'complete breakdown of transport, of the posts and of means of communication generally' had been much aggravated by the 'breakdown of credit'. But, Keynes observed with relief, the 'credit breakdown' had not caused the distress 'which a similar breakdown must have occasioned in England, because the credit system of France . . . is still much underdeveloped'.

Keynes's remarks were strictly for internal consumption, for his masters sitting proudly in the neoclassical splendour of His Majesty's Treasury in Whitehall. He offered a damning portrait, enriched by his trademark use of mock outrage and biting contempt:

> The story of French banking during the last decade is a long one – sordid, corrupt, disastrous and deeply intertwined with the basest feature of French political life . . . [the French] had come to depend more and more for their profits on company promotion and speculative underwriting, and have industriously prostituted their influence with their clients to the end of inducing them to embark their savings in most doubtful enterprises, mines, rubber shares, South American securities . . .[4]

Keynes also noticed in the same memorandum that it was 'still extremely usual in France both for private persons and for traders to keep astonishingly large sums of money in their possession'.[5] This was a point which was frequently made about French money from the time of Bagehot in the 1870s until the outbreak of the Second World War. 'Behind Paris', wrote Hartley Withers, the financial journalist and later editor of the *Economist*, 'stands the enormous power of the thrifty French investor, who probably accumulates a greater proportion of his income than anybody in the world.' For this reason, according to Withers, London had the 'more elastic credit system', since Paris was not 'businesslike', especially in respect of its 'huge store of gold', which the French regarded as 'a precious asset to be sat on and protected'.[6] Of course, British economists and bankers made frequent allusion to this attitude. The French were supposed to place too much reliance on gold hidden underneath their beds, while the British enjoyed well-developed capital markets, backed by the strength and traditions of Lombard Street.

The German capital markets were perhaps better organized than those of the French. Germany, with its longer tradition of independent states, was less centralized than France. The 'inconvertible paper money' which Keynes had spotted as a key element of Germany's war financing was essentially converted into debt, war loans, bought up by a patriotic German public. Borrowing was, perhaps more than in any other country, the principal means by which the Germans funded their war machine.

The struggle, from a financial point of view, was often characterized as a contest between Germany and Great Britain. One of Germany's roles was 'as banker to its allies', a role which Britain had traditionally played in European wars since the eighteenth century. 'We are the grand reserve of the Allied cause,' Winston Churchill boomed in a speech in his constituency of Dundee on 5 June 1915.[7] In the minds of many contemporaries, despite the enormous sacrifice made by French, Austrian, Russian and Turkish soldiers in the first three years of the conflict, Britain and Germany were held to be the principal antagonists. General Groener, the last quartermaster general of the imperial army, wrote that in the First World War the 'German General Staff fought against the English parliament'.[8] This, of course, was a grotesque caricature of the conflict, but it serves to sharpen the issues, particularly when relating to the very different ways in which Britain and Germany financed the war.

The Germans started the war, much like the British, with a large war loan. The first such loan was made in September 1914, just a month after the outbreak of fighting. Other issues of debt followed, twice a year, with impressive regularity every March and September. All the debt issues were successful and raised impressive amounts for the German war effort. The ninth and last loan was raised in the last six weeks of the war, just as the German military machine was on the verge of surrender. While the first loan brought subscriptions of 4.5 billion marks, the second issue doubled this amount, and subsequently no issue fell below 10 billion marks. The biggest loan was undertaken in March 1918, the month of the German spring offensive. This raised nearly 15 billion marks. In total, a sum of nearly 100 billion marks was raised. This contrasts with the total war loan of 350 million marks [US $4.2 million] raised during the Franco-Prussian War, only forty-five years before.[9]

The Germans could not use the sale of foreign securities to finance their war effort to the same extent as the British and, to a lesser degree, the French. Britain and France had before the war made large investments abroad, while most German capital was employed in developing domestic industries. In addition to this, such German overseas investments as there were tended to be in enemy countries. German investments in France, England, Russia and Italy were all unavailable to Germany, and these investments were estimated at 'seven or eight billions [marks]', more than the 'five billions' the Germans had invested in the industries of their allies, Austria-Hungary, Turkey, Bulgaria and Rumania.[10]

The enormous loans Germany managed to secure for itself were accompanied by a large issue of paper money. The phenomenon of German inflation during the war, and in the early 1920s, when people were reported to be using wheelbarrows to carry cash to the shops, is well known. On 23 July, the week before the war started, there were about 2 billion marks in circulation. Just before the war's end, on 7 November 1918, the circulation had reached nearly 27.5 billion marks. By the end of December 1919, this figure had reached 49.6 billion, twenty-four times the sum at the beginning of the war. The German government had resorted to the printing press to a degree unmatched by either France or Britain. Just as in the Napoleonic Wars, the British had managed, despite their use of a paper currency, to keep inflation 'within narrow bounds'. In Germany, by contrast, from August 1914 'an avalanche of [paper] notes destined to continue all though the war' descended on the German people. Inflation was one of 'Germany's chief instruments of war finance', and this led inevitably to big business profits. This was shown by the publication of a table of dividends of the companies quoted on the Frankfurt exchange, published by the *Frankfurt Gazette* on 6 November 1917. In this interesting table, chemical companies were paying dividends of 17 per cent, while machine manufacturers were paying an average of 14 per cent, a very high dividend which was no doubt in line with inflation, but showed the degree to which the owners of capital could shield themselves from the ravages of inflation while ordinary people, most of whose income was spent purchasing goods, and who had no investments, suffered.[11]

Yet the most debilitating failure of German finance was its inability to raise tax revenue. 'The weakest feature of the German war finances was the lack of a vigorous tax policy.'[12] Even before the war, it was estimated that the average Prussian subject paid 42.5 marks in tax per head in 1902. By contrast, the figure per head in France was 79.5 marks and in Britain it was 101.44 marks, nearly two and a half times as much as the Prussian figure. Even the German politicians themselves, men like Karl Helfferich, the German Vice Chancellor between 1916 to 1917, recognized this. As Helfferich put it, 'The British Ministers, at the beginning of the war, called upon their good old tradition, to get money for the war as far as possible through taxes.' He claimed that 45 per cent of the cost of the Napoleonic Wars had been paid for in this way.[13] After the war, Helfferich acknowledged that the war had imposed so many financial demands that even 'England could cover only a modest portion of the costs of war by means of war taxes.' Germany, in his view, was constrained by its Constitution. The German states were very reluctant to surrender their powers of taxation to the imperial government, which had the means of pressure (*Druckmittel*), but had no power of compulsion (*Zwangsmittel*) over the states.[14] When the German empire was established in 1871, several states had 'already appropriated to themselves the most fruitful sources of revenue'. The Constitution marked out a boundary, so that direct taxes and industrial earnings were apportioned to the states, while indirect taxes were given to the imperial government. The states 'fought every move to strengthen the imperial finances at their expense'.[15]

This failure to raise taxes sufficiently to pay for the war was in marked contrast to what was happening in Great Britain. In Britain, the total tax receipts, calculated in marks, were 10.6 billions in the year 1916, while in Germany, a country which was in 1910 as populous as Britain, the figure was only 1.4 billion, not even a seventh of the British total. In addition to the German imperial government's failure to raise tax revenue, the states did not collect enough revenue to compensate for this deficiency. According to a contemporary observer, all the 'German states and municipalities may have increased their tax revenues in 1914–16 as compared with 1913 by [no more than] a few hundred million marks', an increase rendered even less significant given that 'one must not overlook that municipal taxes were also raised in Great Britain'.[16] The failure of Germany to use taxes to extract the most from its people was conspicuous. 'That the German authorities, with their long and thorough study of every aspect of war economy . . . should have fallen so completely into the pitfall of a weak tax policy', wrote the Yale University scholar Fred Fairchild in 1922, seemed 'an anomaly difficult to explain'. Yet the political structure of imperial Germany does go a long way in helping to understand the causes of this anomaly. Britain and France were more successful in this respect. 'Great Britain made unprecedented demands upon her taxpayers from the start,' noted Fairchild. Even France, 'handicapped by a weak and obsolete tax system', did not 'turn her back upon taxation in the German fashion'.[17]

The British also borrowed considerable amounts. And yet, during the period from 1 August to 30 September 1914, the first two full months of the war, Britain had raised 30.5 per cent of its income through taxation. This was a low figure compared with peacetime rates, but was remarkable given the unprecedented need for such large sums of money. The resolve on the part of the British to bear at least a portion of the cost of the war through taxes was expressed in the mood of the House of Commons. For centuries, taxation had been a prerogative of the legislature. This prerogative, after all, had been what the American colonies' cry of 'no taxation without representation' had been all about. The parliamentary nature of British government was an important aspect of the war. The Chancellor of the Exchequer presented the annual budget in Parliament, so there was always an opportunity to debate the government's expenditure.

On 27 November 1914, David Lloyd George, the Chancellor of the Exchequer, gave the Commons a comprehensive review of the country's financial position. 'We have raised the largest loan ever raised in the history of the world for any purpose.' The following February, in another speech to the Commons, the Chancellor mentioned 'figures . . . well calculated to take away the breath of any . . . Parliament', but the 'House of Commons heard them without flinching'.[18] The Chancellor predicted that the aggregate expenditure of the Allies would not be short of £2 billion. Considering that the national debt stood at around £650 million in 1914, this was an enormous sum. After the third budget in September 1915, the *Economist* described it as 'a plain, unvarnished statement of unparalleled revenues, an inconceivable expenditure, and an unimaginable deficit, followed by a list of fresh taxation which placed an unprecedented burden on the country'.[19] In Britain, total government expenditure increased by more than thirteen times in real terms between 1913–14 and its peak in 1917–18.

In all this spending, it was the British willingness to impose greater taxes which aroused admiration. Receipts from the two most significant sources of indirect taxation, customs and excise duties, doubled in nominal terms, but the increases in direct tax receipts were more impressive. Property and income taxes increased by more than six times in nominal terms between 1913–14 and 1917–18. The standard income tax rate was doubled from 6 to 12 per cent in the first war budget of November 1914. It was then increased steadily, finally hitting 30 per cent in 1918–19. The income level at which it was applied was also reduced from £160 to £130 in 1915. This move combined with wage inflation ensured that the number of taxpayers increased from 1.1 million before the war to 3.5 million in 1918. Most of the new British taxpayers were salaried workers who became liable for taxation between 1916 and 1918.[20]

Yet the most successful aspect of the British revenue-raising measures did not come from the income tax or indirect taxes. The most significant wartime fiscal innovation was the 'excess profits duty'. This had been introduced in the third wartime budget, of September 1915. The rate was introduced at a punitive 50 per cent and the duty taxed profits in excess of what was deemed the peacetime standard. We have seen how German corporates made enormous sums of money during the war. In Britain, by contrast, the excess profits duty was an aggressive tax on profits which could otherwise have been ploughed back into the business as capital. More surprisingly, it was raised to 60 per cent in April 1916. Then, finally, it was moved up once again to 80 per cent in May 1917. There was much evasion, but its general success is indisputable. By 1918–19 it was generating £285 million for the Treasury. This was almost a third of the government's revenue for that year.[21] The 'excess profits duty' also showed the single-mindedness with which Britain applied itself to winning the war. The London of 1914 had been the home of Lombard Street, of liberal capitalism, of the upper-class world depicted by writers like P. G. Wodehouse and John Galsworthy. Yet, in a sudden reversal, Britain would tax its capitalists more rigorously than any of the other belligerents.

Despite the considerable demands on British finance, the British government felt confident enough to give loans to foreign governments, to a greater extent than it borrowed from them. Total overseas borrowing by the government during the war amounted to £1,365 million by the end of the financial year 1918–19. Balancing this sum, however, was the £1,741 million that the British government had lent to overseas governments. Some £568 million had been lent to Russia, the biggest recipient of British loans. The domestic debt, owed to British investors, was a much more significant part of the British national debt than any debts to foreigners which had been incurred. Less than one-fifth of the national debt of £7,280 million in March 1919 was owed to foreigners.[22]

Around 75 per cent of Britain's foreign loans came from the United States, despite its being for most of the war a neutral country. It was America, as contemporaries slowly began to realize, that would benefit from the exhaustion of the long-term belligerent powers. According to an American writing in the 1920s, the commitment of New York to keeping gold payments 'provided the plainest possible evidence to the outside world that the United States was at the moment . . . the one locality in which the world's floating capital could be safely lodged without fear of depreciation of its value'. It was revealed that the United States could 'lend on a wholly unprecedented scale to other countries while redeeming its own foreign debt by the thousands of millions'. As foreigners sold their American shares and bonds to raise money for the war, the Americans could buy assets back, while lending more money to the very same foreign powers. New York became a haven for capital. It was said that 'working balances', generally cash on deposit, were 'deposited in American banks, as they had been habitually deposited in British banks'.[23]

Not only did the war provide a significant boost to American finance. The economy of the United States, its agriculture and industry, was supplied with new markets, of almost limitless scope. There occurred, as a result of the war, a collapse of European harvests and agriculture. More particularly, 'the entry of the Ottoman Empire into the war on the German side at the end of October [1914] completed the blockade of Russia'. This was important since the 'wheat consumers of Central and Western Europe' had usually 'drawn in a single year upwards of 150 million bushels' from this source. No more food supplies could be obtained from Russia. The American farmers picked up these markets. 'During the four months beginning with December, 1914, the US exported 98,000,000 bushels.' This was more than five times the 18 million bushels which had been exported in the same period in 1913.[24] The demand for armaments led inevitably to a period of 'unprecedented activity' for the US steel industry. In May 1915, the British government ordered US$100 million worth of goods from the Bethlehem Steel Company for lyddite shells and shrapnel.

In addition to Britain's need for more imports of armaments from the United States, American manufacturers were further supported by the fact that, as Britain itself was a belligerent, British armaments and industrial manufacturers concentrated on meeting the needs of the domestic market. In other words, neutral countries which had relied on Britain for their industrial goods needed a fresh source of supply. 'Through force of necessity they turned to the United States.'[25] US exports to Asia, South America, Mexico and Canada, among other markets, rose from US$2.4 billion in 1914 to US$6.3 billion in 1917, an increase of 260 per cent. The commentator who made this observation concluded with the overstatement that 'whether judged by its magnitude or by the suddenness of its occurrence, it is perfectly safe to say that this achievement . . . was something unparalleled in the world's commercial history'.[26]

The connection between America's ascent and Britain's relative decline as an economic and, more particularly, as a financial centre is made more complicated by the reality that many of the American financiers who benefited from the City of London's eclipse were passionate Anglophiles. No American financier was more of an Anglophile than J. P. Morgan Jr, the son of the man who had founded the eponymous bank. Although he had exactly the same names as his father, J. P. Morgan Jr was known throughout his life as 'Jack', while his father had always been called 'Pierpont', their more unusual and sonorous middle name. Jack was devoted to the Allied cause and was, in the words of a recent biographer, essentially an 'Anglo-American'. He was a personal friend of leading British political figures such as Sir Edward Grey, Winston Churchill and even Lord Kitchener. In fact, J. P. Morgan Jr was so identified with the cause of Britain and its allies that on 3 July 1915 a mentally deranged German sympathizer attempted to kill him and managed to fire two pistol shots into his lower abdomen.[27]

At the beginning of 1915, the British government had signed a Commercial Agency Agreement with J. P. Morgan, placing the firm at the centre of the Allied war effort.[28] The British communicated with Morgans in New York through the British bank Morgan Grenfell, an affiliate bank, in London. J. P. Morgan, as financial agent, organized the purchase of material and the arrangement of loans on Britain's behalf. In some cases, direct negotiations took place between the War Office and the agents of American firms. Some firms, such as the Bethlehem Steel Corporation, had technical experts in London.[29] President Wilson's administration, at the beginning of the war, was committed to neutrality, and William Jennings Bryan, the former Democratic presidential candidate, now Secretary of State, had prohibited a US$100 million loan to France in August 1914.[30] By the time the United States entered the war as a belligerent, however, the government was fully committed to victory. As Keynes wrote in the *Economic Journal* at the end of 1917, the Americans embarked on war with immense focus and desire to prevail. In 'a very short period after the entry of the United States into the war, measures were taken by the Administration for the introduction of new taxation on a very drastic scale'. Keynes observed that 'income tax and excess profits tax are the backbone of the new measure'. The 'tax exemption limit' – that is, the threshold at which income tax applied – was lowered from $3,000 to $1,000 for single people.[31]

Of course, by the time that the United States finally entered the war in April 1917, its economic primacy was assured. The British decision to suspend gold payments in 1914 had far-reaching effects. In January 1915, the British Treasury forbade British loans for 'undertakings outside the

Empire'. This meant that enterprises outside the empire could not borrow from British banks. It was at this point, in the eyes of Alexander Noyes, the noted financial journalist of the 1920s, that London 'ceased to be the money centre of the world'. New York's ascendancy in this context was simple to explain. 'Since gold payments were at the same time being maintained in the United States, alone of all the great markets, New York necessarily took London's place.' This was not only a view shared by the Americans. On 20 January 1915, as a direct response to the British government's order to prohibit foreign loans of British capital outside the empire, *The Times* of London spoke of the 'temporary abandonment of our historic claim as an international money centre'. This made it 'inevitable' that 'much of the international business we have been accustomed to do' would now 'pass to the only other country, the United States, which is capable of doing it'.[32]

Despite suspending gold convertibility, the British authorities attempted to keep sterling at the pre-war parity of US$4.86. Sterling, however, depreciated during 1915, and reached a low of $4.49 in October that year. The entry of the United States into the war saw an appreciation of the pound to $4.76, where it remained till April 1919, after which point sterling fell considerably against the dollar. From the American perspective, it is difficult to see the war as anything other than an economic success. New York had established itself as a leading international financial centre, and new markets had been established for American agricultural and industrial products. Even more fortuitously, America's banking system had been secured by the establishment of a central bank, the Federal Reserve. In 1913, President Wilson had successfully demanded that a system of twelve private regional reserve banks be placed under a central political authority.[33] The 1907 panic had promoted the establishment of central banking in the United States, at the very time when the nation was coming to prominence on the international scene.

For Britain, the end of the First World War was a time for national reflection. Despite a successful taxation policy, the country staggered under an enormous debt. Borrowing contributed 70 per cent of the funds for the British war effort.[34] To be fair, the British position in 1913 had been financially strong. In that year, public debt in Britain was less than 30 per cent of gross domestic product (GDP, the usual measure of the size of a nation's economy), thus 'leaving ample scope for new borrowing to finance the war'.[35] The scale of the war and the high level of spending had transformed Britain's fiscal position. Perhaps the most drastic measure of this transformation was the liquidation of the nation's overseas invest-ments. Before 1914, Britain had been the biggest overseas investor in the world. British capital had developed the vast continental expanses of the Americas; the railroad, the industrial machinery which powered both North and South America, had been financed by British funds. By 1919, most of Britain's financial assets abroad had been sold. 'We have moreover disposed of a vast mass of wealth in the form of our foreign securities,' observed the Liberal banker and fellow of All Souls, Oxford, Robert Brand in December 1918, only one month after the Armistice. Quoting Andrew Bonar Law, who would be Prime Minister briefly in 1922–3, Brand noted that Britain had 'sold or pledged to the United States practically the whole of our American Railway and Industrial investment', which had been 'the finest of our foreign securities'. This was estimated to be worth £600 million, 8.6 per cent of the entire national debt.[36]

In general, the war had ended, from a financial point of view, like the other wars of the previous 150 years. 'In all wars . . . [in the] French revo-lutionary wars in France, England at the end of Napoleonic Wars, or the US after the Civil War' there occurred 'over-expansion of credit and currency, rising prices and depreciated exchanges', recalled Brand in his December 1918 article. This disorder involved 'symptoms familiar also in the history of every South American Republic'. To a late nineteenth-century, Oxford-educated classical liberal like Robert Brand, the only answer to such chaos was a restoration of the gold standard which 'whether or not it can be achieved quickly . . . should be our aim'.[37] Britain's foreign indebtedness would make the gold standard more difficult, but to Liberals and Conservatives alike a restoration of the gold standard in due course was unquestionably the correct policy. To Keynes, inflation was the conspicuous feature of the European economic scene. 'The inflationism of the currency systems of Europe has proceeded to extraordinary lengths,' he wrote in his 1919 classic, *The Economic Consequences of the Peace*. Governments unable, or unwilling, to raise taxes and borrow had simply 'printed notes' to finance the war. The note circulation in Germany was about 'ten times' what it had been before the war; in France it was more than 'six times'.[38]

In wider terms, the First World War in Britain had brought an end to a tradition of public finance which had lasted a hundred years. In his controversial work *The Origins of the Second World War*, A. J. P. Taylor had observed that 'men, reared in the stable economic world of the later nineteenth century, assumed that a country could not flourish without a balanced budget and a gold currency'.[39] In Britain, the First World War had overthrown this assumption. 'Where we spent millions before the war, we have now learnt that we can spend hundreds of millions and apparently not suffer from it,' was Keynes's characteristically pithy comment on the unprecedented era of expenditure which the war had inaugurated.[40] These hundreds of millions had been borrowed, and represented an abandonment of 'Peelite doctrines of balanced budgets' and 'sound money' in the form of a gold currency.[41]

8

Victors and Vanquished

If Britain and Germany had been the principal financial belligerents, it was the United States which emerged, economically and financially, as the principal victor of the First World War. Internationally, for most commentators, however, the end of London's attachment to the gold standard was perhaps the most significant financial outcome of the war. Economists and journalists of many different points of view argued for its restoration. In Britain, writers and economists from every political direction looked back fondly to the steady security of gold, of the world that had been lost. What did the gold standard mean to those middle-aged men whose youth had been passed under its quiet supremacy?

To supply an answer to this question, we can do no better than start with the writings on the subject by contemporaries themselves. The Treasury official Ralph Hawtrey was an articulate and highly analytical commentator on international economics. Born in 1879, Hawtrey had graduated from Cambridge with a first-class degree in mathematics in 1901.[1] He was elected a member of the select intellectual society the Apostles, whose leading lights in his undergraduate days included G. E. Moore, the ethical philosopher, and Bertrand Russell, the logician. Keynes would join the society only a couple of years after Hawtrey had left Cambridge. Hawtrey pursued a career in the civil service, but found time to write on monetary issues from his berth at the Treasury, where he worked from 1904. Essentially a self-taught economist (like Keynes he never earned a degree in the subject), he was less bold, perhaps less flashy than Maynard Keynes, but his contributions to monetary theory and policy have been praised by economists and historians of economics alike. In December 1919, he wrote an article on the gold standard for the *Economic Journal*.

In this article, Hawtrey described the former system in simple but laudatory terms. The gold standard, he argued, 'fixes the price of one commodity', so that the 'monetary unit is equated to a prescribed quantity of the selected commodity'. The commodity was a 'material so durable as to be almost indestructible'. As a consequence of this 'indestructibility', according to Hawtrey, the 'accumulated stocks are very large in proportion to the annual fresh supply'. Put more simply, because all the gold that had ever been mined still existed in private hands or, more likely, in the vaults of central banks, new production could not significantly affect the price. Production of the commodity in one year would add little to the existing global stock of the metal. This meant that it tended 'to have a remarkably steady value'.

Hawtrey looked back to the 'outbreak of war in 1914', when 'the gold standard was in nearly universal operation'. He noted that 'it was universally recognised that paper money ought to be put on a gold basis as soon as possible'. The old currency regime had given 'uniformity to the monetary unit, not only in time, but in space too'. This was a grandiose way of saying that gold was an international standard which ensured the stable value of currency. Inflation had not really been a feature of the international economy in the decades before 1914. In Hawtrey's cogent appraisal of the situation in 1919, he observed that war 'has destroyed this system'. The pressures of war finance had caused the 'Governments of Europe, unable to raise the means of payment by taxation and by genuine loans', to 'pay their way with paper money or with bank credits created for the purpose'. In each country where these expedients were adopted, the 'plethora of credit and money' caused a 'fall in the purchasing power of the monetary unit'.

The dash to paper, to inflation as a means of funding the war, had led to the 'displacement of gold from circulation'. The United States was the principal beneficiary of this trend. During the war itself, 'there had ceased to be a world market for gold'. The war had 'thrown enormous stocks of gold upon the American market'. This had allowed 'America, North and South, to indulge in a currency inflation' comparable to that which had occurred in Europe. In a moment of realism and lucidity, Hawtrey realized that now that the war was over it would be in 'America that the first signs of the re-establishment of a gold market and a gold standard are to be seen'.

Hawtrey's position was thoroughly orthodox. Along with the appeal for a renewal of the gold standard came a plea for balanced budgets. 'Failure to balance the budget' was a symptom of collapse. Hawtrey's assumption was that 'we have to balance our budgets'. The resounding conclusion of this important article was that 'the very moment British currency is re-established on a gold basis', when 'sterling and dollars are at par' (that is, with the pound trading at its old pre-war rate of 4.86 dollars to the pound), 'a beginning can be made' to create a new and stable international monetary system.[2] Hawtrey gave a conventional view of the currency situation as he saw it, at the end of the war, but these views represented a majority opinion among experts and journalists in Britain. Gold as a symbol of stability still fascinated contemporaries. In that sense the contrast was simply one between gold on one side and chaos on the other. As Walter Layton, the editor of the *Economist*, observed in February 1925, just before Britain's resumption of the old currency arrangement, 'the choice which presents itself is not one between a theoretical standard on the one hand and gold with all its imperfections on the other, but between the gold standard . . . and no control at all'.[3] Layton made the argument that, if Britain did not go back to gold, people would 'most certainly transfer their capital to a country with a standard they understood'.

Layton was an economist who had been one of the first graduates of the Cambridge economics faculty in 1907. He was an active Liberal in politics, like his friend Keynes, but unlike Keynes he actually fought parliamentary elections as a Liberal candidate, being unsuccessful three times in the 1920s for seats as diverse as Burnley in 1922, Cardiff South in 1923 and London University in 1929. He praised the gold standard for the 'stability of prices' it preserved. He quoted Professor Arthur Pigou, his former Cambridge tutor in economics, that 'so far as the UK is concerned, until the gold standard has been re-established, more elaborate improvements in our monetary system are not practical politics'. Pigou's view represented, in Layton's assessment, 'British opinion'.[4] Another strength was that the gold standard imposed control on the authorities. Without gold, monetary authorities would have 'too great discretionary power', and the country, Layton perhaps naively believed, would not be 'prepared to entrust so powerful a weapon to anyone'. He concluded that if 'our monetary system were liable to be influenced by a change of government, there would certainly be no assurance of stability in monetary policy'. This argument has frequently been employed by supporters of the gold standard. Government, in this view, is not to be relied upon. Placing monetary policy in the hands of politicians creates instability. This opinion was perhaps most pithily expressed by George Bernard Shaw in his 1928 book *The Intelligent Woman's Guide to Socialism and Capitalism*: 'You have to choose between trusting to the natural stability of gold and the natural stability of the honesty and intelligence of the members of the government. And, with due respect to these gentlemen, I advise you, as long as the capitalist system lasts, to vote for gold.'[5]

The gold standard was desirable not only to British liberals like Walter Layton and Ralph Hawtrey, but even to socialists like George Bernard Shaw. Gustav Cassel, the Swedish economist, railed against the 'complete chaos in the world's monetary system' which had followed the abandonment of the gold standard. This chaos in his view had 'so fully discredited the paper standards in the eyes of the general public that the desire for the return to the gold standard has become very general and powerful'. Cassel's lecture at the London School of Economics in June 1923, entitled 'The Restoration of the Gold Standard', further mentioned the truism that the 'establishing of a gold standard means the value of the currency of the country [is kept] at a constant par with gold'. Cassel concluded that it was 'of the greatest importance for the development of British trade and for the maintenance of London's position as a monetary centre, that the British gold standard should be restored at the earliest possible date'.[6]

Yet, as Cassel observed, there was a problem with London unilaterally resuming the old standard in the assertive and confident way it had been done in 1821. The balance of financial power had, as a consequence of the war, shifted unmistakably to the United States. With regard to the supply of the metal, in particular, the 'gold supply of the United States is so abundant' that almost 'the whole burden of the stabilization of the value of gold has been thrown upon the United States'.[7] Any resumption of the gold standard had to be undertaken by taking American conditions, not British desires, into account. It was in America that the subsequent economic and monetary history of the world would be shaped. The US position in 1919 was, in many ways, analogous to that of Britain at the end of the Napoleonic Wars. The United States in 1919, like Britain a century earlier, was the leading exporter in the world and had the most advanced industrial base of any nation. Unlike Britain in 1815, however, the United States, having been a late entrant to the conflict, did not labour under a staggering burden of national indebtedness. More generally, the economic position of the United States was even more fortunate than that of the British in the 1820s. We have seen in Britain how a resumption of the gold standard had led to a period of deflation, low interest rates and depressed economic conditions. In the United States, by contrast, despite a slight dip in production and prices in the first two years of the decade, the 1920s witnessed an extraordinary period of credit expansion, based on huge export surpluses and the attendant influx of gold.

The extent to which America's exports and its surging gold imports fuelled credit creation in the 1920s was more evident to contemporaries than it has been to subsequent historians and economists, who too often view the 1920s through the lens of the Great Depression of the early 1930s. Yet the 'abundance of gold' in the United States, which Cassel had observed in 1923, was directly, in the eyes of contemporary commentators, connected to the greater provision of credit. Cassel had even suggested that the gold supply in America could 'give reasonable support to a *much more extended* [italics in original] structure of credit'.[8] And this is exactly what happened. Credit expansion in the 1920s was perhaps the most widely observed economic phenomenon of the decade. Increased gold supply emboldened banks, but the credit creation acquired a life of its own. This relationship was best summarized in an article written in 1929: credit was 'not directly related to gold movements . . . but [was] indicative'.[9] There was, evident even in 1929, a loose connection between the increase of the gold supply in the United States and the credit boom of the 1920s. As early as 1923, one American economist had observed that the 'constant influx of gold from abroad' had been an 'influence for credit expansion'. Whether gold came in 'payment of past loans, for current merchandise or . . . to pay for future exports', the effect of its arrival on 'our credit situation will be the same'. Further gold imports would 'increase the amount of loanable funds' leading to credit expansion at home or 'encouragement of investment of funds abroad or both'.[10] To Oliver Sprague, the Harvard economist, the 'enormous increase in the supply of credit since 1914' was not due entirely to the 'operations of the reserve banks', but was a consequence of 'more than a billion dollars in gold . . . imported in 1915, 1916, and the first half of 1917'. This influx of gold 'provided the basis for much credit'.[11] Writing in 1930, C. Reinold Noyes remarked that the 'inflow of gold' between 1921 and 1929 had 'indirectly produced huge increases in bank credit'. He noticed that 'primary reserves of the major part of our banking system increased by [US$]706 million, or nearly 44%' in the same period. He also observed the phenomenon of 'cheap and superabundant credit'.[12]

Looking back from 1930 on the boom years of the 1920s, the American economist Charles Persons gave a vivid description of the 'great field of credit expansion in the last decade', drawing particular attention to the fact that this process had been seen perhaps most acutely in the 'realm of urban real estate mortgages'. More generally, the world of the American consumer, as described by Persons, was one in which an unprecedented range of goods could be acquired by credit. Instalment purchasing, the process of buying radios, cars, washing machines and refrigerators by loans which the consumer paid off by monthly instalments, became almost universal in the 1920s. 'All income classes up to the richest have succumbed to the allurements of easy possession and "pay as you earn".' Companies were also competing with each other to 'secure sales by offering easy terms of possession and payment'.[13]

There followed an account of the extraordinary degree to which goods in America were available on credit in the 1920s – essentially a credit bubble spurred, ultimately, by a significant increase in the quantity of gold. Some 70 to 80 per cent of furniture, according to Persons, 'is now sold in instalments'. This mode of payment was especially popular with 'newly invented commodities with a virgin market'. Electric refrigerators, radios and cars were nearly always bought in this way. In the case of electric refrigerators, or fridges, there was 'an untouched market, an enormous field and a . . . whole-hearted acceptance of the instalment plan for sales'.

The numbers of units sold had increased dramatically from 11,000 in 1922 to 630,000 in 1929. 'Instalment selling with a modest sum down and a lengthy period for completing the payments has been the accepted practice in this industry.' Radios had seen an even greater explosion in sales, and a consequent increase in credit expansion. Only 100,000 radios had been sold in 1922. This figure reached 4.2 million only seven years later, in 1929. This had been an 'astonishing growth' in the market and had led to an increase in debt 'of well over [US$]400 million in this short space of seven years'.

The market for housing loans had grown in an equally spectacular fashion. Long-term 'mortgage bonds', loans from banks with which ordinary consumers purchased houses, were a 'system of finance' that was 'well calculated to lead to credit inflation'. These funds flowed into 'construction and result in business activity and *seeming* [italics in original] prosperity'. The period of rapid expansion in this field had been the 'four years following 1924'. Persons referred to an estimation that the 'volume of real estate securities outstanding' had been US$503 million in 1922 and had, in 'seven short years', increased to US$3.7 billion, a seven-fold increase.[14] The author of this illuminating piece was surely correct in stating that 'some part of our boasted prosperity in recent years undoubtedly rested on nothing more permanent than the process of credit expansion'.[15]

Overall bank lending showed a 'steady increase from 1922 to 1929, inclusive'. The banks had expanded their balance sheets nearly three times between 1914 and 1929, from a total of US$20.8 billion in June 1914 to US$58.5 billion in June 1929. More startlingly, there now existed other credit providers than the traditional banks. In an innovative move, the US car manufacturer General Motors launched a subsidiary, the General Motors Acceptance Corporation, in 1919. The function of this subsidiary was to lend money to instalment purchasers. It was an early form of 'vendor financing', whereby the seller actually lends money to the consumer to purchase the product. The balance sheet of GMAC increased impressively between 1920 and 1929. GMAC's 'notes receivable', the outstanding short-term loans on their balance sheet, rose from US$25.7 million in 1920 to US$400.8 million in 1929. 'Thus, a single corporation, marketing newly introduced commodities on the installment plan, accounts for debt creation to the extent of 400 millions of dollars in ten years.' Moreover, the 'bulk of this impressive total, 300 of 400 millions, was rolled up in the last five years of the period'.[16] Credit was king in America in those exhilarating days of the 1920s. Contemporary economists spoke of the 'abundance of capital', an 'ample supply of cash and credit capital' and even an 'absence of credit strain'.[17]

Undoubtedly, the United States had undergone an immense credit expansion which would inevitably have a massive impact on Europe. Britain's attempt to get back on to the gold standard at the old rate of one pound to US$4.86 was doomed by the shift in the balance of financial power. Between 1914 and 1921 four changes had occurred in the United States economy. Firstly, American exports exceeded imports by 'more than twenty billions of dollars'. Secondly, 40 per cent of the gold coin of the world was now in the United States. Thirdly, the United States was the greatest creditor nation, meaning that it lent money to the rest of the world, as opposed to simply absorbing capital. Fourthly, America engaged with the world.[18] These observations were made in 1922 by John F. Sinclair, an American economist. Against this drastic shift of circumstances which had occurred since 1914, it was unrealistic for the British to attempt to peg the pound at the same pre-1914 rate, since the relative strengths of both the British and American economies had changed.

Yet this was precisely what the British sought to do. On budget day, 28 April 1925, Winston Churchill, the ebullient and somewhat unexpected Chancellor of the Exchequer, announced a return to gold at the old exchange rate of US$4.86 for one pound. This decision he would later regard as the 'greatest mistake of his life'.[19] The rate effectively priced British exports out of the international market. A reduction in wages was required to keep down production costs. The miners resisted this with their cry 'not a penny off the pay, not a minute on the day'. They were understandably unprepared to work longer hours for the same, or even lower, wages.[20] Keynes protested, in a series of articles which appeared in the London *Evening Standard* in July 1925, against the resumption of the old rate, arguing for a lower rate which reflected the actual trading conditions of sterling since the war. This would have meant a rate of US$4.40 or thereabouts. The problem of the resumption was that 'the value of sterling money abroad has been raised by 10 per cent, whilst its purchasing power over British labour is unchanged'. As a consequence, Britain had 'to reduce our sterling prices . . . by 10 per cent in order to be on a competitive level, unless prices rise elsewhere'.[21] Keynes's later rival Joseph Schumpeter could also see in 1928 that Britain's return to the gold standard, '"stabilizing" the pound at what was, viewed from the standpoint of existing conditions, an artificial value, naturally meant dislocating business, putting a premium on imports and a tax on exports, intensifying losses and unemployment'. It led to a situation which was 'eminently unstable'. This had been due to 'the act of politicians, and not to the working of the system which, on the contrary, would have evolved a value of the pound exactly fitting the circumstances'.[22]

Britain and other European powers had seen a complete reversal of their position. Having been American's providers of capital, they were increasingly reliant on American loans themselves. The disaster of the war had meant that 'America has been able to repay the greater part of the capital which she had previously borrowed from Europe' and, in addition, lend 'a very large sum of money'.[23] The indebtedness Britain had incurred as a result of the war would be paid in full. 'They hired the money, didn't they?' was the indignant response of the US President, Calvin Coolidge, to any suggestion that America should relax the conditions of the money it had lent.[24] Europe needed to borrow from the United States in order to continue 'to buy American foods, cotton, minerals and manufactures'. America had to be 'prepared to give additional credit' to Europe. The United States needed to act as the 'world's banker'.[25]

Of the combatants in the world war, none proved to be more dependent on American capital than Germany, whose economic position immediately after the war had of course been dominated by the issue of reparations, the payments which Germany had been required to pay the Allies as compensation for the damage it had caused by starting the First World War. The burdens placed on Germany after the conclusion of the Treaty of Versailles had memorably stirred the mighty pen of John Maynard Keynes into action in 1919. By the early 1920s, Keynes could claim that the centre of gravity in world opinion regarding the issue of German reparations had moved in his favour. It was seen, in 1922, that 'perseverance with the indemnity does now involve practical harm'. Germany essentially adopted a policy of high inflation to reduce its indebtedness. This policy reached its most poignant expression in the hyperinflation of 1922. In order to pay reparations which were, according to Keynes's 1919 estimate, of the order of £8 billion, or US$40 billion, Germany had to ratify the Armistice's expropriations of 'German railway rolling stock'.[26] It was also compelled to 'surrender most of [its] merchant fleet' and 'make large deliveries of livestock to re-stock farms ravaged by the war'. In addition to these swingeing measures, the Germans had to acquiesce in the 'uncompensated seizure of public property and industrial plant in annexed territories such as Alsace-Lorraine'.[27] Of course, there was no way the Germans were able to pay the bill. It is unlikely that any attempt was ever made to do so, though reparations continued to be an issue in international politics throughout the 1920s.

The hyperinflation of the early 1920s has been widely viewed as a symbol of the collapse of the Weimar Republic. Weimar was the city in which the first constitutional assembly of the new German Republic was held in 1919, after the German empire had been replaced. In fact, Weimar lasted another full decade after the inflation occurred. The Reichsmark's value collapsed, it was suggested, because the German government was buying foreign currency to import raw materials from abroad. This account of the hyperinflation is known as the 'balance of payments' explanation. The depreciation had resulted in upward pressure on prices and wages. The central bank in Berlin, the Reichsbank, then simply printed money to meet these wage demands. This was undoubtedly a factor. More obvious, however, was the 'quantity theory of money' explanation which assumed, or rather asserted, a direct relationship between the quantity of money in circulation and the price level. Put simply and crudely, it stated that the more money there existed in an economy, in the form of notes, the higher prices would be, other things being equal.[28]

The hyperinflation was followed by a period in which capital from the United States began to be lent to Germany in considerable amounts. The Rentenmark had been introduced as a temporary currency in November 1923 to halt the hyperinflation. After currency stabilization, American investors began to invest directly into German businesses, or they set up factories in Germany themselves. The Ford Motor Company actually owned a plant in Berlin from 1925 and another in Cologne from 1929. Between 1924 and 1930, Germany borrowed about US$1.7 billion, or 7.174 billion Reichsmarks (using a conversion rate of 4.2 Reichsmarks to a dollar) in bonds, of which 62 per cent or about US$1 billion was borrowed directly from the United States.[29] American writers spoke of the 'great flow of American funds abroad' and the 'striking expansion of American foreign banking'.[30] One American bank which remained aloof from loans to Germany, however, was J. P. Morgan, with Jack himself being known as a 'notorious enemy of Germany'.[31] But Bankers Trust, among other American banks, freely lent to the German government and to German industry.

The German banks themselves were active borrowers of foreign, particularly American, funds. Between 1924 and 1929, the 'shrunken bank balance sheets of 1923–24 were quite rapidly rebuilt'. A large proportion of this capital was supplied by foreigners. With his usual clarity of mind, Keynes quickly identified the risks behind Germany's dependence on American capital. 'Germany', he wrote in an article for the *Nation and Athenaeum* in September 1926, 'is paying on the average 7½ per cent net for foreign loans.' This amount 'in the last two years' had reached about '£10 million per annum'. 'How long can this game go on? The answer lies with the American investor.'[32] So long as American investment flowed to Germany, German development would be on a sounder basis than if Germany had to rely on its own internal resources. Capital shortage was obviously one of the great problems of the Weimar economy. The resources of the German banking system itself had been 'severely depleted by war and inflation'.[33] Hans Luther, briefly Chancellor of the Weimar Republic in 1925, and the later President of the Reichsbank from 1930 to 1933, looking back in 1960 remembered the 'optimism of the Americans', for whom 'Germany seems to be an excellent enterprise [*Unternehmung*] with much promise'.[34]

Although some historians have questioned the connection between American credit expansion and support for the German economy, there does seem to have been some correlation between them. In March of the fateful year of 1929, in a conversation between Irving Fisher and Keynes, printed in the New York *Evening World*, Fisher observed that the direct American interest in the payment of reparations was 'not very great'. America's 'main direct interest nowadays results from the very substantial sums which her citizens have invested in Germany'.[35] Keynes and Fisher, two of the most distinguished economists of the time, took the same view of the relationship between the US and German economies. Even *Time* magazine, at the end of 1927, had noted the 'ominous German trend' of 'large foreign loans being made to German states and municipalities', mentioning a figure of US$940 million outstanding in debts. Most of this foreign capital was American in origin.[36]

Germany's economic descent into the wilderness of depression, however, started slightly before the events in New York in October 1929 and the Wall Street Crash which occurred in that month. To acute observers of the scene German economic weakness had become apparent as early as 1927. The Berlin stock market experienced its own Black Friday on 13 May 1927 after an inept intervention by Hjalmar Schacht, the sharp and self-confident central banker, to dampen the equity market.[37] The boom in Berlin stocks had started in the summer of 1926, as a flood of American money, coupled with renewed optimism in Germany itself, had boosted the market.[38] The slowdown in Germany, though instigated by the Berlin stock market's correction in May 1927, had a further aspect.

Seymour Parker Gilbert, who was the Allied Reparations Commission's Agent General for Reparations to Germany from October 1924 to May 1930, criticized the German government at the end of 1927. It was his criticism and the scepticism he expressed about the German government's commitment to balanced budgets and fiscal responsibility that helped to dampen the flow of American credit. On 20 October 1927, Gilbert, a thirty-five-year-old banker from New Jersey, delivered a memorandum on government financial policy to Heinrich Köhler, the German Finance Minister. In the memorandum, Gilbert charged the German government with 'developing and executing constantly enlarged programs of expenditure and of borrowing, with but little regard to the financial consequences of their actions'.[39] His contention was that the German government was being irresponsible. Gilbert, the orthodox Republican financier, became convinced that if the German government were hindered from borrowing

This gold vase is an example of the fine artistry and material wealth of the Inca civilization which the Spanish conquered at the beginning of the sixteenth century.

Philip II as Crown Prince as portrayed by Titian. As King of Spain he waged wars which depleted the country's resources.

John Law was a rogue but a financier of genius. He was the first real theorist of paper money.

The rue Quincampoix on which the Paris stock exchange was situated, the scene of the dramatic collapse of Law's 'Mississippi System'.

The riots in Boston and other places which greeted the imposition of stamp duty from London in 1765 led ultimately to the Declaration of the Independence of the United States of America in 1776.

Lord Overstone was the archetypal sound money man of the mid-nineteenth century; a pillar of orthodoxy in finance.

Walter Bagehot wrote the classic *Lombard Street* which defined the function of the Central Bank.

Sir Robert Peel was the leading British statesman of the early nineteenth century. His role in the return to gold in 1821 was crucial, as was the Bank Act he passed in 1844.

The House of Commons was the scene of many of the most important debates relating to war and finance in the nineteenth century. It was a committee of the House that returned to the gold standard in 1821.

The US formally adopted the gold standard in 1901, after a period of paper currency during and after the Civil War.

A picture of the area around the Royal Exchange and the Bank of England c.1914. The bank was the main symbol of international financial stability for nearly a century before the First World War.

LONDON: EXCHANGE & BANK.

The American Civil War (1861–5) was the first industrial conflict in which guns, railways and capital were deployed to ensure total victory.

Andrew Carnegie (*left*), the steel magnate, and J. P. Morgan (*right*), the banker, were in their mid-twenties when the civil war bagan. They both made their fortunes from the enormous economic expansion of the US during the late nineteenth century.

The First World War (1914–18) was an intense, all-encompassing struggle in which goverments resorted to paper money. They borrowed unprecedented amounts to spend on armaments.

Ford was a symbol of American industrial might for much of the twentieth century. Ford's successes in the 1920s were built on the back of an unsustainable consumer credit bubble.

German hyperinflation, stoked by paper money, shocked the world during the early 1920s. It has shaped the German preoccupation with a strong currency.

The Wall Street Crash which followed in 1929 rocked the financial world. Wall Street had emerged as the international financial centre after the First World War; its sudden collpase had an equally global impact.

John Maynard Keynes, a scholar of Eton and King's College, Cambridge, was the most influential economist of his time and the head of the British delegation to the Bretton Woods conference.

Harry Dexter White, the son of Lithuanian Jewish emigres to the United States, was a tough negotiator who proved a match for the British at Bretton Woods.

The resort where the global financial system was repaired. The agreement reached at Bretton Woods would last more than a quarter of a century from 1944 to 1971.

on the American markets, it would be compelled to balance its budgets. It has been claimed that he had a 'growing feud with the German government over its financial policies'.[40] Gilbert also recognized that the Germans would not be able to pay their reparations liabilities. In June 1929, the Young Plan, under which Germany's debts were reduced by 75 per cent, was adopted on his recommendation. It was during the winter of 1928–9 that the German economy first showed signs of the weakness that would herald the Great Depression.

By the time of the Young Plan, however, the credit bubble in the United States was nearing its conclusion. Charles Persons in his 1930 article had described in general terms the end of a credit bubble: 'When every potential debtor and installment buyer has assumed the full burden of indebtedness which the new credit policies allow; when every would-be home owning family has purchased . . . as costly a house as its resources will permit . . . in short when the newly tapped credit resources have been fully exploited – there is, of necessity an end to the process.'[41]

This process was perhaps natural, but it had been spurred by America's success as an exporter of goods, which had caused an influx of gold upon which credit had been freely issued. It was also the simple operation of an interest rate policy which had exacerbated the bubble and the subsequent bust. Benjamin Strong, the Governor of the Federal Reserve Bank of New York, had been keen to support Britain's return to the gold standard at the old rate of US\$4.86 to the pound. Although the Federal Reserve had its headquarters in Washington, Strong's personal prestige as the Governor of the New York branch ensured that his opinions were pre-eminent. As a result of Strong's influence, an 'easy money policy' was adopted in the United States to make the dollar less attractive and thus ease the pressure on sterling. To Strong, Britain's stabilization within the structure of the gold standard was the 'cornerstone of European financial reconstruction'.[42] The Federal Reserve in Washington, under Strong's guidance, lowered its discount rate, the rate at which the Federal Reserve lent funds to the commercial banks, from 4 per cent to 3½ per cent towards the end of 1927, before being raised from that low in January 1928 to reach a high of 6 per cent on 9 August 1929.[43] Benjamin Strong had died in October 1928. His successor as Governor of the New York Federal Reserve Bank,

George Harrison, suggested 'an increase in the discount rate of 6% as a warning against the excessive use of credit'.[44] The impact of this rise in rates can be seen in the figures relating to the size of the balance sheets of the American banks. On 31 December 1929, the estimated volume of outstanding bank loans and investments of all banks in the United States was US$58.4 billion. This was a slight fall of about US$57 million from the figure estimated for 29 June 1929. It was only a small decrease, but it was the first half-year in which the figure had fallen since June 1922.[45] The seven-year expansion had ended. Scholars have debated, and will continue to debate, the effects of this somewhat looser policy at the end of 1927, followed by a rapid tightening in little more than eighteen months, between January 1928 and August 1929. Many have maintained that this swing of policy stimulated the bubble and precipitated the ensuing bust which hit the market in October 1929.

What is clear is that the 1920s had seen an unprecedented expansion of American enterprise fuelled by what we have called a credit bubble. This was frequently commented upon by contemporaries, whether adversely or favourably. The contraction in United States lending did have a damaging effect on the rest of the world, particularly Germany, since the United States was, during the 1920s, the biggest exporter of capital. While it is true that the downturn in Germany had started before the stock market crash of 1929, it is also true that any downturn in the United States would aggravate conditions in Germany and the rest of Europe. The position of the United States in the 1920s was a dominant one. America was the world's greatest banker; it lent more money than any other nation. It was the world's greatest manufacturer, exporting more goods than any other country. This is exactly why the abrupt halting of credit expansion in the United States in 1929 exacerbated a global depression.

9

World Crisis

The Great Crash of 1929 is an event which has been seared into the consciousness of three generations of economists and bankers. In his celebrated book describing what happened that year, *The Great Crash of 1929*, John Kenneth Galbraith wrote, 'Some years . . . are singled out for fame far beyond the common lot, and 1929 was clearly such a year.' Galbraith also observed that 'A reference to 1929 has become shorthand for the events of that autumn.'[1] But, beyond the drama, the events of the early 1930s were even more significant than those of 1929. And, of course, the Great Crash of 1929 was itself partially caused by the considerable credit expansion that had occurred in the United States during the 1920s.

The gold basis of this credit expansion was, as we have seen, a widely acknowledged feature of the economic scene. In 1934, in an influential book entitled *The Great Depression*, Lionel Robbins, a British economist, referred to this phenomenon: 'It is clear that the effects of the war and the post-war inflation, which caused so large a proportion of the world's gold supply to be concentrated in New York, laid the foundations for the expansion.' To Robbins, a professor at the London School of Economics, the notion that these gold imports had been 'sterilized' (that is, that their impact had been mitigated by central bank action) was a 'complete misapprehension'. 'Sterilization' means that, if for example a country has a trade surplus, its central bank may sell bonds to banks to absorb the funds derived from the surplus; in simple terms, the bank would be mopping up the liquidity arising out of the high level of exports. The gold imports were the basis of 'a very considerable expansion' of credit and loans.[2] More generally, the 1920s were remembered as a decade of prosperity. Wesley Mitchell, a noted American expert on business cycles, noticed that by 'the middle of the 1920's the intense disorder ended'. As he fondly remembered, 'Budgets were balanced and currencies restored to a gold basis.'[3]

Mitchell pithily summarized the tensions in international finance which had tipped the world into depression: in 'Great Britain resumption was made at too high a parity; Germany depended on huge borrowings; the United States combined foolish foreign loans with an increase of the tariff and unbridled speculation in stocks and urban real estate'.[4] He was unequivocal in blaming the 'critical error' made by the Federal Reserve in the 'summer of 1927' when it 'took the momentous step of forcing a regime of cheap money'. This was the line which Robbins took in his book *The Great Depression*. Robbins was one of the first writers on the subject to describe 1929 to 1933 as the 'years of the Great Depression'.[5] His analysis of the phenomenon was unexceptionable. He noticed the 'enormous volume of foreign loans' from the United States which had 'spread out to other centres and generated expansion there'.

Since Robbins's pioneering study, debate surrounding the causes of the Great Depression has constituted, in the words of Ben Bernanke, Chairman of the Federal Reserve from 2006 until 2014, the 'Holy Grail of macroeconomics'. Given his status as the premier central banker of his time, Bernanke's comments warrant attention. His analysis may be taken as the conventional wisdom at the beginning of the twenty-first century on the subject of the Great Depression. In well-publicized remarks, made in a speech in honour of Milton Friedman's ninetieth birthday in November 2002, Bernanke apologized on behalf of the Federal Reserve. Regarding the Great Depression, he addressed Milton Friedman and Anna Schwartz, co-writers of the important study *A Monetary History of the United States, 1867–1960*, 'You're right, we did it, we're very sorry. But, thanks to you, we won't do it again.'[6]

Friedman and Schwartz had offered a powerful monetarist explanation of the role of the Fed in deepening the Depression. Bernanke, in his laudatory speech, mentioned the 'antispeculative' tightening of 1928–9, when the Federal Reserve's discount rate moved from 3½ per cent at the beginning of 1928 to 6 per cent in August of the following year. Bernanke dutifully talked of the 'falling prices and weaker activity' that ensued.[7] The monetarist argument of Friedman and Schwartz can be quickly summarized. In their view, the Federal Reserve continued a run of tightening policies after the Depression had started. In Schwartz's words, the 'evidence we presented there was that the Federal Reserve System, by failing to act as a lender of last resort during a series of panics, permitted a significant contraction of the money supply that was responsible for the compression of aggregate demand, national income and employment'. This was a roundabout, jargon-laden way of saying that the Federal Reserve did precisely the opposite of what modern central bankers would have done. They raised interest rates when they should have lowered them.[8] From August 1929, when the discount rate hit 6 per cent for the two months until the October crash, 'production, wholesale prices, and personal income fell at annual rates of 20 per cent, 7½ per cent, and 5 per cent, respectively'. After the crash occurred in October, the 'economic decline became even more precipitous'.[9]

Bernanke recounted how, after the depreciation of sterling in September 1931, another round of tightening occurred. The 1929–33 period was called 'the Great Contraction' by Friedman and Schwartz. They showed that, during this period, the three 'successive banking crises which followed' one after the other were 'each more severe than the preceding'.[10] They described the monetary policy of the time as 'inept'. They noticed that the people at the head of the Federal Reserve had not followed the advice offered by Bagehot, by stepping in as the banker of last resort.[11] As a consequence, the United States system experienced 'waves of bank failures'. The percentage of operating banks which failed in America in each year from 1930 to 1933 inclusive was 5.6, 10.5, 7.8 and 12.9 per cent. The number of banks operating at the end of 1933 consequently was just above half the number that had existed in 1929, whereas no serious bank runs had occurred between the First World War and 1930.[12]

Another feature of the crisis in the United States was the 'pervasiveness of debtor insolvency'. In plain terms, borrowers became bankrupt. The 'debt crisis' touched all sectors, as high rates of default created problems for borrowers as well as lenders. In statistical terms, the ratio of debt service to national income – or, in less technical terms, the amount of money being spent to pay debts as a proportion of national income – 'went from 9% in 1929 to 19.8% in 1932–33'.[13] The debt was, of course, aggravated by the falling prices. It was widely appreciated that falling prices make life more difficult for the debtor just as inflation eased the burden of debt. Commodity prices 'in general' had fallen 'by 30 to 40 per cent' in the period between 1929 and 1933, according to Lionel Robbins, while he observed that production in the 'chief manufacturing countries of the world shrank by anything from 30 to 50 per cent'. World trade had collapsed, with the volume in 1932 being 'only a third of what it was three years before'.[14]

The general ineptness identified by Friedman and Schwartz as being characteristic of the Federal Reserve's monetary policy appeared to be infectious among politicians in general. The conditions were so unusual and unexpected that statesmen, bankers and economists seemed adrift and uncomprehending. Keynes, in his usual mode of articulate contempt expressed his dismay at the 'present paralytic policy of the Administration' of US President Herbert Hoover which, he believed, 'must end in some overwhelming disaster for them personally'. In a prescient remark for one who was not gifted with much political foresight, he expressed his view that 'when the Republican Party goes to the polls a year hence, its defeat may be almost comparable with that of our Labour'.[15] These observations had been made in a letter to Walter Case, an American lawyer who was a personal friend, written on 4 December 1931, barely six weeks after the British general election of 1931, in which the Labour Party had lost 231 seats, and was left with a rump in the House of Commons of only forty-six MPs. On 6 January 1932, the great British economist expressed himself in the same trenchant and uncompromising way in a lecture to the International Economic Society of Hamburg. 'Can we prevent an almost complete collapse', Keynes wondered, 'of the financial structure of modern capitalism?' He expressed his pessimism, blaming a lack of responsible leadership and the intellectual deficiencies of the leaders: 'With no financial leadership left in the world and profound intellectual error as to causes and cures prevailing in the responsible seats of power, one begins to wonder and doubt.'

Keynes initially looked to the financial crisis, the problem with the banks and their balance sheets, as the dominant problem to be addressed, before any question of industrial stimulus could be considered. He asserted in his dogmatic way that 'no one is likely to dispute that the avoidance of financial collapse, rather than the stimulation of industrial activity, is now the front-rank problem'. The 'restoration of industry', in Keynes's view in early 1932, 'must come second in order of time'.

In this analysis, Keynes's view was not that different from the reasoning employed by Friedman and Schwartz in their pioneering monetarist study of American economic history published in 1963. He accurately identified and described the phenomenon which they explained in terms of the contraction of the money supply. The 'catastrophic fall in the money value not only of commodities but of practically every kind of asset' had been an 'obvious' immediate cause of the financial panic. In the modern jargon beloved of today's economists and journalists, Keynes initially identified the Great Depression as a phenomenon akin to a 'balance sheet recession'. He continued his assessment that the 'assets of banks in very many countries – perhaps in all countries with the probable exception of Great Britain – are no longer equal, conservatively valued, to their liabilities to their depositors'. This indebtedness, in Keynes's analysis, was widespread in the economy, involving both individuals and governments in the whirlpool of insolvency: 'Debtors of all kinds no longer have assets equal in value to their debts. Few governments still have revenues equal to the fixed money charges for which they have made themselves liable.'

Keynes then dissected the institution which, in the minds of contemporaries, had acquired almost mythical status in the debate about international finance, the gold standard. He noted that in 1932 'France and the US are now the only countries of major importance where the gold standard is functioning freely.' Britain had left the gold standard in September 1931, and this had ensured that 'the decline of prices' had stopped. The division of the advanced economies into two groups – one on the gold standard and one off it – corresponded to the division between 'those [economies] which had been exercising deflationary pressure on the rest of the world by having a net creditor position which causes them to draw gold and those which have been suffering this pressure'.[16]

In an article in the *Sunday Express* which appeared on 27 September 1931, after sterling had left the gold standard earlier in the month, Keynes had famously claimed that there were 'few Englishmen who do not rejoice at the breaking of our gold fetters'. He spoke of the 'enthusiasm' which had greeted the move. 'No wonder, then, that we feel some exuberance at the release.' By contrast, for France and the United States, the gold standard was still, until a comparatively late period, an article of faith. For these nations, argued Keynes, 'the competitive disadvantage will be concentrated'. They had 'already taken nearly all the available surplus gold in the whole world'.[17] In France, according to one recent observer, 'until early 1935 the policy-making establishment was convinced that a liberal economy needed a fixed anchor, namely the gold franc, to allow the price mechanism to operate'. Needless to say, the 'budget had to be balanced'.[18]

The election as President of Franklin Delano Roosevelt in 1932 shifted the mood on the commitment to dollar–gold convertibility. It removed what Keynes had memorably called 'the magic spell of immobility which [had] been cast over the White House' in Herbert Hoover's time.[19] Once Roosevelt was inaugurated in March 1933, he declared a national bank holiday, and immediately suspended gold convertibility and foreign exchange dealings. The Emergency Banking Act was passed on 9 March 1933. The next day, the President issued an executive order extending the restrictions on gold and foreign exchange dealings beyond the banking holiday. On 5 April, an executive order forbade the 'hoarding' of gold and required all holders of gold, including banks, to deliver their gold to Federal Reserve Banks by 1 May.[20] Another feature of the Roosevelt administration's approach to gold was a direct intervention to raise its price. The old rate of the gold standard days had valued gold at US$20.67 an ounce. Beginning in October 1933, the US government started to buy gold from abroad. It also started to buy silver. Buying silver was a way of increasing commodity prices, since pushing up the price of silver, through purchases of the metal, increased general inflation. According to Milton Friedman, the silver purchases from 1932 to 1937 'supported an increase of the general price level of 14%', and, more crucially, in 'farm products of 79%'.[21] The President, under the influence of an agricultural economist, George F. Warren, believed that government purchases of gold would spur inflation and thereby 'reduce debt burdens and raise commodity prices'.[22]

The buying of gold continued from March 1933 to 31 January 1934, when Roosevelt specified a fixed buying and selling price of $35 an ounce for gold. The Gold Reserve Act, passed by Congress on 30 January, the day before, gave the President authority for this action. The $35 price for an ounce of gold essentially devalued the dollar by 59 per cent from the price of $20.67 an ounce which had been established by Congress in 1792. To many classical liberals, the terms of the Act were draconian and redolent of overbearing state power. The Gold Reserve Act also outlawed most private possession of gold, forcing individuals to sell their holdings of the metal to the US Treasury. All gold coins were to be withdrawn from circulation and melted into bullion. From 1 February 1934, the official price of gold was fixed at US$35 an ounce, a price which would be kept, officially at least, for another thirty-seven years.

The move was, as many subsequent commentators have remarked, an exercise in expropriation. The Treasury had formerly valued its own gold holdings at $20.67 an ounce. This was the price it had paid to private individuals and banks for the gold it owned. The new official price of gold fixed at $35 did mark a continuation of the gold standard, though not at the old pre-Depression price. Even more draconian was the prohibition on individuals holding gold coin and bullion, except under restricted circumstances, such as in coin collections.[23] In France, the central bank, despite being the recipient of large gold inflows until 1932, had been constrained from boosting prices. The impact of gold inflow on French prices was 'minimal'.[24] Despite the large gold inflows into the United States and France, both countries experienced an initial fall in prices.

Roosevelt had acted unilaterally. He had ignored the World Economic Conference held in London in June 1933, described by the leading monetary historian Barry Eichengreen as a 'complete and utter failure'.[25] That the United States had acted independently, without any regard for, or consultation with, the international community, led to a disorganized system, in which countries known as the gold bloc suffered. The gold-bloc countries were France, Belgium, Luxembourg, the Netherlands, Italy, Poland and Switzerland, which all retained the gold standard throughout the economic crisis of 1929 to 1933. 'Having severed their golden fetters', by contrast, policymakers in the United States and Britain 'were able to adopt more expansionary monetary and fiscal policies designed to spur the recovery of their economies'. The United States, as already stated, was still on gold, but it had devalued the dollar by over 50 per cent. The 'losers were nations still on gold'. Their currencies had by this time 'appreciated by 67 percent against sterling and the dollar'. This obviously damaged their exports.[26]

Yet, despite the devaluation of the dollar, gold and financial capital 'flowed inexorably toward the United States'. Indeed, between the end of 1934 and the end of 1936, the US consistently held between 65 and 70 per cent of the world's central bank gold reserves. The gold-bloc countries were losing gold, since their exports were falling behind. Their currencies, backed by gold, were too valuable against other currencies which had left the gold standard. This meant that their exports were too expensive to compete. As a consequence, their exports fell. Under this pressure, France, under its leftist Popular Front government, abandoned the gold standard on 26 September 1936, just five years after the British had set themselves free from their 'golden fetters'.[27] This phenomenon of different countries leaving the gold standard or devaluing their currencies has been termed 'competitive devaluation'. As the world economy shrank, countries made their currencies cheaper to render their goods more attractive. This prompted other countries to act in the same way. Barry Eichengreen, who effectively created the conventional wisdom on this period, suggests that once they had 'shed their golden fetters, policymakers had several new policy options available'. They 'could expand the money supply'. They could also 'increase the level of government expenditure' without regard to the exchange rate. Their 'expansionary policies' were facilitated by abandonment of the gold standard.

The country which best typified this new, 'gold-free' approach to finance was probably Germany. Even before Keynes had published his *General Theory of Employment, Interest and Money* in 1936, Germany had adopted expansionary fiscal policies, deficit financing and fiat money. Long before Dick Cheney, the American Vice President between 2001 and 2009, is reputed to have expressed a similar opinion, Joseph Goebbels had confidently asserted that budget deficits were quite safe, since 'no people had ever gone under because of deficits'. Nations collapsed 'only because they lacked weapons'.[28] In 1933 Germany, under the Nazis, embarked on a period which utterly disregarded the principles of nineteenth-century orthodox finance. The key figure in this development was not Hitler himself, but Hjalmar Schacht, a tall, angular and abrasive figure with a keen analytical mind. Schacht's main task was, as he wrote later, 'to provide the necessary finance for the public works programme'. Schacht had been appointed President of the Reichsbank in March 1933. The work-creation mythology of the Nazi regime put a special emphasis on the autobahns, the motorways which were built at record speeds across Germany during the 1930s.[29]

The basic philosophy behind Nazi economic ideas, let alone monetary policy, had been expressed by Hitler in his personal testament *Mein Kampf*. Like the Jacobins in the French revolutionary era, he believed that by force of will and diktat he could overcome the laws of economics. In his conception, economics itself was subordinate to the dictates of politics, whose supreme end was the 'historical struggle of nations for life'. In Hitler's crude, apocalyptic, one might say Wagnerian, vision of this 'historical struggle of nations', the 'nation does not live for the economy, for economic leaders, or for economic or financial theories; on the contrary, it is finance and the economy . . . which all owe unqualified service in the struggle for the self-assertion of our nation'.[30] This view could not be more different from the quiet operation of nineteenth-century capitalism, with its gold standard, its balanced budgets and its essentially international approach – its vision of the man, in Keynes's pre-1914 world, who could 'adventure his wealth' in any part of the globe or could travel anywhere with gold 'on his person'.

Schacht's policy involved making the private sector subordinate to the public sector. There was a tight rationing of credit. He attempted to get the German private commercial banks to help the Nazi government in three key areas. The first of these was to increase the funds available for public investment; secondly, it was necessary to help 'in lowering the rates of interest'. Thirdly, the job of the private sector would be to 'implement the restrictions upon concerns which were refused access to new funds'.[31] This meant that commercial banks would act as agents of government policy, by forcing their clients to conform to the government's public spending plans. Private companies would be starved of funds which would be directed to public spending. Rearmament was the central goal underlying Nazi financial policy. To ensure an 'enormous rearmament' operation was no easy task. A bare look at statistics shows some of the great strides made. The Luftwaffe, for example, was scheduled to raise its strength from forty-eight squadrons in August 1935 to over 200 by October 1938.[32] In a cabinet meeting which took place as early as 8 June 1933, less than six months after Hitler became Chancellor of the Reich, Schacht and others agreed to spend 35 billion Reichsmarks over eight years on the armed forces. This implied an annual spending rate of 4.4 billion Reichmarks, when the annual military spending of the Weimar Republic had been only hundreds of millions of Reichsmarks. Total national income in 1933 had slumped to 43 billion Reichsmarks and, consequently, Schacht's plan amounted to nearly 10 per cent of the national income being devoted to rearming. Even if a recovery was assumed, this figure implied that more than 5 per cent of GDP would be devoted to defence for the eight years after 1933, a much higher figure than that spent by Western European governments in 2012. By comparison, according to its own government, the United States of America spent 6 per cent of national GDP on defence in 2012.[33]

The financing of the Nazi war machine marked a total rejection of the assumptions and complacency of the nineteenth century. Sir Robert Peel would have been bewildered and horrified by the developments in public finance in the ninety years that followed his death in 1850. No regime would, on purely financial grounds, have appalled him more than Hitler's of the 1930s. Perhaps ironically, the Hitler regime, in its deficit financing and its scorn for the gold standard, was imitated by other, more democratic regimes. In his memoirs, published in 1953, Schacht made an explicit connection between Roosevelt and Hitler which a writer from any other nation would have hesitated to make after the Second World War (though before 1939 many did make this comparison). 'Roosevelt and Hitler came to power at the same time. They both owed their election to an extraordinary economic depression. They both had the task of stimulating the economy through State intervention.' Schacht, furthermore, explicitly compared Hitler's economic policies to Roosevelt's 'New Deal', in which the US government substantially increased government spending on public works and welfare payments to produce economic recovery.[34]

Of course, there was nothing really new about the means by which Hitler attempted to stimulate the German economy. The suspension of the gold standard and the running up of government deficits to finance armaments had naturally been the favourite devices of the revolutionary French government in 1792, the British government fighting Napoleon in the early nineteenth century and the federal government of the United States in its struggle against the Confederacy during the American Civil War of 1861–5, among others. The only difference was that the Nazis embarked on these policies before hostilities had been declared; in other words, they operated a 'war economy' in the six years before the outbreak of the actual war in September 1939.

Keynes perceived the significance of this point about war finance. In 1940, after the war had started in Europe, but before the United States entered in December 1941, he observed that it was 'impossible for a capitalistic democracy to organize expenditure on the scale necessary to make the grand experiments which would prove my case – except in war conditions'.[35] These 'grand experiments' had already in fact taken place in Germany and, to a lesser degree, in the United States. Even as early as 1935, the Hungarian-born British financial journalist Paul Einzig had noted that 'President Roosevelt's public works policy has ... created a profound impression in Europe,' but he added that the 'principle involved was by no means an innovation, since several European countries had themselves embarked upon ambitious public-works schemes since 1931 as a means to combat depression'.[36] Einzig supported the public-works programmes of Roosevelt, even though he believed that the President's gold-buying programme of 1933 was a 'crude and brutal method of attaining the desired end'. A prolific journalist during the inter-war years, Einzig also expressed concern about the 'effect of the public-works schemes on the public debt', even though he acknowledged that a 'country with the gigantic resources of the United States can well afford to increase its public debt, especially as its total is still considerably below the figure of the British public debt'.

Einzig's account of international economics and politics, *Bankers, Statesmen and Economists*, is fascinating because of the date when it was written. Published in 1935, years before the war and the violent end of the

Third Reich, this work spoke optimistically about the lessons Europe could learn from America: 'Public opinion in Great Britain has been profoundly impressed by the possibilities of improving the standard of living and reducing unemployment by the aid of public works.' Even more candidly, Einzig compared Roosevelt's initiatives with those of the Nazi government in Germany. He believed that 'National Socialism in Germany stands or falls with the success or failure of the efforts to improve economic conditions.' This was something which, in 1935, the Nazis looked set to achieve. 'There can be no doubt', Einzig argued, 'that economic recovery in Germany since the beginning of 1933 has been greater than in any other country.'[37]

The work of economic theory which knitted these strands together was, appropriately enough, written by John Maynard Keynes. No other theoretical work in the field of economics so firmly bears the imprint of its times and the circumstances under which it was conceived. Keynes's *General Theory of Employment, Interest and Money* was widely anticipated even before it was launched in February 1936. With characteristic self-confidence, born of a lifetime of success and adulation, Keynes had written to George Bernard Shaw on New Year's Day 1935 with proud intent: '. . . I believe myself to be writing a book on economic theory, which will largely revolutionise – not, I suppose, at once but in the course of the next ten years – the way that the world thinks about economic problems.'[38] He was, of course, right. The *General Theory* did completely change the way in which economists thought about their subject.

It is certainly true that Keynes's great work broke new theoretical ground. But, practically, it can be argued that governments had already discovered the secret of his lessons. They had learnt to borrow and 'stimulate' the economy. They had even managed to recreate, in the case of Nazi Germany, wartime conditions without any actual war having been officially declared. Keynes's book brought a new armoury of technical vocabulary into the world. Such terms, or concepts, as 'liquidity preference', the 'consumption function' and the 'multiplier' were introduced to a receptive public. Yet policymakers in the United States and Germany, the 'madmen in authority' whom Keynes often mocked, had already embarked on programmes of economic expansion which would later be called Keynesian.

Keynes's ideas, indeed, became so associated with these kinds of policies that budget deficits have been most commonly considered to be the practical fulfilment of his theories. One historian has gone so far as to suggest that if there 'is one thing that everyone knows about Keynes, it is surely that he favoured budget deficits'.[39]

In recent years, historians and economists, largely still under the influence of his compelling personality and intellectual style, have sought to diminish this aspect of his teaching. Spending resources, however, was something which Keynes had always believed to be the real engine of economic growth. It was not saving but spending that gave to mankind such treasures as the pyramids of Egypt. As early as 1930, in his *Treatise on Money*, Keynes had noticed that it had 'been usual to think of the accumulated wealth of the world as having been painfully built up out of that voluntary abstinence of individuals from the immediate enjoyment of consumption which we call thrift'. This was not the full story, however. It 'should be obvious that mere abstinence is not enough by itself to build cities or drain fens'. Enterprise was the key to economic development. 'If Enterprise is afoot, wealth accumulates whatever may be happening to Thrift; and if Enterprise is asleep, wealth decays whatever Thrift may be doing.'[40] It was not difficult to see how such ideas could lead to the conclusions of the *General Theory*.

The Keynesian Revolution merely gave an intellectual garb to the practical conclusions of statesmen eager to 'do something' about the depression. The techniques these leaders used were not that different to the expedients which had been employed in the wars of previous centuries. It was only that, during the 1930s at any rate, a thinker and writer of real quality, in the form of John Maynard Keynes, had lent an intellectual respectability to them.

Bretton Woods

Bretton Woods is a phrase which denotes an entire era in the monetary management of the world's economy. If the inter-war period can be called the 'age of Keynes', the conference held at the affluent mountain resort town of Bretton Woods, in New Hampshire, was perhaps his most endur- ing practical legacy. Keynes, however, did not dominate the proceedings at Bretton Woods as much as he would have liked. The American delegation, under the direction of Harry Dexter White, was composed of tough, legally trained bureaucrats who would not be bamboozled by the world- famous Englishman. Of course, by 1944, when the Bretton Woods confer- ence took place, Keynes was at the height of his prestige. The advent of the coalition government in 1940 had swept away Conservatives like Neville Chamberlain who remained rigorously attached to Peelite principles of balanced budgets. Churchill's government was much more amenable to Keynes, someone for whom Winston Churchill himself had respect, even if there is little evidence of personal warmth between arguably the two most remarkable Englishmen of their time. As one historian has put it, there was a 'major political shift, once Churchill replaced Chamberlain', which 'unlocked the doors of Whitehall' for Keynes.[1]

To his subordinates on the British delegation, such as the economist Lionel Robbins, Keynes was a semi-godlike figure. Robbins extolled his mentor's 'quick logic, the birdlike swoop of his intuition, the vivid fancy, the wide vision, above all the incomparable sense of the fitness of words' which all contributed to making 'something several degrees beyond the limit of ordinary human achievement'. Robbins acknowledged that Churchill 'in our own age . . . of course, surpasses him'. But 'the greatness of the Prime Minister is something much easier to understand than the genius of Keynes'.[2] Yet some British civil servants, such as Frederick Leith-Ross, a high-ranking Treasury official who had been sceptical of Keynes's public spending ideas in the early 1930s, questioned whether the economist was the ideal negotiator in such fine situations of international diplomacy: '. . . Keynes was not in all respects a fortunate choice . . . [he] could not resist the temptation to score points off his opponents and his professorial tendency to talk down to his class irritated the American representatives.'[3] Unfortunately for Keynes, Harry Dexter White – who was 'blunt and downright in speech' – was equally unimpressed by the Englishman's rather swaggering intellectual arrogance.[4] The contrast between the elegant English economist, with his upper-middle-class assurance, and the hard-headed economists and lawyers who represented the American view was captured by Edward Bernstein, an economist from New Jersey in his late thirties at the time of the conference. Bernstein recounted how, at a preliminary meeting in 1943, Keynes had insisted on rewriting a draft plan, even though he accepted its conclusions, on the grounds that it was written in 'Cherokee'. Bernstein curtly replied, 'the reason it's in Cherokee is because we need the support of the braves of Wall Street and this is the language they understand'. This, to modern ears, was not ethnically sensitive, but the point was well made. Bernstein, recalling this episode in an interview in 1983, concluded that the 'British were well aware that we could have our way no matter what'. A further contrast was supplied by the brusque, direct manner in which the Americans spoke to each other, as compared to the elegant phrasemaking of the Edwardian Keynes. Bernstein remembered Dean Acheson, later a US Secretary of State, murmuring to him later in the proceedings, 'Don't fuck it up, Eddie.' 'I absolutely won't,' replied Bernstein.[5]

Harry Dexter White, the leader of the American delegation, had a completely different background from that of John Maynard Keynes. His father was a Lithuanian Jew, who had arrived in Boston in 1885 and changed his name from Weit to White in the 1890s. Once demobilized at the end of the First World War, White himself only began his study of economics at the age of thirty, and graduated from Stanford. He then embarked upon a PhD at Harvard, receiving his doctorate at thirty-eight, an age at which Keynes was already an internationally renowned writer. In

1934, he took up a job at the US Treasury. It was only a week after Pearl Harbor, on 14 December 1941, that Henry Morgenthau, the US Treasury Secretary, asked White to prepare a memorandum on the establishment of an 'inter-Allied stabilization fund' which, in Morgenthau's words, 'should provide the basis for postwar international monetary arrangements'.[6]

The actual final outcome of Bretton Woods was, to many radicals who did not want to get back to the 1930s, surprisingly conservative. There were respects in which it differed from the old pre-war gold standard, but the Bretton Woods Agreement did, to a certain extent, preserve the fetish of gold worship. According to a modern economic historian of the era, there were three distinct areas in which the Bretton Woods settlement was different from the operation of the gold standard in its classical form. Firstly, instead of each currency being directly convertible to gold, currencies would be pegged to the dollar, which remained convertible to gold, at the rate established by President Roosevelt in 1934 of $35 an ounce. This meant that the exchange rates of each currency were pegged indirectly to gold. The peg to the dollar was adjustable when what the negotiators at Bretton Woods called 'fundamental disequilibrium' took place. Secondly, capital controls were allowed to limit movements of international capital. The third new element was a new institution, the International Monetary Fund, which was designed, in the first instance, to stabilize the exchange rates set up by Bretton Woods.[7] The World Bank would be the other institution associated with Bretton Woods and it would be largely a development bank.

The discussions had been dominated, however, by the dispute between Keynes and White. Keynes was less tied to gold than the Americans were. He preferred 'Bancor', a pun derived from 'bank gold' in French. This, in his conception, would be a substitute for gold itself. Bancor was a fiction, something conjured out of thin air, which need never be in short supply like gold. In its loose way, it gave countries more flexibility and liquidity.[8] The eventual plan was more restrictive and did not abandon the link to gold. The negotiations themselves, though they culminated at Bretton Woods in July 1944, had been taking place for more than two years. It was in July 1942 that a draft of the White Plan had first been sent to London for Keynes's perusal.

From a certain point of view, Keynes's own plan was not that different from White's. Both men prescribed stable exchange rates, which they believed would help both importers and exporters. The crucial difference between the two plans, in addition to the differing roles played by gold in each of them, lay in the bailout funds they prescribed. Keynes wanted a 'Clearing Union' which would provide up to US$26 billion in loans, funded by the United States. White, by contrast, wanted the US to subscribe a maximum of US$3 billion.[9] Keynes's Clearing Union would allow countries which ran balance of payments deficits, where their imports exceeded the amount they exported, to borrow from a fund in order to finance the trade deficit. The Clearing Union would act as 'an international lender of the last resort, just as individual central banks acted as the lender of last resort for their own financial sectors'.[10] The International Monetary Fund would later be designed partly to fulfil this function. The problem with this bailout fund was, of course, the issue of who would pay the bill. The United States, as a leading creditor nation, a state which exported more goods than it imported, would be expected, under the Keynes plan, to provide liquidity to the system, to underwrite the plan.

Reaction in the United States was, understandably, hostile. As one Iowa newspaper commented, 'If we are big enough suckers to swallow the Keynes plan, we shall be swindled out of everything we have left from the war – and we shall deserve to be swindled.'[11] The ventured scheme envisaged that the Clearing Union would only be funded by the Americans to the extent of US$8.5 billion, a considerable sum, but significantly less than the US$26 billion envisaged by Keynes.[12] It was not only in the United States, however, that sceptics about the Bretton Woods arrangement arose. The link to gold had irked a number of people in Westminster. One British politician who expressed himself vociferously against the agreement was the colourful Conservative MP Robert Boothby, who had served as Winston Churchill's Parliamentary Private Secretary in the late 1920s.[13] 'Why, then, this extraordinary hurry to get us all tied up again in an international gold standard?' he asked in an address given in October 1944, after the finalizing of the Agreement in July.

Boothby correctly saw the dividing line between Keynes and White. Keynes, of course, had been less attached to gold and more enamoured with his own idea of Bancor. To Boothby, the White and Keynes plans were 'irreconcilable'. The 'agreement reached at Bretton Woods was achieved only because the original Keynes plan was totally abandoned'. Boothby described the Agreement as not even 'a victory on points for White'. Keynes had been 'knocked out in the third round'. The Agreement, in Boothby's view, had shown with 'startling clarity' that an attempt had been made to 'revert to the economic system of the nineteenth century'. The 'Bretton Woods agreement would put us all back on a gold standard more rigid in some respects than has ever existed in the past'.[14]

This assessment may have owed much to the hyperbole of the political platform, but it hit on an aspect of the truth. Boothby admitted that Bretton Woods allowed sterling to devalue 'up to 10 per cent', but stated that Britain's currency would now be 'in the hands of an international authority, on which our competitors will have a majority vote, and which is to be located in the U.S.A.'.[15] Although Keynes attempted to argue that Bretton Woods was not simply a reversion to the gold standard, he had to admit the link to gold. In a letter to the *Economist*, written in July 1944, he characterized the 'old standard' as 'rigid'. The Bretton Woods regime, which he referred to as the 'proposed standard', would mean that 'all currencies would have a "link" with gold, but it would be "flexible" enough to permit orderly changes in exchange rates' in order to 'avert the breakdown of monetary systems'.[16] In May, Keynes had used his new position as a member of the British House of Lords to defend Bretton Woods against the charge that it was a return to the gold standard. The 'gold standard, as I understand it, means a system under which the external value of a national currency is rigidly tied to a fixed quantity of gold which can only honourably broken under *force majeure*'.[17]

More relevantly to Britain's situation in the mid-1920s, the gold standard involved 'a financial policy which compels the internal value of the domestic currency to conform to this external value as fixed in terms of gold'. In other words, it forced countries to push prices and wages down to make them more competitive, in order to maintain a certain exchange rate against gold. This had actually happened in 1925, when Churchill as Chancellor of the Exchequer had returned Britain to the gold standard at the old rate of $4.86 to one pound. The new Agreement, in Keynes's view, proposed something different. It provided that the 'external value' of the currency 'should be altered, if necessary, so as to conform to whatever *de facto* internal value results from domestic policies'. This meant that domestic policies would be lead partner in the dance; foreign exchange values would respond to domestic policies and not the other way round. Keynes observed in his speech that times had changed. 'Public opinion is now converted to a new model . . . of domestic policy.' Bretton Woods reflected this shift of opinion. It is 'above all as providing an international framework for the new ideas and the new techniques associated with the policy of full employment that these proposals are not least to be welcomed', he added. Of course, he was being uncharacteristically modest. The 'new ideas and the new techniques' he referred to had come largely from his own inspiration and hard work.[18] Keynes was right to emphasize the very restrictive discipline imposed by the old gold standard. Yet the new standard was still dependent on the dollar's connection to gold. Boothby had correctly pointed out that the Keynes plan did not depend on gold. In the 1920s Keynes himself had famously denounced gold as a 'barbaric relic' and had gleefully celebrated the loosening of Britain's 'golden fetters' in September 1931 when it left the gold standard.

The reversion to a 'link with gold' was not something with which Keynes had been associated. To his American sparring partner Harry Dexter White, Keynes expressed characteristic disdain for the parliamentarians who had 'dishonestly' raised the 'bugbear of gold'. The debate which took place in the House of Commons in May 1944 on the Bretton Woods proposals was, in Keynes's view, 'as disappointing as it could be'. The 'discussion was certainly not one which did credit to the mother of Parliaments', was his rather scornful comment about the debate in the lower house. The problem was the gold link, of which he observed that 'the mere suggestion that our proposals can be regarded in the light of a return to gold, is enough to make 99 per cent of the people of this country see red'. By contrast, he had noticed that the 'atmosphere in the House of Lords yesterday [when he made his speech in support of the Bretton Woods proposals] was quite free' from the rather antagonistic mood of the House of Commons.[19]

To modern analysts, however, Bretton Woods was a lot more similar to the pre-1914 gold standard than it would be to the world of freely floating exchange rates of the late twentieth century. Like the gold standard, the Bretton Woods system proposed a regime of fixed exchange rates, though it did allow for some devaluation, if 'fundamental disequilibrium' occurred. In many ways, Bretton Woods was even more rigid than the old gold standard, as it required capital controls, whereas the old system had not. Even more restrictive was the prohibition on exchanging currencies directly for gold. Under the gold standard anyone with a banknote could go to the central bank and exchange it for gold. This facility was precisely what was referred to when the Bank of England suspended 'gold convertibility' in 1797 and again in 1914.

The United States' position as the leading repository of gold ensured that, if gold was still to play a role in the international monetary system, the US dollar would be the chain binding international currencies to the precious metal. The outbreak of war in 1939 had once again, as in the summer of 1914, led to an inflow of gold to the US Treasury. Moreover, the total inflow from January 1934 to August 1939, even before the war had started in Europe, was over $9,000 million. 'Is it probable that the United States will come into possession of virtually the entire world stock of monetary gold . . .?' asked a British economist in 1940, when he estimated that the US owned two-thirds of the world's gold. The once famous Fort Knox became an international symbol of American power when a gold depository was built adjacent to the military fort in 1936. 'This government-owned gold lies buried in a fort in Kentucky.' The United States had become a 'hoarder' of gold.[20]

The gold position of the United States was only a symptom of the power of that country in the world economy. The Second World War, with its huge cost in terms of human lives and capital, had shifted the balance of economic power even more decisively in favour of the United States than the 1914–18 conflict. As for Britain, while its resources were 'quite adequate to meet the liability for the war debt which was assumed in 1923 . . . the amount of lease-lend aid was far greater, and the country's resources far more heavily depleted', wrote Ralph Hawtrey, the retired British Treasury official, in 1946.[21] The prostrate position of Great Britain after the war, in economic terms, has often been seen by historians as a perfect opportunity for America to extend its dominance over the world. Keynes's most significant biographer goes so far as to suggest that 'America's main war aim, after the defeat of Germany and Japan, was the liquidation of the British Empire.'[22] Regardless of the motivations of the Americans, the relative strength of the two countries' position was obvious. The Bretton Woods Agreement reflected White's scheme rather than Keynes's 'not because it was technically superior, but because the Americans had the power'.[23]

Behind the scenes, the British were undoubtedly frustrated by their subordinate position. None was more conscious of Britain's relative weakness than Keynes himself. His letters to friends towards the end of the war express a frustration with the Americans which public pronouncements of co-operation and friendship effectively masked. In a letter to one of his favourite pupils, Richard Kahn, written less than six weeks before his death from a heart attack in April 1946, Keynes reproached the Americans for having 'no idea how to make these institutions into operating international concerns', adding that 'in almost every direction their ideas are bad'. Their superior power meant that the views of other nations, however, would be disregarded: 'they plainly intend to force their own conceptions through regardless of the rest of us'.[24] In a letter to the Whitehall mandarin Edward Bridges, written on the same day as the letter to Kahn, 13 March 1946, Keynes admitted that 'we cannot pretend to be satisfied with the atmosphere here'. This was written in Savannah, Georgia, where the international community of economists and Treasury officials was meeting to conclude the establishment of the International Monetary Fund and the World Bank. The meeting lasted from 8 to 22 March. Some 300 delegates attended from such disparate countries as Guatemala, Ethiopia and Mexico, as well as from the major countries of Europe.

The final source of disagreement between the British, under the guidance of Keynes, and the Americans was the physical site of these international institutions, the IMF and the World Bank. The British had 'not conceived it as possible that either institution would be placed away from New York'. Keynes had favoured New York because those institutions situated in that city would be involved 'in the daily contacts which can be provided by a great centre of international finance'. In New York, further-more, the new institutions would be 'sufficiently removed from the poli-tics of Congress'. But in a stroke of cunning diplomacy the Americans kept their intentions about the location of both institutions secret until the last minute. Keynes remarked, 'No rumour reached us until a day or two before we left Washington for Savannah, when Mr Vinson told me that the American Delegation had decided that both institutions should be placed in Washington and that was a final decision the merits of which they were not prepared to discuss.' Such unilateral and, some might say, arrogant behaviour was justified on the grounds that the 'United States Administration were entitled to decide for themselves what location within the United States was to be preferred'.[25]

This high-handedness was not calculated to endear the Americans to the British. Keynes expressed his usual disdain for the strategic abilities of the Americans. 'It would be a mistake to suppose that the Americans have far-sighted plans, whether good or bad.' Fred Vinson, a Kentucky lawyer and a close associate of the new President, Harry Truman, had been appointed Secretary of the Treasury in 1945. He was, in Keynes's acute assessment, 'a shrewd and ambitious politician' who was 'interested in immediate power and patronage, in personal publicity, and in the appear-ance of successful Americanism [sic]'. It was unlikely, in Keynes's view, that 'he has given ten minutes thought to what he would like the institutions to be doing two years hence'.[26] Keynes's doubts about the sincerity of Vinson's long-term commitment to the institutions of international finance were confirmed in June 1946 when Truman appointed Vinson the thirteenth Chief Justice of the United States. A large, affable man with grey hair and blue eyes, Vinson was the archetypal career lawyer–politician of a kind well known in the public affairs of the United States.[27]

The exasperation Keynes expressed over the American style of negoti-ation was softened by more sentimental recollections of the meeting at Savannah. In one of his last letters, dated 29 March 1946, the great British economist commented wryly on the conference: 'My last memory is of Dr Harry White, with vine leaves (or were they cocktails?) in his hair, leading into the dining room a Bacchic rout of Satyrs and Silenuses from Latin America, loudly chanting the strains of "Onward Christian Soldiers".'

Little more than three weeks after writing the letter, Keynes was dead. He was six weeks short of his sixty-third birthday, and both his parents outlived him. His death was rather premature, but the inter-war period of international economics had been framed and, to an unusual degree, influenced by the products of his fertile and inventive mind. He had burst on to the international scene with *The Economic Consequences of the Peace*, that withering denunciation of what he termed the 'Carthaginian Peace' of Versailles. His *General Theory of Employment, Interest and Money* had been the definitive economic text of the period. Keynes's public career can be neatly fitted into the twenty-seven years between the publication of *The Economic Consequences of the Peace* in 1919 and his death in 1946. His public career had been entirely shaped by the two world wars.

Despite his immense prestige and charisma, Keynes had not managed to stem the tide of American dominance in world affairs. Rather like Winston Churchill, he had been brought up in the high confidence of the upper classes of the British empire. Like Churchill's, his life had been conducted almost exclusively in the elite institutions of British public life. Eton, Cambridge, the Treasury and, latterly, the House of Lords had been the scenes of his life's work. Churchill's life was almost entirely spent at Harrow, in the British army and in the House of Commons. They both reached their age of maturity in the reigns of Victoria and Edward VII. The world of 1946 could not have been more different from that of the late Victorian age. Both Keynes and Churchill, in their own ways, had to react to Britain's diminished place in the world and to the power of the United States.

In economic terms, however, the biggest change wrought by the two world wars had been effected in the fields of currency and government spending. As already noted, Keynes himself had observed after the First World War that where 'we spent millions before the war, we have now learnt that we can spend hundreds of millions and apparently not suffer from it'.[28] The Second World War had been even more costly. In the United States the national debt, which had been only US$40.4 billion in June 1939, rose to US$258.7 billion in June 1945. As a proportion of GDP, the public debt of the United States rose from 43 per cent in 1939 to 112.7 per cent in 1945.[29] The financial position of the United Kingdom was even more desperate. Its total public debt was £24.5 billion in 1945, estimated to be 250 per cent of GDP. This had been the ratio reached in 1815 after the wars against revolutionary France. The national debt of £24.5 billion was more than three times as large as the total reached in 1919 of £7.4 billion. This latter total itself was eleven times the size of the national debt in 1914, immediately before the outbreak of war.

For Britain, the nation of Sir Robert Peel, William Gladstone and Lord Overstone, the two world wars had severely challenged age-old principles of public finance. In little more than thirty years, the Victorian world of a sound currency and balanced budgets had given way to a world of debt and unprecedented levels of government spending. For writers and economists who took a long view of the subject, this development had been extraordinary and of the greatest significance. To sound-money conservatives like Ralph Hawtrey, the changes wrought by world war had been unfortunate and utterly destabilizing. Hawtrey attributed the 'economic catastrophes of the inter-war years, 1919–1939' to 'disastrous variations in the wealth-value of money units', or to what we might term 'inflation'. He pointed out that, as a consequence of Roosevelt's abandonment of the old dollar value of gold in 1934, the 'value of gold in terms of other forms of wealth was *quadrupled* between 1920 and 1935'. More controversially perhaps, Hawtrey expressed a sceptical attitude to the 'expansionist' policy of government which, he believed, was 'likely to end in disaster'.[30] Inflation would ensue from too high a level of government spending, which itself was an almost inevitable consequence of war. As Hawtrey observed, a 'major war nearly always involves the belligerent countries in inflationary finance; they have recourse to paper currency, and their metallic currency is driven abroad'. If excessive government spending and the inflation which followed were the biggest destabilizing influences in the world economy, then the 'need for stabilizing the wealth-value of money is *immediate*', argued Hawtrey.[31]

As for the efficacy of government spending in ordinary times as a means of stimulating demand, Hawtrey remained equally sceptical. He observed that 'President Roosevelt added $24,000 million [*sic*] to the national debt of the United States in the years 1933–9 without ever procuring any but a very incomplete revival'. Roosevelt's experience had been unfortunate, since 'more than once the expansion of the flow of money was robbed of its virtue by an advance of the wage level and resulting increase in costs'. Hitler, by contrast, by 'keeping a tight hand on the German wage level, eliminated unemployment in Germany'.[32] Hawtrey was therefore wary of what we might call 'fiscal policy' as an instrument of economic management. 'Government expenditure is but a clumsy instrument for stimulating demand; and for regulating the flow of money it is definitely unfitted.' This was because government spending could provide 'no means of checking an excessive expansion'. It was no substitute for the bank rate.

Hawtrey favoured monetary policy as a better tool than fiscal policy in the management of an economy. His differences with Keynes, a fellow Cambridge Apostle, in this respect would be continuing themes among the several schools of economists which dominated the late twentieth century. Hawtrey fondly remembered the period between 1874 and 1914, in which the bank rate 'fluctuated between 2 and 5 per cent, with only occasional rises to 6 or 7 per cent'. In this orderly world, the 'true aim' of the bank rate had been 'to prevent an undue expansion of the flow of money'. Despite being an advocate of using the bank rate to stimulate economic activity, Hawtrey acknowledged that 'in the event of an exceptionally severe depression' cheap money could fail 'to evoke revival'. He pointed out that cheap money could continue for 'considerable periods', as had occurred 'between 1894–6 and 1867–8, before any appreciable revival of activity is felt'.[33]

Despite the remonstrations of Hawtrey and others, Bretton Woods was not a radical departure from the principles of the old finance. The gold link was maintained, much to the surprise of many. The desire of people like Hawtrey for stable money values was appeased by the fixed nature of the exchange rates. Bretton Woods tried to impose some degree of order and stability in an uncertain world. From this point of view, as an attempt to create order out of monetary chaos, it was not unlike the gold standard. It was perhaps surprising in this respect. After the most destructive war in human history, and after the immense dislocations of people and capital caused by the war, the economic response of the international community was, as Boothby and others had noticed, one of tepid conservatism. The Bretton Woods system relied, of course, on the United States dollar, but it had not abandoned the link to gold. It marked 'a set of constitutional rules and guidelines for the world economy'. It represented a compromise between the rigidity of the gold standard and the 'wild fluctuations' which economists at the time of the Agreement believed would characterize flexible exchange rates. An element of stability was desirable to promote trade.[34]

More remarkably perhaps, Bretton Woods reflected a degree of international co-operation which had been manifestly lacking in the international politics of the first part of the twentieth century. In May 1944, Keynes himself had observed to Lord Addison, a retired Liberal politician, 'one naturally welcomes the first concrete attempt at international co-operation in the economic field'. 'Surely', he continued, 'it is a considerable thing for the experts of so many nations to have agreed' to the settlement at Bretton Woods.[35] To Camille Gutt, the Belgian politician who would serve as the first Managing Director of the International Monetary Fund, international co-operation in the economic realm was the hardest to achieve. 'If there is one area in which spirits were not prepared for international co-operation, it is certainly in the monetary field,' he wrote. This was because the 'idea of money has always been allied to that of national sovereignty'.[36] The wider significance of Bretton Woods was in its relative success as an effort of co-ordinated international statesmanship. Although it had the stamp of international co-operation, however, it was clear that no such co-operation could have been achieved without the preponderant power of the United States. Bretton Woods itself was a New Hampshire mountain resort. The institutions of Bretton Woods had been located in Washington, the capital of the dominant military and economic nation in the world. The dollar was the basis of the monetary system. Bretton Woods may have marked a turning point in international co-operation, but it was, at the same time, an emphatic symbol and proof of the hegemony of the United States.

PART III

PEACE: THE NEW DOLLAR ORDER, 1945–1973

Pax Americana

In 1945 the United States was by far the most powerful nation on earth. It could even be argued that no nation has ever enjoyed such preponderant influence in the world's affairs as the US did at the close of the Second World War. It was at that time the only power to have an atomic bomb. In the economic sphere, its dominance was no less conspicuous. The most obvious expression of its economic might was the enormous industrial base it possessed, and the most successful company in this context was General Motors, the car manufacturer. When 'World War II began, GM rapidly converted itself from the nation's largest manufacturer of automobiles to the nation's largest producer of war materials'. When the war ended, remembered Alfred Sloan, the noted Chief Executive of the company, General Motors 'rapidly reconverted to peacetime production'.[1]

During America's post-war boom, General Motors, in the eyes of one modern historian of the company, 'did more than simply mirror the American Way of Life – it helped to shape it, and for a time, the story of GM's rise was the story of America's ascendancy'.[2] It was hardly surprising, therefore, if the executives of General Motors sometimes confused the interests of their company with those of the country as a whole. It was the company's President, Charles E. Wilson, who famously mixed up the national interest with that of General Motors at his confirmation hearing as Secretary of Defense in 1953.[3] When asked whether there might be any conflict of interest between his role as Secretary of Defense and such residual loyalty as he might have towards General Motors, Wilson replied, 'for years I thought what was good for the country was good for General Motors and vice versa'. Undoubtedly, the commercial culture of post-war

America was dominated by the big corporation. Harlow Curtice, General Motors' Chief Executive from 1953 to 1958, was even named the *Time* magazine 'Man of the Year' for 1955. Described as a 'trim, lean man with the suave good looks of an ambassador and the cheery smile of a salesman', Curtice was born in Michigan, and his lifelong career at General Motors seemed the embodiment of the American dream.[4]

The burden of responsibility sat heavily on American shoulders after the defeat of the Axis powers. Unlike after the First World War, the United States government knew that it needed to play a part in putting the world back on its feet. Economically, since large parts of Europe and the developed world had been devastated by the war, the United States was the only power capable of leading a general economic recovery. While companies like General Motors were exporting to the rest of the world, the world needed dollars to make those purchases. Economies in Europe and beyond needed to be supported by the United States in order to preserve external markets for the goods which the American industrial heartland was making in such prodigious volumes. William McChesney Martin Jr, a future Chairman of the Federal Reserve, captured the mood perfectly in a speech given at a dinner in New York in November 1946.

At the time, Martin was Chairman of the Export-Import Bank of Washington, a bank set up in 1934 which became an agency of the federal government in 1945, whose function was to support American international trade. A modest and self-effacing Yale graduate, he was only forty, but his experience in government had begun in 1938 when he was appointed President of the New York Stock Exchange at the precocious age of thirty-one.[5] Surveying the wreck of 'a war-torn world' in his 1946 speech, Martin pronounced that the United States was 'bearing the greater part of the initial burden of this gigantic rehabilitation endeavour'.[6] His position was clear. The United States was the only country which had the means to support the global economy. In its weakened and depleted state, world trade needed American dollars with which to buy goods, preferably from America. 'Foreign countries are not in a position to make immediate payment for these vitally needed supplies.' As a result, 'an enormous dollar financing problem arises'.

The 'dollar financing problem' was something which baffled the monetary authorities of the world even before the Second World War had ended.

In Martin's view, this problem had already been anticipated by the American government 'well in advance' of Victory in Japan Day in August 1945. There were three distinct types of dollar financing which had been foreseen. The first was the 'financing of relief', the immediate need to feed, house and clothe the thousands of refugees and people displaced by the war. The second type of financing was required for 'longer-range reconstruction' and development. This referred to the need to build new infrastructure – roads, buildings and the like – to establish Europe's development on a secure basis. The third requirement was perhaps most interesting of all from the point of view of international relations, and the standing of the great powers: 'the financing of the crucial British balance of payments deficit'.

Britain's position after the war was a matter of concern to the Americans. They recognized, according to Martin, that the 'crucial position of Britain in world trade' ensured that it was 'imperative to find some means of meeting the prospective British balance of payments deficit if our post-war international economic objectives were to be fully realized'.[7] The British loan, the terms on which the Americans would lend to the British, had been the subject of the last intense, diplomatic effort of John Maynard Keynes. The final settlement, after many hours of negotiation, included a US$3.75 billion line of credit to Britain. Like many of his background and class, Martin, an urbane Mid-Westerner, who had graduated in English and Latin at Yale University in 1928, was essentially an Anglophile. In front of the House Banking and Currency Committee in May 1946, he declared himself 'unequivocally in favour of the British loan'. To him, the whole point of Bretton Woods was that it provided a solution to the 'British postwar balance of payments problem'. Without assistance in the form of the loan, Martin did not see 'how the British can hope to meet their prospective deficits in the 1946–50 period'.

More revealingly, the only way the British could solve their problem of importing far more than they exported, the so-called 'balance of payments' problem, was by 'continuing their wartime exchange and trade restrictions'. This action would strengthen the ties between the countries in the 'Sterling Area' – that is, countries whose currencies were linked to sterling. The Sterling Area was defined by the British Labour politician Hugh

Gaitskell as a 'group of countries including all the members of the British Commonwealth apart from Canada, and some non-members of the Commonwealth', like Ireland, Burma, Iraq and Jordan. These countries treated 'London not merely as the place where they keep their currency reserves but also as their banking centre'.[8] It would mean that those countries would resort 'to any means at their disposal to push their exports'. This would threaten the interests of the United States or, in Martin's more diplomatic language, 'set up numerous points of friction in the trade relations between this country and the British Empire at a most inopportune time'.[9]

The British loan itself was controversial and split opinion across many levels of American politics. John Wesley Snyder, Fred Vinson's successor as US Secretary of the Treasury, and a close personal friend of President Truman, later recalled that Anglophiles like George Kennan, an official in the US State Department, believed that the 'resources of the United States were inexhaustible and that they should be employed to the greatest extent to relieving some of the economic and financial problems of Great Britain'. Snyder also remembered that the loan was 'very controversial', since many 'of our bankers and congressmen and our businessmen' were 'not at all pleased with the manner in which the loan was set up'. Others, however, 'in our Government . . . felt that it should have been much larger'. A factor which certainly strengthened the scepticism of some Americans was the circumstance that Britain now had a Labour government and was now 'asserting greater state control over the economy and narrowing the area of free enterprise'. Snyder remembered such reluctance borne of suspicions about the march of socialism in Britain as 'definitely' part of 'the thought of a great many of our businessmen, our bankers, and a great many of our congressmen'.[10]

The generosity of the United States to Europe was an instance of 'enlightened self-interest'. 'Private capital could not be expected to meet any substantial part of the emergency post-war needs.' Therefore it was 'essential for the United States [government] to provide the dollar credits required', until 'such time as the International Bank [the World Bank] could take over'.[11] The British loan was necessary for Britain to purchase American goods. If it failed, Martin argued, the 'Bretton Woods program' would fall 'of its own weight', and 'the prospect of repayment of loans already made' would be 'substantially lessened'.[12] The details of the actual loan to the United Kingdom were very simple: the United States would lend US$3.75 billion which would be repaid in fifty annual instalments, beginning on 31 December 1951, 'with interest at the rate of 2 per cent per annum'. The British government was allowed, under the terms of the loan, to 'accelerate repayment of the amount drawn under this line of credit'. The British, under Keynes's direction, had lobbied hard for an interest-free loan, but the six-year waiver on interest payments was all the Americans were prepared to give.[13]

The ultimate expression of American enlightened self-interest was the Marshall Plan. George Marshall himself was a 'homely, reassuring man with compressed, unsmiling lips and deep-set searching eyes'. He was another *Time* magazine 'Man of the Year', for 1947, partly because of his achievements as a soldier and statesman, as a key general in the war, and later as Truman's Secretary of State between 1947 and 1949. It was at Harvard Yard in the summer of 1947 that Marshall launched his ambitious plan to revive a fallen Europe. The Marshall Plan was attractive to a large section of American public opinion because of the circumstances under which it was conceived. The beginnings of a Cold War in Europe, in which different parts of the old continent had fallen under the rival sway of the United States and the Soviet Union, had made the American desire to support Western Europe ever more ardent. Initial support for Marshall's plan was lukewarm in Washington. Hamilton Fish, a former staunchly Republican Congressman who had opposed Roosevelt's New Deal, remarked that the Marshall Plan 'is not a sacred cow'. In February 1948, however, with Czechoslovakia slipping into political uncertainty, a new 'sense of crisis gripped Washington'. After two weeks of debate, at five minutes past midnight on 14 March 1948, the Senate voted 69 to 17 to approve the 'European Recovery Plan', which would, of course, be more popularly referred to as the 'Marshall Plan'.[14] The Plan itself originally did not distinguish between those parts of the continent of Europe that were 'under Soviet control and those that were not', but the thinking that lay behind it 'certainly did'.[15] A fundamental premise of the Marshall Plan was that 'hunger, poverty, and despair might cause Europeans to vote their own communists into office'.

The Plan itself absorbed 10 per cent of the federal budget in its first year, or a sum of US$5.3 billion; over four years, the Plan contributed US$13 billion to the cause of European recovery. From the point of view of a history of currencies and finance, the Marshall Plan contributed to solving the 'dollar shortage', the limited availability of dollars in Europe which hampered the ability of European countries to buy imports from the United States. In this respect, the Marshall Plan performed a similar function to the Anglo-American loan negotiated by Keynes. In order to increase their exports and manufacturing after the devastation of the war, the countries of Europe, in the first instance, needed to import the capital equipment and other materials to produce exports.[16]

The need of war-torn Europe for American dollars with which to buy goods from the United States was a feature of what was subsequently named the 'Triffin dilemma' or the 'Triffin paradox', after Robert Triffin, the economist who wrote about the phenomenon in the early 1960s. In short, the United States had to provide dollars to other countries to promote trade. Those other countries needed dollars to buy goods from America. Yet if the United States provided an unlimited fund of dollars to facilitate trade, confidence in the dollar could weaken. This would be reflected in a run on US gold stocks as holders of dollars converted their dollars into gold, as a consequence of their lack of confidence in the American currency. Such a demand for gold would put pressure on the fixed gold–dollar exchange rate of US$35 for an ounce of gold, the linchpin of the Bretton Woods system.[17]

In the meantime, American bankers and economists had to adjust to the new post-war conditions. According to an assessment by a contemporary economist, the 'Second World War and the preceding decade of depression, deficit financing and expansion of the role of government in economic affairs' had 'profoundly altered the environment of central banking in the United States'. Lawrence Seltzer, a specialist in public finance, remarked that a public debt had emerged which was 'so big' that even 'moderate increases in interest rates ... would produce very sizable increases in the government's interest costs'. Even more fundamentally, the 'climate of opinion' had changed. People now wanted a 'continuous proactive policy'. It seemed to some that the 'whole system of private enterprise is now on trial to demonstrate its capacity to provide a tolerably high level of employment'.[18] This shift of emphasis was 'traceable mainly to the empirical experience of the thirties, but a scientific or intellectual rationale for it has been provided by the doctrines of J. M. Keynes and Alvin H. Hansen'.[19] In this new world, monetary policy would be down-played and the idea of full employment now held sway. The Full Employment Act passed by Congress in 1945 enshrined the idea that it was 'the duty of government to underwrite a stable high level of employ-ment, using deficit spending as a major instrument if necessary'. The debt mountain faced by the United States seemed, at the beginning of the Cold War in 1946, enormous. 'With an interest-bearing public debt already approximating 275 billion dollars, the interest charges alone at present rates will exceed the total budget of the federal government in any peace-time year with the exception of the deficit-financing period of the thirties'. Given such high levels of public indebtedness, it was no surprise that 'the deliberate promotion and maintenance of low interest rates had become an avowed objective of many governments'.[20]

The increase in US public debt in the 1940s actually ensured that bank-ers were more conservative and less daring. They were less likely to lend to the private sector, as they could earn safe, though unspectacular, returns by buying US government debt. As Seltzer observed, with 'the great increase in their earnings from government securities, many commercial banks no longer possess the incentive they once had to seek commercial loans'. By contrast, these banks could 'now make a good living without taking the risks of direct loans to business'.[21] This rather conservative attitude towards lending contrasts vividly with the operation and mentality of banks in the early twenty-first-century United States. What should be remembered is that the holders of US government debt in the 1940s were largely US banks, households and investment funds. The US debt was held domesti-cally, in contrast to the large foreign holdings of US government securities which would develop at the end of the twentieth century.

The conservatism of the American banking sector was not that surpris-ing. Bretton Woods itself had been, as we have already observed, a lesson in conservative statecraft. As the Canadian economist Jacob Viner noticed when commenting on the objections of English critics, 'the program for postwar international economic relations which is contained in the provisions of the Bretton Woods agreements [and in] the Anglo-American loan agreement . . . reverts to nineteenth-century doctrines and practices for its inspiration'. Viner, a classical liberal, felt that this was a good thing. 'It is not prima facie, however, a very damaging charge to make against proposals in the international field that they are more in the spirit of John Stuart Mill and Richard Cobden [noted nineteenth-century liberal free traders] than of Smoot-Hawley [a protectionist tariff passed by the US Congress in 1930] and [Hjalmar] Schacht'.[22]

To other Americans, the post-war years marked not a return to the nineteenth century, but rather the triumph of collectivist ideas regarding big government and state control. In 1946 the American economist Ralph Blodgett spoke gloomily of the likely prospect that 'we shall find ourselves living in a planned and controlled economy long after the war has been officially declared to be at an end'. He painted a picture of creeping socialism. 'To be sure, not many people are advocating a controlled economy as such.' Instead, Americans 'are asked to approve such attractive and innocent-sounding things as full employment guaranteed or underwritten by the government; [or] a system of social security, popularly known as the "cradle-to-the-grave" variety'. Blodgett, a professor at the University of Illinois, spoke apocalyptically about the 'destruction' of 'the capitalistic or free enterprise system' as a result of post-war developments which would, in his words, 'ensure the future existence of a controlled and planned economy'.

High spending was inevitable. Interest on the debt alone, at 2 per cent, would amount to an expenditure of US$6 billion a year. This was 'about twice as great as total federal expenditures in 1930'. The federal government's 'military and naval establishments and the armed forces in general [would] have to be maintained at a high level for some years to come', the cost of which would 'certainly run into several billions of dollars annually'. To this cost 'we must add some billions of dollars for the operation of the ordinary departments of the government, other billions for the maintenance of a complete system of social security . . . and possibly still other billions for providing full employment'. The true magnitude of all this expenditure remained unclear in 1946. 'Some people are thinking in terms of only 18 or 20 billion dollars per year. Others see a possibility that federal expenditures may run to 25 or 40 billions annually.'[23] In a clear-eyed summary of the consequences of increased government expenditure, Blodgett concluded his gloomy prognosis by referring to increased spending which, if Americans did 'not wish to add to the already overgrown federal debt', would have to be funded 'out of tax revenue'. This would require 'a continuation of very high levels of taxation'.[24]

Other commentators were equally pessimistic. They were conscious that the basis of the United States economy had been fundamentally altered. In the introduction to the 1951 edition of his classic work on investing, *Security Analysis*, Benjamin Graham noted that the 'economic structure' of the United States had 'shifted far from its apparently firm laissez-faire and gold standard formation of 1900'. The Second World War had witnessed an 'incredible expansion of the Federal debt from $40 billion to $240 billion'. Nevertheless, observed Graham, instead of rising, 'the bond interest rate fell further during this period', but these 'unorthodox results' were attributable to 'modern artificial controls of the money market by governmental agencies'. The deliberate policy of low interest rates seemed to be working. Ben Graham perhaps was reflecting his own opinions when he and David Dodd, his less well-known co-author of *Security Analysis*, stated that 'businessmen are convinced that the general political climate of the past half century has become increasingly unfavourable to free enterprise and to its profits'. They noticed the 'rapidly ascending personal tax rates', the 'doubled burden imposed by heavy corporate taxes', the 'rapid growth of labour's political and economic power' and, finally, 'the ever-increasing intrusion of government in the affairs of business through regulations, controls, and even competition'. All these developments were 'viewed as unquestionably "bad for business"'.[25]

The increase of government spending was widely accepted by contemporary economists. According to John Williams, 'Since 1914, we have seen the Federal budget grow from under a billion dollars a year to something over 30 billion dollars at present, or about one-sixth of the gross national product.' This was regarded as a 'revolutionary change in the American economy'. During the 1920s, the main focus of US government policy had been on central bank policy. The central bank, by its control of reserves, 'could control the quantity of money'. The 1930s saw a period of 'pump-priming' to overcome the 'inadequacy of central bank policy'. The main significance of this development had been the introduction of 'deficit spending itself'. The idea behind pump-priming, according to Williams, had initially been to create 'new consumer income by means of deficits'. There had been a view that private sector investment, in the first instance, could be promoted through increased spending on consumer goods. Later, the emphasis was placed on 'compensating' for the lack of private investment. In short, the 'chief preoccupation of fiscal theory' in the 1930s and 1940s had been to trust in the 'power of deficit spending to stimulate private investment'.[26]

Despite the generally downbeat assessment from the more trenchant free-market enthusiasts, there remained, during this period, a commitment to balancing the budget. As already observed, it was generally assumed that high levels of spending would be paid for by higher taxation. President Truman, a supporter of Roosevelt's New Deal policies, while accepting the need for increased expenditure, remained committed to the idea, if not the practice, of balanced budgets. In his State of the Union address in 1950, delivered on 4 January, Truman spoke of the need for a 'carefully considered program to meet our national needs'. This programme would 'necessarily' require 'large expenditures of funds'. The requirements for more spending had arisen from the 'costs of past wars' and the need 'to work for world peace'. Government, in Truman's view, also needed to 'make substantial expenditures which are necessary to the growth and expansion of the domestic economy'.

Despite a rather utopian commitment to government spending, Truman paid enough homage to fiscal conservatism to berate the 'ill-considered tax reduction of the 80th Congress', a Republican-dominated assembly which had been returned in the mid-term elections of 1946. These tax reductions, the President argued, had ensured that the government was not 'receiving enough revenue to meet its necessary expenditures'. Truman, at least publicly, defended his fiscal policy as the 'quickest and safest way of achieving a balanced budget'. The need to balance the budget, even after the most expensive war in history, was something to which a Democrat

New Deal President was still openly committed. Truman's statement showed to what extent the idea of the balanced budget continued to have political resonance. Despite deficit spending in the 1930s, it was not a respectable political platform in the early 1950s.[27]

Truman's commitment to balance the budget may have been laudably orthodox, yet events soon upset these aspirations. The onset of the Korean War in June 1950 placed even greater pressures on the President in his attempt to balance the nation's expenditures with tax receipts. He was particularly keen that interest rates should be kept low to help finance the war. The relationship between the Federal Reserve and the US Treasury had been made more complicated by the Second World War. In April 1942, the Fed had publicly committed itself to maintaining an interest rate of 0.375 per cent on Treasury bills (short-dated securities, typically lasting less than a year). The ceiling for longer-term government bonds was a low 2.5 per cent, reflecting the low interest rates favoured by public policy on both sides of the Atlantic in the postwar years. Rising inflation in the early 1950s had made the Federal Reserve more uneasy about keeping the long-term interest rates artificially low and it was anxious to raise the ceiling. The Fed's FOMC (Federal Open Market Committee) now 'chafed at the straitjacket imposed by the rigid regime'.

The fortunes of war, this time in the Korean peninsula, once again had a material effect on monetary and fiscal management. On 25 and 26 November 1950, a Chinese army numbering 300,000 crossed the Yalu River into North Korea. The prospect of war with China and the outbreak of the Third World War, if Stalin came to the aid of his Marxist allies, encouraged American consumers to spend, as they anticipated a reimposition of wartime controls on goods. The inflation rate for the three-month period ending February 1951 reached 21 per cent on an annualized basis.[28] In this context of increasing inflation in consumer goods, Truman was anxious to freeze wages and prices, in so far as he could. He and the Democratic-controlled Congress were committed to balancing the budget and believed that big tax increases would help to achieve this goal. The Congress was particularly keen to raise taxation since it believed that deficit financing had led to inflation during the Second World War. On the

President's insistence Congress passed the Revenue Act in September 1950, one of whose most notable provisions was to increase the top corporation tax rate from 38 to 45 per cent, and an excess profits tax in January 1951. The FOMC, against this background of government interference in prices and high taxes, wished to assert its independence.

After weeks of meetings and discussion, the FOMC, in a letter written at the beginning of February 1951, boldly told the President of what it believed its mandate to comprise. Between fighting inflation and keeping to the low interest rates of the post-war policy, the FOMC chose to fight inflation. 'Today's inflation . . . is due to mounting civilian expenditures largely financed directly or indirectly by sale of Government securities to the Federal Reserve . . . The inevitable result is more and more money and cheaper and cheaper dollars.'[29] The conclusion of this dispute between the White House and the Federal Reserve about its independence and the conduct of monetary policy was the Accord of 4 March 1951. The day on which this agreement was signed has been described as 'Federal Reserve Independence Day'.[30] A former head of the Goldman Sachs economics team has even written of 'an epic struggle between a US president who stood on the verge of a nuclear war, and a central bank that was seeking to establish its right to set an independent monetary policy'. He even paints this 'victory over fiscal dominance' as the 'moment when the modern, independent Fed came into existence'.[31] The Fed's official historian, Allan H. Meltzer, likewise suggested that the Accord of 1951 released 'the Federal Reserve from Treasury control' and began the 'evolution toward the modern Federal Reserve'.[32]

It was perhaps inevitable that the new Chairman of the Governors of the Federal Reserve would be the same William McChesney Martin who at the tender age of forty had been Chairman of the Export-Import Bank. Martin was never a political figure, but was widely believed to have been a fiscally conservative, moderate Republican of a type which was then common on the East Coast. Although he had originated in the Mid-West, an undergraduate degree at Yale and a professional career in New York and Washington had turned him into a quintessentially East Coast establishment figure. He spoke in the language of the classical liberal, influenced by Bagehot and other pillars of nineteenth-century English finance. In an address to the American Bankers Association, barely six months after his appointment, he not only alluded to the 'Frankenstein mechanics of an uncontrolled supply of money', but also affirmed his confidence in central banking. 'Central banking in the United States has been adapted to the requirements of a free people with a minimum of Government interference,' he told his audience.[33]

In consistently lucid and plain language, and in numerous addresses to bankers and economists and even before committees of the House of Representatives and the Senate, Martin articulated the home truths of British central banking in the nineteenth century, with the occasional twentieth-century American twist. In 1953, before the Economic Club of Detroit, he spoke of the 'hard choices left us in wartime', but added that now in peacetime 'that strait jacketing of the economy is wholly inconsistent with democratic institutions and a private enterprise system'. He denounced the Fed's attempt to stabilize the prices of government securities 'up to March 1951'. He hopefully described the federal fiscal situation in 1953 as one that 'does not depend excessively on credit to finance expenditures'. In laymen's terms, Martin thought that the government was doing a good job balancing the books. This state of affairs meant that fortunately 'reasonable stability in the value of the dollar is again a valid assumption in making economic decisions'.

With regard to the power of government to control economic cycles, Martin remained a sceptic. Again, in 1955 before an audience of investment bankers in New York, he looked back to the 'massive problems of the 1930s'. He acknowledged that this period had 'increasingly emphasized an enlarging role for Government in our economic life'. This involvement had been 'greatly extended in the 1940s when the emergency of World War II led to direct controls over wages, prices and the distribution of goods ranging from sugar to steel'. Yet he believed that government's powers were ultimately limited: 'The idea that the business cycle can be altogether abolished seems as fanciful as the notion that the law of supply and demand can be repealed.'[34] Despite his attachment to free markets, Martin was enough of a traditional paternalist in his approach to the economy to preach the virtues of 'moderation' and 'prudence'. Government, in his conception, was not something apart from society. All citizens as well as government had a responsibility to be moderate, and to look beyond mere profit in order to exercise self-restraint:

> If businessmen, bankers, your contemporaries in the business and finan-
> cial world, stay on the sidelines, concerned only with making profits,
> letting the government bear all of the responsibility and the burden of
> guidance of the economy, we shall surely fail ... the fact is the
> Government isn't something apart and remote from you. It is you – all of
> us. If those responsible for major decisions in business, finance, labor,
> agriculture are irresponsible, Government can't compel you, short of
> moving in the direction of dictatorship, to be reasonable, or moderate,
> or prudent.[35]

It was this appeal to prudence which provided the context of Martin's most famous dictum, which also happens to be perhaps the best-known aphorism made by any central banker. Quoting an unnamed writer, he observed that 'The Federal Reserve . . . is in the position of the chaperone who has ordered the punch bowl removed just when the party was really warming up.' These memorable words were an indication of the 'prudent moderation' he aspired to show as leader of the Fed, which he had enjoined his audience also to practise. He concluded his remarks by suggesting that 'unless the business community, leaders in all walks, exhibit moderation, prudence, and understanding, then we will fail and deserve to fail'. This, Martin believed, could not happen, since he had 'a deep and abiding faith in that indefinable yet meaningful phrase we frequently use . . . "the American Way of Life"'.[36]

The figure that emerges from Bill Martin's speeches is a traditional supporter of free markets who took an almost paternalistic moral approach to them. In a speech delivered in New York in 1957, entitled 'Our American Economy: Strength of the Republic', Martin declared that the 'great challenge of our times is to prevent the recurrence of the boom and crash sequence that has imperilled us in the past, and could destroy us in the future'. Noting that markets sometimes failed, he once again, in clear and pithy language, praised the competition while decrying greedy attempts at quick profits. The 'functioning of markets is not always good',

since markets can 'function very badly, particularly when they are dominated by monopoly, by speculative excesses or by inflation'. As a consequence of this, he encouraged the devotion of American 'energies' to 'the
promotion of competition, the restraint of speculative excess, and the
maintenance of the stability of the dollar'.[37] At bottom, Martin remained
a sound-money man of the old school.

To be a sound-money man was a moderately easy task for a Chairman
of the Federal Reserve in the 1950s. The dollar, through the Bretton Woods
Agreement, had preserved the all-important link to gold, which still held
the almost magical value of US$35 an ounce. Although the US gold stock
had reached a peak of US$24,771 million in August 1949, it remained at
US$22,726 million in the summer of 1957. It was at the latter date 'equal
to nearly 60 per cent of the estimated gold reserves of the entire free world'.
America's position with regard to its gold reserves compared very favourably with the British position before 1914, according to one Federal
Reserve memorandum. 'In the days before the First World War, the United
Kingdom acted as banker for virtually the entire world with a gold reserve
that amounted to US$165 million at the end of 1913.' Interestingly, as far
as the memorandum was concerned, such a gold reserve 'would be considered woefully inadequate today', but the 'United Kingdom did not then
suffer from any balance of payments difficulties because it maintained
financial stability and the world had unlimited confidence in the value of
the pound sterling'.

The lessons for the United States were clear. 'Even a small gold and
foreign exchange reserve therefore can prove to be adequate if the country
maintains financial stability and inspires domestic and international confidence in the maintenance of the value of its currency.' The memorandum
went on: 'On the other hand, the largest gold reserve can be dissipated
within a short time if inflation leads to an excessive rise in imports, a sharp
decline in exports and the flight of capital.' The choice for America
remained stark and unambiguous. 'If the United States continues to be
reasonably successful in the struggle against inflationary pressure, and
thereby maintains confidence at home and abroad in the value of the
dollar, the present US gold stock should be fully adequate for its needs.'
The danger would occur 'if the United States were unsuccessful in the fight

against inflation'. In that circumstance, 'even a much larger gold stock might well turn out to be inadequate'.[38]

These words were astute and would eventually prove prophetic, but for the time being, throughout the 1950s, the Eisenhower administration remained committed to the cause of balanced budgets and sound money. George Humphrey, Eisenhower's Treasury Secretary, set the mood at his confirmation hearing, in front of Congress, in January 1953. A successful lawyer, George Magoffin Humphrey established his credentials as a sound-money man from the outset. When interrogating Humphrey, Senator Russell Long simply said, 'I take it you are not in favour of deficit financing.' Humphrey asserted that 'our very first job is to retard and stop the further depreciation of the dollar'. He also pledged to 'eliminate these continuing deficits' which, he suggested, was 'a tremendous job in itself'. Once this had been achieved 'these other things follow', of which he implied the gold standard constituted one element. He stressed the difficulty of balancing the budget.

Humphrey set this as a priority throughout his first year in office. It was a 'real job' to find the US\$9.9 billion savings needed to plug the deficit, he observed at a lunch with the Cleveland Chamber of Commerce in February 1953. He affirmed the administration's commitment to 'attempting to slow down and stop this inflationary tendency that has been going on for all these years that has reduced the value of your dollar down to 53c or 54c, or something of that kind'. At a meeting in Washington, he denounced the budget deficit as 'threatening to our way of life'. Unfortunately, however, 'millions of our fellow citizens do not know this'. He referred to his leader, President Eisenhower, who had recently 'pledged his every effort in a relentless fight against unnecessary spending and loose handling of our fiscal affairs'. The deficit, as Humphrey spoke, was an estimated US\$12 billion, but it seemed shockingly big to earnest Republicans, and Democrats, at the time. In the same speech, Humphrey commented that the United States had created 'over the past 25 years' a 'built-in vested interest in Government spending in large and powerful interested groups widely spread throughout our land'. These groups 'prosper on benefit from the federal purse, and will mightily resist any action that threatens the reduction of their particular participation in the Government spending'.[39]

The positions outlined by George Humphrey all represented orthodox Republican opinions of the era. On the issue of currency, when asked by *Newsweek* in August 1953 about the criticism the Eisenhower administration had incurred because of its hard-money policy, Humphrey denied the charge. 'What we do have is not a hard money but an "honest money" policy. By honest money, I mean money that will buy as much next week, next month, and next year as it will buy today.' This was a perpetual mantra. The next month, in remarks addressed to the National Press Club in Washington, Humphrey again spoke of the administration's attempt 'to make the money of America honest and sound'. Later in the month, in another speech in Washington, he defined sound money as being 'based upon three principal pillars – a proper budget policy, a properly functioning Federal Reserve System, and proper debt management'. Deficit financing he defined as 'spending more than you take in', which meant, according to this orthodox view, 'more and more borrowing and debts which in times of high employment and incomes lead to inflationary pressures and unsound money'.[40]

Deficit financing in wartime had led to inflation in time of peace. The 'excesses of the war years brought inflation and hardship to millions of Americans' when direct controls were removed in 1946. Humphrey objected to the way in which, before the March 1951 Accord, the 'Federal Reserve System, under Treasury domination, contributed substantially to inflation'. This had occurred because of the 'artificial manipulation of the value of government securities' – the low interest rates the Federal Reserve had maintained. Instead of 'allowing the natural increases in interest rates, the Federal Reserve focused major attention on making sure that the Treasury could handle the debt at low rates'.[41]

It is salutary to refer to the public statements of men like Humphrey and Martin who bore responsibility for the economic policies of the United States in the 1950s. Contrary to common perception, backed by the Bretton Woods Agreement's connection of the dollar to gold, the 1950s marked an era of conservative approaches to budgets and currency. It was not a decade in which the deficit financing espoused by Keynes, and pursued during the war years, was particularly applauded. Eisenhower's government adopted fiscal policies which would have been recognized by

Bagehot and Sir Robert Peel. As one distinguished early twenty-first-century economist has noted, '1950s policymakers' views about the economy were very different . . . in the importance they ascribed to a balanced budget.' Economists and policy advisers generally believed that 'persistent deficits were inappropriate and that policy should aim for balance'. For Truman 'this belief almost reached the level of gospel; his Budget Messages are full of references to the principles of "sound" finance'.[42] Eisenhower's administration hardly differed in this respect. Its members were conscious of the tenuousness of the dollar's link to gold. The political prejudices of the time, shared by Democrat and Republican alike, leant towards sound money and its implications for government spending.

Weary Titans

While a triumphant United States gloried in its own pre-eminence in the aftermath of the Second World War, the former belligerents on the continent of Europe were exhausted and demoralized. No country seemed more tired than Great Britain. The City of London, for decades one of the most tangible symbols of British economic power, was not only physically devastated by Nazi bombs, but seemed to retain very little of its former vitality. In the international arena, the dollar was supreme. One-third of Britain's overseas investments had been liquidated. The export trade had ceased to function. British debts were enormous. Indeed, at the end of the war, 'Britain was the world's leading debtor country.'[1] It was generally calculated that Britain 'had lost a quarter of its pre-war national wealth'.[2]

The Englishman who most represented the orthodox view of the City of London between the wars had probably been Montagu Norman, not Keynes, who had been too much of an intellectual and social maverick to win the City's full confidence. Norman served as Governor of the Bank of England for twenty-four years between 1920 and 1944, and it was demoralizing for him when the Labour government decided to nationalize the Bank in 1946. The commitment to nationalize had been part of the Labour manifesto when the party had won the election in a landslide in July 1945, and the new government sought to pursue national reform along overtly socialist lines. Hugh Dalton, the overbearing Chancellor of the Exchequer, praised the measure to nationalize the Bank as 'a streamlined socialist statute', containing 'a minimum of legal rigmarole'. In March 1946, after 252 years, the Bank of England, or the 'Old Lady' as it was sometimes called, fell into government ownership.[3]

Physically, Dalton himself was an imposing and assertive figure. One newspaper report spoke of 'his towering, six-foot-three-inch frame' and referred to the way in which he rolled his 'pale blue eyes so that the whites blaze and flash with an almost Mephistophelian effect'. The four budgets Dalton introduced earned him a reputation as 'the most socialist – or at any rate, the most levelling – chancellor ever to have held office'. As one of his protégés, Anthony Crosland, later observed, Dalton 'maintained, and even extended, the great advance towards income-equality that was made during the war'.[4] The son of a clergyman, Dalton was an Old Etonian who had just failed to win a scholarship to the prestigious school. His aggressive manner was bound up in a welter of social insecurities and pompous self-assertion. Once, when dining in the House of Commons, he interrupted his own monologue to boom in the direction of a Conservative MP, 'What's that suburbanite looking at me for?' His manner reeked of insincerity: he was said to be the kind of man who 'who slaps you on the back . . . and calls you by somebody else's Christian name'.[5]

It was a significant feature of British politics in the late 1940s that it was dominated by a genuinely socialistic Labour Party. Dalton attacked wealth. One commentator noted, after Dalton had left the Treasury in 1947, that it was 'probable that the differences in spendable income [that is, income inequality between classes of people] in this country are already less than those which the Russians consider necessary to provide economic incentives'. At its highest level, tax on income reached 19s 6d in the pound, or 97.5 per cent.[6] Indeed, the whole post-war Labour government has been characterized by a noted historian, sceptical of the post-war settlement, as being dominated by a 'Christian and socialist idealism of the purest late-Victorian kind'. The assumption of this group of leaders had been that they would 'build New Jerusalem by the simple method of redistributing wealth from the *rentier* class', the class of bondholders who had been most enthusiastic supporters of the old gold standard, 'to the working masses'. The problem was that there was precious little wealth to redistribute in Britain immediately after the Second World War. Unfortunately, however, as the distinguished historian Lord Annan acknowledged, 'we were more concerned with how wealth should be shared than produced'.[7] More specifically and ominously, Dalton's own relations with the City were, in the words of a modern historian of the City of London, 'fatally undermined by a mixture of ignorance and emotional immaturity'.[8]

The nature of Britain's post-war problem, a country with little export trade, heavily dependent on imports, with a devastated manufacturing base, was arguably not one which could be tackled by yet more taxation. Even to support a modest standard of living, Britain would be obliged to live partly off the generosity of the United States. 'The conclusion is inescapable', John Maynard Keynes had written in a paper to the cabinet in August 1945, 'that there is no source from which we can raise sufficient funds to enable us to live and spend on the scale we contemplate except the United States . . .'[9] It was clear that any plans for the New Jerusalem would have to be paid for by American generosity, and not from the proceeds of British productive endeavour.

This indebtedness had profound implications for the group of countries whose economies were bound up with sterling, the Sterling Area. This group of countries, however, now constituted a 'legacy of history now too burdensome to carry', since Britain itself now had debts which were owed to the Sterling Area. The one thing, of course, which a currency area needs if it is to function is a reserve. 'It is obviously necessary for the support of such a system' to have a 'considerable volume of reserves in order to allow of the seasonal and other fluctuations that must take place in the trade of the world, including changes in the price of primary products on which the economy of much of the Sterling Area depends.' These remarks were made in July 1948 in a memorandum drafted by the Cabinet Office. Three years later, Richard (commonly known as 'Otto') Clarke, an intellectually capable Cambridge mathematician now working at the Treasury, warned that 'the U.K. cannot live up to its responsibilities as the centre and mainspring of the Sterling Area unless it puts its house in order to the extent of achieving a surplus on its overall balance of payments'. In 'the last resort', argued Clarke, 'every expenditure of sterling by an overseas country (and every credit or loan extended to such a country) involves a call either on the physical resources of the U.K. or on the gold and dollar reserves'.[10]

On top of the commitments to rebuilding infrastructure, schools and hospitals and the like, and to building the New Jerusalem envisaged by Britain's post-war socialist leaders, there also remained a commitment to keeping the Sterling Area afloat. This latter undertaking was an attempt to maintain sterling as an international trading currency. The problems associated with the Sterling Area were typified by what were known as the 'sterling balances', large holdings of sterling outside the UK. The principal problem was that, if countries in the Sterling Area ran deficits, Britain would ultimately be liable for the bill. 'The existence of large sterling balances', so affirmed a report to the cabinet Economic Policy Committee, 'represents a potential direct drain on our economic resources.' In 1944 Keynes himself had noted that 'the maintenance of the sterling area system' would probably 'add to our liabilities on a substantial scale'.[11]

The first sign of trouble regarding Britain's economic position after the war had occurred in the summer of 1947. The American loan of US$3.75 billion, negotiated by Keynes and his team, had been made on the basis that sterling would become convertible on 15 July 1947, a year after the President had signed the loan agreement. As soon as convertibility took place, however, there was an immediate drain of dollars from British reserves, as holders of sterling rushed to exchange their sterling holdings for dollars which were used for international trade and, most crucially, to buy American goods. On 16 August 1947, Hugh Dalton, Chancellor of the Exchequer, produced a memorandum which showed that the dollar drain had amounted to US$868.5 million between the start of July and 15 August.[12]

What had happened was that Sterling Area countries like Belgium had taken advantage of convertibility and had shifted their sterling holdings into dollars. There was, in simple terms, a 'general flight from sterling', and 'so heavy were the transfers from sterling into dollars during the summer of 1947' that the 'sterling area itself might have faced disintegration had the British not suspended convertibility'. An anguished note from the British Treasury, written in early September, shortly after convertibility was suspended on 20 August, explained that the British had 'wanted to maintain convertibility', but that 'if this was to be done it was essential that there be a limit on the demands for dollars which other countries put upon the UK'.[13] This, of course, had not happened, and convertibility had simply encouraged a widespread abandonment of sterling.

Even after sterling convertibility had been suspended, Dalton was writing in an exasperated tone to Sir Edward Bridges, the Permanent Secretary at the Treasury, that the 'weekly drain of dollars is a weekly horror!' Bridges sought to reassure the nervous Chancellor that now that 'sterling is no longer convertible we can hope to ration certain countries in dollars'. Within the Treasury itself, there was an oddly named Dollar Drain Committee which would meet in Sir Edward Bridges's office every Thursday at five o'clock to discuss the desperate situation.[14] Yet still, throughout the latter part of 1947, there continued a constant demand for dollars to buy American goods. On 3 December, the Colonial Secretary in the Labour government was complaining that the 'dollar crisis which besets the United Kingdom and Colonies is so serious that I fear that I must now make certain further drastic requests of Colonial Governments regarding the administration of their import controls', and that 'harsh measures are indispensable'.[15]

In the sphere of economics and finance, an atmosphere of crisis and impotence hung heavily around the institutions of the British government. The final chapter of the post-war episode of British financial incompetence occurred in 1949, when the Treasury finally abandoned the sterling–dollar exchange rate of 4.03 dollars to the pound which had been established at the outbreak of war in 1939. By the time this had occurred, Dalton was no longer at the Treasury. His successor as Chancellor was the austere, fussy barrister Sir Stafford Cripps. His lean appearance, his well-known vegetarianism and his refusal to drink alcohol combined to fix his image in the public mind as one of prim, almost masochistic asceticism. The word 'austerity' clings around his reputation. His own personal circumstances, his background of wealth and privilege, combined with an education at the cerebral Winchester College, had made him an unlikely Labour MP, although Dalton, his predecessor as Chancellor, and Attlee, the Prime Minister, had also been educated at exclusive private schools.

Despite a Master's degree in chemistry from the University of London, Cripps was not really an intellectual. He had certainly not read Keynes, even though he implemented a budget in 1948 'generally considered a landmark of applied Keynesianism'.[16] Yet notwithstanding his well-known self-discipline, practical competence and rigid determination, Cripps could not escape the 'shadow of devaluation' which hung over the London during the summer of 1949.[17] In June that year, the Treasury was once more in its customary post-war crisis-management mode. A draft telegram was composed which would be sent from the British Prime Minister to the prime ministers of the Commonwealth. 'I must tell you of a serious development in our affairs,' it read. 'During the last few weeks the drain in our gold and dollar reserves has increased substantially.' In internal memos at the Treasury, the dreaded prospect of devaluation was referred to as 'Caliban', an apt allusion to the half-man, half-monster in Shakespeare's *Tempest*. The Prime Minister's draft telegram made gloomy reading. 'In the first quarter of this year the dollar deficit of the sterling area was about $25 millions a week,' but in 'the last six weeks it has been running at $50 millions a week'. The consequences were inevitable. The 'reserves are therefore falling fast and the figures which we shall have to publish in the first few days of July will reveal this very noticeable deterioration'. The draft telegram concluded ominously that 'we have no reason to believe that the situation is likely to right itself of its own accord'.[18]

A sense of panic and irresolution among the British establishment was a marked feature of the summer of 1949. The events of that time brought home to the British political class in uncompromising terms how far Britain's power had receded. There were many excuses. In an acute summary of Britain's plight, Douglas Jay, a junior Treasury minister in the Labour government, blamed the United States for the 'basic unbalance' between the 'dollar and non-dollar world' which, he argued, had its origin in the '1914 period'. The causes of this 'unbalance' were clear: after the First World War, the US had 'assumed a preponderance in world production and a positive balance of payments'. This meant that the United States was producing and exporting goods to a much greater extent than it was importing. More crucially, America 'developed neither the completely free import policy nor the foreign investment mechanism which the United Kingdom maintained in the 19th century'. A rebounding United States which was continually selling more goods than it was importing would dominate the world economy. From this would also arise a continual demand for dollars with which to buy those American goods. Like the clever and highly committed socialist ideologue that he was, Jay could not allow the Labour government any share of responsibility for the dire economic condition of Britain. Despite the obvious partisanship in his analysis, there was an element of truth behind it. The United States had been a bastion of protectionism right through the nineteenth century until the 1930s. A protectionist country, with a strong manufacturing and agricultural base, which had won markets from other countries torn by warfare, would necessarily create the trade 'unbalance' Jay described.

Jay even had the temerity to describe the 1949 crisis as a 'dollar crisis not a UK one'.[19] This was indeed a display of wishful thinking which reveals the customary delusions of politicians intent on avoiding any share of the blame when things go wrong. While Jay blamed the Americans for the sad plight of sterling in the summer 1949, Treasury officials were more sanguine and less emotional. Robert Hall, an Australian economist now working in the British civil service, took a prominent part in the discussions surrounding the devaluation of sterling that summer. In a paper entitled 'Caliban: The Future of Sterling', written in June 1949, Hall applied his formidable powers of analysis to the problem of the British currency. He started his memorandum in a defensive way: 'It is often felt that there is something disreputable in changing the gold or other parity of a country.' This was the '19th century view', based on the 'quite proper reason that currency manipulation was usually disastrous in practice, and partly on the feeling that gold was the nearest thing to a fixed standard of value'. In Hall's lucid and delightfully jargon-free account, the view in the nineteenth century had been that 'to write down deliberately the gold content of paper money was in effect cheating all those who had been persuaded to take the money'. The rules of the nineteenth century as described in a highly abstract, though perfectly clear, manner by Robert Hall were elegant in their simplicity: 'The theory of foreign exchanges on the gold standard . . . required all countries to be willing to keep to the so-called rules: to restrict credit when gold was being lost, to expand it when it was being gained, and to accept whatever unemployment was required in order to deflate costs when these were too high to secure a balance of payments.'

This was a succinct and straightforward description of the theory behind the old gold standard. Of course, the events of the 1930s, and the Great Depression, had changed everything. After 1929, there had occurred a complete reversal of what had been established doctrine. 'Almost every Government in the world was overthrown, whatever its political colour, in the Great Depression.' It was also recognized 'by the great majority of economists that costs in different countries might get out of line' and that 'the proper alternative to a reduction in money costs, if these got out of line with other countries, was a devaluation of the currency'. Pointing to the 'articles of the International Monetary Fund', designed to promote 'exchange stability', Hall then quickly justified devaluation in order 'to correct a fundamental disequilibrium'.

After laying out the contemporary justification for devaluing currencies, Hall then moved to consider the case of sterling: 'The arguments for devaluation are in brief that the US costs are lower than ours, and that if we devalue we will become more competitive.' That Britain's costs and prices of exports were too high and, as a consequence, uncompetitive seemed undeniable. 'The Canadians, who are in the best position to know, are constantly complaining that our prices are too high.' Hall's ultimate suggestion in his admirably balanced treatment of the issue was that a devaluation by 'one third' if Britain's 'costs did not rise at all' would obviously make British goods more competitive.

Of course, for an Oxford academic like Robert Hall analysis was easier than actual implementation. There remained the lack of political will within certain quarters of the British establishment, and then an actual timetable for devaluation would have to be drawn up. The principal opponents of the proposed plan to devalue sterling were found in the Bank of England, which had been nationalized only three years previously. The Bank was still, in many ways, the grand and self-confident institution over which Montagu Norman had presided in the 1920s. Its Governor in 1949, Cameron Cobbold, had been a protégé of Norman. At the time of the proposed devaluation, Cobbold himself had been Governor of the Bank for only a couple of months. A big, powerfully built man, who possessed an 'innate presence, solidity and authority', he was anxious to keep the Bank out of politics, but shared many of the assumptions of the City of his time.[20] A 'markets man' who had no real academic training in economics, he was the very epitome of an English central banker of the old school. He was averse to devaluation, and expressed his view to the Labour Chancellor of the Exchequer that the 'fundamental issue about devaluation' was that, even if Britain altered 'the exchange rate within the next month or two', could the government be 'reasonably certain of seeing equilibrium in our balance of payments and avoiding pressure against sterling at the new rate?' Sir Edward Bridges, the Treasury official, made much the same objection, to Stafford Cripps that same day, 18 June. One might add that this hardly seemed a coincidence: most of us 'with differing degrees of emphasis are opposed to devaluation now'. In Bridges's view, 'devaluation is a thing which can only be done once as a remedy for a particular disequilibrium if confidence in the currency is to be maintained'. The risk was that if 'we did it now when the conditions are not propitious, we should have to do it again later on'.[21]

Bridges, an austere but energetic man with a Quaker background, was sufficiently even-handed to acknowledge that many officials, including Robert Hall, thought that 'on balance devaluation now would be to our advantage'. This camp saw 'no possibility of righting the ship without devaluation'. Yet the pressure of events forced the hand of the British government. Throughout the first half of 1949, the perpetually harassed Dollar Drain Committee had been meeting in Bridges's rooms at the Treasury at its usual time of 5 p.m. on Thursday. On 14 July, the prognosis continued to be gloomy. 'The total deficit during the two weeks ending 9th July was again very heavy,' the report read. It was estimated that at the current rate 'our reserves might be used up in rather less than a year'.[22] But what of the loan of US$3.75 billion which a generous Congress had agreed in 1946? The money had been 'spent in about two years'.[23]

The suspicion lingered, among those who opposed it, that devaluation was a soft option, chosen by socialist politicians who did not have the courage to take tough decisions on public spending. Sir Otto Niemeyer, a career civil servant, who had famously come first to Keynes's second place in the 1906 civil service examinations, complained that 'jiggling about with devaluation of Dollar exchange will not help'. In the same note, dated 21 June, Niemeyer voiced the concern of the Edwardian civil servant he always remained: 'devaluation should certainly not be presented as an *alternative* to real measures to reduce costs'.[24] Like Cobbold, Niemeyer (by now an adviser at the Bank) would have preferred spending cuts to devaluation; according to this view, government expenditure reductions, by forcing costs and wages down, would have made British goods more competitive. This had been tried in 1925 to ill effect. The opinions of Niemeyer and Cobbold suggest that there were still many in the Bank of England who had not abandoned the techniques of Victorian central banking. 'Those who opposed devaluation were chiefly concerned to see immediate cuts in expenditure.' They argued that 'without such cuts, devaluation would not work'.[25]

When the devaluation occurred in September, it had been widely anticipated. The rate came down from US$4.03 to US$2.80 to the pound. On Thursday 15 September 1949, Robert Hall composed his diary entry in the air, having flown from La Guardia airport in New York after 4 p.m. He was clutching the 'second last draft of the broadcast, which the Cabinet is to see tomorrow or Saturday'. He was worried that the news of the devaluation would leak. For his part, he was confident that devaluation had been the right thing to do. It had been 'a most interesting period for an economist'. He was sure that the decision would 'set the trading world ablaze'. The operation itself was 'enormous and requires secrecy which will make it very unpopular if kept: and a failure if not'. Hall's conclusion was that devaluation would probably be 'much easier for a small country', but a 'fearful thing' for Britain.[26]

The devaluation itself was accomplished by means of a Sunday-evening broadcast, on 18 September, by the Chancellor of the Exchequer, Stafford Cripps. The move was denounced as 'humbug' by the *Daily Mail*. As so often that newspaper articulated, in strident and uncompromising terms, the views of its largely Conservative readership and its reaction to the policies of the Labour government:

> To listen to the Socialists one would think devaluation was the best thing that has ever happened. It is not. It is a desperate act of a desperate Government whose recklessness and extravagance have helped to push the nation to the edge of disaster as they did in 1931 . . . Sir Stafford Cripps has known for years what really must be done to save this country, but he has refused to face up to it. He knows that only harder work – longer hours with no wage increase, economy in social services and drastic cuts in Government expenditure can restore Britain.[27]

This was an anguished cry, on the part of a popular right-wing newspaper, for economy, in the old nineteenth-century sense of spending less money, and 'cutting your coat according to your cloth', a cry which had been the principal inspiration of nineteenth-century public finance. The twentieth century with its wars had overturned this credo, but there were still many in British public life, not only in the Bank of England, who subscribed to the articles of the old faith.

The British establishment had been divided by the issue of devaluation. The problems of sterling had stood, as is often the case with currencies, as a metaphor for national decline and the ebbing of greatness. The resumption of the gold standard in 1925 at the old dollar exchange rate had been undertaken for reasons of pride. Churchill had wanted the pound sterling to regain its international prestige. This object was achieved at an enormous cost to British wages and living standards. In 1949, the British agonized through the trauma of devaluing their currency, allowing sterling to lose 30 per cent of its value in one day. Meanwhile, another major belligerent of the Second World War, Germany had, under American guidance, adopted a different course.

Germany's predicament as a defeated power had essentially left the country under the control of the victorious Allies. Its position was similar to that of most European countries where there existed a 'dollar shortage in the sense that they lacked the resources and the industrial capacity for producing sufficient goods and services both for home consumption and for export'. With very little industrial capacity and no real currency, Germany was built up by the Allies from low beginnings. Germany, in the wake of the defeat of the Nazis in 1945, had been split into four zones, under the control of the Americans, the British, the French and the Soviet Union. Despite the presence of the three other powers, the United States, as a consequence of its economic strength, was the dominant power in the reconstruction of post-war Germany, and the key figure among its personnel was Lucius D. Clay, a general who was appointed Military Governor of the US Zone in western Germany in 1947. The power of the United States in both Germany and Japan was represented by formidable military figures like Generals Clay and Douglas MacArthur, who were both bureaucrats and warlords. Their education and experience had been entirely within the institution of the United States Army.

Trained as an engineer within the military, Clay brought a technocratic efficiency to his task in Germany. He had played an important role as chief of procurement for the US Army during the Second World War, earning distinction with such feats as procuring 299 million pairs of trousers, 50 million field jackets and 2.3 million trucks, among other large quantities of material essential for the war effort. His general efficiency had been such that James Byrnes, the Secretary of State, had told President Roosevelt that in six months Clay 'could run General Motors or U.S. Steel'.[28] Clay's own account of his role in Germany stressed the chaos and confusion which still prevailed in 1945. 'The black market was rampant,' he remembered, and the currency system had broken down. A coupon book system had been introduced in November 1945, in which coupons had to be purchased in dollars. The German currency itself, the Reichsmark, Clay remembered, was 'worthless' and 'no longer had public confidence'. The old currency was so discredited that, by the spring of 1947, about 'half the value of all commercial trade, at least in the Anglo-American zone, was transacted on a barter or compensation basis'. Many barter transactions were performed 'with the aid of cigarettes'.[29]

The politics of the German currency was set against deteriorating relations between the four powers. On 1 January 1947, the British and American zones were combined to form the Bizone. The economic burden of administering their zone had grown too great for the British to bear, since they were borrowing American dollars to feed the Germans in their zone while food was still being rationed in Britain. It soon became apparent that the Bizone was the 'nucleus of a new political entity',[30] and it pursued a single economic policy under the guidance of Ludwig Erhard, an economist with a strong belief in free-market liberalism.

In response, the Soviets created the German Economic Commission on 14 June 1947. Meanwhile, the responsibility that the Allies felt in regard to Germany was a direct consequence of the terms of 'unconditional surrender' which had been a rallying cry for the Allies since 1943. As Konrad Adenauer, who would later become the first Chancellor of West Germany in 1949, remembered in a speech of that year, the 'unconditional surrender of the German armed forces in May 1945 was interpreted by the Allies to mean a complete transfer of governmental authority into their hands'. Adenauer would have preferred it if the Allies had 'let the Germans order their own affairs'. He believed that the Allies' interpretation was 'wrong from the point of view of international law'.[31]

German currency reform was a matter of serious dispute between Britain, the US, France and the Soviets, and had already been a 'subject of discussion between the representatives of the three Western Powers in London when the Council of Foreign Ministers adjourned' towards the end of 1947. The British Foreign Secretary, Ernest Bevin, and the United States Secretary of State, George Marshall, then issued instructions that if agreement could not be reached in all four zones of Germany, currency reform should be pursued in the bizonal area, governed by the United States and Britain.[32]

After the failure of a meeting in London towards the end of 1947, the situation between the British and American Bizone and the Soviet zone in the east had become tense. On 1 March 1948, the three Western Allies, including the French, decided to introduce a new currency to replace the Reichsmark. In the wake of this reform, price restrictions would be lifted on most goods. The politics of the new currency was immediately controversial, as it would exacerbate the tensions between the zones controlled by the Allies and the zone that was under Soviet control. As Clay remembered, the Allies 'hesitated to introduce a new currency in the bizonal area which would widen the split of Germany'.[33]

Under the tutelage of such men as Lucius Clay, the German economy in the Western zones was guided in a tightly controlled manner. Unlike in some other empires where wide latitude was often given to the man on the spot, it was surprising how closely Clay was monitored from Washington. In March 1948, it was even hinted by the US government that the Americans would not cancel the old debts incurred by the Nazi regime. Clay suggested to his superiors in the US government that cancellation of the old debt was a 'primary necessity if we are to restore confidence in the [proposed] new currency'.[34] The main obstacle to the new currency was not economic but political, in the form of the Soviet Union, which controlled the eastern part of Germany.

Persistent bad relations between the Allies and the Soviets during the first half of 1948 led to the eventual introduction of the Deutschmark in the French, British and American zones on Sunday 20 June 1948. Citizens in these zones were permitted to convert their first sixty old marks into forty Deutschmarks. Beyond this amount, old marks would be converted into Deutschmarks at a rate of 100 to 6.5. Pension, salaries and rents, conveniently enough, would be converted at the rate of 1:1.[35] As so often was the case in periods of monetary upheaval, people who owned hard assets, like factories and property, benefited while many others saw most of their savings disappear as a consequence of the reform.

Clay paid fulsome tribute to his financial adviser Joseph Dodge, a commercial banker from Detroit. 'The success of the issue of the new currency and the effectiveness of the reform were evidence of the careful, painstaking work of the Allied and German experts.' In particular, Clay believed, Dodge's 'leadership and ability were primarily responsible for the outstanding results of one of the major currency measures recorded in financial history'.[36] Together Clay and Dodge had embarked upon tackling the difficult issue of German currency reform as early as the beginning of 1946, even before the Bizone had been created.

Although the three Western Military Governors had agreed to introduce the new currency in their zones, they decided against its introduction in Berlin itself, which like the rest of Germany had also been split into four parts, or sectors. Introducing a currency throughout Berlin, the Allies would later claim, would be too provocative to the Soviets. The 'Berlin situation became more difficult on June 16 when Soviet representatives followed up their withdrawal from the Allied Control Council by walking out of the Kommandatura, which was the quadripartite body responsible for the Government of the City'. This made the introduction of a single currency in the city much harder. The Western Military Governors advised Vasily Sokolovsky, the head of the Soviet Military Administration in Germany, that currency reform would be introduced in the Western areas without an agreement between all four powers. On 20 June Sokolovsky accused the Western powers of 'splitting Germany'. An emergency conference was held on the morning of the 22nd, seven years to the day after Hitler had launched Operation Barbarossa, the invasion of the Soviet Union. The conference had been convened to discuss the Berlin currency situation and to find a way by which trade between the zones controlled by the Western powers and that controlled by the Soviet Union could be continued. The conference did not resolve the matters under dispute. As the mooted currency conference collapsed, both sides, towards the end of June 1948, now viewed each other with an alarming degree of mistrust.

The Soviets unilaterally introduced their own new currency on 23 June. They feared that the old currency, now worth very little in western Germany, would flow into their zone and cause very high inflation. On the same day, they also instructed the acting Mayor of Berlin, Ferdinand Friedensburg, to introduce their currency in all four sectors of the city. The Soviets argued that Berlin should be governed as a single entity because it lay, geographically, entirely within the Soviet zone. The Allies rejected this notion. They viewed Soviet actions as an attempt to integrate west Berlin into their zone and believed that the Soviets were crudely attempting to force the Western powers out of Berlin completely.[37] During this dispute, Clay saw himself as a moderate influence. He was prepared to go along with his French and British colleagues' readiness to accept the Soviet currency in Berlin 'if we could participate in its control'. Sokolovsky 'offered no such participation'. As a result of this stubbornness on the part of the Soviets, Clay knew that their 'proposal was unacceptable to our government'.

Within hours of the introduction of the Soviet currency, the Allies prohibited its use in their sectors of Berlin. They then introduced their new Deutschmark into west Berlin. The Soviets retaliated, believing that this move by the Western Allies was an aggressive attempt to make west Berlin part of the Western zones.[38] The Soviet Military Administration decided to 'close all rail traffic from the Western zones'. This order came into effect at six o'clock on the morning of 24 June. From this point, the three Western sectors of Berlin, 'with a civilian population of about 2,500,000 people, became dependent on reserve stocks and airlift replacements'. Thus began the Berlin Airlift. The crisis had, perhaps surprisingly, emerged as a result of a currency dispute, but had consequences which reached far beyond the confines of monetary economics. For Clay the Soviet blockade of the Western sectors of Berlin represented 'one of the most ruthless efforts in modern times to use mass starvation for political coercion'. Clay noted that the Americans had 'foreseen the Soviet action for some months'. The United States calculated that it could 'sustain a minimum economy with an average daily airlift of 4,000 tons for the German population and 500 tons for the Allied occupation forces'.[39]

The Soviet blockade and the ensuing Berlin Airlift, more than any other event, perhaps marked the definitive start of the Cold War. Any idea of co-operation between the Soviets and the Western Allies had been abandoned in relation to the German currency reforms. While the blockade itself lasted eleven months, until 12 May 1949, it symbolized a wider division and a more chronic suspicion between the Soviets and the Western Allies. It failed in its attempt to integrate west Berlin into the Soviet zone. The French zone joined the Bizone on 8 April 1949 to create a Trizone. This would soon form the new West German state. The 'Federal Republic of Germany' was formally created on 23 May 1949, a mere eleven days after the blockade ended, when the 'Basic Law', which because of the divided nature of the country was not called a constitution, came into force.[40] The economic development of the two entities which would become East and West Germany followed radically divergent lines. The East became a socialist economy. The West, initially under largely American direction, followed a path of free enterprise, the 'free economy' Adenauer alluded to in his memoirs.

The introduction of the new currency in the Western zones effected a stark change in the German economy. The controls on many basic goods fell away. 'Shopwindows and shelves filled up with goods and production lines increased overnight.' An 'immediate buying spree' occurred. Konrad Adenauer himself remembered that until June 1948 'the economy was planned down to the smallest detail, down to trouser buttons and penny items'. In his memoirs, Adenauer, the veteran politician who was seventy-three when he first became Chancellor of West Germany, recommended that 'every economist and every politician who is concerned with questions of the economic order should be urged to study the course of events in the Anglo-American zone [bizonal area] since June 1948'. That was of course the very month in which the new currency, the Deutschmark, later to become renowned throughout the world, was launched. Adenauer played down the role of the new currency itself in establishing order and prosperity. He saw the prosperity of the Anglo-American zone as flowing from a 'free economy'. Of course, the zone was not 'a completely free economy', as there 'never was such a thing in a modern state', but 'as far as possible' the Germans returned to 'a free system of supply and demand while observing certain considerations of social policy'. Adenauer believed that the 'economic upswing can only to a small extent be attributed to the introduction of the new Mark in 1948, or to help given by the Marshall Plan'.[41] The fact that the introduction of the new currency had been significant was demonstrated by the reaction of the Soviets.

Although Adenauer himself had not seen the currency reform of June 1948 in itself as the main instigator of the economic success of West Germany, many American economists at the time thought differently. As Walter Heller, an economist based at the University of Minnesota, remembered in 1950, from 'mid-1948 to early 1949, Western Germany experienced a spectacular economic recovery with the drastic monetary reform of June 1948 serving as the prime mover'. A nearly 'worthless currency' was replaced, leading to a liberalization of controls and an increase in production. 'Recorded industrial production in the Trizone spurted from 50 per cent of the 1936 level in June 1948 to 85 per cent in February 1949.'

Even at this early date exports proved to be the 'lifeblood of the future German economy'. This emphasized 'the importance of avoiding inflation in the home market'. Inflation would inevitably drive up costs making German exports less competitive in foreign markets. Unsurprisingly, coupled with the concern for a 'sound currency', there was reiterated the old warning about the need for balanced budgets: 'A dual prohibition stands athwart the path of budgetary deficits.' The first of these prohibitions was the 'dictate of Military Government currency reform laws that budgets should be kept in balance'. As if this were not enough, there was a prohibition included in Article 115 of the new Western German Basic Law against any borrowing except 'in the case of extraordinary need and as a rule only for expenditure for productive purposes'. In addition to these prohibitions, the 'creation of fiat money' even for investment purposes 'in the form, say, of a central bank credit to the reconstruction loan corporation' was to be resisted. The Allied Banking Commission still exercised final control over the policies of the Bank Deutscher Länder, the new central bank, which would become the Bundesbank in 1957.[42]

The German central bank was to become famous for its determined fight against inflation. In 1977, Otmar Emminger, President of the Bundesbank from 1980 to 1991, could write that the 'struggle against imported inflation has dominated German monetary policy ... over much of the last twenty years'.[43] The word 'struggle' reflected the difficulty of maintaining steady prices, stable monetary values, in a country which enjoyed almost continual balance of payments surpluses. According to classical theory, under the old gold standard a surplus of exports over imports would lead to gold inflows into the country which enjoyed a trade surplus, and thus would push up prices which, in turn, would make exports less competitive abroad. It was what was called a 'self-equilibrating process'. It was revealing, in September 1949, when sterling devalued by 30.5 per cent against the dollar, that the Deutschmark also devalued by 20.6 per cent, achieving a rate of DM 4.20 to the dollar. This rate made the mark relatively cheap, especially when we consider that, at DM 4.20 to the dollar, one pound sterling in 1949 was worth DM 11.76. At this exchange rate, British goods were expensive compared to German products in international markets.

The situation in which Britain and Germany found themselves at the end of the 1940s was somewhat paradoxical. Britain, one of the victors in the Second World War, had in a perfectly democratic process elected a socialist government. West Germany had been given a military government, essentially under US control. Britain adopted socialism, while the Americans imposed a managed form of capitalism on West Germany. Britain had struggled to maintain the historic value of its currency against the US dollar. It had failed. West Germany had been granted a new currency, again under American direction, which had been valued so as to boost its exports. It had been forced, under the shadow of defeat, to adapt itself to a more modern, internationally competitive world of trade. Britain had turned in on itself, in its pursuit of utopian socialism, while still clinging to old glories in the form of an over-valued currency which could only harm its international trading position.

Japan Incorporated

Germany was firmly under the control of the general government of the combined victors after 1945. The other principal defeated power was placed under a jurisdiction which was purely American. Unlike in Germany, where there were other allies to appease, the Americans held an unfettered sway over the destinies of the Japanese people. The man who embodied American control in Japan was the looming figure of General Douglas MacArthur, a man who ruled Japan with as despotic an authority as any emperor in Japanese history. MacArthur is a big name in the history of the United States, although as time passes it has become less clear why he enjoyed such an enormous reputation and fame in his lifetime. Much of this reputation was, of course, due to his flamboyance, his grandiosity and the domineering way in which he made people and circumstances submit to his will. One biographer has described him in melodramatic terms as 'flamboyant, imperious and apocalyptic', a man of 'great personal charm', endowed with 'a will of iron' and 'a soaring intellect'. These epithets might seem exaggerated, but they convey some of the awe in which he was held by contemporaries.[1]

An appreciation of MacArthur is important in order to understand the immediate context of Japan's post-war recovery. The general was revered by the Japanese as he held court on the top floor of the Dai Ichi building in Tokyo. He was noted for his austerity and personal courage, qualities which endeared him to his defeated subjects. In his biographer's rather starry-eyed account he was like a 'medieval Japanese warrior' in his total dedication to duty. He was said never to have taken a holiday in the five years between 'V-J Day and the Korean War'. He left Tokyo only twice during this time, to attend independence ceremonies in Manila, in the

Philippines, and in Korea. In both cases it is reported that he was back before evening. MacArthur was also remarkably free of the racial prejudice and arrogance which many of his compatriots too often displayed.

In many ways, MacArthur was a perfect exponent of American culture, a fitting viceroy to rule over a subject people. He was a military man, tall, lean and athletic, a credit to the education he had received at West Point, from which he graduated at the top of his class of ninety-three students as long ago as 1903. He loved American football and would pore over the sports pages of American newspapers, checking his predictions of results in what seemed to his staff trivial college matches. He came from a tough military family. His father had been a general in the Union Army during the Civil War. His mother, a highly autocratic and strict Southern lady, took up residence in Craney's Hotel for the period during which her son was enrolled at West Point. It was said that she could see the lamp in her son's room from her hotel suite.[2] After the war, MacArthur, now sixty-five, was appointed Supreme Commander for the Allied Powers (SCAP) in Japan. He recalled with some emotion the scene which presented itself to him of Japan's desolation and the loss of hope in that country: 'It was just 22 miles from the New Grand Hotel in Yokohama to the American Embassy, which was to be my home throughout the occupation, but they were 22 miles of devastation and vast piles of charred rubble.' It was not only the scenes of physical destruction which affected the general. He remembered the 'collapse of a faith' and the 'disintegration of everything they believed in and lived by and fought for'. This devastation, physical and mental, left a 'complete vacuum'.[3]

Japan had been an economic success in the 1930s. This was mainly a result of military spending. The Japanese government which took office towards the end of 1931 had abandoned the gold standard and allowed the yen to fall. Government expenditure, funded by borrowing, was increased. Low interest rates led to easy monetary conditions. The index of industrial production shows 'a fall from 100 in 1929 to 92 in 1931 and then a rapid and uninterrupted rise to 151 in 1936 and 171 in 1937'. This impressive growth in output occurred at a time when production in the United States failed to regain its 1929 level, while the United Kingdom, between 1929 and 1937, increased its industrial output by less than 25 per cent.[4]

The leading figure in Japan's 1930s economic boom was Takahashi Korekiyo, a fluent English-speaking government official in his late seventies. Takahashi, Japan's Finance Minister from 1931 to 1936, has sometimes been described as the 'Japanese Keynes' for advocating deficit financing as a way out of the Depression.[5] Indeed, the Japanese war machine had been fuelled by deficit financing, which was used to buy armaments in Japan's rush to become the dominant imperial power in Asia. The military budget, already over 29 per cent of total expenditure in 1931, rose to 65 per cent of spending in 1940. Any notion of fiscal orthodoxy was thrown aside as Japan poured more resources into its military machine. Takahashi himself had thought that 600 million yen would be a 'safe limit for deficits', but he came under mounting pressure from the army to spend more. The soldiers were anxious that their China campaign should be adequately funded. In a macabre coincidence, Takahashi was murdered in the same month, February 1936, which saw the publication of Keynes's *General Theory of Employment, Interest and Money*. A military clique revolted against the government and killed several of its members. Takahashi was eighty-one when he died. He had 'successfully practised, without the benefit of Keynes, a policy in full accord with what was soon to become the new economic orthodoxy'.[6] Although his years in office were known as a period of a 'quasi wartime economy', or *junsenji keizai*, this proved not to be enough for the military warlords bent on ever more defence spending.[7] It has been said that Takahashi was killed for 'trying to apply the brakes to the process he had started'.[8]

Of course, most war machines need an actual war in which they can be tested and used to destruction. The Japanese warlords and military cliques, by launching the Pearl Harbor attack on 7 December 1941, entered into a war that would prove to be far more deadly than any they could have anticipated. The war had ended with the destruction of a large part of Japan's infrastructure and the mental dislocation General MacArthur described as being a feature of the Japanese environment. The organization of the Japanese economy had centred around the great concerns known as the *zaibatsu*, large commercial houses which all had interests in many branches of industry and finance. The *zaibatsu* had naturally been opposed by the military cliques who saw them as a rival source of power and were intent on weakening them.

It is difficult to quantify the physical destruction inflicted on Japan during the war. The two atomic-bomb explosions at Hiroshima and Nagasaki, more than any other single events, may stand as terrible symbols of that destruction. To less sentimental economists, the amount of damage has been described as being equivalent to 'about twice the national income of the fiscal year 1948–9'. The once 'massive export trade' no longer existed. The mercantile marine, 'in pre-war days the third largest in the world', had been reduced to a 'few coasting vessels'.[9]

One of the most pressing problems relating to the Japanese economy was inflation. This had often emerged in the wake of war, from the French Revolution to Weimar Germany. During the war itself, there had been rigid price controls, production controls and other economic controls. By the end of the war, those controls had been relaxed. This relaxation 'irresistibly drove Japan into an inflationary crisis', shaped by deficit war financing and general scarcity. The deficits were blamed by a contemporary Japanese economist for an 'extraordinary currency expansion'.[10] The price level, starting at 100 in the price index on July 1941, had hit 324 by December 1944. By December 1945, it had reached 1,616, quintupling in only one year. Between the surrender in August 1945 and May 1946, 'the average cost of living rose 850 per cent'.[11]

For Japanese people living through this unsettling period, inflation was a chronic and debilitating problem. As the pressure of rising prices on the living standards of the people mounted, there grew 'tremendous popular agitation'. In February 1946, the government under the auspices of the Supreme Allied Command ordered all banks to limit monthly cash withdrawals. This amounted to a ban on withdrawals of more than 300 yen per family head and an additional 100 yen for each dependant. Yet even this limit 'proved to be too high' significantly to reduce the consumer spending that was fuelling the inflation.

For nearly seven years, from August 1945 until March 1952, the Supreme Commander for the Allied Powers – the term designated not just General Douglas MacArthur but the administration in general – held sway. Regardless of MacArthur's own personal magnetism, what is certain is that Japanese officials and businessmen were largely powerless to affect their circumstances. Initially, SCAP seemed rather indifferent to economic recovery. Political reform, and the prevention of the resurgence of Japan's militaristic imperialism, seemed to be the main concern. The immediate post-war period was one of economic stagnation. In 1946, the volume of industrial production was little more than 30 per cent of what had been the annual average in the period 1934–6. In 1947, the figure reached only 37 per cent.[12]

This experience of poor economic growth persuaded the Americans to change course. They quickly realized that, if Japan was to develop along the democratic lines they had envisaged, a thriving economy would be the best bulwark against a relapse into militarism and autocracy. The collapse of Chiang Kai-shek and the anti-Communist Kuomintang in China towards the end of the 1940s also caused a shift in strategic goals for the United States.[13] With customary efficiency and zeal, the American authorities decided to commit their energies to putting Japan's economy on a sounder footing. To this end, Joseph Dodge, the same Detroit banker who had been the architect of the western German currency reforms in 1948, arrived in Tokyo on 1 February 1949. Dodge was a conservative, rather straitlaced banker from the American Mid-West. A man of steady and methodical habits he served for nineteen years as President of the Detroit Bank, an institution which had managed to survive the Great Depression. He was later appointed Eisenhower's Director of the Bureau of the Budget in 1953, where he proved an aggressive cost cutter. Admired by contemporaries 'for his organization, meticulousness and fiscal orthodoxy', he was known for his adherence to the 'banker's conservative philosophy – a sound currency, a balanced budget, and financial stability'.[14]

Dodge immediately set to work on a concrete stabilization programme founded on the philosophy expressed in his dictum 'productivity is decreased and not increased by government spending'.[15] True to this philosophy, he reversed the policy of deficit spending which had been a hallmark of Japanese economic government since 1931. 'For the first time in almost two decades, as a result of a program prescribed by Mr Dodge . . . Japan has a balanced budget,' proclaimed one American economist in March 1950.[16] His reforms revolved around a Nine-Point Stabilization Programme which offered the usual prescription of 'a balanced budget, credit restrictions, and the expansion of trade and production'.[17] Indeed the first target of the Nine-Point Programme was to 'achieve a true balance in the consolidated budget at the earliest possible date by stringent curtailment of expenditures and maximum expansion in total government revenues, including such new revenues as may be necessary and appropriate'. In his nine-point plan, Dodge also alluded, in uncompromising fashion, to the need for 'credit expansion' to be 'vigorously limited to those projects contributing to the economic recovery'.[18] The background to his tough talk was a budget deficit which had increased from 103 billion yen in 1947–8 to 166 billion yen in 1948–9. Meanwhile, government debt had risen more than three times from 150 billion yen in mid-1945 to 531 billion yen in mid-1949.[19]

A further impetus behind Dodge's stabilization programme came from the desire to remove Japan 'from the backs of the American taxpayer', since the US had contributed US$500 million a year to the running of the country. Economic independence from the United States, in Dodge's view, could be achieved only through balanced budgets. On the issue of a 'true balance in the consolidated budget at the earliest possible date' he used the simile of Japan's economy being reliant 'on the support of a pair of stilts, government subsidies and American aid'. Initially, the Dodge mission was greeted with 'fear and suspicion', the main misgivings being that stabilization might mean 'deflation' – that is, falling prices which would bring hardship and unrest in their wake.[20] Eventually, however, the 'Dodge budget' for the fiscal year 1949 was 'thrust down the throat of the Japanese government', and the Diet, the Japanese parliament, approved it in April that year. Inevitably, the Japanese press bestowed on Joseph Dodge during that debate the title of 'Economic Czar'.[21]

Aside from the fiscal discipline – the balanced budget in which Dodge believed as an article of his Mid-Western banker's faith – the other area of significant reform was the currency. The yen itself had been created in 1871, when one yen was worth one US dollar. During the subsequent decades, the yen had steadily lost its value against the dollar. Dodge's tough medicine included a restriction on 'reckless uneconomic credit extension'.[22] His plan for the yen itself was simple. It was announced on 23 April 1949 that Dodge had decided arbitrarily on a single exchange rate of 360 yen to the dollar. He made this significant decision in consultation 'with three confidants', and then a week later left Japan. He had spent little more than three months in the country, and yet had probably influenced Japan as profoundly as any figure in its post-war history.

Dodge's rate of 360 yen to one dollar was probably an undervaluation. It certainly allowed Japan to embark on an export-led growth strategy. In the meantime, many of his reforms proved successful. By the spring of 1950, his policy had 'stopped inflation cold'. There had occurred no real deflation, but prices were stabilized at existing levels. As part of his reforms, Dodge had also abolished the complex system of multiple exchange rates then in use. He returned the yen to a unitary, fixed exchange rate. The stable exchange rate would greatly benefit Japan in the future. It would remain fixed at this rate of 360 yen to the dollar for twenty-two years, until 1971, and it formed the basis of Japan's extraordinary export-led economic growth in that period.[23]

Along with currency reform, the Supreme Commander for the Allied Powers issued a series of directives establishing new institutions which would shape Japan's economic development, including the People's Finance Corporation (established 1949), the Export-Import Bank of Japan (1950) and the Japan Development Bank (1951).[24] One significant institutional reform was the revised Securities and Exchange Law which was based on the Glass–Steagall Act in the United States. This law prohibited commercial banks from underwriting securities, except for bonds. The underwriting of shares, which had been dominated by commercial banks before the war, was now taken over by securities firms. In 1949, the Bank of Japan, the Japanese central bank, was reorganized and put under the control of a Policy Board, reflecting the structure and function of the Federal Reserve System of the United States. These reforms were an import legacy of the United States regime.

The Bank of Japan quickly became the linchpin of the credit system of the country. The 'secular trend in postwar Japan for the city banks' and other 'dominant institutions' was to be 'continuously and heavily in debt to the Bank of Japan'. City banks, in the immediate post-war system, were providers of short-term loans to major domestic corporations. The Bank of Japan's role was much more interventionist than the one which historically had been played by the Federal Reserve and, particularly, the Bank of

England, which had always acted as a lender of last resort, not as the first and principal source of finance. The Bank of Japan, through its 'ability to control directly the availability of its credit to the city banks', could 'strongly influence the availability of commercial bank credit to business'.[25] The relative lack of liquidity meant that the Japanese banking system could easily be controlled by a central authority. The situation was described as one in which the 'illiquid condition of the commercial banks and their dependence upon the Bank of Japan for advances naturally buttressed the power of the central monetary authorities'.[26]

The Japanese economy from the 1950s did not develop exactly on the free-market lines envisaged by Joseph Dodge. His vision of a thriving private sector with minimal state involvement was not entirely realized. From the end of Macarthur's quasi-personal rule, the Japanese government took an active role in pushing the economic growth of the country. Despite Dodge's best efforts at creating a genuinely free system of open competition in the economy, 'monopolistic practices' reappeared, especially after April 1952, when Japan 'regained her independence'. At this point, the government embarked on a 'gigantic industry-financing program' to be effected through governmental development corporations, many of which had been created under the auspices of the Americans. The Japanese government itself allowed tax relief on corporations operating in favoured industries. By the early 1960s, the respected Japanese political economist Shigeto Tsuru could note with apparent frankness that it seemed 'certain that were it not for such a sharing of risk by the government several of the essential industries would not have achieved the level of investment that was recorded in the fifties'.[27]

During the wonder years of Japanese prosperity from 1949 to the early 1970s, government agencies took on a commanding role in the direction of the economy. The principal organs of economic management were the Ministry of International Trade and Industry, the Bank of Japan and the Japan Development Bank. The powerful Ministry of International Trade and Industry, or MITI, became a famous, even if controversial and secretive, force in the economic growth of Japan. Through the Japan Development Bank, MITI 'exercised a predominant policy-making influence'. All loan applications to the JDB were screened by the government department. A strategic view was taken centrally about the industries which needed to be supported, and funds were accordingly found for the purpose. For example, between 1953 and 1955, a total of 83 per cent of the JDB's loans went to four industries – electric power, ships, coal and steel, all identified by the Ministry of International Trade and Industry.[28] It has been observed that the real American equivalent of the MITI was not the Department of Commerce, but the Department of Defense, which, it has been said, shared 'MITI's strategic, goal-oriented outlook'.[29]

The extent of government involvement in the Japanese economy gave rise to the expression 'state monopoly capitalism' employed by Japanese academics to describe their country's political economy.[30] The mechanism by which the Bank of Japan controlled credit was known as 'window guidance', an operation characterized as 'extra-legal and secretive'.[31] It involved the commitment of direct credit allocation according to strict quotas. 'Window guidance' or 'window control' involved a series of tête-à-tête meetings between customers, generally commercial bankers, who would lend the money they had received from the central bank, and officials at the Bank of Japan. This was not 'an open market for securities'. The central bank would use a form of 'moral suasion' to influence the subsequent loan decisions of the commercial banks, which would then have strict instructions about how to allocate credit.[32] The financial system could operate in this tightly controlled manner since Japan maintained a 'highly regulated and protected financial system until the early 1970s'. This financial structure was probably 'one of the most rigidly and administratively controlled in the world' and it relied on the virtual prohibition of 'flows of capital into or out of Japan'.[33]

The ultimate monetary background to this control was of course the Bretton Woods system. Under this system, the Japanese yen kept its exchange rate of 360 yen to the dollar. This allowed Japan to become in the words of a Japanese economist in 1955, 'deeply obsessed with the "export or expire" kind of fatalism'.[34] The initial impetus to Japan's extraordinary performance in exporting goods was provided by the Korean War, which erupted in June 1950. As the United States entered the conflict, extensive orders began to be placed with Japanese firms for ammunition, trucks, uniforms, communications equipment. Between July 1950 and February 1951, the US armed forces placed orders with Japanese firms for over 7,000 trucks with a value of nearly US$13 million. This development was the key to the revival of Japan's automotive industry. Inevitably, the Enterprise Bureau of MITI helped to organize these 'special procurements' and ensured that the dollars which Japan gained in this way were used for further investment in key industries.

These procurements by the American military led to a 'special procurements boom', as it was called, which helped create an atmosphere of economic euphoria. The demands of American troops and their families for Japanese goods contributed 37 per cent of all the foreign exchange receipts of Japan in 1952–3, and even as late as 1959–60 the figure was still 11 per cent.[35] The Korean War itself not only promoted Japan's economic recovery but reminded the United States of how important Japan was as a strategic ally in the new Cold War. If Japan had not been under American control, it is difficult to see how South Korea could have been defended. A strong Japan became, for the Americans, a preoccupying consideration in their 'Eastern strategy'.[36]

The combination of strong government control and military backing from the United States, coupled with a stable and weak currency which drove greater exports, led to impressive growth. For nearly two decades after 1945, the Japanese economy maintained consistently 'an annual rate of growth higher than nine percent'. No one standing in 'the midst of the debris wrought by wartime destruction as Japan surrendered in August 1945' could ever have believed even in their wildest dreams the extent of Japan's transformation.[37] To a later commentator who lived through the period, the 'rise of the Phoenix' might have been 'an apt phrase for the dramatic renascence of the Japanese economy'. The 'rise of the Phoenix' from the 'hopelessly prostrated nadir of the immediate postwar period to the top-rank position in per capita GNP [had taken place] within less than a generation'.[38]

The successes of Japan in the economic sphere first became a subject of public debate in the international arena in 1962. In that year, the British weekly the *Economist* ran a series of articles on Japan, which was later published as a book in 1963 with the title *Consider Japan*. It was in this series of article that by 'common agreement among the Japanese' the term 'miracle' appeared for the first time. In its issues of 1 and 8 September, the *Economist* spoke of dramatic economic expansion, at a time when the Japanese themselves were expressing doubts about the sustainability of the boom and worrying about potential crises. Interestingly, Japanese economists and pundits expressed concern about 'irresponsible budgets', while the *Economist*, a paper of a marked classical liberal bent, referred to the 'expansion of demand'.[39] The *Economist* pointed to Japan's 'very expansionary budget policies, with large planned increases in government expenditure and sizeable reductions in personal taxation', which were 'a regular feature of most recent years'. The magazine also noted that, in Japan's armoury of economic management at the time, monetary policies and rises in interest rates were 'the main restraining weapons when and if any restraints are needed'. With regard to the Bank of Japan's role in the allocation of credit, the *Economist* outlined the process by which commercial bankers had to come 'begging' to the central bank when they needed funds to increase their own loans. Furthermore, the 'entire credit structure of Japan' now seemed to the 'visiting foreigner to lie snugly under the Bank of Japan's control'. The British weekly now described the Bank of Japan as 'one of the most powerful central banking organisations in the world'.[40]

The magnitude of this central bank control represented a reversal from what had occurred in Japan before the war. In the 1920s, for instance, Japan's economy was the scene of 'fierce competition', 'takeover battles between large companies' and an active stock market which raised equity finance for economies. The consequence of the war and the American-led reconstruction had, perhaps paradoxically, given a different complexion to Japan's capitalism. One recent assessment of the post-war period is that 'Japan did not use free markets to become the second largest economy in the world.'[41] The authors of the *Economist*'s September 1962 report would have agreed with that assessment. In describing the 'window guidance' or 'window operation' which typified the relationship of the Bank of Japan to the commercial banks, the *Economist* noted the 'regular consultations' with the commercial banks, the review of the 'likely trend of advances of each bank for perhaps a month ahead'. Then the central bank might warn individual banks that they 'should please start to restrain their advances'. The central bank might even suggest an 'overall loan level' for the big banks 'as a whole'.[42]

In order to facilitate lending to favoured sectors, the Bank of Japan would 'offer favourable discount rates on particular types of lending'. In particular, the Bank would often 'help indirectly to subsidise Japanese exports in this way'. In short, it was a highly managed process, often affected by 'political considerations'. The system was one of 'rationed capital', in which fiscal policy, or government spending, could be used to stimulate demand, while monetary policy, notably in the form of high interest rates, could be used to impose restrictions that would curtail lending to businesses which, for whatever reason, were not favoured. It was during this period, between the end of the Second World War and the early 1960s, that the curious reliance of Japanese companies on banks for their funding was first noted. 'This peculiarity of industrial firms depending on banks even for their long-term investment funds is . . . more marked in the postwar Japan than in the pre-war', observed the veteran Japanese economist Tsuru Shigeto in 1964. Tsuru quoted a study from 1963 which observed that 'in the United States of all the sources of financial funds' only '5–8 percent was accounted for by loans from banks'. By contrast, the ratio in Japan was as high as 31.6 per cent. These sums also included the retained earnings, or profits, of a business which could be used for reinvestment. In West Germany, another country which was noted for the dependence of companies on bank finance, the figure was only 18.8 per cent.[43] Even when interest rates were low, credit rationing would often mean that companies unlucky enough not to be favoured simply could not borrow money. The loan market was 'often in disequilibrium'.[44]

The Bretton Woods settlement and its institutions were crucially important for Japan. The General Agreement on Tariffs and Trade, or GATT for short, signed in 1947, was also significant in providing a framework of stability in which Japanese exports could flourish.[45] GATT was a general undertaking on the part of its signatories to lower tariffs and promote global free trade. The stable exchange rate, chronically undervalued as it was at 360 yen to one US dollar, made it 'easier and easier' for Japanese industries to expand their export markets. There also occurred a high degree of 'technology transfer' whereby the technology from which Japan had been cut off during its period of isolation in the 1930s was adopted and used in such industries as electronics, petrochemicals, automation devices and new materials.[46]

The rise of Japan was probably the greatest legacy of the Pax Americana. The seven years of direct American rule shaped the country's subsequent political and economic development. Of course, under the canopy of American support and friendship, Japan did not have to embark on the ruinous defence expenditure which had overburdened its budgets in the 1930s. Additionally, it enjoyed a major export market in the United States and cheap transfers of technology.[47] Its economic development was driven by policies of its own making. Yet the overarching framework had been supplied entirely by the United States. The United States helped to create modern Japan even more than it did Germany, where the other Allies had played a role in the government. Germany had also been split, and would remain split for forty years. Japan was entirely under American influence and control. The Americans had fulfilled their quasi-imperial duty by creating a stable framework for Japanese economic development. This was achieved through the years of direct rule by SCAP, the reforms of Joseph Dodge and the Bretton Woods system itself.

Imperial Retreat

American leadership had effectively reconstructed both Germany and Japan. Meanwhile the economic climate in the United States itself began to grow more turbulent at the end of the 1950s. Truman and Eisenhower had, rhetorically at least, been committed to balanced budgets and to meeting expenditure, in so far as they could, with increased taxation revenues. Deficit finance, it must be stressed, was not a legacy of the Second World War, given that governments in the United States and Europe reverted very much to the balanced budgets of the pre-Depression years as a matter of policy. As Christina Romer, an American economist and supporter of President Obama, observed in 2007, it was the 1960s which 'represented the beginning of a long dark period for macroeconomic policy'.

This was largely, in Romer's view, a consequence of the laxity of budgetary discipline which occurred in that decade. In the 1950s, 'Dwight Eisenhower shared Truman's fundamental commitment to long-run budget balance, and emphasized the importance of fiscal prudence for economic growth.'[1] Although the 1950s had witnessed an extensive military commitment by the United States in Korea, this expenditure had been met by increased taxation. US policymakers in the 1950s had 'often raised taxes to pay for particular spending they wanted'. An extreme case of this was 'the fact that Truman fought the Korean War almost entirely out of current revenues by imposing huge wartime tax increases'. Equally, 'expansions in social security benefits and the building of the interstate highway system were financed with dedicated tax increases'.[2] As Romer has argued, one way that 1950s policymakers' views about the economy 'were very different from those of many modern policymakers was in the importance they ascribed to a balanced budget'. During that decade, the 'actual surplus' was 'positive', since the 'budget was allowed to go into deficit in bad years, but it was forced to be in surplus in good ones'.[3]

There occurred, however, a 'crucial change in economic beliefs' in the early 1960s. This led to the 'danger of persistent deficits'. By the 1960s, Romer argued, 'The 1950s emphasis on the benefits of fiscal discipline was replaced by a view that deficits, even over several years, could be salutary.'[4] The policymakers of the 1960s 'expressed confidence that deficits would largely take care of themselves by generating rapid growth and hence increased revenues'. Lyndon Johnson, US President from 1963 to 1968, repeatedly asserted that 'deficits would take care of themselves'. In his 1965 budget, the President declared that a tax cut would stimulate growth and 'should hasten the achievement of a balanced budget in an economy of full prosperity'.[5] This statement by Johnson began the rather circular argument which could be used to justify perpetual deficits. Once a deficit occurred, it was often argued, governments should allow it to continue so that growth would return which, so the argument went, would close the deficit. This view was accompanied by a strong predisposition against unemployment and an enthusiasm for ambitious social programmes. In the 1966 economic report from the President's office, a number of key goals of public policy were outlined. 'Stabilization, expanding opportunity, social welfare, even equilibrium in the balance of payments' were all mentioned. No mention was made of the aspiration for 'long-run budget balance'.[6]

Herbert Stein, a fiscal conservative, recalled in his book *The Fiscal Revolution in America*, published in 1969, that, by the time of the 1964 tax cut, 'budget-balancing had ceased to have an important influence on fiscal decisions'. By then, 'compensatory finance' had taken its place as standard doctrine. The rather old-fashioned term 'compensatory finance' has been defined as just another term for deficit financing, in which there occurs a 'use of borrowing to finance an excess of expenditure over income'. This is generally used to refer to governments who 'often spend more than they can raise in taxation'.[7] During the discussion, Stein remembered, there were 'repeated respectful references to budget-balancing as a goal, by the President and his economic advisers as well as by conservatives'. These references, however, were 'ritualistic', in that no decisions followed from them.[8]

Contrary to his expressed beliefs about the need for fiscal prudence, President Eisenhower had run a $12.4 billion deficit in 1958–9, towards the very end of his two-term presidency. President Kennedy and his advisers, however, 'in 1961 and 1962 still thought there was a budget-balancing function to be reckoned with', only to prove weak in their implementation of this vaunted ideal. When 'they finally decided to take the plunge to deliberate deficit creation they found that the opposition they [had] feared was a shadow'.[9] Fiscal discipline had given way to a much more relaxed approach.

The main contributors to the loosening of fiscal restraints were of course the twin needs for 'guns and butter', the old phrase referring to the demands for military and civilian spending. These two forms of expenditure were represented by greater commitments to the Vietnam War and to the needs of the Great Society, a social programme which President Johnson launched in 1965. In August of that year, the Defense Secretary Robert McNamara asked for and received a US$1.7 billion emergency appropriation from Congress to help pay for the Vietnam War. At that time, it was generally assumed that American involvement in the conflict had reached its peak, and that the US economy would adapt to the new wartime conditions. Congress continued to be uneasy during those early years of the war. John Stennis, a Mississippi Democrat, and one of the Senate's leading voices on military affairs, warned of sharply increased spending in 1966 unless something was done to contain the war. Gardner Ackley, the Chairman of the Council of Economic Advisers, told Johnson, late in 1965, that the President could not have 'the war, the Great Society programs and a stable price level all at the same time'. Ackley argued that 'something would have to give'. He also urged the President to ask the Congress for 'a tax increase'.[10]

In the winter of 1965–6 President Johnson was struggling to identify the principal themes and strategic goals of his administration. In the words of one of his excellent biographers, the President's eagerness to do the right thing 'convinced him that the country was rich enough and committed enough to have guns and butter'.[11] In his State of the Union address in

January 1966, he renewed his commitment to the war and to creating the Great Society, a society in which poverty and deprivation would be abolished. 'This Nation is mighty enough,' he thundered, 'its society is healthy enough, its people are strong enough, to pursue our goals in the rest of the world while still building a Great Society here at home.'[12] None of the Congressmen present could have doubted the strength of the President's conviction or the vigour of his idealism. In the course of his address, Johnson challenged Americans to 'prosecute with vigor and determination our war on poverty'. He urged them to 'rebuild completely, on a scale never before attempted, entire central and slum areas of several of our cities'. But his address acknowledged the continuing effects of the Vietnam War. Despite his enthusiasm for the Great Society, the war meant that he could not achieve 'all that we should', or indeed all that 'we would like to do'. In his conclusion, Johnson used the most emotionally charged rhetoric he could muster to rouse the liberal Congressmen, who had risen to their feet to applaud him. He appealed to the Congress, 'representatives of the richest Nation on earth . . . the elected servants of a people who live in abundance unmatched on this globe', to bring 'the most urgent decencies of life to all of your fellow Americans'. The *Washington Post* summarized the address aptly with the headline 'US can continue the "Great Society" and fight in Vietnam'.[13]

The costs of the Vietnam War, however, like those of many such conflicts, far exceeded initial estimations. In mid-1965 McNamara had thought that there would be 300,000 American troops in Vietnam by the end of the following year and that he would need US$10 billion to fight the war in 1966. In November his estimates had risen to 400,000 men and between US$15 billion and US$17 billion. Ackley and his colleagues on the Council of Economic Advisers were also urging tax increases.[14] Johnson's 1966 budget called for increased Vietnam spending while he wanted additional funds for Great Society programmes. All through 1966, Ackley and others continued to encourage White House support for a general tax increase, but Johnson resisted these calls. Even at the time, the President knew that defence spending would rise and be greater than had been anticipated.[15]

During all this time, from 1951 right through to 1970, the urbane William McChesney Martin Jr continued to preside in a benign and patrician fashion over the Federal Reserve. As the longest-serving Chairman of the Board of Governors of the US Fed, Martin looked on as the world of balanced budgets and fiscal restraint of the 1950s changed into a scene with which he felt less comfortable. Giving a speech in Virginia in October 1969, he reflected on his career of nearly forty years in the financial world. He remembered the 'day in September 1931 when England went off the gold standard – a memory made vivid for me by the fact that I had just gone on the floor of the Stock Exchange'. Martin went on to describe the important years in his career. He recalled the day in December 1941 when America was 'plunged into World War II'. He also remembered the time in December 1965 when the Federal Reserve 'raised the discount rate. The raise was only from 4 to 4½ per cent.' This, in 1969, seemed to Martin like 'a bargain basement rate'.[16]

Martin remembered how the slight increase in interest rates at the end of 1965 earned him an unwanted invitation to President Johnson's ranch in Texas, where he had to explain himself to an irritated President. Early in his administration, Johnson told him that 'he came from a part of the country that liked low interest rates'. That was how Johnson believed 'interest rates should be'. Martin responded in a combative tone to a President known for his bullying manner. 'I, too, like to see interest rates as low as conditions of inflation . . . permit them to be.' The difference was just that Johnson 'liked them to be low . . . all the time'. During his presidential interview Martin cited the traditional tenets of the conservative banker. 'Mr President, I want to tell you how you can have low interest rates, and the *only* way you can have low interest rates,' Martin began. He continued, it 'is with budgetary responsibility, both in respect to Government spending and taxing, and a fiscal policy that makes that responsibility plain'. He concluded, if 'you will see to that, you can have moderate interest rates'.

Of course, as Martin observed, 'that wasn't the way things went'. The war in Vietnam began to 'escalate sharply around mid-1965, when we were also embarking on many new, sizable and worthy welfare programmes'. The consequence of all this was that the United States government became 'increasingly over-committed and over-extended, especially because nothing was being done about taxes even though expenditures were mounting'.[17] Martin was echoing the approach of Eisenhower and other conservatives who, in the 1950s, were not afraid to raise taxes to balance the budget. In fact, a commitment to balancing the budget in the 1950s and 1960s was still understood to entail a willingness to raise revenues through taxation if necessary.

Martin, as might be expected from a fiscal conservative, coupled his warning for budgetary responsibility with a plea for the maintenance of a sound currency. He argued that no 'modern country can have stability and sustained growth without some basis of sound currency'. His views about the need for preserving the value of a currency might seem quaint to a subsequent generation of politicians and bankers, but he believed that currency stability was the reason for having central banks. 'That is why all modern countries have central banks.' More particularly, in the case of the United States, it was the reason why the 'Federal Reserve is charged with the duty of doing all it can, within its limited powers, to help maintain the dollar's value'. By the end of the 1960s, Martin was becoming obsessed by the spectre of inflation which, he believed, remained 'the great problem'. The Federal Reserve needed to 'check deterioration' of the dollar.[18]

Martin's strongly held convictions regarding the efficacy of sound money, even then still backed by gold, had been expressed in a talk entitled 'Good Money is Coined Freedom', delivered before the Economic Club of Detroit in March 1968. In his fulsome introduction to the speech, Raymond T. Perring, Chairman of the Detroit Bank, described the sofly spoken Federal Reserve Chairman as 'the arch enemy of inflation', as 'a symbol of orthodox money' and 'a sound money man' who nevertheless wanted 'interest rates as low as possible, without having inflation'. In his remarks to the Economic Club, Martin squarely addressed the problem of government spending. 'What we're confronted with today is a budgetary problem that's been getting progressively worse. I have said this repeatedly.' The danger, as he saw it, was that 'what we are moving toward gradually is not deficit finance for a temporary period, but perpetual deficit'. The natural consequence of perpetual deficit, a situation in which government spending outstripped tax revenues in every single year, was a weak currency. 'This is a very sad progression toward undermining the currency.' Martin observed that 'deficit finance can be properly used, but it should be used only for the purpose of obtaining a balance at some point'.[19] The problem occurred when '"surplus" gradually comes to be a bad word and "deficit" becomes a good word'. This is what he believed had happened 'in this country over the last decade'.

The heart of the budgetary problem was that the United States was, in Martin's gloomy view, 'overextended and overcommitted'. 'We have commitments in Vietnam, we have commitments in South Korea, we have commitments in the Middle East.' The United States also had 'military forces stationed in Western Europe'. He rejected the notion that the United States could 'fulfil all these other commitments and at the same time not in any way change our way of life at home'. It would be extraordinary in the early twenty-first century for a Chairman of the Federal Reserve Board to express his or her views so publicly and with such unequivocal lucidity. In regard to the US currency, Martin always remained committed to the dollar's link with gold. In the address in Detroit, he paraphrased sympathetically the sentiment of George Bernard Shaw that 'if it was a choice between trusting gold or governments, he would take gold any day'. But the Chairman of the Federal Reserve was enough of a practical realist to suggest that, in order to preserve the gold link, ultimately 'a government has to be relied upon'.[20]

Sterling had been devalued in November 1967. People then assumed that 'the United States was going to go blindly on its way in the same direction'. The reason for sterling's devaluation, from US$2.80 to the pound to US$2.40, Martin stated, was that the 'British people were not willing to face up to these budgetary implications'. The British had lacked the political will to restrain their spending. Martin spoke darkly of the world not having 'the same degree of confidence' as it was accustomed to having in the past. There are people today 'who are doubtful whether we have the capacity as a nation to handle our affairs'.[21]

Even as late as 1968, the power and allure of gold as the anchor of the international monetary system remained strong. Martin said he was 'well aware of the mystique and the fetish of gold in the world'. He had 'no thought of demonetizing it tomorrow', but he did acknowledge that eventually there would 'not be enough gold in the world for use as the basis for currencies' in terms of the Bretton Woods agreed dollar value of gold. The

French in the late 1960s were constantly putting pressure on the Americans with regard to the issue of gold. 'What the French are saying to us', continued Martin, was that 'we are not showing any capacity for leadership; that we are not showing any capacity to handle our own affairs'.[22] He was quite right that the French were hesitating to put their confidence in US leadership of the international monetary regime during the late 1960s. Charles de Gaulle had been making a nuisance of himself at a series of press conferences where he had complained of the primacy of the dollar, which allowed the US what de Gaulle's finance minister Valéry Giscard d'Estaing called an 'exorbitant privilege'.[23]

All through the late 1960s, Martin sounded his usual message to anyone who cared to listen. He seemed to be most relaxed in front of audiences in his native Mid-West. In Toledo, Ohio, in June 1967, he had made his customary plea for a balanced budget. Unlike many later anti-tax conservatives in the United States, he was unsurprisingly anxious to raise taxes in order to meet the country's expenditures in its war effort. Interestingly he also believed that there would be popular support for tax rises to pay for war expenditure. 'The public recognizes that the war in Vietnam – which after all accounts for the major share of added Government expenditures . . . must be paid for.' As a consequence of this realism, he believed that 'a tax increase now deserves, and will receive, broad support'.[24] The Toledo remarks are particularly revealing in the connection they show, in Bill Martin's mind, between fiscal responsibility and the maintenance of the gold link, at the fixed Bretton Woods Agreement price of US$35 an ounce of gold. In these remarks, Martin paid tribute to the success of Bretton Woods:

> The readiness of the US Treasury to buy and sell gold at the fixed price of US$35 in transactions with foreign monetary authorities has greatly contributed to the willingness of monetary authorities and private foreign residents to hold dollar reserves . . . As a result, the dollar has attained a unique position in international commerce and finance, and the universal acceptability of dollars has greatly facilitated the record expansion of international trade. Since 1950 world trade has tripled, rising from less than $60 billion to $180 billion last year.[25]

The success of the dollar as an international currency, however, was dependent on sound budgetary and financial management at home in the United States. In this context, 'the availability of US monetary gold holdings to meet international convertibility needs is a matter of vital importance not only to the United States but to the entire present system of international payments on which the free world relies'. The idea of being able to convert the dollar to gold was a fixed point of the system. Yet, for this system to function properly, the United States needed to be responsible. 'In the end, our nation cannot have sound money unless its monetary and fiscal affairs are well managed.' The United States, with its enormous economic wealth and even greater potential, was a 'great and a prosperous nation' which could 'undertake whatever programs we feel we need'. This ability was dependent, however, on a willingness 'to assume the financial obligations involved'. If America were to 'fall into the habit of perpetual deficit financing the soundness of our currency and the strength of our economy will eventually be undermined'.[26] To his detractors, however, Martin remained 'a symbol of conservative fiscal policy and "sound" finance'. The more acerbic of his contemporaries often portrayed him in caricature wearing a high starched collar 'looking like a refugee from the nineteenth century'.[27]

The US commitment to maintaining the dollar link to gold was something which many foreign governments had begun gravely to doubt in the 1960s. Most of all, the French, under Charles de Gaulle, were suspicious. At a press conference held in February 1965, de Gaulle himself had launched an extraordinary attack on the dollar's primacy, calling for the eventual return of the gold standard and effectively 'inviting other countries to follow France's lead and cash in their dollars for gold'.[28] Just before he spoke, Johnson's Treasury Secretary Douglas Dillon made the first public admission that the US balance of trade deficit – the level of trade imports over exports – had moved higher than anyone expected. This figure was US$3 billion, all of which the United States government was legally committed to exchange for US gold on demand. At the same time, the Federal Reserve announced that the US gold supply had declined at the beginning of February 1965 by US$100 million, to a twenty-six-year low of US$15.1 billion.

France converted US$150 million into gold in January 1965 and planned another US$150 million conversion imminently. Spain had 'quietly exchanged US$60 billion of its dollar reserves for US gold'. The fear, even among US Congressmen, was that the 'gold-laden truckloads [would continue] rolling out of Fort Knox'. De Gaulle with characteristic good timing intervened in this monetary debate. At his February 1965 press conference, he argued that the 'time has long since passed' when the currencies of any one or two nations can enjoy 'this signal privilege, this signal advantage'. The present-day world, he said, needs 'an indisputable monetary base, and one that does not bear the mark of any particular country. In truth, one does not see how one could really have any standard criterion other than gold.'

Under the gold standard, as envisaged by the French President, the United States would no longer be able to pay its foreign debts in dollars. Such payments would have to be made in gold. The Americans would not be able to maintain endless trade deficits, since they would run out of gold. The gold standard would force American consumers to reduce their purchases of foreign goods which would curtail the US trade deficit. De Gaulle dubbed his plan the 'Golden Rule', in which the value of money would be guaranteed by the immutability of gold.[29] He pointed out that the situation of the 1960s had radically changed from that which had prevailed in 1945. At the end of the Second World War, nearly all the gold reserves of the world were held by the United States, which could, as a result, defend the Bretton Woods rate of $35 per ounce of gold. Without ample gold reserves, such a rate would be under pressure as foreigners acquired more gold reserves, by selling their dollars for gold. This American dominance in regard to the actual possession of physical reserves of gold did not correspond to the 'realities of the present'. The currencies of Western Europe, which had been dislocated by the war, were now in a different position: the gold reserves of the six nations that were members of the European Economic Community were now equal to the gold reserve of the Americans. If the countries of the EEC converted all the dollars they possessed into gold, their gold reserves would easily surpass those of America. De Gaulle's view was that the balance of world trade was such that a dollar link to gold could not be maintained.[30]

The capacity of the United States, with its huge spending commitments and lax budgetary policy during the 1960s, to sustain a gold link was severely constrained. For some years, the dollar value of an ounce of gold – prescribed at Bretton Woods at US$35 – seemed to undervalue gold. Unofficially, gold was trading at US$40 an ounce as early as October 1960. As a response, the United States 'fed gold into the market via the Bank of England'. This caused the price to drop back to US$36. To stop this price instability from occurring again, in November 1961 the Bank of England, along with six central banks of Western European countries and the USA, joined together to form the 'Gold Pool' which was designed to supply all the gold necessary to keep the market stable at the stated Bretton Woods price of US$35 an ounce. The United States share of the pool was 50 per cent. The Gold Pool was closed in 1968, after which there was established a two-tier market in gold. 'One tier was the official market which dealt with gold held by central banks and governments. This kept gold fixed at $35.' The other tier was the 'free' market', in which gold 'was left to find its own price level'.[31] The economist Harry Johnson believed that the 'present "two-tier" price system for gold was touched off by short-run speculation on a rise in the price of gold derived from uncertainties gener-ated by the devaluation of sterling, the extraordinary deterioration of the US balance of payments' and, above all, 'growing disbelief – justified in the event – in the willingness and/or ability of the gold pool countries to hold the market rate at $35 an ounce'.[32]

By the late 1960s, the US dollar was under pressure from all sides. The trade balance was moving against the United States, as strong European economies, in particular Germany, coupled with Japan were exporting goods, thereby earning dollars. Allan Meltzer, the US economist and the official historian of the Federal Reserve, gives the orthodox view that finan-cing 'the war and the president's Great Society by increasing money growth created inflation'. The inflation rate, as measured by consumer prices, 'remained below 1.5 percent until the middle of 1965'. In 1969, the rate reached 5.5 per cent: 'The Great Inflation was under way.' It was 'sustained by rapid money growth to finance the government budget and pay for the Great Society and the War in Vietnam'. Martin, the Chairman of the Federal Reserve, likewise believed that 'budget deficits caused inflation'.[33]

Meltzer, an adviser to both Presidents Kennedy and Reagan, has accurately described the 1960s in his magisterial history of the Federal Reserve published in the first decade of the twenty-first century. 'The years 1961–71 were a part of the Keynesian interlude dominated by a strong belief that government was responsible for an unruly private sector.' As we have observed, this 'vulgar Keynesianism', a belief in the efficacy of deficit financing on the part of the government, was not something which had been a real legacy of Keynes's direct influence, since in the 1950s governments had sought to balance the budget. The great man had died in 1946, but 'Keynesianism' became a key term of reference, and then of justification for 'big government', only in the 1960s. In Meltzer's succinct formulation, the main events of the 1960s that 'dominated politics and monetary policy' were the Vietnam War and the expansion of the welfare state. President Johnson's Great Society also 'expanded programs in health, education and welfare that redistributed income' and 'increased social spending'. The result of these policies, both foreign and domestic, was that between 1960 and 1970 the spending of the US government 'doubled in nominal terms and rose 50% in real terms'. All of the increase in military expenditure came after 1965, rising 60 per cent from 1962 to 1969. Spending on education and health increased 'five or six fold' in the decade.[34]

Dramatically increased government spending and mounting inflation, coupled with a worsening trade balance, was the situation of the United States economy which confronted Richard Nixon on his inauguration as President of the United States in January 1969. From the start of his presidency, Nixon began to take 'a hard look at how to cut defense costs', so that he could use some of the funds for 'higher welfare spending'.[35] The 1960s with their increased government spending and worsening trade balances had damaged the power of the United States. As early as 1964, the 'dollar holdings of foreign central banks exceeded the value of all the gold in Fort Knox'.[36] They could have cleared out the United States gold reserves by presenting their dollars for gold in any one instant.

Nixon himself was an odd mixture of conservative pragmatist and hyperactive interventionist. He believed passionately that the economy had cost him the presidential election in November 1960. He blamed the recession of that year for his defeat.[37] His appetite for power was legendary and made him the supreme pragmatist in politics. Despite his toughness, and the seeming readiness with which he could shift position on policy, the bare facts of the US economy, towards the end of 1968, did not presage a particularly attractive future. When Nixon was elected in November 1968, the inflation rate at 4.7 per cent was the 'highest since the Korean War'. Wages had increased 6.5 per cent in 1968 and 'showed no signs of slowing'. The economy was clearly overheating, as indicated by the very low unemployment figure of 3.3 per cent. Interest rates, by contrast, were at their highest level since the Civil War, as the prime rate, the rate which US banks generally charge to their most creditworthy clients, had jumped from 5.75 per cent in October to 6.5 per cent in late November. The 'overheated American economy had generated a flood of imported goods' which damaged America's trade balance.[38] A continuing adverse trade balance would, as de Gaulle had foreseen, make the dollar link to gold increasingly untenable.

The final break with gold was dramatic and, as much as any other development of monetary history, can almost be entirely attributable to the actions of one man, the President of the United States, Richard M. Nixon. It was Nixon's decision in August 1971 which substantially altered the course of monetary history and inaugurated a period, for the first time in 2,500 years, in which gold was effectively demonetized in most of what had been understood to be the Western world. In January 1971, the President had declared, 'I am now a Keynesian'.[39] Yet, unlike his newly professed intellectual guru, Nixon was bored by the intricacies of international finance. He saw them as irrelevant when considered against the background of the cosmic political forces he believed to be shaping the world. Like Keynes, he believed gold to be a 'monetary anachronism'. Unlike Keynes, he 'did not wish to waste his time on a topic that seemed to him inconsequential and boring'. After a year in office, the President wrote to his aides, 'What really matters in campaigns, wars, or in government is to concentrate on the big battles and win them.' He had little concern for the details of monetary arrangements. 'I do not want to be bothered with international monetary matters.'[40]

Nixon did, however, surround himself with officials of force and character more engaged in monetary affairs than the President himself. Arthur Burns was appointed Chairman of the Federal Reserve in 1970 in succession to William McChesney Martin Jr. In his latter years as Chairman of the Fed, Martin had been increasingly frustrated by the developments in American budgetary policy. His views on the need for balanced budgets, and the inability of the Federal Government adequately to prosecute war abroad and promote the Great Society at home, had been largely ignored. He spoke eloquently about the importance of fighting inflation, even after he had given up his position at the head of the Federal Reserve. In September 1970, at a conference in Basle in Switzerland, he identified inflation as 'the biggest problem', and spoke of a global economy 'beset by inflation'. 'Today, we are seeing around the world a wage explosion of major force,' he said. He believed that 'over a long enough period of time, we will demonstrate that the only real possibility of having . . . high levels of employment is to have relative stability in prices and to resist those inflationary trends'.[41]

Martin's successor, Arthur Burns, was, intellectually at least, very different. Burns was the first Chairman of the Federal Reserve to have an academic training in the 'dismal science' of economics. Martin had graduated from Yale in the humanistic disciplines of English and Latin, and had acquired his knowledge of markets and economics within the institutions where he had worked over four decades. Burns had been born in Stanislau, Austria, in 1904, the only child of Nathan Burnseig and Sarah Juran. His parents emigrated to the United States when Arthur was ten years old and settled in Bayonne, New Jersey. Nathan worked as a paint contractor, while the young Burns studied economics at Columbia University, right up to doctorate level, supporting himself as 'a waiter, shoe salesman, house painter, postal clerk, and summer sailor'.[42] By the time of his appointment as Federal Reserve Chairman, Burns had long before shed any bohemian student tastes he might have acquired and had become a staid figure of the Republican establishment.

Despite his formal training in economics, Burns was more of the literary type of economist than the mathematically fluent technocrats who would dominate the subject by the end of the twentieth century. In the middle of his career he had written that 'a subtle understanding of economic change comes from a knowledge of history and large affairs, not from statistics or their processing alone – to which our age has turned so easily in its quest for certainty'. He had an academic style. It was said of him in 1980 that he 'can wear tweeds easily, smokes those pipes (he has over a hundred of them) and, when the occasion calls for it, can mask his thoughts with complex rhetoric and jargon'.[43] Behind the scholarly exterior, he had a subtle politician's instinct for power and mastered the art of swaying people. 'If God were an economist,' said one of Burns's contemporaries, 'he would be like Arthur Burns.'

Another key figure of Nixon's economic team was the former Texas Governor, John Connally. Appointed Treasury Secretary by the California Republican Nixon, Connally, a Southern Democrat, liked to portray himself as a bipartisan figure with broad appeal. In contrast to Arthur Burns, and to Nixon himself, 'Big Jawn' was a tall, swaggering Southerner with the charm and force of personality of his one-time mentor, Lyndon Johnson. Comparisons were constantly drawn between these two Texans. One wit described Connally as 'LBJ with couth'. Others observed that the younger man's 'physique, accent and general presence were direct reminders' of the former President.[44] Connally's most dramatic moment had been when, in November 1963, he had ridden in the car in which John F. Kennedy had been shot. The shock of this experience had caused him to give up smoking cigars, but he continued with the habit of chewing them. Nixon relished the former Governor's 'well-groomed, big man, easy going manner'.[45] In Henry Kissinger's acidic assessment, 'Connally's swaggering self-assurance was Nixon's Walter Mitty image of himself. He was one person whom Nixon never denigrated behind his back.'[46]

Despite his winning, 'big man' persona, Connally was notoriously short on experience in banking or economics. When a reporter asked him his qualifications for the job of Secretary of the Treasury, he replied flippantly, 'I can add.' He was first and foremost a politician, not a monetary theorist, which was precisely why Nixon had appointed him.[47] His instincts on the international stage were strongly nationalistic, which rather undermined the spirit of international co-operation, under American leadership, which had characterized Bretton Woods. His nationalistic poses also chimed well with Nixon's views of himself as a 'tough guy', a man of action and decisiveness. Connally's assertiveness with international financiers at high-level conferences quickly became the stuff of legend. He described himself, with pompous self-conceit, as the 'bully boy on the manicured playing fields of international finance'. A contemporary historian, writing in 1972, stated that Connally's outlook on the world 'gave American policy a more nationalistic trend than it has ever had since World War II'.[48]

By 1971, described as the 'climactic year of his economic management', Nixon had abandoned the 'postwar liberal ideal of a harmonious trade world in favour of a nationalist conception of US interests'. In the summer of 1971, the *Wall Street Journal* reported that the 'United States government is getting ready for a new cold war against the rest of the free world'.[49] The right of foreign governments, or their central banks, to 'show up at any time at the "gold window" of the US Treasury and insist on trading their dollars for gold' was something which Nixon was beginning to reconsider.[50] The 'death watch for Bretton Woods' had begun. On 3 May, the German Finance Minister Karl Schiller set off market concern by hinting at the 'revaluation of the mark'. In July, it was reported that the US trade balance, which had produced a US$2.7 billion surplus in 1970, had in June yielded a deficit of US$597 million.[51]

Above all, the emergence of Japan from 1965 onwards as an exporting giant had aggravated the US balance of trade. The United States had paid little attention to the matter before 1965, when Japan's exports to the world had reached US$7 billion. It was in that year that the US trade balance with Japan slipped into deficit for the first time. By 1971, Japan's exports to the rest of the world had increased to US$23 billion, while the US trade deficit with Japan had climbed to US$3 billion. The cause of American monetary problems was the 'continuing deterioration of the US trade and payments position'.[52] Throughout 1971, there were rumours of the lack of confidence that foreign governments now had in the dollar. There was a dark suspicion that the Bank of England had asked for a guarantee against devaluation of its dollar holdings, which were now some US$3 billion. Other sources claimed that the British Ambassador himself had turned up at the Treasury Department to request that US$3 billion be converted into gold.[53] British officials denied this rumour. Yet in his diary entry for 12 August 1971 H. R. Haldeman, the President's Chief of Staff, mentioned that the British had asked 'for \$3 billion to be converted to gold'. 'If we gave it to them, other countries might follow suit. If we didn't, they might wonder if we had enough gold to support the dollar. In either case, it was a major crisis,' Haldeman noted.[54]

With inflation rising in the summer of 1971 and an insistent appeal for the government to take action, Nixon and his officials organized a weekend meeting on 13–15 August. The President and fifteen advisers went to Camp David to discuss potential policies. From this session there emerged a 'New Economic Policy' which would, it was hoped, for a ninety-day period 'freeze wages and prices to check inflation'. More dramatically, with longer-lasting consequences for the financial world, the gold window would be closed.[55] Burns argued vociferously against the closing of the window, which would decouple the dollar from gold. He warned that '*Pravda* would write that this was a sign of the collapse of capitalism.'[56] Burns was also said to have observed that 'the closing of the gold window' would make it seem as if the United States was 'murdering the international monetary system without proposing to put anything in its place'.[57]

The President, however, immune to such objections, boldly pursued the policy. In a televised speech relayed on the Sunday evening, interrupting the hit show *Bonanza*, Nixon declared, 'I have directed Secretary Connally to suspend temporarily the convertibility of the dollar into gold.' He observed that this 'action will not win us any friends among the international money traders. But our primary concern is with the American workers, and with fair competition around the world.' For good measure, as a demonstration that he would now be thinking of America first, the President imposed 'an additional tax of 10 percent on goods imported into the United States'.[58] This was the old protectionist tradition of Hamilton and the nineteenth-century Republicans being enlisted to support the dollar by eliminating the trade deficit. The various proposals outlined by Nixon constituted, according to *Time* magazine, 'the most comprehensive New Economic Policy to be undertaken by this nation in four decades'.[59] The Dow Jones stock market index reacted well to the news the following day, even though, in the view of the magazine, 'Nixon's measures threatened a serious reversal of the post-war trend toward freer trade.'

The day after the broadcast, Nixon paid lavish tribute to Connally, asserting in front of some of his less high-profile officials that this 'kind of program doesn't come off the top of a President's head'. Characteristically adopting the 'tough guy', sports-fan image he wished to project, he adopted a metaphor from American football: the radical policy, he added, had been 'developed by a great team quarterbacked by Secretary Connally'. Nixon himself, he went on, had been 'more like the coach' of the team. He concluded by saying that he had 'learned as much from the quarterback as he learned from me'.[60] Closing the gold window was indeed a momentous step in the history of the world's economic system. The dollar's link to gold had existed since the drafting of the United States Constitution. It had been suspended as a consequence of the Civil War, and then resumed. It had now finally been broken. The Bretton Woods Agreement, which had been predicated on a conversion of dollars into gold at the fixed rate of US$35 an ounce, had been unilaterally terminated.

In his 1993 book *The Death of Money*, Joel Kurtzman, a former editor of the *Harvard Business Review*, asserted that 'closing the gold window, although buried in a long laundry list of essentially useless economic policy changes, represented the biggest challenge to the world economy since the Great Depression'. From this time, the 'value of the dollar was no longer linked to the amount of gold in Fort Knox'. In a stern judgement, Kurtzman also alleged that by 'closing the gold window Nixon destroyed the carefully crafted post-World War II economic system and replaced it with what former German Chancellor Helmut Schmidt . . . called a "a floating non-system"'.[61] The end of Bretton Woods was noted as a significant event at the time. In 1972, Henry Brandon, the Washington correspondent of the British *Sunday Times* newspaper, observed that devaluation of the dollar, 'unthinkable in 1964, had become not only quite thinkable in the summer of 1971, but was effectively carried out by the year's end'. The fall of the 'once Almighty Dollar from its uniquely high pedestal' had caused 'no political shock waves for the President at home, although it caused some around the world'.

The change in the United States' position had been remarkable. 'The days when American pride was such that the United States had to be first in everything had gone.' The reason for this change, Brandon believed, was the 'acute sense of overstrain and a new perspective on the limits of power brought home with such a vengeance in Vietnam'. The old order had been overturned. The 'old confidence of power' had been replaced 'by a new maturity, an awareness that even supreme power has its limits'. The recognition of the limits of power had been accompanied by a more rugged attention to America's national interests as opposed to any international responsibilities. This was 'a reversal of the post-World War II settlement'. 'After twenty years of generosity (it was argued) and an outward-looking policy, the United States had to switch to a policy that would give priority to America's own national interests.'[62] Import tariffs and the end of the dollar's historic gold link, as announced in the President's broadcast of 15 August 1971, symbolized, in dramatic terms, the retreat of American power.

PART IV

PAPER: THE END OF GOLD, 1973–

The Impact of Oil

Shortly before 2 p.m. on 6 October 1973, 222 Egyptian jets took off, with the aim of bombing Israeli command posts on the eastern bank of the Suez Canal and in the Sinai peninsula. The day was Yom Kippur, the holiest day of the Jewish Year. This assault by the Egyptians began the fourth of the Arab–Israeli wars. One weapon was 'unique to the Middle East'. It was the oil weapon, 'wielded in the form of an embargo', which would induce production cutbacks and restrictions on oil exports.[1] The war itself had come as a shock to an unsuspecting world. The events of the summer of 1971, when President Nixon had ended the dollar's link to gold, were still fresh in the minds of international policymakers.

Nixon had followed his closing of the gold window in August 1971 with a devaluation in December, when he announced that the dollar, which had been pegged to a gold value of US\$35 an ounce, would be devalued by 8.5 per cent to US\$38 an ounce. The new gold price had been agreed on the Azores at a meeting held between Nixon and Georges Pompidou, a fastidious former Rothschilds banker who was now the President of France. During the meeting Pompidou had dominated the discussion, and had given the hapless Nixon a Gaullist lecture on the primacy of gold and the evils of a dollar standard.[2] The new monetary arrangement outlined in the Azores was agreed by representatives of the major economies at the Smithsonian Institution in Washington in December 1971. Nixon claimed that the compact constituted the 'greatest monetary agreement in the history of the world'. The Smithsonian Agreement had settled on a dollar standard, 'Bretton Woods without the gold'.[3]

According to Paul Volcker, who served as Chairman of the Federal Reserve from 1979 to 1987, the two years during which the Agreement held were 'the most economically turbulent of the postwar period up to that point'.⁴ Of course, events in the Middle East would soon alter the perception of what 'economic turbulence' really involved. The Yom Kippur War of October 1973 had been preceded by 'near-panic buying [of oil] by US and European independents [oil companies] as well as the Japanese'. These purchases sent 'oil prices sky-rocketing'.⁵ For years, the Arab world had spoken in hushed tones of the hazily defined 'oil weapon' that could be used to achieve their various objectives in the politics of their region. This threat had been disregarded so long as American oil production still had spare capacity. The oil fields of Texas, Louisiana and Oklahoma could always, it seemed, be relied upon to increase oil production, if demand increased. By the early 1970s, however, the United States had hit 100 per cent in terms of production rates. Arab oil production had now become the 'supply of last resort'.⁶ The United States could no longer increase production to supply its allies in the event of a crisis.

Meanwhile, the impact of the Gulf states had grown in the oil markets. Saudi Arabia's share of world exports had risen rapidly from 13 per cent in 1970 to 21 per cent just three years later. The Saudis had pushed up their daily production of oil. The average production in July 1973 had reached 8.4 million barrels per day, 62 per cent higher than the previous July. Given Saudi Arabia's vast reserves and the scale of its oil production, Anwar Sadat, the Egyptian President, in the spring of 1973 urged the Saudis to use this 'weapon' as a way of supporting Egypt in its struggle against the 'Zionist oppressor', Israel.

The travails of the dollar, its devaluation and the general lack of confidence that international markets were beginning to show towards the American economy had irritated the Arabs. Devaluation of the dollar had 'abruptly cut the worth of the financial holdings of countries with large dollar reserves, including Saudi Arabia'. As the Kuwaiti Oil Minister had put it, 'What is the point of producing more oil and selling it for an unguaranteed paper currency?' Even before the outbreak of war in October, Arab oil wealth had become a topic of fervent speculation and even envy in the West. In April 1973, *Time* magazine quoted James Akins, an energy expert in the US State Department, who later became US Ambassador to Saudi Arabia: 'With the possible exception of Croesus, the world will never have seen anything quite like the wealth that is flowing and will continue to flow into the Persian Gulf.'[7] The dollar's currency woes had continued after Nixon's announcement in August 1971. Although the dollar could no longer be exchanged for gold, there was still a fixed rate in operation. When gold was revalued at US$38 an ounce in December, it marked a dollar devaluation by 8.5 per cent. In February 1973, the dollar was devalued again, by a further 10 per cent. The dollar price of gold was now US$42. It was widely believed that the Arabs' sale of dollars had been a contributory factor in the second devaluation. In April of that year, *Time* magazine was already reporting that 'international bankers are deeply concerned about the effect the Arabs' growing financial power may have on the west in the next few years'.

Other writers and analysts began to remark on the new assertiveness which could be seen throughout the Arab world, and which, in their view, constituted a threat to Western and particularly American hegemony. In Libya, the young leader Colonel Gaddafi had begun a new phase of Arab self-assertion by rejecting the prevailing royalty rates, and forcing the oil companies to increase Libya's oil royalties by 20 per cent. Libyan oil revenue grew from US$1.1 billion in 1969 to US$2.07 billion in 1971. Gaddafi used his surging revenues to amass the 'largest gold and hard-currency reserves in the Arab world today' (April 1973), which amounted to US$2.9 billion.[8]

The oil embargo which was introduced at the end of October 1973 has been a matter of controversy ever since. On 16 October OPEC, the Organization of Petroleum Exporting Countries, imposed a dramatic price rise. In what has been described by Henry Kissinger as 'a stunning and unprecedented move', six Gulf states unilaterally raised the price of oil by 70 per cent from US$3.01 a barrel to US$5.12. At a meeting in Kuwait the following day, the Arab members of OPEC agreed to cut their production of oil by 5 per cent and to continue reducing it by an additional 5 per cent every month until Israel was induced to withdraw from all occupied Arab territories. Nixon responded, perhaps insensitively as far as the Arabs were concerned, by asking the Congress on 19 October for a US$2.2 billion package of assistance to Israel. This would be used to pay for the military equipment the Israelis were deploying against their Arab foes. In

Kissinger's measured words, the 'timing of the aid request could not have been more unfortunate'.[9] As the *Economist* in London observed on the 20th, the 'Arabs brandished their oil weapon on Wednesday'. It was clear to the *Economist*'s editorial team that the Arabs' 'only aim' was 'to bring about a change in America's policy towards Israel'.[10] Towards the end of 1973, the atmosphere of panic and unease began to disturb international markets.

The price of oil continued to climb to new heights. At the beginning of December, the *Economist* reported that 'oil men have been swarming into Lagos to see what extra supplies of non-Arab oil they can pick up'. On 15 November, the price of oil had hit US$16.80; in Wall Street the Dow Jones in the six weeks from mid-October to the end of November had fallen 15 per cent. The *Economist* even entitled its article on the nervousness of Wall Street, '1929 and all that'. Amid the political uncertainty, the gold price also continued to climb. By the middle of December 1973, the price of gold had reached 'around $105 an ounce', from only $90 an ounce a month earlier.[11] On 8 December, the *Economist* commented gravely that it was 'the big policy decisions that make money for investors': that was why 'those who decided to buy gold shares a year ago are still laughing'. The gold price had been helped by the rumour that 'the Arabs might insist on payments in gold'.[12]

The demise of Bretton Woods led to the beginning of the modern period, in which currencies, unpegged to any gold value, freely 'floated' in value against each other, like any other commodity. It was at the beginning of 1974 that the vulnerabilities of the newly floating currencies, and the relative security of gold, become more obvious. In April the European Economic Community (EEC), forerunner of the European Union, expressed concern about the instability of dollar values. The London *Financial Times*, in an article about the nine member states of the EEC entitled 'Nine to seek US backing for gold price plan', explained that the price of gold had been fixed 'for over 30 years' at $35 an ounce. The paper recalled that 'throughout the 1960s suggestions for dealing with what was then a shortage of world liquidity' by increasing the official dollar price of gold had been 'greeted with derision, particularly in Washington'.[13] It referred to the devaluation of the dollar under the

Smithsonian Agreement of December 1971 which raised the official price of gold to $38 an ounce, and to the subsequent devaluation in February 1973 which saw an official gold price of $42.22 an ounce. The 'speculative explosion in the private gold market', however, had made these small incremental increases in the official gold price into 'material for the financial museum'.

The official gold price was now a meaningless anachronism, as the gold price soared. On 9 January 1974, the *Financial Times* reported that the gold price had hit historic levels, rising US$4.75 to reach its 'highest ever closing price of $127 an ounce'.[14] This meant that the US$35 an ounce established at Bretton Woods had more than tripled. The 1970s would be the greatest decade for the gold investor in all history. From a high of $127 in January 1974, the price increased steadily through the ensuing months to reach $197.5 an ounce on the last trading day of that year. The gold price continued to rise through the decade before hitting US$850 an ounce in January 1980, as Soviet tanks rolled into Afghanistan.[15]

The central banks' inability to contain gold speculation had been the reason for the creation of the Gold Pool in 1961 and the establishment of a two-tier market in 1968. In a summary account of the gold reserves of different industrial countries, the *Financial Times* valued the gold holdings of the various economically powerful nations at the end of 1973 using an anachronistic official price of $42.22 an ounce. The United States was the biggest holder of gold reserves, but, with a value of US$11.7 billion, the 1973 figure was significantly below the value of officially held US gold in the 1950s and 1960s. The Germans' stocks were the next most valuable with US$5 billion, with the French not far behind with their US$4.3 billion stock. Per head of population, Switzerland with its US$3.5 billion reserve easily held the most gold. Japan and the United Kingdom, perhaps for historic reasons, held only US$891 million and US$886 million respectively. Gold was interesting but did not necessarily confer prosperity. Yet it had become increasingly apparent that the rise in its value had been spurred by the more uncertain economic environment. 'It is distrust of currencies which has driven the value of gold upwards,' the *Financial Times* article of April 1974 concluded.[16]

Meanwhile, the spring of 1974 saw the end of the embargo on

shipments of oil to the United States. The embargo had remained in effect for only five months, but when it was finally lifted in March the cost of crude oil had increased four times. It now cost around US$12 per barrel as against a pre-embargo level of US$3 per barrel. An assessment of the oil embargo written in 1978 showed that the 'subsequent quadrupling of the world price of oil set into motion inflationary forces that are still rippling through the world economy'. The mood throughout the mid- to late 1970s was gloomy and depressed. Contemporaries spoke of the 'Great Recession'. It was recalled that the 'price of oil had actually been falling through most of the postwar period, both absolutely and in relation to other world prices'.[17] The oil shock of 1973 led to 'visions of financial disaster for the west'. The spike in oil prices had increased all costs in the Western economies, which were heavily dependent on oil. 'Prices were higher and employment lower' as a consequence of the oil shock.[18] Despite the arguments of a later generation of economists, contemporaries were very clear about the direct causal link between higher oil prices, increased inflation and stagnant economies. The Harvard economist Otto Eckstein wrote in 1978 that the 'erosion of purchasing power caused by higher energy prices affected all categories of consumer spending'. At the same date, he also stated that the 'energy crisis was the single largest cause of the Great Recession'.[19]

The economic downturn of the 1970s, perhaps even more than the Vietnam War itself, typified for a generation of Americans how far their country had fallen. The Arabs' increase in the price of oil was a vivid indicator of the new forces shaping global politics, forces which were less controllable by a beleaguered White House. The Watergate affair, in which President Nixon was suspected of ordering an illegal entry by members of his staff into the Democratic Party headquarters, had further undermined confidence in one of the United States' most revered institutions. The *Economist* spoke for the financial community when it observed in November 1973 that 'American investors have been watching Watergate and the oil crisis and not liking what they have seen.'[20] A couple of months later, in January 1974, the same newspaper, in a perceptive analysis, referred to the 'shift in the balance of economic power' which had been witnessed in 1973. For 'more than twenty years

Western Europe and Japan have prospered on plentiful dollars and cheap oil'. Abundantly cheap oil had 'powered the growth of industry (particularly in Japan)'.[21] This had been stopped abruptly by the Arabs' actions in October 1973.

The shifting economic power balance in the world was a subject on which journalists of the time continually discoursed. The once mighty dollar seemed to have been eclipsed by the power of oil. None represented this new power better than the staid King Faisal of Saudi Arabia, whom Sadat had encouraged to use the 'oil weapon' in the spring of 1973. Faisal was one of the sons of Ibn Saud, the founder of the kingdom of Saudi Arabia. He was a mild, rather austere figure who described himself as a 'staunch friend of the United States'.[22] One of his favourite proverbs was 'God gave man two ears and tongue so we could listen twice as much as we talk,' and, true to this precept the King was himself taciturn and reflective. The simplicity of his manners, his seeming disdain for the trappings of wealth and luxury, were attractive to his people. In a profile in *Time* magazine, whose 'Man of the Year' award he won in 1974, Faisal was described as a hard-working, modest monarch who had shown enlightened liberalism by permitting 'Saudi women to be educated in schools for the first time'. As a result of a series of ulcer operations on his stomach, the King's diet was simple, consisting mainly of boiled rice.[23] After his assassination in March 1975, the King was also described as 'a rare mixture of piety, shrewdness and inner calm'.

This almost spiritual figure, however, played a significant role on the world stage in the last couple of years of his life. It was in the 'past 18 months', his obituary recorded, 'since the Arab–Israeli war in October 1973, and its economic consequences, that the power of this absolute ruler had stretched out so far beyond his own kingdom to touch the lives of people almost everywhere'.[24] Faisal fell victim to one of his nephews in a blood feud. The source of his country's newly acquired wealth continued to soar in value. Oil, throughout the 1970s, became a symbol of wealth and power. Outside members of the royal family, the man who most symbolized the international prestige of Saudi Arabia was Sheikh Ahmed Zaki Yamani, a strictly observant Muslim who had been educated briefly at New York University and Harvard Law School.

Yamani's prominence in the realm of international diplomacy stemmed from the oil power of the kingdom he represented, in which he served as Oil Minister. As Faisal's closest adviser, he had been showered with gifts and favours by a grateful King and it was fitting that when the King was shot he lay dying in Yamani's arms. It was after the Saudi oil embargo to the United States had ended in the spring of 1974 that the boom time really came to Saudi Arabia. From 1974 until well into 1976, 'with oil flowing like Manna from heaven, Saudi Arabia was the California gold rush in spades'.[25] The Saudis themselves were spending their new-found wealth with abandon. Sir John Witton, a British diplomat who arrived at the Embassy in Riyadh in 1976, remembered how 'Saudi prosperity manifested itself in a total blockage of the ports.' He spoke of the 'incredible sight' of 'hundreds of ships queuing off Jeddah, waiting to unload'. This was also the time when tales were told about 'piles of merchandise, rusting, rotting, being eaten by rats on the quayside'. The Saudis had bought 'all over the world and they sent the goods home', but then they 'couldn't get anything off the ships and into use'.[26]

Increased revenues, which flowed into the treasuries of the oil-exporting countries, altered the international economic environment. David Rockefeller, scion of the wealthy dynasty and Chairman of the Chase Manhattan Bank, recalled that the 'most immediate effect of the oil shock was the surge in the flow of dollars from oil-importing nations into OPEC's coffers. Between 1973 and 1977, the earnings of the oil-exporting nations expanded 600 percent, to US$140 billion.' There lay the problem confronting the world monetary system. The enormous dollar reserves acquired by the oil exporters needed to find some outlet. Rockefeller, somewhat self-importantly, remembered that the 'task of recycling [these] dollars and maintaining the system of global trade and finance fell to the major international commercial banks, including Chase'. A graduate of Harvard, he was the archetypal moderate conservative banker, complete with a grey business suit and a large network of high-level connections. His elder brother, Nelson, gave his name to the 'Rockefeller Republicans', a group of moderate, high-spending, patrician Republicans. David Rockefeller, as a conservative banker, expressed 'uneasiness about the process' of recycling petrodollars. Others, like Walter Wriston, the Chairman of Chase's arch-rival Citicorp, were more enthusiastic about issuing general loans at low interest rates to sovereign borrowers in Latin America.[27]

The dollars amassed by the Gulf states confronted them with a serious problem. Each state solved this problem in its own distinctive way. Saudi Arabia, the world's largest exporter of oil, 'placed most of its enormous new revenues with US banks . . . or in US Treasury bonds'. The Kuwaitis, 'less conservative', invested 'most of their revenues in the US and European money and stock markets'.[28] Meanwhile both the Shah of Iran and Saddam Hussein, the Iraqi Vice President, used their new oil revenues to build infrastructure, to invest in education and, more ominously, to buy military hardware.[29] Chase Manhattan and its American competitor banks were active in recycling the so-called 'petrodollars', the dollars earned by oil exports, as loans to foreign businesses. Loans were also extended to Latin America, Africa, East Asia and other parts of the developing world.[30]

Other American bankers and senior officials began to express anxiety about the political and economic outlook. Paul Volcker, the future Chairman of the Federal Reserve, remembered that by mid-decade the 'combination of accelerating inflation and the oil shock late in 1973' went far in 'establishing floating currencies as the . . . international monetary system'. The mid-1970s were marked by 'what was then the most serious of the postwar recessions' and by ever-higher inflation. Floating currencies, and the end of any link to gold, were a novel feature of the period. It had been assumed that 'both exchange rates and economies would stabilize as the world gained experience' with floating rates. This hope, as the 1970s progressed, proved delusional. Meanwhile, changes in the US administration in 1974 brought William Simon, a former bond trader, to the position of Treasury Secretary.

Simon adopted an aggressively pro-market approach to the problems of currency and public finance which confronted the US and many of the advanced economies of the world in the 1970s. In Volcker's words, his 'experience and free market ideology were of one piece'.[31] William Simon came into government from Wall Street, where he had been a high-ranking executive at Salomon Brothers, the investment bank, which had supported Nixon's re-election in 1972. Appointed Treasury Secretary in May 1974, he was one of the disgraced President's last cabinet appointments. Nixon's successor, Gerald Ford, however, confirmed the appointment and the Treasury Secretary remained in post for a further two and a half years. Simon's perspective on the growth of government was somewhat unorthodox for the mid-1970s, but men of his opinions would find greater voice and influence in the 1980s. His analysis of the problems facing America, as set out in his 1978 memoirs *A Time for Truth*, very much chimed with what would become the prevailing philosophy under the leadership of President Reagan in the United States and Margaret Thatcher in the United Kingdom.

Simon was no great intellectual. In his memoirs he recounted his college days at Lafayette College, Pennsylvania, where 'such ambitions' as he possessed and all his 'capacity for gruelling self-discipline were directed into sports'. 'Virtuoso performances as a card player' were also happily remembered. Despite a less than stellar academic record, Simon found success on Wall Street and had very clear ideas about the economy when he became a member of Nixon's cabinet. In his formulation, the problem facing America was essentially simple. It was government itself which was the problem. 'When we see this monstrous growth of government, we must realize that it is not a matter of narrow economic issues,' he declared to a House of Representatives subcommittee in April 1976. 'What is at stake is the fundamental freedom in one of the last, and greatest, democracies in the world.'[32]

The problem, as Simon saw it, extended beyond the wide shores of the United States. 'Just look at what has happened in other countries today,' he told the members of the House subcommittee, 'whether it be Italy, or the United Kingdom or Argentina or Uruguay or Ceylon. Look at what has happened there when the so-called "humanitarians" try to create "Great Societies" by taxing and promising and spending.' Using a form of analysis which would become popular in the 1970s, he looked at figures relating to the supply of money, the nominal amount of cash and deposits in the economy. It was certain that 'the government was printing money hand over fist to help finance its expenditures'. 'From 1956 to 1965', Simon pointed out, 'the money supply expanded at an average of 2.3 percent.' But 'between 1966 and 1975, as the government engaged in runaway spending . . . the average annual money growth rate rose to 5.8 percent'.[33]

Increased government spending was also accompanied by increased lending by the commercial banks which, having been 'encouraged by government policies, [were] caught up in the go-go craze, both at home and abroad'. Simon also complained about the high level of company indebtedness, caused by the irresponsibility of politicians who 'were telling them [US companies] that the business cycle was dead, that the government could now keep the economy expanding indefinitely'. In sum, he concluded, it was not just 'federal government that was on an inflationary spending binge'. The binge had 'extended to the populace at large'.[34] In Simon's robust analysis the difficulties of the 1970s had been a natural consequence of the 'suicidal policies of the past'. Government debt-fuelled spending was, as ever, the root cause of this malaise. 'It took us [the United States] a hundred and seventy-one years to get a federal budget of a hundred billion dollars a years . . . That was 1960. Within nine years we had reached two hundred billion dollars. And two years from now, if present trends are not reversed, we will reach four hundred billion dollars. The very existence of our free economy depends on getting government spending under control.'[35]

Simon's views on public spending were aligned to the changing intellectual mood of the 1970s. It was in 1976, after all, that Milton Friedman received the Nobel Prize for economics. Friedman was a doctrinaire free-trade advocate who had been instructed in economics at Rutgers by none other than Arthur F. Burns, Nixon's appointee as Chairman of the Federal Reserve. Isaiah Berlin, the British philosopher, famously categorized intellectuals as either hedgehogs or foxes. The 'fox knows many things but the hedgehog knows one big thing'. Friedman was a hedgehog who championed the same ideas about money for more than fifty years. The core of his thinking was that government should 'keep its hands off the economy, to let the free market do its work'.[36] It was against this background that his well-known and enduring commitment to monetarism must be understood. Monetarism allowed the government only one lever to influence the economy, the control of the supply of money. Friedman, of course, had been renowned for many years for his work on the causes of inflation. He objected to the way in which post-war policymakers had loosened monetary policy by deficit spending in order to reduce unemployment. As the

Economist remembered in Friedman's obituary notice published in 2006, in the 1970s 'rich economies suffered rising inflation and higher, not lower, unemployment, despite governments' efforts to inflate their way out of trouble'. To deal with this phenomenon, Freidman recommended a 'stable monetary framework'. By this phrase he meant 'setting a target for the growth of the money supply, a rule known as monetarism'.[37] As if to emphasize his political affiliations, Friedman even contributed the preface to William Simon's memoirs *A Time for Truth*. 'This is a brilliant and passionate book by a brilliant and passionate man,' he wrote.[38]

To many economists bred on the cosy post-war Keynesian consensus, Friedman's ideas seemed exciting and novel. To a historian with even a cursory knowledge of monetary history, monetarism was simply a way of providing a stable monetary environment in a world of floating currencies. It was an attempt to recover the certainty of the gold standard. The policy prescriptions of Milton Friedman, his desire for stable monetary growth and his scepticism about government spending, particularly with regard to deficits, would have been entirely familiar to Sir Robert Peel and William Gladstone. The nineteenth-century mantra of a sound currency and balanced budgets was not, in reality, far removed from the ideas of the monetarists.

The emergence of monetarism as a theory in the 1970s was really a cry of despair. Years of deficit financing, the final collapse of the Bretton Woods Agreement, now compounded by a sharp hike in oil prices, had led to a world of reduced optimism and weaker economic prospects. The inelegant word 'stagflation', which, as its name implied, meant a combination of economic stagnation and inflation, was a characteristic concept of the time. Monetarism was a theoretical attempt to bring order back to a distracted economic world. In much the same way, the development of the gold standard itself had been a response to a familiar problem, the tendency of governments to spend beyond their means and print money – which, of course, historically had been a result of fighting wars. The United States in the 1970s, with its dramatic spending on defence in the context of the Cold War with the Soviet Union, its commitment to the Great Society and its rising inflation, in some ways had the characteristics of a war economy.

Nineteen-seventy-six was also significant as a presidential election year. In November, James Earl Carter defeated the incumbent Gerald Ford by a slim 2 per cent margin in the popular vote. During the campaign itself and afterwards, the victor emphasized 'the long and deep recession in 1974–1975 and the slow recovery'. Yet Carter, a liberal Southerner, focused on promising full employment, without paying any attention to the dangers of inflation. He explained that he had never been asked about inflation during the entirety of the campaign, but 'only about employment'.[39] He tried to impose his priorities on the government and met resistance. Arthur Burns openly opposed the administration's policies, by claiming that 'budget deficits and labor unions' were 'major causes of inflation'.[40] Carter's programme had not been influenced in any way by the monetarism espoused by Milton Friedman which was then beginning to become fashionable. As Paul Volcker remembered, Jimmy Carter's appointments to the 'main economic posts in the Treasury, the Council of Economic Advisers, and the State Department were of a quite different breed from the monetarists predominant during the later Nixon–Ford years'. Carter's people all had 'professional training in economics and had seen substantial governmental service in the 1960s'. These advisers and officials supported 'floating exchange rates' and shared, by 'instinct and experience', the 'Keynesian faith in the ability of governments to maximize the performance of the economy and indeed of the market itself'.[41]

The persistence of inflation in the second half of the 1970s well into the Carter presidency created yet more uncertainty and despondency. The years 1976–8 saw the return of higher inflation.[42] Paul Volcker, who would be appointed Chairman of the Federal Reserve by Jimmy Carter in 1979, spoke in 1978 about the recession of 1974 and 1975 which had 'sprung on an unsuspecting world with an intensity unmatched in the post-World War II period'. 'Now,' he said, 'three years later, the industrialized world is still faced with a combination of high levels of unemployment and inflation.'[43] Volcker went on to suggest that the 'very severity of the recession also helped expose some financial weaknesses that were not characteristic of earlier post-World War II recessions'.[44]

It is difficult, perhaps, for a generation which witnessed the financial crisis of 2008 to understand the gloom and pessimism of the 1970s. In the

United States, in particular, the 1970s were a decade of self-doubt and economic failure. This mood is captured in many of the presidential speeches and congressional debates of the period. No other public statement of this type captured the mood so well as President Carter's own addresses to the nation. In a remarkable television address from the White House delivered in July 1979, he declared that the 'erosion of confidence in the future is threatening to destroy the social and the political fabric of America'.

This was an extraordinary utterance from a United States President. Whereas Roosevelt had projected sunny optimism in the 1930s in the depths of terrible economic hardship, Carter did the opposite in his address, admitting that 'For the first time in the history of our country a majority of our people believe that the next 5 years will be worse than the past 5 years'. The President reminded the American people of their violent history, particularly with respect to the previous decade, during which the naive hopes nursed by an optimistic nation were shattered. 'We were sure that ours was a nation of the ballot, not the bullet, until the murders of John Kennedy and Robert Kennedy and Martin Luther King Jr.' The country, in the President's rather bleak summation, had failed in the sphere of armed conflict. 'We were taught that our armies were always invincible and our causes were always just, only to suffer the agony of Vietnam.' In his wide-ranging survey of American institutions and their relative decline, Carter even included the office of the President. 'We respected the Presidency as a place of honor until the shock of Watergate.' Even America's currency arrangements did not escape the withering glare of his irony. 'We remember when the phrase "sound as a dollar" was an expression of absolute dependability, until 10 years of inflation began to shrink our dollar and our savings.'[45]

In this address, which lasted little more than half an hour, President Carter gave what was perhaps the most downbeat assessment of their country that any American President had ever delivered to the American people. His words were echoed almost continually in the press in the course of the late 1970s. Early 1979 witnessed the deposition of the Shah of Iran in the wake of a radical Islamist revolution. The economic effect of these dramatic events was a second oil shock, in which the price of oil rose

30 per cent in a week, from US$13 a barrel to US$17. The disruption of Iranian oil supplies was significant for America, because they accounted for about 5 per cent of US petroleum needs. The impact, however, was more pronounced in other countries of the developed world, since Iran normally supplied 'about 20% of the total petroleum imports of all the consuming nations', with Japan and Western Europe being particularly exposed to any shortfall in Iranian oil production.[46] The 'chaos in Iran, plus another sharp OPEC boost in oil prices, added up to what the Japanese increasingly referred to as "the second oil crisis"'.[47]

The mood at the end of the 1970s was one of resigned defeatism in the United States, the architect and protector of the post-war capitalist system. As Soviet tanks rolled into Afghanistan in December 1979, Americans were openly questioning the basis of their economic model. The Cold War can never be disregarded by anyone considering the global economic situation during that period. In October 1979, *Time* magazine in an article entitled 'The Squeeze of '79' pronounced the 1970s 'the decade of recurring recession, relentless inflation and repeated runs on the no longer almighty dollar'. It was in the realm of the currency and stock markets that the decline of the once proud United States could most vividly be captured. *Time* described in lurid terms how in 'just five days, the market dive left investors with some $55 billion in paper losses and sent the Dow Jones industrial average plunging a total of 58.62 points to a week's close of 838.99'. Many Americans were left wondering 'whether they were about to be flattened by a 50th Anniversary replay of the October 1929 Wall Street collapse'.

The nerves in the market had been shaken by some 'coolly deliberate steps that the men who manage the US's money had made in hopes of stabilizing the wobbly dollar and pulling down inflation, now running at a blistering annual rate of 13.1%'. The *Time* article expressed the determination behind Volcker's policy in dealing with inflation. Volcker himself, appointed Chairman of the Federal Reserve in August, was a bureaucrat, an economist who had spent most of his career in public service. Now aged fifty-two, he described himself as a 'pragmatic monetarist' who was unafraid to make tough decisions in fighting inflation. From the point of view of the politicians, a renewed focus on fighting inflation would prove costly and unpopular. Volcker's 'pragmatic monetarism', argued *Time*, was 'bound to make the nation's developing recession deeper and thus further cloud the re-election chances of Jimmy Carter'. Yet there was a widespread appreciation that the 'Fed's new anti-inflation activism' was 'one of the most hopeful signs in a decade that Washington is at last becoming serious about combating the economy's debilitating price spiral'. Volcker's policy was straightforward. Interest rates would be 'going up, perhaps to levels that would have seemed wholly unimaginable only a few months ago'.[48] Higher interest rates and a squeezed money supply would tackle the problems of surging inflation and the depreciation of the dollar. From November 1978, the Fed had initiated a number of moves designed to support the value of the dollar in international markets, but 'inflation kept rampaging domestically, and eventually the dollar began to crumble all over again'. In the meantime, the price of gold scaled new highs, reaching a record US$447 an ounce in October 1979, before settling back and rebounding. Gold would reach an all-time high in January 1980 of US$850 an ounce, a level which would not be attained again for nearly twenty-five years.[49]

The Fed's discount interest rate rose from 13.5 per cent to a new peak of 14.5 per cent in October 1979, and commercial banks like Chase Manhattan increased their rates in response. Controlling the money supply would prove challenging for the Federal Reserve. One considerable danger continued to be 'the threat of an outright credit crunch', in the words of *Time* magazine in its October 1979 piece. Such an eventuality would occur if the 'Federal Reserve's tightening up of money, and the resulting rise in interest rates, reach such levels that borrowers found it impossible to get money on almost any terms'.[50] The situation outlined in this scenario was classical in its character. A rise in interest rates had notoriously forced Wall Street into the death spiral of the end of 1929. It was widely accepted that tight money could strangle business investment, and that the most effective means of achieving this outcome was through an overly aggressive increase in interest rates. *Time* recalled that such a 'squeeze [had] occurred in the summer and fall of 1974, and almost immediately forced businesses to lay off upwards of 2 million workers'.

With admirable realism, the article proposed that 'something like a credit crunch may be the only thing that can break the nation's addiction to easy money'. Volcker, *Time* concluded, 'had brought monetary policy-making fully into the fight to hold prices down'. The President had insisted at a press conference towards the end of October 1979 that 'whatever it takes to control inflation, that's what I'll do'. This marked a change from the rhetoric with which he had begun his presidency, when the main worry was employment. Nobody had talked about inflation on Carter's campaign trail, yet it was inflation which had become his principal concern at the end of 1979. Volcker personified this determination to fight inflation. According to *Time*, it was the 'first genuine hope of the Carter administration that someone might have both a will and a way to deal with the inflation menace'.[51]

While Volcker, along with his increasingly beleaguered President, was fighting the 'inflation menace', one of his predecessors, Arthur F. Burns, was publicly meditating on the nature of the central banker's art. In a lecture entitled 'The Anguish of Central Banking' delivered in September 1979 in Belgrade, the capital of what was then Yugoslavia, Burns reflected on the 1950s. He remembered them as 'a decade of great prosperity, a decade in which we had a stable price level, and also as an era of social tranquillity'. He believed that the time was now ripe to adopt some of the home truths which had been neglected in the intervening two decades. There had been a 'recognition', he suggested, 'by the United States that the persisting deficits in its international currency account must be eliminated'. 'Benign neglect' of the external value of the dollar had to be discontinued. 'Even Germany and Switzerland', paragons of monetary orthodoxy in the past, could 'no longer qualify as islands of stability'.

Burns shared his successor's view that inflation was the principal economic misfortune of the age, a view endorsed by President Carter himself towards the end of his presidency. The 'current instability in international finance is largely a consequence of the chronic inflation of our times and . . . stability will not return to the international monetary system until reasonably good control over inflationary forces has been achieved in the major industrial nations – and especially in the United States'.[52] Burns went on: 'One of the time-honored functions of a central bank is to protect the integrity of its nation's currency, both domestically and internationally.' Yet central bankers had 'failed so utterly in this mission in recent years'. According to Burns, in this paradox lay 'the anguish of central banking'.[53]

Burns offered a damning indictment of American economic policy since 1950. In his historical account, a 'tradition of individualism was shattered by the cataclysmic events of the 1930s and 1940s'. A 'persistent inflationary bias' had emerged from 'the philosophic and political currents that have been transforming economic life in the United States and elsewhere since the 1930s'. He spoke of the 'breakdown of economic order during the Great Depression' which had been 'unprecedented in its scale and scope'. This had 'strained the precept of self-reliance beyond the breaking point'. The federal government had then taken on a 'far larger responsibility in the economic sphere than it had hitherto assumed'.

These remarks were uncontroversial, but Burns then suggested that since the war there had been 'a strong inflationary bias to the American economy'. This had been caused in part by the 'proliferation of government programs' which had led 'to progressively higher tax burdens on both individuals and corporations'. Despite increased taxation, the 'willingness of government to levy taxes fell distinctly short of its propensity to spend'. Since 1950, the 'federal budget has been in balance in only five years'. More alarmingly for Burns, since 1970 a deficit had occurred 'in every year'. Moreover, the deficits had 'been mounting in size'. Budget deficits had 'thus become a chronic condition of federal finance; they have been incurred when business conditions were poor and also when business was booming'. In Burns's analysis government deficits led directly to the inflation which had been the curse of the decade. When 'the government runs a budget deficit, it pumps more money into the pocketbooks of people than it withdraws from their pocketbooks'. As a consequence, the 'demand for goods and services there tends to increase all around'. This was the mechanism by which the 'inflation that has been raging since the mid-1960s first got started and later kept being nourished'. This had been not only an American phenomenon, as other industrial countries had subscribed to very much the same 'philosophic and political currents that transformed economic life' in America. These currents had introduced what Burns called 'secular inflation in the United States'.[54]

As a concluding remark, Burns observed how among economists 'the Keynesian school has lost much of its erstwhile vigor, self-confidence, and influence'. In many ways, he was talking long after the shift had happened. Across the Atlantic Ocean, in Britain, the Prime Minister James Callaghan had already in 1976, at the Labour Party conference in Blackpool, asserted that 'We used to think you could spend your way out of a recession, and increase employment by cutting taxes and boosting Government spending.' He continued, 'I tell you in all candour that that option no longer exists.'[55] Callaghan went on to be defeated by Margaret Thatcher at the general election held in May 1979. Thatcher herself remembered her victory as a change which defined an era. Her government would be conducted under different lines. Her election was a political realization of the shift in economic thought, embodied by Milton Friedman and his school, which had occurred in the mid-1970s.

Thatcher and Reagan

The victory of Margaret Thatcher in the British general election of 1979 was an historic event. For the first time in a Western country, a woman had been elected to the highest office. Yet Thatcher herself was less affected by the implications for gender equality of her success. She was motivated more by the force of her ideas. In her memoir of her premiership, *The Downing Street Years*, published in 1993 less than three full years after her departure from the office, she stated her convictions in stark, unequivocal terms. Her ideology was clear and emphatic. 'No theory of government was ever given a fairer test or a more prolonged experiment in a democratic country than democratic socialism received in Britain. Yet it was a miserable failure in every respect,' she claimed.[1] The extent to which she was committed to an ideological path, when she was first elected in 1979, has been contested, but certain hallmarks of her philosophy and style were immediately apparent.

Regarding her first budget, Thatcher believed that her 'general approach was well known'. Monetarism, the tight control of the money supply, as advocated by Milton Friedman, was the order of the day. 'Firm control of the money supply', in Thatcher's own crisp words, 'was necessary to bring down inflation.' Coupled with the stern approach to inflation implied by a strict adherence to monetarism was the commitment to curb public spending. 'Cuts in public expenditure and borrowing were needed.' This 'need', in Thatcher's later view, arose from the desire to 'lift the burden on the wealth-creating private sector'.[2] The ideological commitment can be seen in the way in which her administration removed controls on foreign exchange which had been introduced in 1939. As she subsequently recollected, she 'took greatest personal pleasure in the removal of exchange

controls', which in her view had been maintained by successive governments 'largely in the hope of increasing industrial investment in Britain
and of resisting pressures on sterling'.

Her opponents within the Conservative Party and outside were equally
happy in ascribing ideological motives to her decision to remove these
controls. Ian Gilmour, an aristocratic member of her first cabinet who was
quickly dismissed in her first reshuffle in 1981, remembered that her decision to abolish exchange controls was due to the 'Thatcherite's ideological
belief in the invariable beneficence of market forces'.³ Thatcher's Chancellor
of the Exchequer, Geoffrey Howe, was a quietly spoken barrister with
great determination. He later recalled that Denis Healey, the former
Labour Chancellor, had damned the decision to eliminate exchange
controls as 'reckless, precipitate and doctrinaire', and that William Keegan,
an economic commentator for the liberal-left *Observer* newspaper, had
rashly predicted that unless 'economic miracles occur, we shall have
controls reimposed in some form by 1985'.⁴ Nigel Lawson, Howe's successor as Chancellor in 1983, remembered the abolition of exchange controls
as a 'radical and highly controversial step', since it was 'impossible to
predict the scale of the capital outflow which might result'. Abolition was
'a leap in the dark'.⁵

Lawson was as ideologically motivated as Thatcher. As a junior minister
in the Treasury in 1979, he was a staunch supporter of the Prime Minister's
programme. For him, the abolition of exchange controls was the 'first
significant increase of market liberalization undertaken by the Thatcher
Government'. Without this important step, he believed, 'the City would
have been hard put to remain a world-class financial centre'. More broadly,
he saw implementation of this policy as an 'important blow for freedom',
since it was part of a worldwide advance towards the goal of 'freedom of
capital movements'. This new-found freedom 'changed the entire international financial and economic environment'. It was a fine instance, in
Lawson's recollection, of 'defying consensus', and he warmly praised
'Geoffrey Howe's courage and determination in seeing it through'.⁶

The free movement of capital was an ideological notion which underpinned the neo-liberal philosophy espoused by Margaret Thatcher and her
supporters within the government. There were, however, within the

government itself dissentient voices. Thatcher seemed to thrive on the conflict and tension generated by debate within her government. Her style was that of a crusader fighting for a holy cause against infidels too weak or too stubborn to grasp the truth. Combined with a commitment to the free movement of capital, there was the rhetoric about expenditure cuts, which many critics have suggested was more argued in principle than achieved in practice. But the rhetoric was powerful, and Thatcher herself remembered that in striving for such cuts she was determined to 'make as vigorous a start as possible'.

It was in the realm of public spending that many of her most public disagreements with other members of her government arose. 'In July 1979,' as she recalled, 'when the crucial decisions were being hammered out, we had a series of particularly testing (and testy) Cabinet discussions on the issue.' The government's goal was to 'bring public expenditure back to the 1977–8 level in real terms'. Ministers hoped to achieve this by 1982–3. But despite the reductions they had achieved, Thatcher believed, 'public expenditure was already threatening to run out of control'. Nevertheless, 'there was strong opposition from some ministers to the cuts'. These were 'the so-called "wets" who over the next few years took their opposition to our economic strategy to the very brink of resignation'.[7] Thatcher was explicit in her disavowal of the Keynesian consensus. For her opponents, on the other hand, 'who had not heard that Keynes was dead, the prospect of reducing expenditure and curbing borrowing as we and the world sank into recession was undoubtedly alarming'.

Thatcher was also committed to retreating from spending commitments made by the outgoing Labour government. She was adamant that an increase in public sector pay 'which was forecast to be 18 per cent, and which would cost another £4.5 billion', should not take place. 'We had to make reductions of £6.5 billion in the expenditure plans for 1980–81, just to hold the PSBR [Public Sector Borrowing Requirement] in that year down to £9 billion.' The Public Sector Borrowing Requirement was simply the amount the government needed to borrow to pay for government spending. It was the old name for the budget deficit. For Margaret Thatcher this figure was 'in itself too high', but 'the "wets" continued to oppose the cuts both in Cabinet and in the indecent obscurity of leaks to the

Guardian'.[8] Underlying this stern commitment to curb public spending, there lurked in the mind of Margaret Thatcher and her more ardent supporters a deep suspicion of the public sector, which she herself never hid. 'We had to make further attempts to curb public spending and borrowing – no matter how difficult – because otherwise private enterprise would have to bear a crushing burden of public sector profligacy.'[9]

Thatcher's very language, the metaphors she often employed, in the service of her arguments were moralistic and, some might say, almost religious in their tone. 'Profligacy' was a potent word to describe the public sector of which, as Prime Minister, Thatcher was the nominal head. Again, writing about 1980, she said that 'the most bitter Cabinet arguments were over public spending'. This opposition, in her view, was partly the consequence of ministers 'trying to protect their departmental budgets'. But the theoretical opposition was directed against the whole idea of monetarism, which was linked to the notion of controlling the money supply and thus, indirectly at least, to reining in public spending. As already observed, these features of monetarism were not that different, in their practical force, from the old Peelite mantra, emanating from the City of London in the nineteenth century, of a sound currency and balanced budgets.

It has almost become a cliché to suggest that Margaret Thatcher, a grocer's daughter, brought the values of a provincial shopkeeper into government, but such an assessment is very plausible. The values of her Methodist upbringing, the emphasis on thrift and good housekeeping which she imbibed almost from her cradle, were derived largely from the nineteenth century. In Gilmour's rather sneering judgement, 'Thatcherism largely consisted of nineteenth-century individualism dressed up in twentieth-century clothes.'[10] This was something of which Margaret Thatcher would have been proud. As one of her biographers, the left-leaning historian John Campbell, has written: 'Growing up in a shop is a very particular upbringing . . . the shopkeeper makes his living very visibly: there is no mystery or reticence about it. Every penny is taken over the counter, and reckoned up the same evening . . . A small shop thus displays the working of the market in its purest form.' According to Campbell, the 'child of a shopkeeper cannot grow up ignorant of the facts of economic life', and a grocer was also dependent on 'international trade'. The Lincolnshire grocer's instincts were those articulated by such nineteenth-century luminaries of liberalism and free trade as John Bright and Richard Cobden. In relation to groceries, John Bright had called for 'a free break-fast table'. He wanted to 'get rid of the heavy duties upon tea, coffee, and sugar'.[11] It was hardly surprising, given her upbringing in a shop in Grantham, that Thatcher grew up to be 'a passionate believer in global free trade, impatient of protectionist tariffs and political cartels'.[12]

Thatcher understood the nature of the Keynesian objections put forward by the 'wets'. 'The "wets" argued that because we had embraced a dogmatic monetary theory that inflation could only be brought down by a fierce monetary squeeze, we were squeezing the economy in the middle of a recession.'[13] Indeed this was the main charge levelled by the 'wets' against what Ian Gilmour in his memoirs called the 'monetarist frenzy'. Gilmour went on to describe monetarism as the 'guiding doctrine and principle' of Thatcherism.[14] To him, Thatcher was 'very much the First Lord of the Treasury', the historic title of the British Prime Minister, though a number of post-war Prime Ministers, notably Anthony Eden and Churchill himself, had not bothered themselves with the finer details of economic policy. To Thatcher, the 'wets' made the connection between a fanatical adherence to monetarism and the desire to cut public spending. 'Such dogmatism . . . [the wets] argued, similarly prevented our using practical tools of economic policy like prices and incomes control and forced us to cut public spending when, as Keynes had argued, public spending should be increased to lift an economy suffering from lack of demand.'[15] Tight control of the money supply in Thatcher's mind, as well as those of the 'wets', was connected with a tight control of public spending, and the desire to introduce tough 'cuts', if necessary.

The moral crusade behind monetarism, for many Thatcherites, was inspired by a visceral hatred of inflation. In the House of Commons, in February 1980, Thatcher explicitly declared that her 'first priority is to restore sound money and conquer inflation'.[16] Sound money, in the 1980s, meant monetarism. In her speech to the Conservative Party conference in October 1980, Thatcher voiced the most stinging condemnation of infla-tion ever uttered on a public platform: 'Inflation destroys nations and

societies as surely as invading armies do. Inflation is the parent of unemployment. It is the unseen robber of those who have saved.' She continued,
'No policy which puts at risk the defeat of inflation – however great its
short-term attraction – can be right.'

The speech is remembered for its phrase 'the lady's not for turning'.
Thatcher's commitment to sound money was also on display in what was
one of the most significant declarations of her government's programme
during her entire first term. She was never noted for her historical understanding, but in the same speech she gave an account of the success of
European countries which praised the soundness of currency as the anchor
of European prosperity. She said, 'some people talk as if control of the
money supply was a revolutionary policy. Yet it was an essential condition
for the recovery of much of continental Europe.' She reminded the audience of Conservative activists that those 'countries knew what was required
for economic stability. Previously they had lived through rampant inflation; they knew that it led to suitcase money, massive unemployment and
the breakdown of society itself. They determined never to go that way
again.' As a consequence of tight control of their money, 'after many years
of monetary self-discipline', as she put it, 'much of continental Europe'
enjoyed 'stable, prosperous economies better able than ours to withstand
the buffeting of world recession'.[17]

Across the Atlantic, one of Thatcher's intellectual heroes, Milton
Friedman, fulminated against inflation in equally lurid terms. In his popular book *Free to Choose*, he denounced inflation as a 'disease, a dangerous
and sometimes fatal disease' which, if left unchecked, could 'destroy a society'. In one of those populist analogies that helped make him famous, he
compared inflation to alcoholism. 'When the alcoholic starts drinking, the
good effects come first; the bad effects come the next morning when he
wakes up with a hangover.' The parallel with inflation was 'exact'. He reiterated his old dictum. 'There is only one cure for inflation: a slower rate of
increase in the quantity of money.'[18]

The problem for politicians was that it was very difficult, in a modern
economy, to define what money was. In Thatcher's case, monetarism had
mixed success. 'The difficulty Howe and Lawson had was in measuring the
growth of money.' The problem lay 'not in the principle but in the

practice'.[19] There were different measures of money in circulation – M0, M1, M3, M4, each of which represented different types of money. M0 was the narrowest definition and just included notes and coins in circulation, while M4, the broadest definition in the British context, included bank and building society deposits. Of course, critics also suggested that monetarism, by squeezing the money supply, constricted economic growth and exacerbated recessions. Similar problems in defining money and in the practical application of monetarist ideas were also encountered in the United States.

Ronald Reagan had been elected as the fortieth President of the United States in 1980. Born in Illinois in 1911, Reagan was nearly seventy when he was inaugurated in January 1981. He had a showman's gift for communication and could win an easy rapport with almost any audience. Intellectually, perhaps as a consequence of his age, he did not pay such close attention to the musings of economists as did Margaret Thatcher. As David Stockman, his first Budget Director, remembered, 'Reagan's body of knowledge is primarily impressionistic: he registers anecdotes rather than concepts.'[20] The fortieth President exuded the bonhomie and warmth of a Franklin Delano Roosevelt, while maintaining a philosophy radically different from that of FDR's New Deal. While Roosevelt saw government as the solution to the economic problems of the 1930s, Reagan believed government was the 'problem, not the solution'. Reagan's sunny optimism was of course what most connected him, in the minds of many Americans, to Roosevelt. In the words of one of his biographers, 'People who listened to Reagan tended to feel good about him and better about themselves.'[21] His presidency, despite being a theatrical performance in many ways, was anchored 'in the fundamental themes of lower taxes, deregulation and "peace through strength"'. Reagan had articulated his basic philosophy as early as 1964, in his 'A Time for Choosing' speech, in which he railed against government programmes and what he saw as socialism. He was an inherent 'anti-statist', who quipped that 'a government bureau is the nearest thing to eternal life we'll ever see on this earth'.[22]

Reagan's well-known scepticism about government was a more elemental philosophy than a technical view about controlling the money supply. Yet the two ideas, monetarism and the free market, were entwined in the

public mind in both Britain and America in the early 1980s. Reagan's
agent of monetary discipline was Paul Volcker, the man Carter had
appointed Chairman of the Federal Reserve. Volcker, who had emerged as
an anti-inflation hawk in the last days of the Carter administration,
displayed an impressive commitment to beating inflation through rigorous interest-rate hikes and a fanatical adherence to monetary targets. At 6
foot 7 inches, he was a looming figure with slightly drooping eyelids and
rumpled suits. He was described as a 'hard money type', who like most
central bankers viewed the inflation of the 1970s with dismay.[23]

Both Volcker and Reagan were stubborn characters. Reagan remained
confident, even in the depth of the recession, that his policies were sound.
Volcker believed that 'the Fed was following the course necessary to throt-
tle the menace of inflation'. His tough approach coincided with Reagan's
almost Calvinist conviction that America would have to pay a price 'for a
half century of living beyond its means'. Reagan, like Friedman in his
earlier analogy regarding inflation, compared fiscal incontinence to drinking alcohol: 'We've been on a binge for thirty years. This is the price you
have to pay.' The son of an alcoholic, he thought of the government
programmes of Lyndon Johnson's Great Society as 'a terrible drinking
spree from which the nation was suffering a monumental hangover'.[24]
Similarly, at a lunch in New York in January 1982, the President admitted
that the United States was in a recession but that his administration was a
'cleanup crew for those who went on a non-stop binge and left the tab for
us to pick up'. At another meeting in Montana, held in October 1982,
before the mid-term congressional elections, he again drew on the imagery
of a temperance campaign. The election would decide whether America
would 'stay the course' or 'stagger off on one more economic binge – a
binge that we and our children would have to pay for, and we'd pay for it
with another pounding hangover'.[25]

Volcker remembered his attempt to curb inflation with pride. 'In
September 1979, the markets seemed to be confident of only one thing:
Bet on inflation.' He added, 'both unemployment and inflation were
rising, and further delay in dealing with inflation would only ultimately
make things worse'. To him, a quintessential technocrat, it was obvious
that there was a connection between the money supply and the rising

prices. 'People don't need an advanced course in economics to understand that inflation has something to do with too much money.'[26] He moved interest rates relentlessly upwards. There were, of course, constant complaints about Volcker's tight-money policies from Western and Southern Republicans. Howard Baker, the Republican Senate Majority Leader from Tennessee, told party strategists late in 1981, 'Volcker's got his foot on our neck, and we've got to make him take it off.' Nineteen-eighty-one saw the highest interest rates in American history. Until mid-October, banks kept their basic loan rate at 19 per cent.[27] Indeed, as one historian of financial speculation has written, 'for the eighteen months of Reagan's presidency the bond and stock markets remained depressed as interest rates were raised to record levels in order to squeeze inflation out of the system'. Bank interest rates 'peaked at over 20 percent and the yield on long-term bonds climbed to over 15 percent'. It was only in the summer of 1982 that Volcker reduced the discount rate.[28]

Volcker himself saw his role as that of a surgeon. Austere and frugal in his private life, he would often complain about high prices in 'swanky' Washington hotels.[29] He was intense, secretive and lacked the polish of more sophisticated financial types. By the standards of the United States financial elite, he was not wealthy. His successor, Alan Greenspan, who had set up his own economic consultancy in the 1950s, remembered that since Volcker had been a 'civil servant most of his career, he didn't have much money. He kept his family at their house in suburban New York for the entire time he was Fed chairman. All he had in Washington was a tiny apartment – he invited me over once in the early 1980s.' The place, Greenspan was rather horrified to discover, was 'filled with piles of old newspapers and all the other clutter of a bachelor apartment'.[30]

It was during the early 1980s, at the height of the high-interest-rate-induced recession, that some on the right of the Republican Party began to yearn for a return to the gold standard, or at least to the pre-1971 Bretton Woods arrangement. In 1982 Ron Paul, a Texas Congressman, denounced Nixon's severance of 'the last link between the dollar and gold'. The 'present crisis' had 'not developed in the past year', but had been 'growing for at least a decade'. The '10-year experiment with paper money has failed; it is time that the Congress recognize that failure'. Paul denounced paper money, which he saw as an extension of government power. 'For the past 10 years we have had a monetary system unique in our national history: no circulating silver or gold coinage, but a government monopoly of politically managed paper money.' This process was described, in unambiguous terms, as 'outright theft on the part of the federal government', which sought to 'substitute a managed irredeemable paper money system for a gold standard'.[31]

Paul, and his co-author Lew Lehrman, were members of the US Gold Commission in 1981, which had been appointed by the Secretary of the Treasury, Donald T. Regan, to 'conduct a study to assess and make recommendations with regard to the policy of the U.S. Government concerning the role of gold in domestic and international monetary systems'.[32] Their minority report, entitled 'The Case for Gold', was a robust articulation of the need to maintain some link between the dollar and gold. The majority of the Commission were not so convinced of the need to go back to a gold link, but the setting up of the Commission itself was a measure of how seriously the Reagan administration considered a return to gold. Paul and Lehrman were particularly anxious about the surge in inflation. 'Since 1971 America's monetary unit has been both undefined and undefinable. The meaning of the term "dollar" has changed from year-to-year, month-to-month, even day-to-day.' They urged a return to a gold standard, suggesting that for 'too long the federal government has been playing with Monopoly money'.[33]

Reagan's economic fortunes as President improved. With the advent of better economic conditions, talk about a return to gold inevitably receded. He won re-election in 1984 against a backdrop of recovery. His slogan 'Morning again in America' proved to be widely popular and projected the image he had always crafted so well, that of the sunny optimist, a 'happy warrior' who represented an idealized picture of how Americans saw themselves. In that election, Reagan carried forty-nine states, receiving 525 votes in the Electoral College. The Democratic candidate, Walter F. Mondale, barely managed to carry his home state of Minnesota by one percentage point. He also won the District of Columbia.[34]

Despite the ease with which Reagan was re-elected, there remained some discomfort underneath the smooth confident exterior. The poorest one-fifth of American families saw their average income decline nearly 8 per cent, 'from $6,913 to $6,391' (using 1982 dollars), even though average annual income for American families had risen 3.5 per cent during Reagan's first term.[35] More worrying for Reagan, a self-avowed fiscal conservative, who continually objected to government spending, was the mounting budget deficit. Attempts to balance the budget were discarded during the 1980s in the face of a wider commitment to even greater tax cuts and increased military spending. The Reagan era marked the time when conservatives believed that tax cuts, regardless of budgetary conditions, were an essential article of faith. For much of the preceding two decades, statesmen who would describe themselves at least as fiscal conservatives did not hesitate to put up taxes in the name of balanced budgets. In the United States, both Truman and Eisenhower actually justified tax rises in the interest of balancing the budgets. In Britain, during the eighteenth and nineteenth centuries, William Pitt, Sir Robert Peel and William Gladstone had all introduced, reintroduced or increased income tax in order to balance the budget. It was only really in the 1980s that American conservatives adopted the 'supply-side revolution', in which tax cuts formed an important part. Indeed, talking of the proposals for tax cuts in the early part of the decade, Herbert Stein, a Republican economist, remarked that a 'tax cut that would greatly increase the deficit was not acceptable to the Republicans or salable to the country'. It was at that point, Stein argued, that 'supply-side' economics 'came to the rescue'.[36]

David Stockman, Reagan's Budget Director, was an enthusiastic thirty-four-year-old when appointed to his role in 1981. He was a strong, idealistic budget hawk, who like his master saw government as 'the problem not the solution'. He hated government spending, and was openly ideological in his support for what he called the 'Reagan Revolution'. Revolutions, as described by Stockman in his 1987 account *The Triumph of Politics*, were characterized by 'drastic, wrenching changes in an established regime'. This was not 'Ronald Reagan's real agenda in the first place'. It was Stockman's mission, however, and 'that of a small cadre of supply-side intellectuals'. 'The Reagan Revolution, as I had defined it, required a frontal assault on the American welfare state.' In Stockman's radical analysis, 'forty years' worth of promises, subventions, entitlements, and safety nets issued by the federal government to every component and stratum of American society would have to be scrapped or drastically modified'. Ideologues like him passionately believed that 'A true economic policy revolution meant risky and mortal political combat with all the mass constituencies of Washington's largesse.' Beneficiaries of this largesse included 'Social Security recipients, veterans, farmers ... the housing industry, and many more'.[37]

Stockman gave up on the possibility of radical reform. He quit Reagan's service in 1985. He believed that the 'true Reagan Revolution never had a chance'. True revolution 'defied all of the overwhelming forces, interests, and impulses of American democracy'. The supply-side revolution was all about lower taxes. In Stockman's simple formulation, higher taxes 'caused less work', while low tax rates 'caused more'. More generally, 'supply-siders' favoured deregulation and labour-market flexibility, characterized as easier 'hire and fire' policies in order to boost production, or the supply side. This contrasted with the Keynesian emphasis on aggregate demand, often promoted by government spending, as a key driver of economic growth. As early as November 1981, Stockman became convinced that the Reagan administration had 'locked the door on its own disastrous fiscal policy jail cell' and had thrown away the key. The problem was that leading administration officials, from the President downwards, were unwilling to give up pet projects which inevitably cost money. 'Cap Weinberger [the Defense Secretary] hung on for dear life to the $1.46 trillion defense budget.' As a consequence of such intransigence, the United States' 'huge fiscal imbalance was never addressed or corrected; it just festered and grew'.[38]

In terms of numbers, the position was stark. Stockman, in the disillusionment he felt in the mid-1980s, complained that 'we were not headed toward a brave new world'. The United States was headed 'toward a fiscal catastrophe'. In the heady days of the President's first year, in February 1981, it was said 'you could have a big tax cut and big defense buildup, and still have a balanced budget by 1984'. The Republicans around the White House in 1981 believed that the balanced budget of 1984 would be 'followed by a $28 billion surplus by 1986'. But that depended on what Stockman called the 'Rosy Scenario' – which did not happen. Over the five years from 1981 to 1986, the actual path of the economy led to even more indebtedness. The deficits in 1985 and 1986 were US$223 billion and US$226 billion respectively, leaving a cumulative increase of indebtedness in the Reagan presidency of nearly a trillion dollars. With regard to the welfare state, Stockman's idealistic commitment to wholesale reform came up against the realities of democratic politics. The 'half-trillion-dollar budget' which existed in 1986 'after five years of sustained ideological challenge is there because the rank and file of GOP [Grand Old Party – that is, Republican] politicians want it for their constituents no less than their Democratic counterparts do'.[39]

George Soros, a Hungarian Jewish émigré to the United States and an asset manager, published a book, *The Alchemy of Finance*, in 1987, in which he gave a lucid account of the dilemma which confronted Reagan's White House. 'The large and growing U.S. budget deficit', argued Soros, 'emerged as the unintended consequence of conflicting policy objectives. On the one hand, President Reagan sought to reduce the role of the federal government in the economy by reducing taxes; on the other he wanted to assume a strong military posture in confronting what he considered the communist menace.' These objectives, however laudable individually, 'could not be pursued within the constraints of a balanced budget'.[40] The Americans, under Reagan, had committed themselves to expansionary finance. Tax cuts and increased spending were, of course, the classic Keynesian response to a slump. Performing both at the same time was no way to balance the budget.

At the very moment when the Reagan administration's budget plans began to unravel, the dollar itself was riding high in the foreign exchange markets. By 1984 and early 1985, the recession of the early 1980s was 'long over', and the 'stratospheric levels of the dollar in the exchange market were provoking complaints by exporters'. By the end of 1984 the Japanese yen and the German mark were trading at their pre-1973 levels, or below, against the US dollar.[41] By the mid-1980s, the dollar and its fortunes were the most hotly debated issue in international finance. Otmar Emminger, the former President of the Bundesbank, wrote in September 1985 that 'the dollar's exchange rate is at present the most important price in the world economy'. Emminger added the parenthetical remark that 'ten years ago one would probably have attributed this role to the oil price'. The high dollar had had 'an enormous impact on the world economy'. It had 'affected the competitive position of other industrial countries versus the United States, the U.S. trade balance . . . and price inflation both in the United States and elsewhere'.

The high dollar during 1985 which Emminger defined at US$1 to DM 2.80 had defied all 'conventional wisdom'. 'At least until the beginning of 1985, we could watch a rather paradoxical, if not "perverse," spectacle: the more the American budget deficit and trade deficit increased, the higher rose the dollar.' Emminger observed that 'What would have made all other currencies weak seems to have strengthened the dollar.' He felt that there had existed a 'strange connection between high budget deficits and a strong dollar'. The powerful position of the dollar was due to its unique role as a world currency.

Contrary to what many had expected, the end of the 'gold–dollar standard' in 1971 had not 'finished the key role of the dollar in the world monetary system. When President Nixon suspended the gold convertibility of the dollar in August 1971, Emminger noted, 'experts' had believed that 'the dollar had become a normal currency like all the others'. More strikingly, they believed that the United States, by ending the convertibility of the dollar to gold, had lost what the French 'had called the "exorbitant privilege" of financing its external deficits with its own domestic currency'. These assumptions had proved 'thoroughly wrong'. The dollar had, contrary to expectation, 'not only maintained its special position' but in some fields even 'enlarged it'. Since 1971, the dollar had remained 'by far the most important reserve and intervention currency'. Central banks had nearly 'quadrupled their reserves of inconvertible dollars'. The international banking system had built up even larger dollar holdings since the beginning of the 1970s. The dollar consequently remained the 'main provider of international liquidity'.

Even without gold convertibility, the United States could afford the 'luxury of a passive balance-of-payments strategy'. This meant that America could with impunity run balance of payments deficits, importing goods far more than exporting. This was because foreigners were willing to lend the US government money, buying bonds from the US Treasury. Emminger believed in 1985 that this phase was 'probably over'. This would turn out to be a premature judgement, however. Capital movements, the ability to buy dollars and purchase American shares and bonds, had meant that the dollar would be purchased regardless of the actual conditions of the American economy. The dollar had become an 'international investment asset'.[42] Foreign capital remained attracted to dollar assets. There was a 'high return on financial assets' in the United States and there also existed confidence which, in Soros's opinion, had been 'inspired by President Reagan'.[43] Emminger observed that between 'the United States and a group of other industrial countries' there had now arisen 'a queer kind of mutual interdependence . . . over the last few years'. These 'other countries' had supplied 'large amounts of capital to the United States'. In return the United States had 'supplied additional demand to them'. The other industrialized countries were lending money to the United States which the United States would then use to buy goods from the 'other countries'. 'Is this going to be a new structure of the world economy – a big capital gap in the United States standing opposite a capital surplus in Japan and other countries?' A key cause of this dependence was the 'low private savings ratio' in the United States and the 'very high ratio' of savings in Japan. Emminger stated with an air of frustration that it was not 'very satisfactory that the richest country is drawing huge amounts of capital from the rest of the world'. Such a phenomenon 'cannot possibly remain a durable position', he naively concluded.[44]

The strength of the dollar in the mid-1980s was ended by a series of government interventions in the foreign exchange market. The Plaza Accord was signed in September 1985. This confirmed a commitment on the part of the G5 group of countries – West Germany, Japan, France, Great Britain and the United States – to sell dollars, and thus weaken the American currency. A motivation behind trying to push down the dollar was the desire to head off 'protectionist legislation', which the US Congress was threatening against countries like Japan and West Germany as a result of the 'damage' that the high dollar rate 'inflicted on domestic producers'.[45] Protectionism was never far off the agenda in American administrations. In 1983 President Reagan himself had famously bailed out the American motorcycle maker Harley-Davidson by slapping Japanese motorcycle makers with a 49 per cent tariff on large bikes. By 1986, needless to say, Harley-Davidson's cycles were among the most widely sold in the United States. The American company, feeling the effects of the 1982 recession, had protested to the federal government about the Japanese 'dumping' their excess production in American markets.[46]

The Reagan administration was ideological in its inspiration, but often, as we have seen, it failed to follow its vaunted ideals in practice. Thatcher was probably more doctrinaire in her application of free-market principles to practical policies. Her government, after striking a militant, 'no turning back' pose in the early 1980s, pursued with undimmed vigour a raft of free-market-friendly policies. Her aggressive promotion of the free market led to a number of deregulatory moves in the corporate and, perhaps most memorably, the financial structures of the United Kingdom. The hallmark of her government's policy was the process of privatization, which involved divesting state-owned industries and transferring them, by means of stock market flotations, to the private sector. In the words of the political journalist Peter Riddell, as quoted by Nigel Lawson, Margaret Thatcher's long-serving Chancellor of the Exchequer, privatization represented 'the Jewel in the Crown of the Government's legislative programme'. It was also an idea that had been 'taken up, and copied, with explicit acknowledgement of the British influence' in many other countries of the developed and developing world.[47]

Nigel Lawson remembered with pride that, by the 1992 general election, 'about two thirds of the formerly State-owned industries in the UK had been transferred to the private sector'. He boasted that 'forty-six major businesses, employing some 900,000 people', had been 'privatized'.[48] Privatization was controversial, but it was not reversed. Indeed, when the financial crisis of 2008 hit the world, there were some in Britain who were quietly thankful that major state assets, which had been a large cost to the public purse, had already been divested. A Britain which still had a vast quantity of state-owned assets on its balance sheet would probably have been forced to sell them at very low prices in the wake of the global recession which descended in 2008–9. State assets would undoubtedly have made Britain's poor public finances in the aftermath of the events of 2008 even worse.

In addition to privatization, there also occurred the regulatory reform of the City of London. In 1986, 'Big Bang' changed life within the Square Mile for ever. The 'traditional and class-based' culture of the City was swept away. Big Bang itself happened on 27 October 1986, but for three years, following the 1983 agreement between the Stock Exchange and the Department of Trade and Industry, 'the structure and the form of the City' underwent a revolution.[49] As one historian explains: 'A new dealing system was established together with a new regulatory framework to police it. New firms were created out of businesses that had been required to be arm's length for decades . . . Relationships with clients had to be redefined. Within firms a new contract between employer and employee had to be created.'[50]

There were inevitably cultural tensions as big American banks acquired more traditional English brokerage firms and merchant banks. The initial 1983 deal between the Stock Exchange and the government had been an undertaking, on the part of the City of London, to drop fixed commissions and to open itself to competition. These steps had ushered in the market reforms of 1986 known as Big Bang. In the light of the events of October 1987 in which international markets crashed, many questioned the pace and efficacy of the reforms that Mrs Thatcher's government had introduced.[51] Yet, as in so much else associated with her government, the direction and philosophy were clear. Policies flowed consistently from a set of ideological premises. There was a good deal of pragmatism, but the Thatcher governments were noted for their ideological fervour. Thatcher herself reportedly used the phrase 'one of us' to denote people who shared her deeply held convictions. She had always said that she had only gone into politics 'to do things', and she did indeed accomplish many 'things' whose legacy is still fiercely disputed.[52]

In the United States, another committed free-market disciple, Alan Greenspan, was appointed Chairman of the Federal Reserve to replace Paul Volcker in 1987. While Volcker had been a technocrat and career civil servant, Greenspan combined an entrepreneur's experience of running his own economic consultancy since his late twenties with a firm ideological belief in individualism and markets. More intriguingly, the so-called objectivist philosopher Ayn Rand, who preached a naked form of individualism, was a personal friend and mentor of the young economist. Rand, in Greenspan's own admission, introduced the young New Yorker 'to a vast realm from which I'd shut myself off'.[53]

Greenspan remembered the 1950s with affection as a time when 'you were supposed to balance your budget and make ends meet'. He recalled that one year 'President Eisenhower actually apologized to the American people for running a $3 billion deficit.'[54] Greenspan was therefore a free-market, balanced-budget-supporting economist who voted loyally for Republican candidates and supported the party avidly in government. Paradoxically, as is often the case in the history of money, the first act which defined him as a central banker, and set the course for much of his subsequent performance in his role as Chairman of the Federal Reserve, was a programme of market interventions. On Friday 16 October 1987, the Dow Jones average dropped by 108 points. Greenspan believed that 'the Fed's job during a stock-market panic is to ward off financial paralysis – a chaotic state in which businesses and banks stop making the payments they owe each other and the economy grinds to a halt'.[55] The following Monday, the Dow Jones fell 508 points, a 22.5 per cent drop from 2,250. This was the biggest one-day loss in the New York Stock Exchange's history, bigger even than Black Friday in 1929.

Greenspan's response was to become hyperactive. 'We manned the operations center around the clock.' He and his team 'tracked markets in Japan and Europe' in order to get 'a preview of what the New York markets were likely to do when they opened'.[56] In the midst of the crisis, he had declared that 'The Federal Reserve, consistent with its responsibilities as the nation's central bank, affirmed today its readiness to serve as a source of liquidity to support the economic and financial system.'[57] The way in which the Federal Reserve supported Wall Street was simple. Traders at the New York Fed, one of the Fed's twelve regional banks, were instructed to buy billions of dollars of Treasury securities on the open market. 'This had the effect of putting more money into circulation and lowering short-term rates.' In a move that Greenspan would repeat many times in his eighteen years at the head of the Federal Reserve, he eased interest rates 'to help keep the economy moving'. In the following months, the 'economy held firm'. Growth hit a 2 per cent annual rate in the first quarter of 1988. 'By early 1988 the Dow had stabilized at around 2,000, back where it had been at the beginning of 1987 . . .'[58]

Greenspan's success, as he saw it, in stabilizing the markets was a lesson he would never forget. Ideologically at least, he was the Federal Reserve Chairman most committed to the operation of the free market. Yet none of his predecessors ever intervened so directly to stabilize the supposedly free operations of the New York stock market. This circumstance was one of the many paradoxes of the Reagan years.

By 1988, despite having vehemently denounced government spending in his ascent to the highest political office, Reagan left the United States with an enormous national debt. As Greenspan himself recalled, 'Huge government deficits under Reagan had caused the national debt to the public to almost triple, from just over $700 billion at the start of his presidency to more than $2 trillion at the end of fiscal year 1988.' Yet the battle against inflation had been largely won. At 3.6 per cent, inflation was 'far milder than the double-digit nightmare people remembered from the 1970s'.[59] In Britain too, inflation had been tamed. Nigel Lawson could boast that inflation 'was down to 3.5 per cent in 1986', a startling change from the 1970s when the inflation rate had hit over 20 per cent.[60] Thatcher's attempts to balance the books were probably more successful than those of Ronald Reagan, although such public-finance figures were flattered by the asset sales known as privatizations. By 1988, Thatcher could boast of a £14 billion projected surplus for the 1988–9 fiscal year,[61] though this may have been somewhat misleading as it reflected very buoyant economic conditions.

Looking back at the Thatcher era in Britain and the Reagan era in the United States, many people have drawn different conclusions. What is commonly held is that both leaders were highly ideological in their approach to politics. They adopted clear policy positions which had been derived from a set of simple beliefs about the world, about society and about the economy. Their world view was characterized as neo-liberal. In their rhetoric, they spoke of government spending in terms usually associated with household budgets. Both leaders referred to 'sound money' and denounced inflation. This rhetoric was merely a throwback to an earlier age, to the world as it had existed before 1914, when government spending was small, and taxation, by modern standards, almost non-existent.

The cry for sound money was, after all, what had underpinned the gold standard. The attempt to recreate the pre-1914 world was perhaps unrealistic by the end of the twentieth century, but the Thatcher and Reagan revolutions aspired to return to a simpler age. Both leaders, to a certain degree, repudiated the legacy of the post-war years. In fighting the Cold War, Reagan did not manage to curb government spending. Thatcher successfully privatized many of the industries which a post-war Labour Party had nationalized. Inflation in the 1980s in both Britain and the United States fell. The Thatcher and Reagan era was mixed in its success, but its goals were nothing if not ambitious.

The Creation of the Euro

While Margaret Thatcher and Ronald Reagan were attempting to reshape the destinies of their countries, the nations of Western Europe began to construct their own vision of an economic future. Ironically, because of the rather different philosophies underpinning both the European Union and neo-liberal monetarism, both approaches attempted to answer the same problem, the chaos of monetary instability. The Europeans after 1971, in particular, were coming to terms with a world of floating currencies as they tried to impose monetary order on a chaotic world. Even before the fateful decision of Richard Nixon to suspend gold convertibility of the dollar, the Europeans had sought to embark upon the road of currency union. Pierre Werner, the Prime Minister of Luxembourg, was entrusted with producing a plan for currency union in 1970. The backdrop of Werner's report was a 'full monetary storm' in the early 1970s, which saw the advent of floating currencies for the first time.[1] 'Disorder was present on the Foreign Exchange Markets,' remembered Jacques Delors, a future President of the European Commission.[2]

The dream of peace in Europe consolidated by political and, eventually, monetary union was something which had been articulated since 1945. Jacques Rueff, the French politician and monetary expert, had asserted as early as 1950 that 'Europe will make itself by money or not at all.'[3] Rueff, a lifelong advocate of the gold standard, and a sceptic about dollar leadership in international financial affairs, would have welcomed the subsequent path towards monetary union in Europe. Following the Werner Report of 1970 which recommended a European currency union in the long run, a number of countries of the EEC created the 'snake' which, from 1972 to 1977, constrained the fluctuations of currencies.[4] The snake was launched alongside the Smithsonian Agreement of 1971.[5] It was always explicitly recognized that the undertaking by the Europeans to create a common currency was an attempt to recreate the lost stability of the Bretton Woods system, which itself harked back to the pre-1914 gold standard.

The Werner Report had sketched out a path to economic and monetary union by 1980. This in itself demonstrated that the European common currency had 'long been a grand integration project'.[6] The consistency with which senior officials and politicians pursued the single currency in Europe represents one of the most remarkable strategic successes in international politics. For thirty years, these officials and politicians never lost sight of their long-term objective. They strove for the single currency despite setbacks and the wild gyrations of markets. In the meantime, many hurdles had to be overcome. Which countries would join the monetary union, how these currencies would be linked and at what rates, what would the rules of the game be – these were all questions that took years, if not a couple of decades, to resolve. It was perhaps to be expected that the large country which would give the euro project the most problems would be Great Britain.

The British had always maintained an ambivalent attitude to European integration in its widest sense. It was no surprise that the issue of a single currency stirred resistance. London took pride in its traditions of finance and commerce. The pound has often been described as the single oldest currency in continuous existence. The pound's unbroken history of nearly 1,400 years, combined with the position of London as a centre of global finance for 300 years, gave the arguments about the merits of a single European currency a peculiar intensity in Britain.

Yet, despite the emotions aroused in the debate surrounding a common currency, the British did participate in the snake and its successor the ERM, or exchange rate mechanism, which had been introduced in March 1979. The snake itself had been dissolved in 1977, in which year it had essentially become a Deutschmark zone, with only the Belgian, Dutch, Danish and Luxembourgeois currencies tracking it. The ERM was an attempt to recreate the snake. ERM was also a system designed to limit exchange rate volatility. It was explicitly constructed to be a forerunner of full European economic and monetary union, or EMU, which would require a single currency. The peculiar relationship of Britain with the nascent institutions of European monetary union was described by Jacques Delors as 'le problème britannique', or the 'British problem'.[7] The tensions aroused by British involvement in the single European currency were felt within the heart of the British government itself. Margaret Thatcher asserted plausibly that she had always been against any move for Britain to join the ERM. In her words, 'I could see no particular reason to allow British monetary policy to be determined largely by the Bundesbank rather than by the British Treasury . . .' Revealingly, she added that such a course would be justified only if Britain 'had no confidence in our own ability to control inflation'.[8] Her hostile attitude to ERM put her at odds with her Chancellor Nigel Lawson.

Lawson was unapologetically in favour of British membership of the ERM. In his 1992 memoirs *The View from No. 11*, he declared that British failure to join the ERM in 1985, 'five years before we did eventually join', was the 'greatest missed opportunity'. He believed in ERM on sound fixed-rate principles. He believed in the 'advantage of rules over discretion'. This was a similar rationale to that espoused by all advocates of fixed rates in currencies from the gold standard to the beginning of the twenty-first century. In 1992, Lawson believed that joining the ERM in 1985 would have had a far better outcome than the eventual British entry into the ERM in 1990. He took the view that, if Britain had joined the ERM in 1985, there would have been 'a clear run of five or six years during which the Deutschmark would have served' as a 'very satisfactory low-inflation anchor, without the strain of the relatively high interest rates that unification [German unification in 1990] was eventually to impose on the system as a whole'.[9]

Lawson and Thatcher worked with relative cohesion for six years as Chancellor of the Exchequer and Prime Minister respectively. Lawson eventually resigned in 1989 over the very issue of ERM membership and the excessively powerful role of Alan Walters, Margaret Thatcher's special economic adviser, who was denounced by members of the Labour opposition as an 'unelected Chancellor'.[10] Alan Walters had been at Thatcher's side during the memorable 1981 budget in which she raised taxes and cut spending in the depths of a recession. About that budget she wrote, 'If you believed, as they [her critics] did, that increased government borrowing was the way to get out of recession, then our approach was inexplicable.'[11] Walters, a man from a working-class background in Leicester, was a professional economist who left Thatcher's side after the 1983 general election. While living in America in the 1980s, he became increasingly irritated by the prospect of a single European currency.[12] The idea of Walters being recalled to Thatcher's side as her personal economic adviser dismayed Lawson, the elected MP and long-serving Chancellor of the Exchequer. By late 1989 Walters's 'job as the Prime Minister's personal economic adviser' was making Lawson's position 'as Chancellor impossible'. The markets, as a consequence of Walters's influence, 'heard two voices, and did not know which to believe'.[13]

It was their approach to the single currency, initially in the form of the ERM, which divided Walters and Lawson. John Smith, the Labour MP, and shadow Chancellor of the Exchequer, described the conflict between the two men as provoking 'confusion and disarray in the formulation and explanation of Government economic policy'. Lawson replied with contempt that Walters was 'a part-time adviser and his views on the ERM are not the views of the Government'.[14] Thatcher remembered Walters as having 'trenchant views', but stuck by her adviser. On 18 October 1989, the *Financial Times* of London reported Walters as having described the ERM as 'half-baked'.[15] By contrast, Lawson had publicly expressed a desire for Britain to join it. On 26 October, Lawson submitted his resignation to the Prime Minister. She retorted that if 'Alan were to go, that would destroy *my* [italics in original] authority'. He told her that this idea was absurd. Her authority 'owed nothing whatever to Walters'. Lawson presented his leader with an ultimatum. 'I reiterated my conclusion that, if she were not to get rid of Walters by the end of the year, I did not see how I could possibly remain as Chancellor.'[16] According to Thatcher's own account, she 'made it clear that Alan Walters was not going and hoped that Nigel would reflect further'.[17]

Lawson nevertheless stuck firm to his decision to resign. The problem Thatcher now had was that Lawson's successor, John Major, was equally committed to British membership of the ERM. Major was an emollient, mild-mannered man who did well in politics because he was well liked. He also had a chameleon-like quality which convinced any audience that he shared their views. To Margaret Thatcher John Major, a man who came from humble origins in Brixton, was 'one of us'. His friends detected a softer edge to his politics than was evident in the strident militancy of the Prime Minister. Major was certainly ambitious, but he was not as intensely and obviously driven to power as some of his colleagues. His reflections on being appointed Chancellor on Lawson's resignation were characteristic-ally modest. 'I accepted the chancellorship,' he recalled. 'Yet again political Christmas had come early for me.' The chancellorship was the job Major 'most coveted', but he had obtained it 'under the most unhappy circumstances'.[18]

Major and Douglas Hurd, the new Chancellor of the Exchequer and the new Foreign Secretary respectively, were keen to convince their reluctant leader of the 'merits of entry into the ERM'. In the spring of 1990, Major along with Robin Leigh-Pemberton, the Governor of the Bank of England, were 'as one on the need to join the ERM'. The Governor, 'a jovial, well-mannered' cricket lover, was impressed by the ERM as 'an anti-inflationary weapon'.[19] All through the summer of 1990, Major believed that the foreign exchange markets were propping up the sterling exchange rate in the expectation that the pound would imminently join the ERM. Even at this stage, in early June 1990, Major was beginning to harbour some doubts as the Bundesbank, anticipating the reunification of East and West Germany, had set a rate 'for monetary reunion of one ostmark to the deutschemark – a politically driven and unrealistic rate which put pressure on interest rates across Europe'.[20] This, of course, had been the central point of Margaret Thatcher's objec-tion to the ERM, and to deeper monetary union. 'Why should the Bundesbank, and not the British Treasury, set the path of British monet-ary policy?' she had asked.

But Major remained committed to ERM, and Thatcher was well aware that, with public opinion turning against her government, she could not afford to lose another Chancellor. She acquiesced in British entry. On 5 October 1990 Britain finally joined the ERM. At this point it looked as though Britain would take part in any further monetary union which might occur. It needs to be stated emphatically that the various structures devised from the time of the Werner Report, the snake of 1972 and then ERM in 1979, were designed with the distinct prospect of monetary union at the end. This was a view clearly shared by the French and the Germans, even if the British had not fully understood the final implications of the snake or the ERM.

In the opinion of its European partners, the significance of sterling in the history of finance had always given the British an inflated sense of their own importance. Despite British equivocation about the ERM, the initial response to joining the mechanism was generally positive. The *Sunday Telegraph* welcomed the 'strong discipline' imposed by it, while the *Independent* said that the British government had seized the 'political and economic initiative'. There were, however, questions about the rate at which sterling had entered the mechanism. Some commentators believed, that at 2.95 Deutschmarks to the pound, the exchange rate was too high. Yet John Major himself, in a self-exculpatory vein, suggested that there was no real alternative to that particular rate. Other European countries, he later argued, would not have permitted sterling to enter the ERM at a lower rate. Those countries, in Major's words, 'would not have allowed us to gain a competitive advantage upon entry by an artificial devaluation'. Even more emphatically, in a tone of almost petulant denial, Major argued that 'Any suggestion that we could have entered at a significantly lower rate is utterly unrealistic.'[21]

There was good reason for Major's insistence that there had been no alternative. The decision to join the ERM was one which would scar his own tenure of the Prime Minister's office as the policy unravelled in the autumn of 1992. At that time, the Bundesbank under the grip of its President, Helmut Schlesinger, decided to keep interest rates high at a time when both the Italian and British governments were pressing for interest rate cuts. In Jacques Delors's recollection, September 1992 was a 'terrible month' in which 'everyone appealed to the Germans' to lower rates. Schlesinger's eyes, however, were 'riveted as always on the internal German situation'. Interestingly Delors stated clearly in his memoirs that, in his opinion, 'the credibility of the European Union remains bound to the success of economic and monetary union'.[22]

John Major, having succeeded Margaret Thatcher as Prime Minister in November 1990, won his own mandate in the general election held in April 1992. Norman Lamont, the Chancellor of the Exchequer under Major, remembered how as early as June 1992 the 'pressure on sterling had returned'. Like many of the other leading figures of the time, he did not believe that the rate at which sterling had entered the ERM was the problem. The problem for Lamont was that interest rates 'could not be lowered below the levels of the anchor currency in the ERM, the Deutschmark'. Lamont, a former Rothschilds asset manager, was an experienced politician who had first been elected to the House of Commons in 1972. After leaving Major's government in 1993, he became an articulate opponent of plans for European integration. His hostility to the wider project of European monetary and political union created a dilemma for him as he attempted while still Chancellor to defend sterling's position within the ERM. 'At the same time', he admitted later, 'that I was feeling increasingly trapped by the ERM, I had to carry on arguing in public for the policy, constantly assuring MPs that there was no alternative.' In a memorable conclusion to this section of his memoirs, Lamont made the obvious but significant remark that 'Politicians do not have the luxury of airing their doubts in public.'[23]

The interest rate problem arose because Britain's inflation rate had been falling while 'in Germany the opposite was happening'. This has been widely accepted. The problem, in Lamont's view, was that the German government had decided to unify the West German Deutschmark and the East German Ostmark on a one-for-one basis, when the East German currency was significantly weaker than that of West Germany. Partly as a consequence of this monetary union, but largely as a result of the physical union of the countries, the federal government in Bonn had also been 'pumping huge amounts of money into the East German economy'. The results of this injection of money were unsurprising to any monetarist. In March 1992, inflation in Germany reached '4.8 per cent' which was 'high by German standards'.[24] It was this need to curb German inflation which determined Schlesinger's policy to raise interest rates in September 1992, that 'terrible month', in Delors's words, which precipitated the final departure of sterling from the ERM.

Lamont, like many Conservative British politicians, 'did not believe in the ERM at any time as a step towards monetary union'. He had always accepted it 'as a monetary device for lowering British inflation'. This opinion would be considered a typically parochial British view by Europeans, particularly by the French, for whom monetary union had always been part of the master plan for Europe's future. The late summer proved testing for sterling and the Italian lira in the international currency markets. On 14 August 1992 sterling 'plunged to its lowest level ever in the ERM, down to DM 2.815'. At this rate, sterling was only '3 pfennigs [there were 100 pfennigs to a Deutschmark] above its floor', the lowest level it could trade at within the ERM. In an almost farcical scene, Lamont remembered having to telephone Nick Brady, the US Treasury Secretary under President George H. W. Bush, 'from the depths of a yacht belonging to the Italian representative' of the British merchant bank Schroders. The British Chancellor of the Exchequer was especially careful that 'the other passengers, several of them bankers, did not hear [his] . . . conversation'.

The fateful month of September arrived with no improvement in sterling's position. The storm which swept the foreign exchange markets was unforeseen by most of the British officials whose policy it destroyed. Lamont, rarely for a politician, admitted that he 'did not in any way foresee the scale of what was to happen'.[25] On 3 September, the British government announced that the Bank of England would borrow 10 billion ecus (the European currency unit, the unit of account for the ERM), equivalent to £7.25 billion, and sell them for sterling. In effect, the Bank of England would use the borrowed money to buy pounds, to prop up sterling within its prescribed range in the ERM. After this announcement, sterling 'did rise quickly above DM 2.80 for the first time in two weeks'.[26] The range in which sterling could trade without a devaluation in the ERM was within 6 per cent either side of DM 2.95 to one pound. This meant that sterling had to trade between DM 3.12 and DM 2.778.[27] As a consequence, a value of one pound to DM 2.80 was a danger signal. The fight to keep sterling within the ERM was a struggle waged by the British government against the impersonal markets. This struggle was aggravated from the point of view of the British government by the equally intense struggle that the Italians were fighting to keep their lira within the same mechanism.

On 13 September, John Major received a telephone call from Giuliano Amato, the Italian Prime Minister. The telephone call was unusual because Major and his wife, Norma, were staying with Queen Elizabeth II at Balmoral and the entire phone conversation took place while a piper was playing the bagpipes outside the British Prime Minister's bedroom window. Amato wanted to talk to Major about a planned devaluation of the lira, to be agreed by other participant countries of the ERM. The Italian Socialist also wanted a parallel cut in German interest rates. Major welcomed this as he believed that the Bundesbank's increase in interest rates on 16 July had helped to 'cause the recent problems'. Indeed, Major remarked rather acidly that 'From the beginning of 1991 – a matter of weeks after sterling entered the ERM – to July 1992 the German discount rate rose by 2.75 per cent', a rise which 'neither the Treasury nor the City had anticipated when we entered the ERM'.[28] Of course, the Bundesbank, ever mindful of the domestic needs of the German economy, did not oblige Amato and Major. Later that Sunday, 13 September, the devaluation of the Italian lira was announced. With startling lack of sensitivity, Schlesinger, President of the Bundesbank, was reported as saying that 'the tensions in the ERM are not over', adding that 'further devaluations are not excluded'. This was interpreted by Major as a signal to 'sell sterling', which is what investors did. In Major's pained recollection, a 'swift and authoritative rebuttal from the Bundesbank was essential. It did not come.'[29]

The consequence of this palpable lack of confidence in sterling from the Bundesbank was inevitable. 'Carnage began,' as Major put it. In New York trading on Tuesday afternoon the pound fell below its ERM floor. Wednesday 16 September started very badly. Despite the Bank of England's intervention, sterling had been widely sold, Major was told at seven in the morning. After speaking to Lamont, Major was convinced of the need to raise interest rates and buy sterling if there was to be any hope of keeping the British currency within the ERM. At 12.45 a.m. 'a white-faced Norman Lamont hurried to see' Major. He was accompanied by the Governor of the Bank of England. The news was 'awful'. None of their plans had

worked, as markets were relentlessly selling the pound. 'They're still selling,' said Terry Burns, the Treasury's top civil servant. At 2.15 that afternoon, Major spoke to Helmut Kohl, the German Chancellor, and
informed him that the pound would have to leave the ERM unless additional support, in the form of market support for sterling, was given by
European central banks. The Bank of England had increased interest rates
by 2 per cent to 12 per cent at 11 a.m. This was followed by an announcement that interest rates would be raised to 15 per cent that afternoon.

By 7.30 that evening, the game was up. Lamont, in a brief statement
outside the Treasury, announced the suspension of sterling's ERM membership. The rise in interest rates from 12 per cent to 15 per cent would not
now be implemented. Indeed, interest rates went back to 10 per cent, still
a historically high level. In his characteristically frank memoirs, Major
described the 'collapse of sterling' as 'a catastrophic defeat'.[30] But there
were winners. While the British government had been humiliated, speculators, most notably the Hungarian Jewish émigré based in New York,
George Soros, had made billions of pounds. Soros, on the back of his
aggressive selling of sterling, gained an international notoriety and enjoyed
an almost Hollywood celebrity status during the 1990s. He remembered
the British government's increase of the interest rate by 2 per cent as 'an act
of desperation' that had the reverse effect of its intention. It merely encouraged the speculators 'to continue selling sterling even more aggressively'. It
signalled to the market that 'the British position was untenable'. After that
memorable day, Soros proudly recalled, he became known as 'the man
who broke the Bank of England'.[31] This was a remarkable occurrence,
when we consider the Bank's solidity and the confidence which it had
inspired in much of its history. More than any institution, the Bank of
England represented stability and unruffled tradition in the turbulent
world of international finance. Its history since the Second World War
may have been less glorious, but it still stood for certain ideals in global
finance.

The reaction of the British political press was caustic. The somewhat
leftward-inclined *Financial Times* (it had supported the Labour Party in
the 1992 election) remarked that Wednesday 16 September had been the
'first time in modern history that the Bank had raised interest rates twice

in one day'. The article went on to relate that the Bank of England had 'spent an estimated £7bn – roughly a third of its foreign currency reserves – in buying sterling for D-Marks'. Contrary to the complaints of Major and other British politicians involved in the debacle, the *Financial Times* claimed that both the Bundesbank and the Bank of France had co-operated in the intervention to 'prop up the UK currency'. They spent 'an estimated £2bn'.[32] This action, by any measure, was a generous expenditure of French and German taxpayers' money in the interests of European solidarity. In an excellent piece of reporting, the *Financial Times* meticulously observed that sterling had closed in London on 16 September at DM 2.75, down 3 pfennigs on the day and below the all-significant floor of DM 2.778.

The departure of both sterling and the lira, which left ERM the day after sterling, did nothing to halt the march towards a single currency. It was at Maastricht, in December 1991, that the path to monetary union had been set in what would turn out to be an irrevocable process. The British experience with the ERM, the subsequent devaluation of the pound and the recovery of the British economy that followed meant that Britain would be an unlikely participant in the first wave of monetary union. This fact seemed rather to accelerate rather than hinder the process. The Delors Committee had been established in 1988 to plan for European economic and monetary union, and its report led in 1991 to the Maastricht Treaty, which could be regarded as EMU's constitution.[33]

The Maastricht Treaty had committed Europe to full monetary union even before the crises which undermined both the lira and sterling in September 1992. As the Italian bureaucrat and economist Tommaso Padoa-Schioppa wrote in 1999, Maastricht 'established the legal and institutional basis of the single currency and of the Eurosystem'.[34] Padoa-Schioppa served as a member of the first executive board of the European Central Bank when it was established in 1998. To Otmar Issing, the German economist who also served as a member of the ECB's first executive board, Maastricht represented the end of a process, not the beginning. In his book *The Birth of the Euro*, published in 2008, Issing dutifully outlined the conditions under which countries would be allowed to join the single-currency project. There were three principal characteristics: first, a 'low inflation rate'; second, 'sound public finances'; third was a more specific commitment, by which countries needed at least 'two years' membership of the fixed exchange rate mechanism' without exhibiting what Issing referred to as 'any tensions'.[35]

As a schoolboy Issing had been a Bavarian sprint champion or *Meister* over 100 and 200 metres. He had studied classics at Würzburg University, where he developed an interest in the works of Aristotle, before switching to economics, in which he obtained his doctorate at twenty-six. He spent nearly thirty years on the staff of the same university before he became chief economist at the Bundesbank in 1990. At the Bundesbank, he would warm up for the Central Council's fortnightly meetings by swimming in the bank's pool.[36] As a formidable German bureaucrat with a highly disciplined and academic approach to his career as a central banker, Issing had a very clear idea of what the single currency involved and how it should operate.

Naturally enough, to elite figures like Issing, the 'option of flexible exchange rates was never seriously entertained in the context of European integration'.[37] It was only natural too that Issing spoke of monetary union in terms of 'discipline' regarding public finance and the criteria imposed by membership of the new single currency. In his book on the euro, Issing described with obvious pride how the 'discipline exerted by the conditions for entry into the monetary union came late in certain cases, but all in all, it was timely enough'. If, as I have argued, the project of a single currency is viewed as an attempt to return to some of the rigour of the gold standard, or at least to the relative monetary order imposed by Bretton Woods, it was not surprising that Maastricht prescribed that the ratio of national debt to GDP should be less than 60 per cent. It also prescribed that annual deficits should not be more than 3 per cent of GDP.

Issing admitted that as regards the criterion of public sector indebtedness – the ratio of government debt to GDP – 'the progress made, if [there was any] at all, was much more modest' than the figures governments announced relating to their budget deficits. Total national debt figures of the aspirant eurozone countries remained high, even though annual deficits seemed to be kept low, by official figures, in the 1990s. Rather ominously, he also admitted that the deficit figures had been 'massaged in certain instances by acts of "creative accounting"'.[38] Issing's gravest fears about monetary union, however, were the lack of political union accompanying it, a reservation shared by many German technocrats and politicians during the 1990s. In two important areas, 'regulation of the labour market, on the one hand, and government tax and spending, on the other', national governments had been allowed sole discretion. Some of the fears which Issing expressed about monetary union were articulated before the euro was born. In his later work on the euro, Issing summarized the problem of 'moral hazard' which the euro created.

'Moral hazard' is a term in economics which has been defined as the 'presence of incentives for individuals or institutions to act in ways that incur costs they do not have to bear'.[39] One common instance of moral hazard exists in the case of insurance. Economists have observed that possessions which are insured are less well looked after than those without insurance. In 2008, just before the Greek sovereign-debt crisis, Issing wrote that the nations of the eurozone were conducting their fiscal policy under the condition of moral hazard. He wrote: 'In a single currency area, the political benefit from deficit spending (gaining votes) is enjoyed by *national* [italics in original] players, while the potential negative effects in the form of higher interest rates (due to increased government borrowing) are felt by *all* [italics in original] member states.' This state of affairs ensured that 'the resistance to deficit spending is reduced, and the propensity to pursue an (inappropriate) expansionary fiscal policy increases – a typical case of what is known as *moral hazard* [italics in original]'.[40] Observations similar to those made by Issing in 2008 were made by Germans sceptical about the single-currency euro project at the very beginning of the 1990s. Indeed the scale of initial German distrust of the single currency is something which is often overlooked as the German economy came to be regarded as the anchor of the eurozone, and the German political elite began to see themselves as guardians and guarantors of the euro. Proud of their own currency, the Deutschmark, which they believed had underpinned their country's enormous economic progress, German politicians and economists had initially been reluctant to surrender it.

As François Mitterrand, the French President, and Giulio Andreotti, the Italian Prime Minister, met at Mitterrand's out-of-town hotel on 8 December 1991 on the eve of the final Maastricht negotiations, a time-table for monetary union was yet to be agreed. The Germans did not want a firm date. They feared that 'some countries wouldn't be ready'. Under the influence of the Italian delegates, the Maastricht negotiators cleverly came up with two dates as the deadline for monetary union. These were 1997 and 1999. If a majority of the twelve member states of the EEC did not meet the criteria by 1997, then the project would begin by default in 1999, even if only 'a minority of countries qualified'.[41] On 9 December 1991, Mitterrand and Andreotti ambushed the Germans with this idea. It was reluctantly accepted by leading German politicians, who were unwilling to be cast as the guests who spoiled the party.

Inevitably, elements of the German press furiously denounced the proposals. *Der Spiegel*, the respected news magazine, and the tabloid *Bild* both carried lead articles asking why the beloved German mark should be sacrificed to the cause of European solidarity.[42] Indeed *Der Spiegel* in December 1991 pointed out that Chancellor Kohl had referred to the Deutschmark as 'the treasure of our country'. It also quoted Theo Waigel, the German Finance Minister, as saying that the 'Deutschmark is and remains the symbol of German political stability'. *Der Spiegel* went on to assert authoritatively that 'the mark is a symbol in fact, and . . . it embodies values such as diligence and thrift. The mark is German and, for many, it is Germany.'[43] But the magazine was in no doubt that, as a consequence of monetary union, 'suddenly Germany's trade partners [will be] forced to regulate their own currencies according to the stable German currency'. This would prove to be a naive hope.

If any nation could be said to be the principal driver of the single-currency project from the start, it was France. Even before the Maastricht Treaty was signed in February 1992, the French quality newspaper *Le Monde* was excitedly anticipating the treaty 'inaugurating economic and monetary union'. In a piece published on 1 December 1991, the 'sole problem' it foresaw regarding the treaty was the 'opt-out' the British would no doubt demand. *Le Monde*, unlike many commentators in Britain and, more surprisingly, in Germany, was very clear about the implications of the impending Treaty in Maastricht. 'We are on the way therefore towards the adoption of a treaty at Maastricht that will introduce step by step, in three stages, an Economic and Monetary Union between the countries of the E.E.C. [this became the European Union in 1992 as a result of the Treaty], according to a scheme close to that proposed in April 1989 by the council of experts, presided over by M. Delors.' Even before the meeting at Maastricht, *Le Monde* had seen with admirable clarity the development towards currency union as a natural process which had evolved from the establishment of the Delors Committee in 1988. The newspaper described the Germans as being 'obsessed by the fear of being dragged, by association, into an economic and monetary operation with little merit'. The Germans, like the Dutch, *Le Monde* predicted, would want the euro currency to be a 'kind of club reserved only to those member states which were rich and disciplined'. Despite tacitly supporting a wider definition of the currency, admitting all the then twelve member states of the EEC, the newspaper recognized that the Treaty would have 'to monitor excessive budget deficits', which were 'incompatible with the good functioning of a single currency'.[44]

The march to European monetary union, despite some German doubts and despite the ERM debacle of September 1992, proceeded smoothly. As early as 1991, Chancellor Kohl had described the process as a railway journey: 'In Maastricht the train may travel slowly through the station . . . and whoever wants to get off now, can get off.' As *Der Spiegel* reported in December that year, Kohl remained deeply committed to the vision of monetary union. The Chancellor, the magazine claimed, is 'quite sure that in a few years everybody will be sitting in the train'. They quoted Kohl at his most grandiloquent: 'History has a quite clear trend and a clear evolution towards Europe.' He added, 'There is no turning back.'[45] Kohl's assertiveness, his sense of destiny and the prestige he had attained by becoming the Chancellor who reunited West and East Germany were obvious advantages in promoting the single currency.

A towering figure, both physically and politically, Kohl projected an intense willpower that became a key motor behind the creation of the euro. A report in the British *Independent* newspaper in July 1997 observed that, although 'Germany has no chance of keeping its budget deficit below 3 per cent this year, Mr Kohl insisted the goal remained within his reach'. These words, the newspaper reported, had been directed at Edmund Stoiber, the Bavarian Prime Minister, who led Kohl's sister party, the Christian Social Union. Stoiber emerged as a powerful opponent of EMU, urging postponement of the single-currency project if the Maastricht Treaty's criteria were not met. He promised 'fierce resistance' to any attempts on the part of the German government to 'fudge the criteria'.[46] Stoiber's openly expressed doubts contradicted Kohl's own assurances, given at a meeting in Chicago in June 1997, that the 'European train', hurtling towards financial and political union, 'is firmly on track'. Kohl's insistence on the project was almost too emphatic to be wholly credible: 'The euro will come. I am absolutely certain.' Yet, that summer of 1997, the shape and scope of the single currency remained unclear. 'How many countries will be part [of it], I am not able to say,' the German Chancellor conceded.[47]

The fiscal situation of the European countries which aspired to join the single currency did not inspire confidence. All through the late 1990s, the lack of preparedness of certain EU countries to join the euro was a subject of open debate. 'There has, of course, been some sleight of hand,' wrote Rupert Cornwell in the *Independent* in February 1998. 'It remains mysterious quite how Italy, which for years regularly ran double-digit budget deficits, conveniently slashed last year's to a mere 2.7 per cent of GDP.' It was obvious, even before the euro was launched, that the single currency was an almost purely political project, which would be pursued without any real regard for the underlying economic reality. As the Frenchman Jacques Rueff had said, 'Europe will make itself by money or not at all.'[48] The words of the Portuguese Prime Minister António Guterres at the Madrid summit in December 1995 were even more grandiose and emphatic: 'When Jesus resolved to found a church, he said to Peter, "You are Peter, the rock, and upon this rock I will build my church." You are the euro, and upon this new currency we will build our Europe.'[49]

There was never any idea that the people of Europe, the citizens of the individual states, would be consulted before this momentous step was taken. As Issing himself later admitted, it was 'doubtless in Germany that resistance to EMU was the greatest'. The decision to 'abandon the D-Mark required a great deal of political courage', he remembered. In opinion polls conducted as late as the autumn of 1995, only 34 per cent of Germans were in favour of the single currency, while 45 per cent were against. Needless to say, these figures were reversed as the decade wore on and the single currency became more imminent. By the spring of 1999, some 55 per cent of Germans now supported the single currency while only 36 per cent continued their opposition.[50]

In the same poll from 1995, the Finns were shown to be the least in favour of the currency among the nations which eventually joined: 53 per cent of Finns were hostile to the currency, while only 33 per cent approved. It is important to grasp the extent to which Europe's political elites were committed to the single currency. The reasons why numerous political figures and bankers became strong advocates of the euro differed. For the Germans, it was often as much a symbol of fiscal discipline as a badge of European unity. For Issing, the benefits of the euro were explicitly focused on the need for fiscal discipline. This was a view widely held in Germany and the Netherlands.

The people of Europe, of course, had not been consulted before the single currency was officially launched on 1 January 1999. The euro was always conceived as an elite project, conjured up by technocrats, to be foisted upon a largely acquiescent and amorphous European public. There was as yet no European superstate, a fact which worried Germans, unsure of whether a monetary union was possible without a political union.

These concerns reveal the prime function of the single currency, aside from its role as the ultimate symbol of European unity and co-operation. Repeatedly, during the 1990s, the single currency was hailed as a mechanism which would tame wild deficit spending. Otmar Issing himself, in a speech in May 1999, admitted that even though there had been some progress, 'government deficit and debt levels remain on a level in many euro area Member States which is too high and not sustainable'.[51] *The Political Economy of Monetary Union: Towards the Euro*, a book on monetary union published in 1998, suggested that 'reducing budget deficits has become every politician's obligation'. This goal was justified by the trends in the 'debt to GDP ratio' which had been 'striking'. In the period 1980–95, the authors of this book noticed, 'the average gross public debt in industrial countries swelled from about 40 per cent to about 70 per cent of GDP'. They went on to state that 'most countries, including France, Germany, Italy, Japan, the Netherlands, Sweden and the United States, experienced roughly a doubling of their debt [as a percentage of GDP] over this period'. When their book was published, among 'the highest debt countries, Belgium and Canada, with Greece and Italy, have debts near or over 100 per cent of GDP'.[52] In conclusion, the Maastricht Treaty was described as the 'biggest pan-European attempt to limit budget deficits by imposing legal constraints'.[53]

The single currency was a grandiose political project. It was also designed to impose limits on deficit spending. The 'mechanisms of the political process stand in the way of such discretionary fiscal policy action', Issing wrote in 2008. The 'long-term objective of sound fiscal policy is easily lost sight of' and the consequence of democracy was that there was a 'tendency towards rising budget deficits and increasing public debt, as was observed in Europe in the 1970s'.[54] Such scepticism about the ability of democracies to deal with the problems of public spending and borrowing was perhaps to be expected of a German bureaucrat such as Issing, who had enjoyed immense power within Germany and in Europe without ever being elected to any official position. It was the attitude of such men that largely determined the nature of the single currency. It was their determination and drive which converted the dream of a European single currency into reality.

The currency was successfully launched in January 1999, and notes were first issued in January 2002. *Der Spiegel*, the German current affairs magazine, saw the launch of the euro notes as a 'Departure into the Unknown'.[55] The London-based *Economist* had described the earlier launch of the euro as a trading currency as 'Europe's adventure', and the 'biggest risk the EU has ever taken'. In its rather grandiose way, the British weekly added that the launch of the euro was 'arguably the most momentous currency innovation since the establishment of the United States dollar in 1792', though public support for it had been 'thin, to say the least'. It also acknowledged the boldness and ambition of the project: 'As recently as ten years ago, the idea of merging the European Union's national monetary systems seemed fantastic. A plan for doing it was drawn up nonetheless. Then . . . the forerunner of the single currency [the ERM] . . . collapsed, casting new doubt on the whole enterprise.' This, it turned out, did not deflect the determination of the protagonists. 'No matter. The prime movers, Helmut Kohl in Germany and François Mitterrand in France, carried on regardless.' The *Economist* concluded that on 'January 4th [1999] their remarkable vision becomes a reality'.

The creation of the euro was no doubt, as the *Economist* suggested, 'an amazing political feat'. More interestingly, it had been achieved without much popular enthusiasm. 'Nobody can claim that EMU was forced upon Europe's governments by force of events, still less by popular demand.' The single currency thus represented the triumph of bureaucratic planning. It had been, in the *Economist*'s words, 'an elite project'. 'Europe's governments are saying: Our people may not be convinced of the euro's benefits just yet, but once it is in place and they come to understand it, they will change their minds.' Such an attitude was evidence of a high degree of self-confidence among the pioneers, the bureaucrats, the politicians, particularly Kohl and Mitterrand, and economists who pushed the countries of Europe towards the euro in the late 1990s.

The self-confidence of the European political class should perhaps have been tempered by doubt about the suitability of some of the participant countries. Doubts had been raised through the 1990s about the ability of such countries as Italy and Belgium to put their fiscal house in order. That Greece should have joined the single currency was not, as late as 1997, even contemplated. In April that year, Yannos Papantoniou, the Greek Finance Minister, travelled to Brussels for a meeting of his European Union counterparts. In a discussion about the lettering on the coins, Theo Waigel, the German Finance Minister, had asked him, 'What ever makes you think you will ever be in the euro?'[56] The Germans had always wanted a hard currency. Over the course of the next four years, Papantoniou nonetheless steered Greece towards the euro. The Greek adoption of the euro currency was late; it joined in 2001, while the other currencies had been pegged to the currency in 1999. This proved to be a fateful event which made the lives of investors, politicians and, most importantly, the Greek people less comfortably secure than might otherwise have been the case.

The Rise of China

At the end of the twentieth century, the most significant global development, strictly in terms of international currency, was undoubtedly the
creation and successful launch of the euro. More widely, the greatest
economic phenomenon of the time was almost certainly the growth of
China. After adopting a peculiar brand of Marxism with the victory of
the Chinese Communist Party in 1949, China abandoned doctrinaire
Communism as an economic philosophy in 1978. It was in this year that
Deng Xiaoping finally seized the reins of power in China and began a
process which continued to propel that country in the early twenty-first
century.

Deng was born in 1904 and was already seventy-four when he became
China's 'paramount leader' in 1978. At such an age, many people thought
he would be 'too old to be anything but a transitional figure'.[1] Deng's
journey had been tortuous. Mao had first placed him in the upper reaches
of the party in the early 1950s. As early as 1954, Deng had become General
Secretary of the Chinese Communist Party. His career, however, saw sharp
reversals, as an increasingly paranoid Chairman Mao purged rivals during
the 1960s. In October 1969, Deng and his wife, Zhuo Lin, were taken by
a special plane to Nanchang in Jiangxi province, an inland province in the
south-east of China. In this new location, Deng was forced to engage
in physical labour. He was also made to undergo a programme of 're-
education' in 'Mao Zedong Thought'. He and his family were allowed to
bring personal belongings and several cases of books with them, although
Deng's request to see Mao before his exile was not granted.[2]

By the time Deng took over the government in 1978, Mao had been
dead for two years. Despite the 're-education', Deng's years of exile had

made him less committed to the thought of Mao. To understand the transformation of China, it is perhaps instructive to consider the experience of Japan at the end of the nineteenth century when, under the Meiji restoration, a deliberate plan of modernization was initiated. From December 1871 to September 1873, fifty-one Japanese officials travelled by ship and rail to a number of different countries to study the ways of the world. They returned to Japan to implement the lessons they had learnt. Likewise in China, one hundred years later, many separate 'study tours' took place. Senior Chinese officials were similarly eager to learn from their travels and to introduce reforms in their home country. Deng himself had embarked on a five-day visit to France in 1975. He had taken with him a number of technical bureaucrats, in the transport and industry sectors. The tour was not so significant in terms of what Deng learnt. Rather, it converted him to the whole process of tours, which he undertook with enthusiasm, while encouraging other study groups to travel abroad. It was some months after Mao's death before foreign travel could be organized, but in 1978 Chinese officials, under Deng's encouragement, began to make those visits. They were exhilarated by what they saw.[3]

As Deng himself observed towards the end of 1978, the 'more we see, the more we realize how backward we are'. Prominent Chinese bureaucrats and other technocratic figures visited such diverse parts of the world as 'Eastern Europe, Hong Kong, Japan, and Western Europe'. It was obvious to them that China had to change. Japan, in particular, was a source of interest. The Japanese recovery after the disaster of the Second World War showed the Chinese how a 'strong central government' could direct an economy rapidly to catch up with the West. In a report to the Politburo on Japanese economic progress since 1945, Chinese officials recounted with awe and admiration how the Japanese 'had boldly introduced foreign technologies, made use of foreign capital, and vigorously developed education and scientific research'.[4] A trip to Western Europe, undertaken in May 1978, made an even more profound impression. A visit to the United States was out of the question, given the dispute over the Republic of China on Taiwan, which until April 1979, the United States recognized officially as the only legitimate Chinese government.

Deng's reforms have been characterized as essentially pro-capitalist. The story often told is one of China, a country ruled by avowed Communists, turning its back on Mao Zedong and Karl Marx and embracing the free-market capitalism of the West. This, of course, is a simplification of what happened. The type of capitalism which China adopted was distinctive and, in many of its features, differed widely from the capitalism preached by the neo-liberals who dominated US and British administrations in the 1980s. The key to understanding China's impressive economic growth in the 1980s and 1990s starts inevitably with the state. China did not grow like neighbouring Hong Kong, as a free-market trading area, whose political economy was governed by the 'invisible hand' of Adam Smith. While free-market impulses were given some leeway, China's path to success was dictated by the state. In this way, China represented a triumph of 'mercantilism', a concept which needs to be understood fully to grasp what happened in that country in the last quarter of the twentieth century.

Mercantilism was a term used to describe the economic policies of European countries in the sixteenth to eighteenth centuries. Despite the work of Adam Smith and the continuing efforts of other liberal economists, mercantilism, with its emphasis on exports, has remained widely practised in the modern world. Eli Heckscher, the Swedish economic historian, outlined the early modern European states' approach to political economy in his two-volume work *Mercantilism*, first published in Sweden in 1931. Very simply put, mercantilism was a system which sought to boost exports in order to gain gold, which would form the basis of a state's power. 'With a large population and low wages,' wrote Heckscher, 'it was hoped to effect a large export surplus of manufactures and a large import surplus of gold and precious stones, and this desire became itself a part of the state's policy of power.'[5]

To many critics and observers of Chinese economic policy, particularly in the United States, Heckscher's account perfectly summarized Beijing's approach to economic development. As late as December 2009, the Nobel Prize-winning economist Paul Krugman, a leftist commentator, asserted in his *New York Times* blog that 'we know that China's pursuing a mercantilist policy'. Having made his accusation, Krugman then explained what this policy entailed. The Chinese, he maintained, were 'keeping the renminbi [the Chinese currency] weak through a combination of capital controls and intervention leading to trade surpluses'.[6] He presented as accurately as Heckscher had done, almost eighty years previously, the essential logic of mercantilism, spelling out the link between keeping a currency weak and promoting exports. By keeping your currency under-valued against, for example, the US dollar, you would make your exports cheaper for Americans to buy. This undervaluation of a domestic currency compared to the currency of a trading partner would achieve the 'large export surplus of manufactures' which Heckscher believed to be the main object of mercantilism.

The accusation that China had manipulated its currency, known as the renminbi or the yuan, by keeping it artificially low in order to price its exports competitively was widely made by Americans from both wings of the US political divide. It was natural that Americans should be the most concerned about a cheap Chinese currency. Throughout the last two decades of the twentieth century and the first decade of the twenty-first, Americans of all political persuasions often complained that the United States' trade balance, the difference between imports and exports, was always in deficit, with imports far outstripping exports. The principal beneficiary of these trade deficits was China. Patrick Buchanan, a populist right-wing commentator on American politics, also observed China's mercantilism, but, unlike Krugman, he had nothing but praise for the Chinese. In July 2010, in a piece entitled 'Yankee Utopians in a Chinese Century', Buchanan noted with alarm that for 'a decade' China had been 'running history's largest trade surpluses with the United States' and had by July 2010 'amassed a hoard of $2.3 trillion in foreign currency'.

To Buchanan, China's policy was one which should be adopted by the United States. 'How has China vaulted to the forefront in manufacturing, trade and technology?' he asked. He supplied the answer to his own ques-tion: 'Export-driven economic nationalism.'[7] He then proceeded to give a partial and highly abbreviated history of how Beijing had managed to engineer such a beneficial outcome for Chinese exports. 'Beijing cut the value of its currency in half in 1994, doubling the price of imports, slash-ing the price of exports and making Chinese labor the best bargain in Asia.' The natural consequence of this dramatic cut in the value of the yuan was that foreign firms 'were invited to relocate their plants in China and told this was the price of access to the Chinese market'.[8]

Buchanan's account of the way in which foreign firms were supposed to have 'relocated' to China, the famous outsourcing of American jobs denounced by populists of both left and right, was perhaps inaccurate. Yet a look at the movement of the value of the yuan against the US dollar since 1980 gives credence to his and Krugman's claims that the Chinese had indeed depreciated their currency as an act of deliberate policy. What is nearly always forgotten in discussions about China's export-led policy is that, as recently as the mid-1980s, the Chinese, like much of the Western world, actually had a trade deficit. A 'consumer-goods spending spree in 1984' caused the 'government to lose control over imports'. China's trade deficit, in terms of goods, 'shot up to US$15 billion in 1985, while foreign exchange reserves plummeted from US$14.42 billion in 1984 to US$11.19 billion in March 1986'. The mid-1980s were years when China was sucking in imports, as the country 'borrowed from abroad to finance its visible-trade deficit, which averaged between US$1 billion and US$1.5 billion a month'.

In this condition, running a chronic trade deficit, China in the mid-1980s was merely 'moving along the path that so many developing . . . economies would follow over the next decade'. The Chinese government believed that, along with trade deficits, would come the 'loss of self-reliance'.[9] As was to be expected, the Chinese leadership acted to improve matters. Indeed from 1980 the Chinese yuan experienced 'substantial depreciation against major currencies'. Between 1980 and 1992, the yuan 'devalued by 74 percent versus the US dollar, 85 percent versus the Japanese yen, 71 percent versus the ECU (European Currency Unit) and 60 percent versus the Hong Kong dollar'. The devaluation of China's currency was manifestly a deliberate policy. It was, 'without doubt, intended to promote exports and to restrain imports so as to improve China's current account position'. In 1980, the official value of the yuan was 1.53 to a US dollar. By 1985, this rate had fallen to 3.2 to a US dollar. After successive devaluations in July 1986, December 1989, November 1990 and January 1994, the rate had fallen to 8.72 yuan to a US dollar.[10] Looked at another way, 100 yuan in 1980 had been worth about US$65. In 1994, 100 yuan was worth only US$11.5, a mere 17.5 per cent of its value fourteen years before. This inevitably made Chinese goods considerably cheaper for American consumers to buy. These successive devaluations were a cause of great concern to American administrations at the time. The Chinese currency's relationship with the US dollar was complicated by the fact that there were two types of currency: the renminbi, or yuan, issued to locals, and a foreign-exchange certificate issued to foreigners which was the only convertible currency.[11]

As late as December 1989, the *New York Times*, commenting on yet another Chinese devaluation, made the obvious point that 'devaluation will make exports cheaper and imports more expensive, and hence should improve China's trade balance, which, according to customs figures, ran at a deficit of $7.7 billion' in 1988.[12] At the time of the *New York Times* article, however, China's trade situation was changing. It was in the late 1980s that the Chinese state 'stepped up efforts to provide preferred access both to raw materials and to credit'. These measures were taken to 'assure the continued growth of exports'.[13] The effect of these policies, coupled with well-timed devaluations, ensured that China would now be export-ing more goods than it imported. In the final quarter of 1989, its trade deficit was only $100 million. During the following year, 1990, China achieved trade surpluses 'that grew greater in each quarter'. For the year as a whole, the trade surplus was '$8.74 billion'. By the end of 1990, Chinese foreign exchange reserves had risen to $28.6 billion, more than twice the level of mid-1989.[14]

Even in the early 1990s, China's accumulation of such large trade surpluses irritated the American government. In Washington's view, China's 'trade strategy had changed fundamentally from a genuine policy of openness and freer trade towards a policy of "continued export growth without import liberalization"'. The United States' share of China's exports had grown significantly. The proportion of China's exports going to the United States went up from 6 per cent in 1979 to 26 per cent in 1991. American policymakers, by the early 1990s, were increasingly concerned and initiated a series of bilateral discussions, in which they urged China to open up its markets. They principally wanted the Chinese to 'reduce the number and severity of administrative barriers they imposed on imports'.

These restrictions included 'import licensing requirements', quotas on imports and other onerous regulations relating to product testing and the need to acquire appropriate certificates.

China's steady devaluation of its currency was concluded in 1994. With the yuan then worth little more than a sixth of its dollar value in 1980, there had been depreciation of about 8.4 per cent every year against the US dollar. The currency rate of 8.72 yuan to a US dollar was reached in 1994, but a rate of 8.28 was then maintained for eight years from 1997 until 2005. In July 2005 the rate was allowed to appreciate slightly to 8.11 yuan to a US dollar. Naturally enough, it was during the mid- to late 1990s that China's exports to the United States really took off. The US trade deficit with China went from US$39.5 billion in 1996 to US$124 billion in 2003. Falling dollar values against the euro, for example, made no difference since China had pegged its currency to the dollar.[15] The Chinese knew where their main export market lay. They remained unwilling, despite intermittent urging by the Americans, to allow their currency to appreciate against the dollar.

It was during the late 1990s that the West first started to take China seriously as an economic power. As is often the case, one person came to symbolize, for many observers in the West, the immense strides towards prosperity which China made in this period. Zhu Rongji became Prime Minister of China in March 1998. Zhu had been born to a family of landowners in Hunan province in 1928, and his bourgeois background created suspicion among the higher levels of the Communist Party. Like many of the people who have filled the most senior political and administrative offices in China, he studied electrical engineering and had a sharp, technocratic approach to problems. In a flattering profile in *Time*, he was said to be 'tall and sharp with the features of a falcon', dominating meetings 'with his quick mind'. '"His IQ must be 200," deputy US Treasury Secretary Lawrence Summers once said.' The favourable magazine article referred, in tones of reverence, to Zhu's 'rolodex memory' and 'endless energy'.

Zhu was also something of an intense, controlled obsessive. He read, *Time* assured its readers, 'many of the 16,000 letters' he received every year from citizens with grievances. To the magazine this seemed a trivial use of his time: 'he should not be doing that too often', because a man of his importance 'should be dealing with the big problems'.[16] It would be a mistake, however, to believe as many did that Zhu was a committed capitalist, always ready to defer to the law of the free market. He had been 'brought up through the system of command, not through market economics'.[17] His approach to economic management was a curious hybrid of 'both monetary and fiscal intervention tools accepted in a Western market economy' and 'the high-handed administrative measures characteristic of the command economy'.[18]

One of the first challenges facing Zhu as he took over as Prime Minister in 1998 was the aftermath of the Asian crisis which started in the summer of 1997. The crisis itself, precipitated by the sudden devaluation of the Thai currency, the baht, has spawned a substantial literature discussing its causes and consequences. The causes of the crisis should be familiar. The famous search for yield, in which low interest rates at home prompted investors to seek better returns in more distant markets, was the initial engine of the boom in the newly named 'emerging markets'. As Paul Krugman expressed it, in the early 1990s 'interest rates in advanced countries were exceptionally low, because central banks were trying to boot their economies out of a mild recession'. Investors 'went abroad in search for higher yields'. In 1990 'private capital flows to developing countries were $42 billion'. At that time, the financing provided by private investors was exceeded by official agencies like the IMF and the World Bank. Asian markets gained an increasing share of this investment in the course of the 1990s.

The rush of foreign investment caused a speculative boom in Southeast Asia in the middle of the decade. In Krugman's words, by 'early 1996 the economies of Southeast Asia were starting to bear a strong family resemblance to Japan's "bubble economy" of the late 1980s'.[19] Japan's asset bubble had ended in the early 1990s when the Bank of Japan started increasing interest rates to 'let some air out of the balloon'. From 1991, as Krugman recounted looking back over the whole of the 1990s, 'land and stock prices began a steep decline, which within a few years put them some 60 percent below their peak'.[20] Looking back from 2000, Fumio Hayashi and Edward Prescott, who was to be the 2004 winner of the Nobel Prize in economics, depicted the 1990s in Japan as 'a lost decade', in which there had occurred 'economic stagnation'. The authors pointed to Japan's 'average annual growth rate of 0.5 percent in the 1991–2000 period', while the United States enjoyed growth at an annual rate of 2.6 per cent.[21]

The Asian crisis was, if anything, even more dramatic than Japan's years of stagnation. It blew up over a few months in the summer of 1997. There was essentially a panic among foreign investors in Thailand. At the beginning of July 1997, the Thai baht went into free fall, the 'baht price of a dollar soared 50 percent over the next few months, and would have risen even further if Thailand had not sharply raised interest rates'. The baht's dramatic collapse had very predictable consequences. The panic created more panic in a process Krugman said was similar to a microphone in an auditorium generating a 'feedback loop': 'sounds picked up by the microphone are amplified by the loudspeakers'.[22] These sounds are then amplified and increased until a deafening noise is created. The idea that a panic creates its own momentum is implicit in the phenomenon of a 'bank run', in which the prospect of a bank collapse actually causes this to happen, as depositors, doubtful of a bank's solvency, remove their deposits, thereby damaging the bank.

The feedback loop or bank run is essentially a circular process: it might be called a vicious circle. In the case of Thailand, the loss of investor confidence and the ensuing collapse in the value of the baht forced the central bank of Thailand to increase interest rates to defend the currency. Inevitably, both higher interest rates and a devalued currency created serious problems for Thai businesses and financial institutions. 'On one side, many of them had dollar debts, which suddenly became more burdensome as the number of baht per dollar increased; on the other, many of them also had baht debts, which became harder to service as interest rates soared.' The risk behind the sudden panic which rocked the Thai economy was that, by a process known as 'contagion', other countries in the region would be affected.[23] 'Contagion' has been defined as a 'domino effect, such as when economic problems in one country spread to another'.[24] This is what occurred in the Asian crisis in 1997–8, a period of 'plunging crises, failed banks and recessions'. It is suggested that the experience led many of these countries, such as Thailand,

Malaysia and Singapore, to concentrate on 'export-led policies in the 2000s'.[25]

Of course, an 'export-led' economic policy was one which China had been pursuing since the late 1980s. One of the most remarkable features of the Asian crisis was the role of China as a pillar of stability amid the unfolding uncertainty. 'What spared China', Krugman observed, 'was the fact that, unlike its neighbours, it had not yet made its currency "convertible": that is, in China you still needed a government license to change yuan into dollars.' This 'lack of convertibility meant that the kind of high-speed currency crisis . . . in which everyone rushed to convert domestic currency into dollars before a devaluation . . . could not happen'. It also meant that China, unlike other countries in the region, could effectively 'print money at will'.[26]

During the crisis, the yuan remained stable. It seemed 'miraculous that the regional contagion did not result in significant reduction in the value of China's renminbi (RMB)', a commentator wrote in 2000. While there had existed 'downward pressure on the Japanese currency' during 1998 'the top leaders of the People's Republic of China (PRC), including President Jiang Zemin and Premier Zhu Rongji, on many occasions pledged themselves to maintaining a stable RMB'.[27] China's leaders were adamant that they would not devalue the currency. They knew that to do so would 'knock a psychological prop under the Hong Kong dollar', which was pegged to the American dollar via a currency board, a monetary authority in one country whose sole aim is to maintain a fixed exchange rate with the currency of another country. The Chinese leadership quickly grasped the depth of Asia's problems. In the summer of 1997, they agreed to contribute to a fund to help bail out Thailand. They also 'reintroduced tax rebates for exports' to aid their exporters who might otherwise be expected to lobby the government to devalue the currency. The Chinese leaders also 'noted with shock the ability of a convertible currency to take a country's ropy banking system to the point of collapse'.[28]

The stance of China's leaders is ironic, given that the same Americans who intermittently criticized China for being a currency manipulator applauded its stability in 1997. The Chinese were praised by US officials during the crisis for 'holding the line', even though in Beijing they just thought they were being consistent. In the summer of 1999, the *Economist* of London stated that a devaluation of the yuan was 'now increasingly likely'.[29] In February 1998, the magazine *Business China* confidently expected that 'the present RMB: dollar exchange rate can last until the last quarter of 1998 or the first quarter of 1999'. Then, the magazine believed, the rate would 'be adjusted down about 11% to RMB 9.3: US$1'.[30] The Chinese leaders themselves would have found the comments of the Western press amusing. On the one hand, they were accused of being currency manipulators and keeping their currency undervalued. On the other, when most foreign commentators widely expected the Chinese to devalue their currency even further during the crisis, they did not in fact do so. The Chinese, however, had always maintained that their policy of pegging the yuan to the dollar was not 'meant to favour exports over imports, but instead to foster economic stability by tying its currency to the US dollar at a constant level'. This may have been rather disingenuous, but it is incontestable that stability was a prime concern for the Chinese. The Chinese Communist administration admirably pursued a consistent policy, over decades in which successive American administrators adopted different attitudes, now threatening, now more conciliatory, to the rising superpower across the Pacific Ocean.

In December 1997, Zhu Rongji, then Deputy Prime Minister and often referred to as the 'nation's economic czar', said in a newspaper interview that 'China will not devalue its currency'. By the end of 1997, Thailand, Indonesia, Malaysia and the Philippines had experienced sharp drops in the value of their currencies, thereby improving the competitive position of their exports as against China's products. The goods with which they competed with China included shoes, toys and electronic goods. Both this group of countries and China competed for the same markets in the United States, Europe and Japan.[31] It would have been natural to expect the Chinese to follow these currencies by devaluing their currency. The stability of the yuan in 1997–8 demonstrates more clearly than perhaps any other economic phenomenon the strategic quality of China's economic policymaking. The Chinese leaders, unaccountable to anything like a domestic electorate, planned for the long term and refused to be swayed by short-term considerations.

Of course, the real devaluation had already taken place. The steady depreciation which China introduced in the 1980s was followed by a remarkable period of currency stability between 1997 and 2004. This stability coincided with a phase of astonishing economic growth. By the middle of the first decade of the twenty-first century, commentators were beginning to speak of Chinese economic growth as an unprecedented phenomenon in human history. A British writer, James Kynge, compared the growth of many cities in China to the growth of the United States in the nineteenth century. Chongqing, a relatively new city, whose municipality was created as recently as 1997, was likened to Chicago. 'The raw human effort that girded nineteenth-century Chicago and propels Chongqing today underpins the two cities' most revealing similarity.' This likeness stemmed from 'the speed of their expansion'. Yet Chicago, known as the fastest-growing city on earth in 1900, had taken fifty years until 1900 to increase its population to 1.7 million people. Chongqing was growing at 'eight times that speed'.[32]

There is a popular, but apparently mistaken, belief that the Chinese word for crisis is composed of two characters, one representing 'danger' and the other 'opportunity'. Despite this misapprehension, it is now clear that the Asian crisis was used to great effect by the Chinese to quicken the pace of their reforms. Zhu Rongji, once again, was identified as the main driver of these measures. 'State enterprises' were 'given just three years to sort themselves out' in 1998, even though this may have meant sacking millions of workers. The state banks were also given three years 'to clear their books of bad loans' and to begin 'lending on purely commercial terms'. In the face of protests, Zhu was believed to show 'a steely intelligence and an impressive force of character'.[33] Anyone who attended his press conferences would realize that he was still very much a party bureaucrat, an apparatchik who relied on giving orders and drawing up plans, rather than the liberal capitalist figure many in the West portrayed. At his first press conference as Premier, Zhu spoke in arcane terms about the 'Three Implementations'.

The first 'Implementation' was the commitment to 'turn around most of the large and medium-sized loss-making state-owned enterprises in about three years, and then to establish a modern enterprise system'. This,

Zhu stressed, had to be accomplished 'within three years'. The second element of the programme was the decision to 'thoroughly reform' China's financial system. This once again would be completed 'within three years'. The main feature of financial reform would be the strengthening of the Chinese central bank's 'supervisory and regulatory role'. Commercial banks, Zhu confirmed, would have 'to operate autonomously'. The third plank of his ambitious programme was the 'reorganization of government agencies'. He aimed to reduce the number of ministries and commissions overseen by the State Council 'from forty to twenty-nine'. Half of the staff of these ministries would, in Zhu's telling phrase, be 'reassigned'.[34]

It has been an open question to what extent Zhu actually managed to achieve all he set out to do. Like many politicians, he was skilful at advertising his accomplishments. In a press conference in Beijing in March 2001, he recalled the crisis years of 1997 and 1998. China's economy had experienced difficulties in those years, he conceded, but he added proudly that around '10 million workers in state-owned enterprises were laid off'. These remarks offered an interesting perspective on the highly centralized and dirigiste nature of Chinese policymaking. Some people had suggested that 'we devalue the renminbi to boost our exports'. Meanwhile others had suggested that 'we could get through the crisis by selling state-owned assets'. Against these arguments, however, China's masters held firm: the 'Party Central and the State Council made a firm decision to pursue an expansionary fiscal policy along with a steady monetary policy'.

The fiscal policy which the Chinese embarked on at this time would be familiar to students of the 1930s. They invested '1.5 trillion yuan [US$180 billion] in infrastructure construction over the past three years [1998–2001]'. From the vantage point of 2001, Zhu was proudly confident of the efficacy of these policies. The 'results are now very obvious'. Then like the centralizing bureaucrat and statistical enthusiast that he was, he proceeded to reel off the number, size and scale of all these gigantic achievements in building the infrastructure of his country. His list of statistics sounded like something taken from one of Stalin's Five-Year Plans, which indeed provided part of the inspiration for the Chinese Communist Party's bid to industrialize China. In 'these three years, we built 170,000km of highways, including 10,000km of high-speed expressways'. Zhu also boasted of building 10,000 kilometres of 'new or upgraded . . . electrified rail-roads'. His accurate and retentive memory enabled him to recite all the statistics of the government's programme with great fluency. As someone steeped, purportedly at least, in the teachings of Mao Zedong, he showed an admirable grasp of Keynesian economics. 'It is true', he added, 'that China's fiscal deficit has increased, and the increase is significant, but the entire added deficit was used to finance infrastructure construction.'[35]

One year later, at another press conference in Beijing, held in March 2002, the Chinese Premier noted that China's estimated deficit for the year would be 309.8 billion yuan (US$36.7 billion), which at that time was 'around 3 percent of GDP'. The total debt figure which Zhu revealed was only 2.56 trillion yuan (US$309 billion), a mere '16 percent of GDP'. This last figure was remarkably low given that Great Britain's debt-to-GDP percentage in 1914, just before the outbreak of the First World War, after nearly a hundred years of paying down debts incurred in the Napoleonic Wars, had been 25 per cent. China's low debt-to-GDP figure was a func-tion of an economy growing at 8–10 per cent a year over more than twenty years. Debts were dwarfed by economic growth.

Zhu was particularly defensive about deficit spending. The 'most important thing', he maintained, was that China's deficit was not being 'used to make up shortfalls in the regular budget'. It was being used exclu-sively for 'infrastructure construction'. He proceeded to rattle off a number of projects which had been constructed making use of a '2.5 trillion yuan' fund. This time he stressed Chinese achievements in energy: 'We've built 95 million Kw of power stations and completely rebuilt the rural power grids across the entire country.' As always in the case of China, the sheer scale of some of these projects challenges the imagination. Zhu almost casually observed that there were now '320 million subscribers for fixed line and mobile telephones', a figure which covered only a quarter of the total Chinese population, but which comfortably exceeded the number of people in the United States. Zhu boasted, in defence of his programme of public investment, that he wouldn't merely be leaving behind debt for the next administration (his five-year term was ending the following year, in 2003), but that there would 'be more than 2.5 trillion yuan of high-quality assets' to show for this lavish expenditure.[36]

The Chinese authorities were not afraid to spend public money, but their public spending was part of a wider economic strategy: exports would earn foreign currency reserves, and borrowing would be spent almost exclusively on building up the infrastructure of the large territories which constitute China. The Chinese government had not developed a comprehensive system of public welfare provision, although it was often suggested that many of the most inefficient state companies, by supplying jobs and salaries to workers, offered a crude form of welfare provision. As a final tribute to the success of his programme of public spending, Zhu declared that he was 'very proud' of his adoption of an 'expansionary fiscal policy'. This policy, in his opinion, had ensured that China 'not only overcame the impact of the Asian financial crisis, but was able to use the opportunity to achieve unprecedented economic growth'.[37]

In a sense, the Chinese had acted more consistently with Keynesian principles than many other governments would in later crises. Keynes had been brought up in the late Victorian era. His basic assumption had been that governments would try to balance their budgets. He advocated the financing of public spending through borrowing only in exceptional circumstances, as a way of stimulating the economy whenever a downturn occurred. His ideas were developed in the 1930s, a decade of exceptional economic crisis. Naturally, he implicitly assumed that governments would run surpluses or at least balance their budgets in ordinary times. This is broadly what the British had achieved in the century between 1815 and the start of the First World War. A similar fiscal discipline characterized the Chinese government. The deficits it ran, it must be remembered, were moderate. In 2002, Zhu Rongji referred to a deficit of 3 per cent of GDP; this was the figure prescribed by the Maastricht Treaty which, even in times of economic prosperity, many eurozone countries struggled to achieve.

Despite China's careful stewardship of its public spending programme, the Chinese currency continued to be an object of complaint by many in Washington. Throughout the first decade of the twenty-first century, China's currency arrangements remained a source of frustration to American administrations, grappling with ever-increasing trade deficits. Constant pressure from George W. Bush's administration between 2001 and 2005 was a contributory factor in China adopting a cautious upward revaluation of the yuan. The revaluation was effected in July 2005 and was only 2.1 per cent, which resulted in the exchange rate of the yuan rising from 8.28 to a US dollar to 8.11. This was a small step, but the US Treasury Secretary John W. Snow described it as 'the start of an awfully important process' which might resolve one of the principal sources of dispute between China and the United States.[38]

The yuan's revaluation in July 2005 did not lead to the freely floating currency desired by the Bush administration. A member of that administration noted that 'Chinese leaders continued to describe their currency as "managed".' The background to this pressure on the part of the American government on the Chinese to float their currency was, of course, the mounting US trade deficit with China. As the *New York Times* explained in July 2005, with 'the United States building up a trade deficit with China that could exceed $180 billion this year, anti-China sentiment in both parties', Republican and Democrat, was 'so high' that even 'ardent free-trade advocates' were considering 'new restrictions'.[39] It was the objection which US administrations had been raising since the early 1990s: 'China was giving itself an unfair trading advantage by keeping its currency at an artificially low value against the dollar, which made its exports to the United States cheaper than they would otherwise be.'

The move to revalue the yuan was widely dismissed by American Congressmen of both parties. Benjamin Cardin, a Democrat Congressman from Maryland, contemptuously dismissed the Chinese policy announcement as 'inadequate'. Phil English, a Republican Congressman, said, 'If this is a last best offer, it is unacceptable.' US politicians continued to threaten retaliatory measures, in the form of tariffs and added protection for their domestic manufactures. But other economists, notably Alan Greenspan, were more reluctant to blame China alone for the United States' chronic trade deficit with the rest of the world. Greenspan argued that 'America's bloated trade deficits probably wouldn't be helped by China revamping its currency as the Bush administration has been pressing Beijing to do.' The Federal Reserve Chairman observed that US companies would be likely to turn to other countries 'such as Thailand or Malaysia' for goods they were buying from China. The US, in Greenspan's view, would simply be 'importing from a different area' and would be importing 'the same goods'.⁴⁰ He was arguing that, if the Chinese currency appreciated, causing Chinese goods to be more expensive, US companies would simply buy goods from other South-east Asian countries, whose currencies, and hence whose exports, remained cheap. The US trade balance would remain unaffected in this case.

To the American politicians, however, with their powerful interest groups to appease, China remained a favourite object of attack. Even as late as February 2010, President Obama stated that China's undervalued currency put US firms at a 'huge competitive disadvantage'. In the perennial language of the politician seeking to affirm his or her sense of urgency, Obama 'pledged to make addressing China's currency policy a top priority'. Again, eighteen months later in November 2011, he asserted that the Chinese needed to 'go ahead and move towards a market-based system for their currency' and that the United States and 'other countries' now felt that 'enough is enough'. By then, this cry had been made fitfully by US governments for twenty years. The Americans had achieved some concessions. Indeed, between 2005 and 2011 the yuan had appreciated by about 30 per cent against the dollar.⁴¹ (The average rate was about 6.5 yuan to the dollar in 2011, as opposed to 8.28 before the revaluation of July 2005.) In November 2012, the US administration decided not to declare China 'as having manipulated its currency to gain an unfair trade advantage', even though the US Treasury expressed its belief that the yuan remained 'significantly undervalued' and urged the Chinese 'to make further progress'. The Republican candidate in the 2012 presidential election, Mitt Romney, had declared that he would have branded China 'a currency manipulator' on his first day in office.⁴² Romney's stance was in tune with the Republican Party's traditional support for economic nationalism, as demonstrated in its consistent support for protective tariffs throughout the nineteenth century.

The Chinese themselves unsurprisingly began to show growing exasperation over US attempts to increase pressure over the currency issue. The Xinhua News Agency, the official press agency of the People's Republic of China, reported in March 2010 that some 'politicians in the West are playing the game of politicizing China's RMB exchange rate again'. Astutely,

Once again, the demands of war forced governments to print more money and borrow huge sums to spend on military hardware.

The Berlin airlift of 1948–49 symbolised the start of the Cold War between the US and the Soviet Union. The origins of the crisis in a local currency dispute is often forgotten.

As Labour Chancellor of the Exchequer, Hugh Dalton (*above*) oversaw the nationalisation of the Bank of England (*right*) in 1946. After more than 250 years as a private institution it became an instrument of government.

Austerity Britain: the late 1940s were particularly tough in Britain as the government attempted to balance the books after years of wartime expenditure.

General Douglas Macarthur's military bearing and authority overawed contemporaries. He was fanatically committed to the army. As the Supreme Commander of Allied Powers in Japan, he was the ultimate arbiter of the fate of the Japanese people between 1945 and 1952.

The Bank of Japan was a symbol of continuity in a country which had been devastated by the Second World War. The original building dated from 1896 and was a deliberate imitation of the Bank of England.

The United States government remained committed to alleviating poverty through the 'Great Society' programme (*below*) while at the same time escalating the war in Vietnam (*above*). Spending on both social security and defence led to the demise of the Bretton Woods System in the early 1970s.

King Faisal of Saudi Arabia became a figure of global importance in the eighteen months before he was assassinated in March 1975. Oil was the key to his wealth and power.

Thatcher and Reagan formed a formidable partnership. They shared a similar economic vision of free enterprise and small government. It was sometimes unclear who the real leader of the pair was.

New York's Plaza hotel was the scene of an international currency agreement to weaken the dollar in September 1985. The intervention was successful and a good example of international cooperation after a period of US dominance.

The European single currency was launched in 1999, but physical coins and notes only appeared in 2002. At first, all seemed to augur well.

Buoyed by the strength of her national economy, Angela Merkel, the German Chancellor, became the undisputed leader of Europe. For the Greek Prime Minister, George Papandreou, German dominance was hard to bear.

Greek discontent over austerity measures imposed by the Eurozone spilled over into violent clashes in May 2010.

Alan Greenspan, Chairman of the Federal Reserve for nineteen years, stepped down in 2006. He was praised on his retirement but there were some who accused him of having created a credit bubble.

Anthony Mozilo created Countrywide, which would become the biggest issuer of mortgage lending in the United States. *Time* magazine featured Mozilo, the son of a Bronx burcher, at number one in their 2009 piece '25 People to Blame for the Financial Crisis'.

Florida was the centre of a huge boom and bust. Here properties are being sold, as hard times hit.

China remained the manufacturing hub of the world. Chinese goods continued to flood Western markets because of the cheap Chinese currency.

Supported by its natural resources, Australia remained relatively prosperous. A gold mine is as potent a symbol of the real economy as any.

the Chinese news agency noted that as mid-term elections approached in the United States, 'some US Senators have proposed legislation . . . to press China to appreciate its currency'. The Chinese, under a one-party government, were particularly sensitive to, as well as contemptuous of, the electoral cycles to which Western governments were subject. Xinhua added wryly that it had been 'customary practice for Western politicians to press for appreciation of the yuan when their domestic economy is in trouble'.

The Xinhua agency's news item constituted a crisp rebuttal of the notion that the US's chronic trade deficit had anything to do with the value of other currencies against the dollar. Quoting Steven Forbes, the American publishing billionaire, Xinhua recalled that the 'United States started in the 1970s to put pressure on Japan to change the value of the yen'. The result of this pressure was that 'the dollar today [2010] has fallen 75 percent against the yen, and we still have a trading deficit'. China's successful export policy, its continuing trade surpluses with the United States, had more to do with the 'trade policies and structure' of the United States than with the exchange rate. Once again, Chinese officials emphasized the benefits of stability as opposed to the free-floating exchange rates which had been a feature of global currency markets since the collapse of Bretton Woods: 'A stable yuan is of vital significance to the global economic development and the stability of the international monetary system.'[43]

The consequence of China's exporting success was the accumulation of trillions of dollars of reserves. At the beginning of 2012, it was reported that Chinese reserves had slipped 0.6 per cent in the last quarter of 2011. This was the first quarterly decrease since 1998, but at US$3.18 trillion Beijing's stock of foreign currencies was still by 'far the biggest' in the world.[44] These reserves would be invested in different types of securities, but it was the purchase of US government debt, known as US Treasuries, which would divert the attention of the world, and would have profound consequences for the global economy in the first decade of the twenty-first century. In 2003, the *Economist* noted that 'China and other Asian countries hold their reserves largely in American government securities,' and that if 'Asians lost their appetite for dollar assets the greenback would fall even further, and American bond yields would rise'. It was Chinese capital in particular which kept American bond yields so low in the 2000s. The explanation for this phenomenon can be easily grasped. A popular borrower, whose debt is widely sought, will command lower interest rates than a less favoured borrower. Chinese capital kept US Treasuries 'well bid', in market jargon. US interest rates remained very low, with fateful consequences as the 2000s unfolded.

Delusions of Debt

As the twenty-first century began, the United States remained a buoyantly confident nation. China was using its trade surpluses to buy US Treasuries, but in 2001 US government debt was hardly a matter of concern. On 25 January 2001, Alan Greenspan, in his fourteenth year as Chairman of the Federal Reserve, gave important testimony to the Senate. He spoke in bland but self-assured tones about the US fiscal position. He argued, in those heady days, that 'a tax cut is needed now to prevent the government accumulating large stocks of private assets when the stock of public debt is paid off'. This showed extraordinary faith in the future of the United States government. The late 1990s had seen budget surpluses in the United States, so Greenspan's testimony looked forward to a time when the federal government would still be 'running a budget surplus'. In this happy circumstance, the government would be receiving more in tax revenue that it would be spending. Greenspan reflected on what it might do with these excess funds. He concluded that it 'would have little choice but to spend the excess revenue buying up other assets like municipal bonds and, eventually, chunks of the private sector'.[1]

For Greenspan, the notion that a US government, overflowing with tax receipts, would buy up private sector assets with its surplus revenue was a 'disturbing prospect'. To avoid this distressing outcome, he argued that it would make 'sense to start cutting taxes'. This would be done to provide 'a pre-emptive smoothing of the glide path to zero federal debt'. This was the state of affairs, in relation to a discussion about the United States fiscal position, at the beginning of 2001. It would be difficult to imagine an assessment which was so utterly wrong. The testimony which Greenspan gave to the Senate was reflective and visionary. Incredibly, it might seem, he posed the question, 'when does the debt actually disappear?' His answer was that 'it could be as early as 2010'. This view, he pointed out, was actually quite conservative, since the 'rosier forecasts from the Congressional Budget Office suggest it could be sooner', in 2006.

The forecasts Greenspan alluded to pointed to a world of make-believe, in which the United States had eliminated its entire national debt. The problem with such optimistic prognostications was that the seeds of doubt were already manifest in 2001. As the London *Economist* concluded, the 'only possible economic justification of Mr Greenspan's view' was that 'the new economy has produced a productivity miracle'. Greenspan's optimism could only be predicated on 'a permanent increase in the underlying rate of productivity growth'. The *Economist* was more cautious: 'such a miracle may be occurring', but 'no one is sure'. The magazine argued with admirable circumspection that to 'justify ten years' worth of huge tax cuts on the basis of a guess about productivity growth derived from a few quarters' figures can only be considered a reckless gamble'.

The 'glide-path' to zero federal debt proved to be a cruel fantasy. It is salutary to remember that the Congressional Budget Office suggested that the budget surplus would be almost $6 trillion over the ten years from 2001. Greenspan quoted this figure rather too credulously. As the *Economist* opined, 'Mr Greenspan's "glide-path" is an unnecessary exaggeration, rather like a fat man starting on a diet and worrying about anorexia.' Even in 2001, it was clear to economic journalists that, if the government accumulated private assets, the US public finances would 'swing rapidly back into deficit again' because of the 'costs of Social Security and Medicare' which would 'soar as the baby-boomers [defined as people born between 1946 and 1964] retire'.[2] There were already signs that the remarkable fiscal successes of the late 1990s would be short-lived.

The late 1990s had indeed been a remarkable era for the US economy. Greenspan himself, perhaps with the benefit of hindsight, described the situation as a highly unusual one: 'in the late nineties, the economy was so strong that I used to get up in the morning, look in the mirror, and say to myself, "Remember, this is temporary. This is not the way the world is supposed to work."' As he later admitted in his memoirs *The Age of Turbulence*, he 'loved watching the economy flourish, as well as the strange new challenges this prosperity brought on'. In his memoirs, Greenspan spoke of the 'emergence of a federal budget surplus' as a 'wondrous happening' which first occurred in 1998. In its fiscal peak year 1992, the deficit had reached 'almost $300 billion'. The causes of the surplus, in Greenspan's analysis, were factors 'we thought we understood'. They were, in the Chairman's own words, 'fiscal conservatism' and 'economic growth'. The scale of the change, however, went 'far beyond that'. As he remembered, no one at the Fed or elsewhere had 'anticipated the emergence in fiscal year 2000 of the largest surplus (relative to GDP) since 1948'.

Greenspan's memoirs were published in 2007, when the world economy was less secure, and prospects of economic growth stretching for years to come seemed unrealistic. His testimony before the Senate in January 2001 implied that he really had been taken in by these delusive hopes. In his later memoirs, the 'maestro', as he was dubbed in a biography published in 2001, modestly noted that 'history told us booms like this couldn't and wouldn't last forever'.[3] He behaved, during the period itself, with much less circumspection than the prudent modesty of his memoirs subsequently suggested. He was, as has already been noted, a doctrinaire advocate of the free market, who believed passionately in the 'spontaneous order' of the market place.

Towards the end of a historic tenure of the chairmanship of the Federal Reserve, a *New York Times* profile of the great central banker pithily summed up Greenspan's philosophy: 'The doctrine was not to have one.' The article appeared on 25 August 2005, less than six months before Greenspan finally departed the Federal Reserve. It claimed that the Chairman was about to leave 'a brilliant record but a murky legacy' and went on to give a graphic, if somewhat nihilistic, account of his management style. Greenspan, the *New York Times* suggested, 'abhorred rules'. He was 'sceptical about economic models and jettisoned practices' that had been enshrined by the likes of 'Paul A. Volcker and Milton Friedman', the stern monetary heroes of the early 1980s. Contrary to the doctrinaire approach of a Milton Friedman towards controlling the money supply, Greenspan, at least to the *Times*, represented a form of loose anarchy in the sphere of economic management. 'If Greenspan stood for anything it was flexibility and the freedom from dogma.'

When some economists referred to the 'Greenspan standard', according to Alan S. Blinder, a Princeton professor who had served as Vice Chairman of the Federal Reserve, 'for the most part [they] meant what Greenspan wanted to do'.[4] It became fashionable to blame Greenspan after the financial crisis of 2008 had damaged the US economy. Indeed, in February 2009, *Time* magazine listed the former central banker at number three in their list of '25 People to Blame for the Financial Crisis'.[5] Yet, even before the memorable events of 2008, some critics had already begun to blame him for overheating the economy. In its August 2005 article, the *New York Times* accused him of presiding over 'a stock market bubble that burst'. His attempts to mitigate the collapse of stock prices had led, in turn, to the 'housing boom' and to the 'potential bust'. The *Times* also pointed to the accumulation of 'heavy foreign debt'. This had a simple cause: the Federal Reserve 'drove interest rates so low that Americans borrowed more and saved less'.[6]

Greenspan's belief in the efficacy of free markets had led him to a relaxed view of regulation, and to a scepticism about rigid control of economic variables. 'He had little faith in widely accepted concepts like the "natural rate of unemployment".' the newspaper averred. 'He jettisoned the practice of basing policy on growth in the money supply, a concept enshrined by Mr Friedman as the best way to prevent inflation.' A natural scepticism inclined Greenspan 'to roll with the punches'. In his youth, he had been a jazz musician. An accomplished saxophone player, he had adopted the same talent for improvisation in his handling of economic policies. 'I idolized the great improvisers like Benny Goodman and Artie Shaw,' he remembered.[7] His sterner critics, however, contended that he had 'relied too heavily on his own judgement and not enough on consistent principles'.[8]

To blame Greenspan for his lax, 'light touch' approach and his devotion to free markets is a little too harsh. The real problem that the United States faced was the development of chronic indebtedness at the level of the federal government. To understand the change in position, we need to consider the condition of the United States public finances, just before the tragic events of 11 September 2001, when more than 3,000 people died in an unprecedented attack on mainland America. The best way to try and recover the prevailing atmosphere before the 11 September attacks is to look at the articles and popular press concerning the issue of the US budget. Revealingly, an article which appeared on 3 September 2001, eight days before the terrorist attacks, in *Time* magazine was entitled 'Who Swiped the Surplus?' This article spelt out in clear terms the fact that, even before 11 September, the US fiscal position had deteriorated at an alarming rate.

The article was emphatic: 'It seems like only a few months ago that the federal budget surplus was unfurling like a vast, star-spangled security blanket, a cushion of cash that stretched farther than the eye could see.' As recently as April 2001, the White House had projected a surplus of US$281 billion for the 2001–2 fiscal year and a total of US$3.4 trillion 'for the next ten years'. By early September, such optimism appeared 'too good to be true'. At the end of August, the White House admitted that '$123 billion of this year's surplus had somehow evaporated.' The question was then asked, 'Who killed the surplus?' The President, George W. Bush, denied that his policies had been responsible for this sudden reversal. His proposed tax cut, passed by Congress in June 2001, was 'jump-starting' the economy, he claimed. It was the 'big-spending Democrats' who were 'squandering the surplus', the President maintained. Bush remained, at this point, committed to what he called 'fiscal sanity in the budget'. Even though, to his Democratic opponents, the President himself had been responsible for fiscal irresponsibility by pressing ahead with tax cuts. Kent Conrad, a fiscally conservative Democratic Senator from North Dakota, questioned the President's fiscal record at the time: 'He [the President] claimed we could afford his massive tax cut, a major defense buildup, more money for education, while paying down the debt and protecting Social Security and Medicare.' The President, Conrad added, 'was wrong'.[9]

The fiscal position had been deteriorating throughout 2001. Democrats pointed to Bush's Economic Growth and Tax Relief Reconciliation Act, passed in June of that year, as a sign of the President's lack of fiscal discipline. In the years to come, both Bush's tax cuts of 2001 and 2003 would be highly contentious subjects of political debate among Democrats and Republicans. Contrary to subsequent mythology, the 2001 tax cuts

were not simply for the rich. The core of the 2001 legislation was a simplification of the code in which a 'five-bracket income-tax system of 15
percent, 28 percent, 31 percent, 36 percent and 39.6' was reduced to four
lower rates of '10 percent, 15 percent, 25 percent and 33 percent'. Clearly,
the rich benefited from the new 33 per cent rate: 'rich folk, who pay the
most taxes, reap the most rewards'. Yet everyone who paid taxes benefited.
The problem, however, was whether the country could afford it. Bush
would have to convince sceptics that the 'nation can afford a cut this size'.[10]

Bush's critics articulated the authentic voice of the balanced-budget
approach to public finance. Tax cuts would have to be paid for. It was the
traditional approach that had been practised in both the Truman and
Eisenhower administrations. This view of public finances had been assailed
from the left, by those who believed that deficits were self-financing.
Essentially, many on the left believed, as President Johnson had argued in
the 1960s, that deficits incurred in order to spur growth would cure themselves. On the right, a conviction had taken root that tax cuts would
stimulate growth which, in turn, would eliminate any temporary shortfall
in revenue that the cuts caused. It doesn't take much reflection to see that
this argument was very similar to the notion that deficits financed themselves. They were both, in their way, circular arguments. The traditional
view, espoused if not always practised by Peel in Britain in the 1840s, and
by Eisenhower in the United States in the 1950s, had been to raise taxes,
or cut spending, when the government ran a deficit.

By contrast, Bush's government cut taxes and increased spending. It has
been argued that both these actions damaged the United States' fiscal position. The general impact of the Bush presidency is still contentious, but
over his fiscal legacy there is a strange alliance among commentators on
both the left and the right. To Paul Krugman, admittedly writing with the
benefit of hindsight, Bush's administration was highly culpable. In 2009
Krugman castigated the Bush regime's approach to public finance. Bush's
presidency represented '8 years of gross fiscal irresponsibility'. Krugman
pointed to two developments which had deepened the hole in the federal
government's finances. 'There were two big-ticket Bush policies. One was
the tax cuts, which cost around $1.8 trillion in revenue.' With interest
costs, Krugman suggested that total debt would be 'more than $2 trillion'.

The other major policy development with a large impact on the debt was the Iraq War, which had cost '$700 billion'. The fiscal irresponsibility of the Bush years, according to Krugman, had left the United States 'poorly positioned to deal with the current crisis, turning what should have been an easily financed economic rescue into a more difficult . . . process'.

A more surprising feature of the debate is the extent to which Bush's fiscal incontinence was reviled by the conservative commentators and self-appointed guardians of the flame of small government. Paul Weyrich, an American conservative and co-founder of the Heritage Foundation, in an article published after his death, candidly observed that in spite of the 'positive impact' of many of his foreign policy initiatives, Bush's fiscal legacy had been damaging. 'The most prominent' of Bush's mistakes had been 'recklessness in fiscal policy'. Weyrich noted with frustration that Bush 'did not veto a single budget bill, in his first term, though many were saddled with pork and unnecessary spending'. 'Pork' was a colloquial American term for government funds supplied for local improvements designed to ingratiate members of Congress with their electorates. Bush, in Weyrich's acidic appraisal, 'did not begin to veto spending bills until 2007'.

Bush's reluctance to use the President's right of veto, in the assessment of many conservatives, led to a dire state of affairs. Weyrich observed that 'in his entire eight years Bush only used his veto power twelve times'. He compared Bush's record as a wielder of the veto with the records of his predecessors: 'Ronald Reagan vetoed 78 bills, George H. W. Bush vetoed 44, and William J. Clinton used his veto 37 times.' As a consequence of Bush Junior's relaxed attitude to congressional spending, Weyrich concluded, 'both the Federal deficit and the national debt have ballooned to unsustainable levels'.[11]

It was not just voices on the left or the far right that sharply criticized Bush's fiscal profligacy. Alan Greenspan, the man many blamed for the financial crisis of 2008, also noticed the surprising failure to use the presidential veto in the Bush years. Not 'exercising veto power', wrote Greenspan, 'became a hallmark of the Bush Presidency: for nearly six years in the White House, he did not throw out a single bill'. Such a policy of benign neglect was 'without modern precedent'. Greenspan recalled that

'Johnson, Nixon, Carter, Reagan, George H. W. Bush, Clinton – all had vetoed dozens of bills. And Jerry Ford had vetoed everything in sight – more than sixty bills in less than three years.' George W. Bush, known as 'Dubya', was an easygoing Texan businessman who owed his good fortune in life more to his family circumstances than to any powers of intellect or sustained application. He translated much of his good-natured bonhomie, the 'frat boy' charm, into government. He was simply a President who could not say no. Like many born to high position in life, he hated confrontation. Greenspan, a lifelong Republican, believed that 'Bush's collaborate-don't-confront approach was a major mistake.' It 'cost the nation a check-and-balance mechanism essential to fiscal discipline'.[12]

Greenspan asserted that after the Republicans had gained 'a sweeping victory' in the November 2002 mid-term elections 'the situation got worse'. He quoted Glenn Hubbard, Chairman of the President's Council of Economic Advisers, as suggesting that budget deficits made little difference. Hubbard had indeed expressed the hope that 'the discussion will move away from the current fixation with linking budget deficits with interest rates'.[13] To Greenspan, Hubbard's relaxed attitude to budget deficits was at one with the attitude of the Republican President and Congress who 'viewed budgetary restraint as inhibiting the legislation they wanted'. To the Republicans in the early years of the twenty-first century, 'deficits don't matter'. This had 'to my chagrin', Greenspan admitted, become 'part of Republicans' rhetoric'.

Greenspan was a conventional 'balanced-budget' conservative. He looked back fondly to the administrations of both Truman and Eisenhower during the 1950s. The approach of the new Republicans startled him. 'It was a struggle for me to accept' that the idea that 'deficits don't matter' had become the 'dominant ethos and economic policy of the Republican party'. He remembered a lunch he had enjoyed in the 1970s with Jack Kemp, then a 'young congressman from upstate New York'. Kemp, in an interesting observation, complained that the Democrats were 'always buying votes by boosting spending all over the place'. His frustration was that the resulting deficits would 'land in the lap of a Republican administration'. 'Why can't *we* be a little irresponsible ourselves?' Kemp asked. 'Why can't we cut taxes and give away the goodies before they can?' At the time Greenspan felt that his 'sensibilities as a libertarian Republican were offended'. More depressingly for him, he believed that this attitude was now the prevailing orthodoxy among his fellow Republicans in 2002.

As already noted, Greenspan's memoirs were published in 2007. Bush's lax approach to fiscal issues, however, had been criticized by American conservatives during the President's first term. These strictures acquire a certain pungency from the fact that they were contemporary observations, made well before the crisis of 2008. The criticisms of Bush's fiscal record were fiercest from the right-wing think tanks. In an extraordinary polemic of 2006, entitled *Buck Wild: How Republicans Broke the Bank and Became the Party of Big Government*, Stephen Slivinski, an economist at the Cato Institute, railed against Bush and against the Republican Party. He focused, of course, on all the additional spending. 'As conservatives had discovered in the late 1990s,' he remarked bitterly, 'the budget surplus had turned the GOP into a party without any motivation to cut government.' Slivinski, and others like him, expressed horror that Republicans in Congress were 'sounding like spendaholics . . . begging for an intervention by Bush'. A Republican Senator from New Hampshire, Judd Gregory, told a *Washington Post* reporter as early as 2001 that 'Congress has a fiscal discipline problem.' Gregory noted that the 'huge increases in spending' had been supported by 'all segments of Republicans'. 'We have seen the enemy', he concluded, 'and he is us.'[14]

Slivinski's sharp critique of Bush and his fellow big-spending Republicans was written only a few years after the terrorist attacks of 11 September 2001, popularly known as 9/11. The right-wing Republicans' criticism of their leaders acknowledged that in the 'wake of the 9/11 terrorist attacks, there was naturally a widespread consensus that more money would be spent on defense and homeland security'. The unfortunate consequence, however, of such a consensus, as far the Republican ideologues were concerned, was that 'suddenly, there was a mad rush to spend more on just about every federal program, whether it was related to defense and homeland security or not'. This development was summed up well by a Democratic Representative for a Californian congressional district, Robert Matsui: 'we have basically opened the door for anything'.[15] To the

Republican right, 9/11 represented an historic opportunity to redefine the core role of government, to restrain government spending. This opportunity was squandered. In Slivinski's view, Bush failed to use 'the political honeymoon period to call on Congress to make cuts to non-essential programs to pay for the needed increases in military spending'.

A source of frustration to many Republicans was that most of the increase in spending in Bush's first term had nothing to do with the requirements of America's security. Bush was complicit in a spending spree whose net result was a 'one-year 10% discretionary spending increase after adjusting for inflation – the biggest real rate of growth since 1967'. The Congressional Budget Office estimated that the amount of money actually assigned to the 'war on terror and the invasion of Afghanistan only amounted to $17 billion' in 2002, less than a quarter of the overall spending increase. According to this view, Bush had 'missed one of the best opportunities he would ever have to show' that he was serious about 'restraining spending'. In April 2002, the President declared, 'I've got a tool and that's called a veto.' His reluctance to use this effective tool was the cause of much disappointment among many Republican supporters.[16]

The raw statistics marshalled against Bush by Slivinski were damning from the standpoint of the fiscal-deficit hawk. 'In Bush's presidency so far [Slivinski's book was written in 2006] the federal budget has grown by 27% after adjusting for inflation. That's more than twice as fast as during the eight years of President Clinton.' Bush's tenure, Slivinski concluded, had been a 'return to the Johnson and Carter philosophy of budgeting: across-the-board increases in everything'.[17] The grumbling about excess spending had arisen since the events of September 2001. In February 2004, Tom Schatz, President of an organization known as the Citizens Against Government Waste, expressed frustration with the President's reluctance to use his power of veto, the same criticism which Bush's own Chairman of the Federal Reserve, Alan Greenspan, had made. Schatz understandably blamed Congress for its role in increasing the spending of the federal government, but Bush was equally culpable: 'if he's not going to veto any bills, he has to share the blame'.[18] As early as 2004, the Republican right had lost faith in President Bush. As James Bovard wrote in his polemic *The Bush Betrayal*, published that year towards the end of the President's first term, Bush 'browbeat Congress into exacting the biggest expansion of the welfare state since Lyndon Johnson'.[19]

Bush had defined himself as a 'compassionate conservative' when he sought the Republican Party's nomination to be its presidential candidate. More relevantly, other commentators labelled him favourably as a 'big government conservative'. Fred Barnes, a respected conservative commentator, proudly defended the President's notion of a dynamic role for the federal government in an important article in the *Wall Street Journal* published in August 2003: 'The case for Bush's conservatism is strong. Sure, some conservatives are upset because he has tolerated a surge in federal spending, downplayed swollen deficits, failed to use his veto, created a vast Department of Homeland Security, and fashioned an alliance of sorts with Teddy Kennedy on education and Medicare.' According to Barnes, the 'real gripe' of the conservatives, however, was that Bush simply 'isn't their kind of conventional conservative'. Rather, he was 'a big government conservative'. By contrast, the Republican idol, Reagan, in Barnes's analysis, was 'a small government conservative who declared in his inauguration address that government was the problem, not the solution'. In this respect, wrote Barnes, 'Bush begs to differ.' 'Big government conservatism', argued Barnes, was a 'trade-off'. In order to gain 'free-market reforms and expand individual choice', Bush was willing to 'broaden programs and increase spending'. Barnes concluded by suggesting that the 'Big government conservatives are favorably disposed toward what neoconservative Irving Kristol has called a "conservative welfare state".'[20]

This was an unambiguous assertion of Bush's political philosophy, in so far as he could be said to have one. It was revealing that early in his administration spending was regarded as a virtue, something of which to be proud. What was particularly galling to older traditional conservatives was that increased spending was allied, in Bush's first term, to tax cuts. Bush seemed to combine the worst of all approaches to public finance. A traditional conservative, like Eisenhower, would be inclined to raise taxes to balance the budget. A supply-side advocate for lower taxes, like Jack Kemp, would have sought to cut spending while cutting taxes at the same time.

Bush, on the contrary, as we have seen, increased spending and cut taxes, both of which would exacerbate any deficit, at least in the short term.

It was in 2003, the very year that Fred Barnes celebrated President Bush's 'big government conservative' approach to administration, that a major round of tax cuts was announced. In Greenspan's recollection the new budget was 'a little more discouraging'. Federal government spending exceeded $2.2 trillion and 'the bottom line was a projected deficit of more than $300 billion in both 2003 and 2004 and another $200 billion in 2005'. As Bush's officials were quick to point out, a '$300 billion budget deficit was the equivalent of only 2.7 percent of GDP, relatively modest by historic standards'. It was surprising that such a deficit should have occurred when the economy was growing, however, and, in Greenspan's later view, the federal government should have been preparing itself 'for the retirement of the baby boomers with balanced budgets or surpluses for the difficult years ahead'.

The 2003 budget, needless to say, 'did not include funding for the looming war in Iraq'. The budget's centrepiece was the round of tax cuts. Greenspan was dubious about these cuts. The result of the tax package in 2003 was, in his analysis, 'to add $670 billion . . . over ten years to the $1.35 trillion cost of Bush's first round of tax relief [in 2001]'. Once again, Greenspan portrayed himself as a guardian of fiscal conservatism. His 'main concern', he wrote in his memoirs, 'was the failure to address the longer-term path of promised benefits that are going to leave a very large hole in future budgets'. The Greenspan who, in 2001, had looked forward to the elimination of the entire national debt of the United States was now a fearful old man, bewailing reckless tax cuts. 'Far more urgent than tax cuts', he argued, 'was the need to address the threat posed by the soaring new deficits.' Such a statement shows how dramatically the budgetary outlook had changed for the United States in the two years between 2001 and 2003.[21]

The 2003 Bush tax cuts became the focus of a media circus in which hundreds of economists wrote letters either in support of, or opposed to, the planned tax changes. Four hundred and fifty economists, including ten out of the twenty-four American Nobel Prize laureates in economics, signed a statement in February 2003 urging the President not to enact the cuts. 'Passing these tax cuts will worsen the long-term budget outlook, adding to the nation's projected chronic deficits,' they argued.[22] Needless to say, in reaction to that statement 250 other economists wrote in support of the President's tax policies. The extraordinary thing about Bush's tax cuts was that they alienated budget hawks on the right as well as eliciting more predictable hostility from self-styled Keynesians on the left. Greenspan recalled that 'It quickly became clear that there was no room in the administration for an outspoken deficit hawk like Paul O'Neill', who had spent 'much of his two years as treasury secretary feuding with the Bush economists, especially Larry Lindsey, the primary architect of the tax cuts'.[23]

For Greenspan, bad policies typified by 'tax cuts and spending increases' had considerably damaged the United States' budgetary position. Quite rightly, he suggested that 'The costs of the Iraq war and antiterrorism measures do not explain the gap' between the projected national debt and the actual outcome. In 2001, the US national debt projected for the end of September 2006 was $1.2 trillion. The actual outcome was $4.8 trillion. This constituted, in Greenspan's measured phrase, 'a rather large miss'. The US debt was steadily mounting even before the events of the credit crunch in 2008. As a consequence of more borrowing, classic economic theory would expect higher interest rates for the borrower. A low interest rate was traditionally a sign of a respected and trusted borrower. This had been the case, perhaps most conspicuously, in the nineteenth century, when British government bonds, known as gilts, had often been issued paying less than 3 per cent interest.

Despite the increased borrowing, and the chronic budget deficits, the United States enjoyed interest rates which were extremely low by historic standards. One of the effects of the terrorist attacks of September 2001 had been a cut in interest rates by the Federal Reserve. The Federal Funds rate (the rate at which banks lend funds to each other) was cut to 2.5 per cent from 3.0 per cent, the lowest level since 1962. One of the criticisms aimed at Alan Greenspan, as the credit crisis of the latter part of the decade escalated, was that he had presided over a low-interest-rate environment. His critics argued that he had always been overly keen to lower interest rates in order to keep up economic activity. More ominously, he was accused of having a special eye on the markets; he was charged with cutting interest rates in order to lift the stock market, something which orthodox central bankers like William McChesney Martin Jr would never have contemplated doing.

The reaction of Greenspan to the events of 11 September was widely praised at the time, but it is easy to forget that the cuts in the Federal Funds rate were part of a wider move which took place throughout 2001, even before the terrorist attacks supervened. This was in response to the internet company bubble and bust, the so-called dot-com bubble, which lasted roughly from 1997 to 2000. The legacy of that particular bubble was the 'wiping out within two years' of '$5 trillion in paper wealth on Nasdaq', the stock market on which the shares of many of the new technology companies were traded. The market value of Nasdaq companies peaked at $6.7 trillion in March 2000 and hit a bottom of $1.6 trillion in October 2002, although by July 2006 the value had rebounded to $3.6 trillion.[24]

Against this background of sharply falling stock prices, Greenspan applied his familiar trick of interest rate cuts. There were an unprecedented nine cuts in 2001. The Federal Reserve's goal was easy for commentators to surmise. Greenspan and his colleagues wanted to 'make money more available to consumers, who drive two-thirds of America's economy, and keep them spending'.[25] Even before 2008, economists, politicians, bankers, market professionals and many ordinary Americans were very conscious of the unusual interest rate regime which now prevailed. Commenting on Bush's fiscal policies in July 2004, Mark Zandi, a market economist, spoke of an 'unprecedented combined monetary and fiscal stimulus'. The 'magnitude' of the monetary stimulus was evident, Zandi claimed, 'from the sharp decline in the federal funds rate target from 6.5% in mid-2000 to a low of 1% that prevailed through this June'. The peculiar nature of low nominal interest rates was exacerbated by inflation rates which hovered between 2 and 4 per cent from 2002 to 2006. With nominal interest rates being lower than inflation, there existed a 'negative' real federal rate which, to put it simply, essentially paid people to borrow money. As Zandi recalled, the 'real funds rate first turned negative soon after 9/11'; this, in July 2004, was already 'the longest stretch of a negative real funds rate on record'.[26]

The consequences of a negative real funds rate were far-reaching. The most conspicuous result of this period of low rates was a sharp increase in borrowing of all kinds. The credit explosion in almost all segments of the market – credit cards, mortgages, vehicle finance – was remarkable and drew extensive comment. Already in 2004, it was obvious in the United States that the 'vehicle and housing markets have been the principal beneficiaries of the extraordinarily low rates'. After the credit crunch had arrived, it was inevitable that mortgages should be the principal focus of attention. It was true, even to an observer in 2004, that 'generational-low mortgage rates [had] sparked record-shattering home sales' and had even 'ignited a mortgage borrowing binge'. The extent to which the US economy was driven by consumer debt could also be seen in the auto market, where auto manufacturers were able to 'offer wildly popular zero percent financing deals' because their own borrowing costs were 'so low'.[27]

The heavy indebtedness of the American householder was a phenomenon widely observed. Commentators viewed such debt with differing degrees of wonder, confusion and insouciance as new records were broken. A particularly perceptive contemporary analysis of the American love affair with debt was supplied by Richard Duncan, a Singapore-based banking analyst, whose book *The Dollar Crisis* was published in 2003. Duncan described in lurid, even apocalyptic terms the consequences of America's addiction to debt-fuelled spending. His focus was narrowly on the future of the dollar, which he believed would crash in value, crushed by an avalanche of dollar-denominated debt. The credit crisis that eventually descended was not strictly a currency crisis. Despite the 'dollar crisis' perhaps not materializing, much of Duncan's analysis stands the test of time.

Americans, Duncan warned, were embarking upon a 'buying binge'. In the twenty-three years since 1980, 'household debt' had risen from '50% of GDP to 78%'. Borrowing had 'never been easier or cheaper'. One bank chairman, Duncan revealed, had recently said, 'You'd have to be an insolvent arsonist not to get a loan now.' The observations Duncan made were time-old truths. 'Debt cannot continue to expand more than income indefinitely.' Yet by the end of 2001 income was going up by only 2.5 per cent, while debt was rising by more than 8 per cent 'for the fourth year in a row'. By historic standards, the outlook for the American consumer looked bleak even as early as 2001. The wonder was that the good times lasted as long as they did. By the years 2000 and 2001, Americans had stopped saving. 'The personal savings rate in the United States fell to its lowest recorded level during the final days of the New Paradigm [dot-com] bubble in 2000 and 2001.' At this point, during 'seven out of 24 months, Americans saved less than 1% of their income'. This pathetically low figure contrasted with the average savings rate 'between 1959 and 1998' which was 8.4 per cent.[28] Low savings rates were accompanied by a high level of indebtedness. There can be 'no doubt that the American consumer is over-extended financially.'

Duncan prophesied in 2003 a sharp reversal in the property market. As personal incomes were depressed and unemployment was beginning to rise, it would not be long, he believed, for the 'property market to become unaffordable to many'. 'Every Ponzi scheme', he observed, 'ends in crisis. The Great-End-of-the-Century Consumer Credit bubble will be no different.' He went on, 'When the consumer folds and begins to rein in his debt, there will be ramifications throughout the debt market.' The consequences of such retrenchment would be severe. 'Hardest hit will be the financial sector.' This was because 'The federally related mortgage pools, government-sponsored enterprises (GSEs), issuers of asset-backed securities and commercial banks all depend on the expansion of consumer credit for their growth.'

What was particularly ironic was Duncan's beacon of hope. The one agency which, he felt, could surmount the enormous problem of indebtedness was the government itself. 'The ability of the government to spend generously may be the only factor that keeps the US economy from falling completely into crisis.' This, of course, assumed that the federal deficit and debt levels could sustain any attempted rescue of the overly extended and 'heavily indebted corporate and household sectors'.[29] Duncan, from the relative safety of 2003, declared that of all the 'major sectors issuing debt in the US credit markets, the US government is the least over-extended financially'.[30] In the light of subsequent events, such a judgement might seem hopelessly optimistic. The other remarks relating to household debt and over-issuance of credit were well vindicated by later events.

It became fashionable after the events of 2008 to suggest that the credit crunch was something which happened out of the blue, that it was an event which was sudden and unexpected. In fact, the opposite case could be more plausibly argued. There never was a bursting of a bubble that was so widely predicted, anticipated and dissected as that which engulfed the world in 2008. The wonder, as has been remarked in this book already, was how the bubble lasted so long. As early as 1999, a British market economist, Peter Warburton, published a book entitled *Debt and Delusion: Central Bank Follies that Threaten Economic Disaster*. Through his vividly titled book, Warburton intended to give a 'wake-up call for those sound sleepers who have found no cause to question the authenticity of the economic and financial achievements of North America and Western Europe since the mid-1980s'.[31]

Warburton described the world of the 1990s as a 'realm of financial fantasy' which had been created in the mid-1980s. He depicted a world in which there remained very few restraints on the supply of credit. In the 1980s and 1990s, loans and bonds had been issued in seemingly limitless quantities. 'The world bond market has grown from less than $1 trillion in 1970 to more than $23 trillion. It has tripled in size since 1986.' Warburton linked the development of this market to the 'financing of government budget deficits in almost all western countries since the mid-1980s'.[32] In this analysis of overextended credit bubbles written in 1999, Japan's example in the late 1980s was cited as the 'object lesson'. Japan had witnessed a 'rapid, credit-induced inflation in property and financial asset prices in the late 1980s' which had exploded in January 1990, 'leaving massive personal and corporate debts'. The consequences of this reversal had been a 'prolonged economic slump and deflation of consumer prices'. Japan had experienced 'a phenomenal upsurge in the demand for bank borrowing between 1983 and 1989'. The consequences for Japan, Warburton observed, had been stark. 'In 1998, eight years after the credit bubble, land was worth less than half as much as at its peak.' This rather apocalyptic book was quick to point to parallels between other Western capitalist countries and Japan. Since 1990, 'the USA and several other western countries have gone a long way towards emulating Japan's reckless credit expansion'.[33] Indeed, the declared argument of the book was that the 'leading economies of North America and Western Europe have fallen victim to a dangerous illusion, related to the anarchic development of global capital and credit markets'.[34]

Many of Warburton's prophecies would prove to be uncannily accurate. The only problem was that the time period in which these dire warnings were realized was more extended than the author had anticipated. 'How much time' did 'institutions . . . have to change course?' he asked. Answering his own question, he suggested perhaps until 'the end of 2003'.[35] This 'would take a miracle'. Predicting collapse and downfall is always a risky business. The fact that the 'realm of fantasy', which Warburton so vividly described, lasted a further five years beyond 2003 only proves a reputed, though unsourced, saying of John Maynard Keynes that 'markets can remain irrational longer than you can remain solvent'.

The important point to remark upon was that the nature of what may be termed the 'explosion of credit' problem was terrifyingly clear to a perceptive British market economist in 1999. Unlike many such insights which are often not articulated or merely form the basis of arcane trading strategies, Warburton's analysis was written up in a highly readable and engaging book. One of the three scenarios he envisaged was an outcome in which 'the slow-burning erosion of consumer credit quality suddenly erupts into a domestic crisis'. In words which will resonate for all those who witnessed the events of 2008, he concluded that when 'the illusion of prosperity fostered by stellar equity market performance and indefinite borrowing facilities is ultimately blown away, a sober reality will dawn'.[36]

A legitimate question would be 'Why did the "realm of fantasy" endure as long as it eventually did?' A simple answer would perhaps be 'China.' It was the Chinese exporting phenomenon, and the need of the Chinese to recycle their dollar surpluses, earned from those exports, which underpinned American borrowing. This relationship was well described in 2007 by Niall Ferguson, the British historian, and Moritz Schularick, an economist then based at the Free University of Berlin. In a paper entitled '"Chimerica" and the Global Asset Market Boom', they suggested that China and America could be viewed as one country, 'Chimerica'. This one country was a fantasy land but it illustrated the deep symbiotic connection between the two nations. Chinese excess savings had 'depressed US and global interest rates'. These 'savings', Ferguson and Schularick argued, had derived from surging corporate profits in China due to 'increasing exchange rate undervaluation'.

In effect, China's export strength, particularly in the United States market, had led to a surplus of US dollars which were then reinvested in the purchase of dollar-denominated securities. The primary financial object which Chinese excess dollars bought was the US government bond, known in the market as US Treasuries. Ferguson and Schularick observed that China's current account surplus increased from about 2 per cent of GDP in 2000–3 to about 10 per cent in the first half of 2007.[37] This increase, interestingly, happened at a time when the yuan had been revalued, that is deliberately strengthened, against the dollar, from 8.28 yuan to a US dollar to 8.11 in July 2005. It was then allowed to float up to a rate of 7.6 in 2007. All of this suggested that the weakness of the yuan was not the only factor driving the surge of Chinese exports to the United States. Chinese demand for US securities boosted asset prices, but also, by pushing up the price of US government bonds, kept interest rates low. There is a well-known inverse relationship between interest rates and bond prices which follows the simple intuition that the greater the demand for a borrower's debt, the less interest the borrower will have to pay; only needing to pay low interest rates and having a high price for your debt means the same thing. This is known as an 'identity relationship'.

The low-interest-rate environment created the climate in which there was a search for yield. Investors speculated in higher-interest-yielding securities because traditional investments, like US government bonds, gave such low returns. Historians could look back to the circumstances in 1825, when there was a bubble and panic. As John Horsley Palmer, the Governor of the Bank of England in the early 1830s, remembered, the 'reduction of interest . . . created that feverish feeling in the minds of the public at large, which prompted almost everybody to entertain any proposition for investment, however absurd'.[38] We have already encountered Palmer's remark in Chapter 4, but it applied with as great a force to the credit conditions of the early to mid-2000s. The 'absurd propositions' of Horsley Palmer's dismissive phrase would be the increasing number of credit products, mortgage-based securities, derivatives and the like which proliferated in finance during the 1990s and early 2000s.

More generally, after the events of 2008 some commentators also observed that the burgeoning of credit had something to do with the prevalence of paper (fiat) money. Warburton, in his 2000 polemic, had denounced the central banks of the world's leading economies for presiding 'over an unprecedented explosion of financial credit'.[39] He had not considered the nature of the currency regime which had facilitated the 'explosion' he so passionately deplored. There were a minority who questioned the very basis of the paper money system which had prevailed in global finance since 1971, arguing that paper money allowed the very credit creation which had brought about the bubble and exacerbated the credit bust. As gold prices soared to new heights, even moderate observers who would have vigorously opposed a return to a full gold standard noticed that the explosion of credit had occurred partly as a consequence of the severance of the link to gold. Gold itself from the old Bretton Woods price of $35 an ounce reached $1,671 at the end of 2012, six times more than the average price during 2001 of $271 an ounce, and nearly forty-eight times the pre-1971 price of gold. In terms of its value in gold, the US dollar was little more than 2 per cent of what it had been during the Bretton Woods era.[40]

'The world now operates with a system where money can be created at will or by decree ("fiat money" as it is known in the jargon),' declared the British financial journalist Philip Coggan in 2011. 'It is no coincidence that debt levels have exploded in the last forty years, culminating in the credit crisis of 2007 and 2008 from which the world is still recovering.'[41] The very title of Coggan's book, *Paper Promises*, hinted at the fickleness of the new global monetary order. Other commentators were more vitriolic in their denunciations of paper money. In another work published in 2011, James Rickards, a former banker, noted that, '[t]ime and again paper money currencies have collapsed'.[42] One book, of the hundreds spawned by the crisis of 2008, was even entitled *Paper Money Collapse: The Folly of Elastic Money and the Coming Monetary Breakdown*. In this tirade against paper money, Detlev Schlichter, a London-based former trader, lamented that today people lived 'in a world of "paper money"'. 'Today, money is nowhere a commodity. It is everywhere an irredeemable piece of paper that is not backed by anything.' Schlichter observed that it was 'simply a historic fact that commodity money has always provided a reasonably stable medium of exchange, while the entire history of state paper money has been an unmitigated disaster when judged on the basis of price level stability'.[43]

It was the explosion of credit, easy money and excessive loans which created a world that was financially unstable. From the point of view of some of the themes of this book, war, notably commitments in Afghanistan and Iraq, had put pressure on US government spending. Yet many of the spending commitments had been driven by a 'big government' ideology which was repudiated by many of the Republicans President Bush aspired to lead. It was clear that paper currencies, not backed by any commodity standard, had facilitated unprecedented credit expansion. In this context, the soaring gold price, measured in US dollars, partially showed the extent to which investors were losing faith in the American currency. The US dependency on Chinese goods had created a precarious balance, or symbiosis, in which Chinese capital was supporting credit expansion in America. The resulting low interest rates brought about an environment in which the search for yield became a major motivation for investors in the United States. These investors sought greater returns and turned to riskier assets. It was in the purchase of these riskier securities that the origins of the eventual crisis of 2008 can be found.

Crises and 'Bailouts'

On 4 June 2009, Angelo Mozilo, a mortgage lender, was accused by America's Securities and Exchange Commission of securities fraud. Mozilo was the former boss of Countrywide, the United States' largest mortgage lender before 2008. His story in many ways showed the boundless optimism of America as well as revealing the precarious nature of fame and fortune. In *Time* magazine's article '25 People to Blame for the Financial Crisis', Mozilo featured at number one. He had earned this dubious accolade because as head of Countrywide he had done much to 'legitimize the notion that practically any adult could handle a big fat mortgage'. *Time* admitted that Countrywide had not been the first company to 'offer exotic mortgages to borrowers with a questionable ability to repay them'. It simply acknowledged that Mozilo's firm had embraced this market with an enthusiasm and vigour unmatched by its competitors.[1]

Mozilo had been born in New York, the son of a Bronx butcher. From modest beginnings, he earned a degree from Fordham University which later, in 2005 at the height of his prosperity, gave him a 'Founder's Award'. In accepting the award, he thanked his mother for encouraging him to pursue a college education against his father's expressed wish for the young boy to follow his own vocation as a butcher. Mozilo founded Countrywide in 1969. In 2004, when interest rates had hit new lows, and when none other than Alan Greenspan was extolling the merits of the adjustable-rate mortgage, Countrywide finally became America's 'largest home mortgage originator'. In that year alone, the company generated $8.6 billion in revenue, more than twice the amount it had achieved only two years previously. With his permatan, Hollywood smile and easy charm, Mozilo was a driven salesman who constantly strove to win market share from rivals. The problem with an almost infinite supply of credit was that the only way to gain share was to apply less strict underwriting standards – in other words, Mozilo and his colleagues did not look too closely at the credit-worthiness of the people to whom they were issuing loans.

This loosening of standards was at the heart of the SEC's charge. They alleged that Mozilo, together with two of his colleagues, deliberately misled investors. The Countrywide executives failed to inform investors about the risk of the mortgage loans the company was making in its bid to win market share. In public, Mozilo praised the quality of his firm's loans. He even went so far as to describe Countrywide as a 'role model to others in terms of reasonable lending'. In private, he was said to be 'increasingly alarmed at the poor quality of the mortgages and their chances of blowing up'. He was accused of issuing 'dire assessments' about the quality of the mortgages to his colleagues. In a series of internal emails, Mozilo was quoted as describing one of Countrywide's mortgage products as 'toxic'. Another product was portrayed in equally acerbic terms as 'the most dangerous product in existence'.[2]

Mozilo's firm adopted lax loan-underwriting standards, even when its own chief risk officer was warning about such practices. A further allega-tion of the SEC was that Mozilo had been guilty of insider trading, using private knowledge from his position as the CEO of the company, when he sold nearly $140 million worth of Countrywide shares.[3] Eventually in October 2010, Mozilo agreed to repay $45 million of his 'ill-gotten prof-its' and a further $22.5 million in 'civil penalties as part of a settlement with the SEC'. Neither he nor his colleagues admitted any wrongdoing, but they agreed to the settlement all the same. It was an undignified end to a long and lucrative business career, but, for the man who had been *Time* magazine's number-one culprit for the financial crisis, the fine was a far better outcome than a lengthy prison term.

The market which Mozilo had sought to dominate was the 'subprime' market, which took on a mythology of its own as the crisis unravelled. As the subprime debacle unfolded, many conservative commentators sought to blame government for creating subprime mortgages in the first place. The National Housing Act of 1968, a part of President Johnson's Great

Society programme, 'provided government-subsidized loans to expand home ownership for poor Americans'. It was observed, often in a derogatory tone, that liberal policymakers had believed that these loans, called section 235 loans, could 'enable poor Americans – urban blacks in particular – to buy their own homes'.[4] The writer of these words, which appeared in the *New York Times* in December 2007, was the economic historian Louis Hyman. In his history of American debt, *Debtor Nation: The History of America in Red Ink*, Hyman made the same point: 'Legislators of the Great Society program sought to help welfare recipients gain a stake in owning their housing, only to inaugurate the era of subprime mortgage loans.' The current financial crisis, he noted, was rooted in 'those credit instruments'.[5] Yet Hyman also pointed to the overarching environment which had incubated the crisis. Interest rates were low, with the Federal Funds rate hovering at little more than 1 per cent between 2003 and 2004. As a consequence, there followed 'a frantic drive for yield',[6] the 'feverish feeling' described by the early nineteenth-century British central banker John Horsley Palmer. Even without sophisticated, mortgage-related credit instruments, investors would surely have found other risky assets which potentially gave better returns on investments.

The explosion in subprime mortgages was driven not so much by the demand from African-Americans or Mexicans as by men such as Angelo Mozilo who were pushing these products to gain market share. Other bankers were also eager to satisfy the demand of their clients for higher-yielding assets in a world where US Treasuries were paying only 2 per cent for ten-year bonds. In the 2008 edition of his book *The Return of Depression Economics*, Paul Krugman noted the 'complete abandonment of traditional principles' of lending.[7] It is true that some individual families were motivated by dreams of owning their own spacious home, but the explosion of credit was as much driven by the suppliers of credit who created such novel instruments as Collateralized Debt Obligations, or CDOs for short, to satisfy the need for higher yields.

This so-called 'securitization' of assets has been described as the act of 'turning an expected future cash flow into tradable bond-like securities'.[8] A famous example of securitization occurred when Bowie Bonds were created in 1997. The original bond sold that year raised $55 million for the rock musician David Bowie. Future album sales of his music generated the revenue stream for the securities. In 2004, Bowie's bonds 'fell to earth' when Moody's lowered its rating on them to 'just one notch above "junk", citing lower-than-expected revenue'.[9] The bonds collapsed in value as people stopped buying Bowie's music, but the bond illustrated the potentially broad application of the principle. CDOs were bonds which bundled together lots of mortgage loans. It was the quiet, though speedy, disruption in this market, and with subprime mortgages in general, that was the immediate cause of the events of 2008. 'When the 2006–7 loans started to default,' write Philip Coggan, 'the whole system froze.'[10]

The Marxist historian Robin Blackburn provided as good a description as any of the actual events leading up to the crisis of 2008. His account, entitled 'The Subprime Crisis', is implicitly hostile to financial capitalism. Despite its obvious bias, the account is interesting because it was published in April 2008, five months before the dramatic fall of Lehman Brothers in September of that year, which was the moment when the crisis took on truly global dimensions. 'The trigger for the credit crunch', wrote Blackburn, 'was rising defaults among US holders of subprime mortgages in the last quarter of 2006 and early 2007.' This led to the failure of 'several large mortgage brokers in February–March 2007'. The analysis shows the impact which the credit crunch had on a frightened world at the end of 2007.

'The subprime debacle and the drying up of credit, themselves the consequences of deteriorating conditions, were hastening the slide to recession in the US and the global economy.' The 'credit crunch' itself came as 'the climax of a long period of gravity-defying global imbalances and asset bubbles'. It was 'Fear of recession that had prompted the US Federal Reserve to keep interest rates low in 2001–06.' This, people now recognize, 'set the scene for cheap and easy loans'. In the eyes of the Marxist analyst, 'The world's financiers and business leaders looked to US householders, the "consumers of last resort", to keep the global boom going.'[11] This is only partly true. Despite repeated warnings from a number of writers, the 'world's financiers and business leaders' and politicians genuinely believed that the good times would never end. They were not 'looking' for a 'consumer of last resort'. Everyone was consuming and was believed to be able to continue to do so, seemingly for ever. Between 2001 and 2006, for most professionals working in the financial markets of London or New York, there was no atmosphere of panic, even though some perspicacious observers recognized the first signs of trouble.

The period between 2001 and 2006 can be pinpointed as the true era of the 'realm of fantasy' that Peter Warburton had identified as early as 1999. During this period, new subprime mortgages rose from $160 billion in 2001 to $600 billion in 2006. It was a period in which brokers happily signed off on 'ninja' loans – loans to people with 'no income, no job and no assets' – by the 'hundred thousand'.[12] It was in 2007 that the crisis began. Another writer has spoken of how, during the 'murky and curious period from early February to June 2007', the subprime mortgage market 'resembled a giant helium balloon'.[13] The balloon was, however, moored to a phenomenon in the real world. As a consequence of loose lending stand-ards and keen competition among mortgage providers, as well the 'frantic search for yield', loans were handed out with abandon. This naturally forced up the prices of houses. According to one assessment, the 'sheer scale of the housing bubble' in the United States meant that housing was 'probably overvalued by more than 50 per cent by the summer of 2006'. To eliminate this 'overvaluation' prices would have to fall 'by a third'.[14]

Many were surprised that what started as a crisis in the United States housing market ended up being such a global problem. The Federal Funds rate crept upwards. From June 2006 to September 2007, the rate was held at 5.25 per cent, having risen from a low of 1 per cent in June 2003.[15] This increase, between 2003 and 2006, would eventually put pressure on mort-gage holders. Yet by late August 2007 it was already too late to supply relief. At that time, funds and banks around the world had already 'taken hits' because they had purchased bonds backed by US home loans, 'often bundled into financial instruments called collateralized debt obligations, or CDOs'. An Australia-based professor of finance observed that it was 'amazing how much ignorance and fear are out there'.[16] In the spring of 2008, the former 'maestro', Alan Greenspan himself, writing in a blog on the *Financial Times*'s website, referred in his jargon-filled academic prose-style to the 'dramatic fall in real long-term interest rates' which 'statistically explains, and is the most likely major cause of, real estate capitalization rates that declined and converged across the globe'. All this meant was that low interest rates had pushed up the price of real estate. In practice, a 'capitalization rate' could be seen simply as the return on an asset. For instance, a property which cost $100,000 and produced a yield of $10,000 would have a 10 per cent capitalization rate. If it still yielded $10,000 but went up in price to $200,000, its capitalization rate would fall to 5 per cent. Falling capitalization rates meant higher prices.

Greenspan observed in the same piece that by 2006 'long-term rates for all developed and major developing economies declined to single digits, I believe, for the first time ever'. This was the background to a global bubble. In the United States, the 'core of the subprime problem' lay with 'the misjudgements of the investment community', Greenspan maintained. In his recollection, subprime 'did not break from its localized niche status until 2005'. Like nearly everyone who has commented on the causes of the bubble and the bust, Greenspan, quoting Ben Bernanke, his successor as Chairman of the Federal Reserve, blamed looser standards of lending: 'The deterioration in underwriting standards appears to have begun in late 2005.' He also attributed the demand for subprime securities to the fact that they were 'seemingly under-priced' or 'high-yielding'. These securities appeared to offer 'great profit opportunities'. The demand for these mortgage-backed securities and CDOs was what was driving the promotion and sale of the underlying mortgages to people who could not really afford them. 'Investors of all stripes pressed securitizers [the banks who constructed and marketed these bonds] for more MBS [mortgage-backed securities]. Securitizers, in turn, pressed lenders for mortgage paper with little concern about its quality.'

Self-justifyingly, Greenspan said, 'I admit to being surprised and appalled at the recent collapse in bank underwriting standards.' In an equally defensive remark, later in the article, he confessed to having 'an ideology'. Once again, using the technical and opaque jargon of which he was a master, he admitted that his 'view of the range of dispersion of outcomes has been shaken, but not my judgement that free competitive markets are by far the unrivalled way to organize economies'.[17] What happened later in 2008 may well have posed a greater challenge to Greenspan's confidence in the free-market system. The market turbulence and dramatic events of September that year would leave their lasting impression on the memories of traders, bankers and politicians.

On Monday 15 September 2008, Lehman Brothers filed for bankruptcy protection and 'hurtled toward liquidation after it failed to find a buyer'.[18] The firm was not as reputable as some on Wall Street, since it had always had an image as one of the hustlers on the Street, where a brash, abrasive culture prevailed. It was a firm with a tight, almost cult-like sense of internal loyalty. As the wife of one executive remarked, 'If you made a personal choice that hurt Lehman, it was over for you.'[19] The culture at the firm was one of excessive consumption and little caution in the pursuit of profits. Subsequent investigations undertaken by journalists and reporters revealed a 'series of incidents stretching back decades', in which 'Lehman's traders routinely hid the riskiness of their trades from senior managers and the public'. The superficiality of such a culture was captured by the fact that one of the firm's leading female executives 'annoyed her colleagues by becoming blonder, more toned and better dressed as she rose through the ranks'.[20]

The Lehman bankruptcy became one of those symbolic events which define the end of an era. As Peter Peterson, co-founder of private equity firm the Blackstone Group, remembered, 'I've been in the business 35 years, and these are the most extraordinary events I've ever seen.' With respect to Lehman Brothers, investors had 'become increasingly nervous about whether major financial institutions can recover from their losses'.[21] Of all these major financial institutions, Lehman Brothers had been among the most heavily exposed to property lending. As the property market bubble started sharply to deflate, 'Bear Stearns and Lehman Brothers were the smallest of the big investment banks and the most heavily exposed to the housing market.'[22] Other banks, knowing the exposure of these two, became 'reluctant to provide the short-term funding' that the pair needed. Bear Stearns was an equally aggressive firm which had collapsed in March 2008. Lehman's demise had wider repercussions, the reverberations of which were felt, and argued about, for years.

Lehman's problems raised the issue of moral hazard, which has already been referred to in connection with problems associated with the creation of the euro. It was decided, as Lehman tottered and eventually fell, not to 'bail out' the bank in order not to create moral hazard. 'The idea that borrowers should be allowed to escape is one example of "moral hazard",' wrote Philip Coggan. 'Let the borrowers believe they will be rescued from their folly . . . and they will never meet their responsibilities.' It was this sentiment which prevented US officials from rescuing Lehman Brothers, a decision which, arguably, led to the near-collapse of the global financial system. Such a decision was, of course, a finely judged matter. If officials had leapt in to protect Lehman, some of those who had criticized the government for letting Lehman sink would have, no doubt, complained about government intervention.

It was perhaps doubly unfortunate that the man who was finally responsible for the demise of Lehman was Hank Paulson, a staunch free-market Republican who also happened to have spent his entire banking career working for one of Lehman Brothers' arch-rivals, Goldman Sachs. Appointed Treasury Secretary in 2006, Paulson was a man who had climbed to the top of Goldman because of his efficiency as a deal maker. As head of the investment bank – the part of the bank that put together deals and offered advisory services to corporate clients – Paulson was wary of the trading side of the bank, and had a disdain for the culture of trading. By contrast, the head of Lehman, the man who more than any other had been responsible for building up that firm, was Richard Fuld, a veteran bond trader and salesman. Fuld was brash and aggressive, a stereotypical bond trader.

A conservative banker by temperament and by intellectual conviction, Paulson was averse to the very idea of 'bailouts'. The term 'bailout' itself was a word which was often heard in the media and the discussions of that time. It was popularly used in the American media and owed its origins perhaps to the legal phrase: a prisoner pays bail and is thereby released from prison. The phrase, in a modified form, is Shakespearian. Thus in *Titus Andronicus*, dating from 1598, the King says to Titus, when he offers himself as a surety for two suspected murderers: 'Thou shalt not baile them, see thou follow me.'[23] The word 'bailout' came into its own during the crisis as billions of taxpayers' money were spent in trying to support a stricken international financial system. Paulson was conscious that, as a public servant, he needed to be mindful of public money, the taxpayers' dollars.

The drama which surrounded the fall of Lehman – the all-day meetings, the brinkmanship and hard-nosed deal making – has been admirably described in a series of accounts of the financial crisis. From the perspective of an enquiry into the history of money in the last 500 years, the significance of the meetings and the drama is perhaps less obvious. The reaction of Paulson and his colleagues in the Bush administration is more important. It was later in the same week that Lehman crashed to earth, on Friday 19 September 2008, that Paulson announced his Troubled Asset Relief Program in the press room of the Treasury Building. TARP itself was 'a vast series of guarantees and outright purchases' of what Paulson himself described as the 'illiquid assets that are weighing down our financial system and threatening our economy'.[24]

Paulson, a tall, slim man, was not a natural performer on the public stage. His career had thrived in the corporate culture of Goldman Sachs, a bank not especially known for its skill in media relations. Paulson now gave a vague account of his plan which did little to allay the market's fears. He was open to the press, telling them what they all knew: 'The underlying weakness in our financial system is the illiquid mortgage assets that have lost value as the housing correction proceeded. These illiquid assets are choking off the flow of credit.' In simpler terms, the bad mortgages were preventing banks from lending any more money. Paulson 'intentionally chose not to mention how much the program would cost'. After the hesitant press conference, now back in his office, he met with one of his officials. They debated what the precise cost of the TARP programme might be. 'What about $1 trillion?' asked Paulson's colleague. 'We'll get killed,' was Paulson's dejected reply. 'Okay,' responded the official. 'How about $700 billion?'[25]

As Paulson later acknowledged, there had been little in the way of scientific calculation in arriving at the vast amounts of money now being considered. He admitted in his memoir of the episode that 'the $700 billion figure shocked many Americans – and Congress'. He attributed his failure to anticipate such a howl of protest to the fact that he was now becoming 'inured' to the 'extraordinary numbers associated with the prospect of an all-out financial meltdown'. He remembered 'being pilloried for the proposal', not least because the document embodying it (a mere three pages) was 'so short'. He had naively asked for 'broad power to spend up to $700 billion to buy troubled assets, including both mortgages and mortgage-backed securities, under whatever terms and conditions we saw fit'.[26] In the United States, where there existed a strict separation of powers, Congressmen were understandably wary of transferring so much power over the public purse to an unelected official, appointed by the executive. In the midst of what then seemed a tightly fought presidential race, such issues became highly contentious.

The Republican presidential candidate in 2008, John McCain, a foreign affairs and Vietnam veteran, addressed a town-hall meeting in Scranton, Pennsylvania. He told the crowd, 'I am greatly concerned that the plan gives a single individual the unprecedented power to spend one trillion . . . dollars without any meaningful accountability.' Then, as if carried away by his own rhetoric, he started to adopt the cadences of the British statesman Winston Churchill. 'Never before in the history of our nation has so much power and money been concentrated in the hands of one person,' he thundered. By Monday 22 September, the Dow Jones had fallen 373 points, as a consequence, in Paulson's own words, of the 'uncertainty caused by Republican disenchantment with TARP'.[27] By Thursday the 25th, Paulson himself was now the protagonist who felt disenchantment: 'We'd devised TARP to save the financial system. Now it had become all about politics – presidential politics.'[28]

The beleaguered Paulson then received support from an unexpected quarter. A committed free-market Republican, he was reluctant to approve any measures which could in any way be interpreted as constituting excessive government interference. He was especially reluctant to do anything which would lead the banking system to fall under state control. His mind naturally resisted any notion of the state directly injecting money into the banks' capital reserves. This would involve the government buying shares, or taking a direct stake, in the banks. Yet this was precisely what Gordon Brown, the British Prime Minister, was suggesting by the beginning of October. It was early on Tuesday morning on 7 October that Paulson recounted walking to the White House for a conference call with 'President Bush and British prime minister Gordon Brown'. Brown told Bush and

Paulson that 'his government planned to inject capital into U.K. banks'. He wanted their support.[29]

As if under the spell of some enchantment, Paulson changed his mind. He now 'firmly determined that the Treasury should make direct investments in banks'.[30] On 13 October 'the nine biggest U.S. banks had agreed to accept $125 billion in capital from the government'.[31] Brown's own plan for the United Kingdom involved investing the equivalent of $87 billion in the small number of banks which dominated Britain's highly concentrated financial sector. It was Brown who won plaudits for devising a clear and workable plan, in favourable contrast to Bush and Paulson.[32] Brown remembered with pride how, on Monday 13 October, as markets opened, his government 'announced a £37 billion recapitalisation of RBS [Royal Bank of Scotland], Lloyds, and HBOS [Halifax Bank of Scotland]'. A committed socialist and Labour Party activist from his youth, he added that the British government 'would take a 57 percent stake in RBS and a 58 percent stake in HBOS'.[33] He had shown a command of the situation which the Bush administration, in its twilight days, had not displayed. In the weeks just preceding the US presidential election in November, the economist Paul Krugman did not miss an opportunity to lash the dying Bush administration's indecision: 'The Brown government has shown itself willing to think clearly about the financial crisis, and act quickly on its conclusions ... this combination of clarity and decisiveness hasn't been matched by any other Western government, least of all our own.'[34]

One of the interesting outcomes of the financial crisis has been the large number of first-hand accounts which have been published by many of the leading protagonists. Both Gordon Brown and Hank Paulson have written readable, though of course highly subjective, books which recount their parts in this memorable episode in financial history. Another such protagonist was Alistair Darling, Gordon Brown's Chancellor of the Exchequer. In his version of events, Darling recalled that on 26 September Mervyn King, the Governor of the Bank of England, had asked to see him. King told Darling that 'unless the banking system as a whole was recapitalized, further failures were inevitable'. Darling added, 'The only realistic source for that capital was unfortunately the government.' Historians will no doubt have different opinions about who ultimately was responsible for the idea to recapitalize the banks. Clearly, both Darling and Brown, in their own way, take the view that they were individually responsible for it, and they both believe that, if drastic action of this kind had not been taken, the entire global financial system would have collapsed in the ensuing landslide. As Darling's account pointed out, the British government 'would be providing billions of pounds . . . to banks that, until now, had been owned entirely by their shareholders'.[35] It was a move that involved an unprecedented degree of state control.

Darling and other politicians often expressed a sense of wonder at the huge sums of money they found themselves spending in this attempt to save the world from financial collapse. Yet it was the very size of these bailouts, which ultimately had to be paid by taxpayers, that caused concern – particularly in the Republican heartlands in the United States. The issue of bailouts would perhaps not have been so toxic if the public finances of both the United States and Great Britain had been better managed in the years immediately preceding the crisis. The position of the US national debt was a matter of fierce debate in the months after President Obama took office in January 2009. The American national debt, which had stood at US$5.7 billion on 30 September 2000, had more than doubled by the same date in 2009 to $11.9 billion, an increase of 109 per cent in just nine years.[36]

Many Americans now wrongly believed that the country's federal government had always been a spendthrift and debt-engorged leviathan. Yet this was simply not the case historically. In a perceptive and timely article entitled 'The U.S. Deficit' which appeared in *Time* magazine at the end of August 2009, it was observed that the 'United States' checkbook hasn't always been in the red. Aside from periods of war or economic turmoil, the federal budget was actually in surplus for most of the nation's first 200 years.'[37] This may have been a slight exaggeration, but it was true to suggest that, after the Civil War of 1861–5 and the Spanish–American War of 1898, a series of balanced budgets had meant that the debt shrank every year as a proportion of the United States' GDP. Remarkably, the federal debt, which had stood at $2.77 billion on 7 January 1866, was still only $2.91 billion on 7 January 1914.[38] These were nominal figures. In terms of the size of the economy, the 1914 figure was much smaller than that of 1866. It represented a nominal increase of barely 5 per cent in nearly fifty years, even though the US economy in 1914 was five and a half times (or 550 per cent) bigger than it had been in 1866.[39]

The unprecedented degree of indebtedness that America experienced in the years after the crisis shocked many Americans, and infused an added bitterness into much of the political debate. But, if Americans were stunned to find themselves grappling with unimagined levels of debt, it was in Europe that a real sovereign debt crisis occurred in the early 2010. If there was one country which typified this problem, it was Greece. The Greek sovereign debt crisis, which started to upset markets in 2009, in many ways eclipsed even the severity and alarm caused by the initial financial crisis. The Greek crisis became a highly contentious subject of debate across Europe and, somewhat surprisingly, in the United States. Different political persuasions took different lessons from it. To Republicans, and other fiscal conservatives, the woes of Greece were a dire warning of what might happen, if public spending was not restrained, in the United States. To commentators on the left, Greece was an exceptional case, made worse by the total breakdown of the Greek state, proved by its chronic inability to raise tax revenues: for the left, the situation of Greece was utterly unlike that of America.

Greece's problems stemmed from the fact that it had joined the euro at a time when it was not ready. The euro, it had been widely anticipated, would lead to greater fiscal discipline from participant countries. As it turned out, it was only really Germany which adopted more stringent policies as a consequence of the creation of the new currency. The Greek crisis began, as a market crisis, in October 2009, but its origins lay in the decade preceding that unhappy month. As George Papandreou swept into power after the elections of 4 October 2009, he promised a new beginning. Behind the optimism and the vague and cloudy phrases lay the reality of 200 years of Greek financial history. 'From 1800 to well after World War II, Greece found itself virtually in continual default,' noted Carmen Reinhart and Kenneth Rogoff in their important history of financial crises, *This Time is Different.*[40] Such a history would perhaps have disqualified Greece automatically from ever being considered as a full participant in the euro. But it became such a participant, because political considerations were paramount in the promotion of the European single currency; economics played only a minor part.

The Greek panic began when Papandreou, to discredit his political rivals, the nominally centre-right New Democracy, soon after taking office revealed that the budget deficit had reached 12.5 per cent in 2009. By contrast, the outgoing government had estimated its 2009 budget deficit at 3.7 per cent. In reality, the figure turned out to be closer to 14 per cent.[41] Greece had joined the euro in 2001, a couple of years later than other participant countries. At first, the new currency seemed to inaugurate an era of prosperity and success. Since joining, 'the country had averaged an annual growth rate of 4.2 percent . . . second only to Ireland'. But, even as the economy seemed to expand, the trade deficit worsened. This showed that Greek imports exceeded exports by 14 per cent of GDP by 2009. The trade figures painted a picture of a country with little in the way of productive enterprise, with nothing to export, but greedily devouring imports with its inflated currency, the euro. The failure to nurture any exporting base whatsoever suggested that the euro was too expensive a currency to allow Greece to be competitive. Fatally, in retrospect, though welcomed at the time, entry into the euro caused interest rates in Greece to reduce 'dramatically'. This meant that the country rode on a wave of cheap debt, since it was now 'able to borrow money on the global markets on virtually the same terms as Germany'.[42]

As well as a large trade deficit, Greece developed large budget deficits, as government spending soared. As a result of chronic failure to cut expenditure, Greek public debt exploded as a proportion of GDP. In 1990, public debt had been 74 per cent of GDP. By 2004 that figure had soared to 102 per cent.[43] Meanwhile, one of the principal reasons why the government budget was always in deficit was that 'the Greek economy had become a massive exercise in tax evasion'. It was said that not paying your taxes had become 'a way of life for middle-class Greeks'. One example of this delinquency which acquired an almost legendary status was the case of the swimming pools of Ekali, a prosperous suburb to the north of Athens. In the municipality of Athens, a permit was required to own a pool. Such a permit could cost up to 5,000 euros a year, and so the affluent residents of Ekali simply refused to pay. It was alleged that only 324 people checked the box on their annual return, while later satellite evidence revealed nearly 17,000 swimming pools. This implied an evasion rate of 98 per cent.[44]

Doctors, surgeons, lawyers and other professionals would declare incomes of as little as 3,000 euros a year on their tax returns, an income which seemed utterly implausible, given the amounts they had paid to attend medical and other professional schools. Even more seriously, the Greeks had created lavish entitlements for their citizens. A state retirement age of fifty-eight meant very substantial pension costs to the Greek state. The Greek railway system was another state structure which seemed to exist solely for the benefit of its employees. To one journalist, the function of Greek railways seemed 'more about preserving jobs for its 6,500 workers, more than half of whom are over 50 and are looking forward to generous pensions, than it is about moving either staff or people around the country'.[45]

Papandreou, the head of the Greek Socialist Party (Pasok), was the son and grandson of former Greek prime ministers. His party's populism, with its generous spending and seeming inability to collect tax revenues, was partly responsible for the Greek crisis. He was, in his first months, however, 'under intense pressure' to curb Greece's 'soaring budget deficit'. In December 2009, in a much heralded speech to business groups and labour unions, he used all the weapons of modern political rhetoric, declaring, 'we need to move immediately to a new social deal'. He accepted the need for change: 'We must change or sink.' He used slick soundbites, twisting words to suit his rhetorical message: 'Our biggest deficit is the deficit of credibility. Markets want to see action, not words.' His avowed aim, expressed in this admirably phrased speech, was to 'reduce state spending by 10 percent and to bring the budget deficit to less than 3 percent of gross domestic product in 2013'. The deficit target of 3 per cent of GDP had, of course, been enshrined as a precondition for European monetary union in the Maastricht Treaty as long ago as 1991.[46]

Papandreou's rhetoric was matched by some tough measures, but these were not enough to close the 'deficit of credibility' he had so eloquently described. By the spring of 2010, demonstrations were frequent occurrences in Greece. In early May of that year, hundreds of demonstrators took to the streets of Athens, unfurling banners over the Acropolis to protest against their government's 'austerity measures'. Pasok's Yannos Papantoniou, the respected former Finance Minister, holder of an economics doctorate from Cambridge University, described the situation very simply: 'Now we are paying the price for the fact that we lived above our means, with amazing profligacy, and failed to reduce the role of the state.' It was a sign of the extraordinary nature of the crisis that a nominally socialist Greek politician could speak openly about 'reducing the size of the state'. Another economist who ventured into Greek politics, again on the side of the socialists, commented in 2010 that Greece had entered into the euro as 'an invitation to party'. Yannis Stournaras, a polished product of Athens University and Oxford, where he earned his PhD in economics, observed that instead of 'cutting the deficit and liberalizing the economy . . . the country continues to spend'.[47] Stournaras would be appointed Finance Minister in June 2012.

As can be inferred from looking at the experience and educational attainments of the Greek elite, Greece's problems stemmed more from a failure of political will than from any intellectual shortcomings. It is difficult to see how the Greek elite could have been ignorant of the likely consequences of their policies. Yet the Greek government, under administrations of both left and right, could not stop spending. The tragedy of Greece was that both parties had acquiesced in a system of public finance which everybody could see had been disastrous. It was apparent to them that spending would have to be drastically reduced, but it also became clear that Greece could not drag itself out of its difficulties on its own. Some form of assistance or 'bailout' would be needed.

The Greek crisis was genuinely a European crisis. Greek irresponsibility had raised the old theme of moral hazard, which meant people being able to behave irresponsibly and then expecting others to pay the bill. This was the issue which had condemned Lehman Brothers, because Hank Paulson had been reluctant to play the role of the white knight, or provider of the bailout – only to find himself writing even bigger cheques in the aftermath of Lehman's collapse. In the case of Greece, the Treaty governing the European Union explicitly contained a 'no bailout' clause, forbidding countries from assuming the debts of others. The clause had been inserted on German insistence when the Maastricht Treaty was signed in 1991. During 2010, intense pressure was applied for some kind of arrangement to be made which could somehow breach the stern provisions of the Treaty. 'One remedy', the *Economist* suggested, 'would be for Greece to arrange a bridging loan from another eurozone country in good credit, such as Germany.' Such an outcome, the British weekly recognized, might or might not be legal, but 'it would certainly make for terrible politics'. It was clear to British journalists as early as February 2010, when the *Economist*'s editorial 'A Very European Crisis' appeared, that if 'Germany steps in [to solve the Greek crisis], there will be people on the Athens street who will say the *Wehrmacht* is back'. Another potential saviour was the IMF, but European officials were generally 'horrified at the thought' of calling in the Washington-based Fund to solve what Europeans felt was a domestic problem. 'To turn to the fund for aid would be a humiliation for Europe.'[48]

The Germans, under the direction of their cautious and analytical Chancellor, Angela Merkel, were understandably perplexed by this turn of events. Greece in itself was a negligible factor in the European economy. According to Evangelos Venizelos, speaking in July 2011 when he was Greek Minister of Finance and Deputy Prime Minister, Greece made up only 2.5 per cent of the eurozone economy.[49] Yet, as Greek yields continued to soar into double digits, Merkel, in the run-up to state elections in Germany, was reluctant to approve the big spending deal which would save the Greeks. Eventually, in May 2010, a €110 billion 'bailout package' was agreed. This comprised three-year loans from eurozone countries and, to the embarrassment of the Eurozone fanatics, the IMF. Greece, in return, was expected to embark on further rounds of expenditure cuts, dubbed 'austerity measures'. Furthermore, a €750 billion scheme was established. It was given the bureaucratic and portentous-sounding name of the European Financial Stabilization Facility (EFSF). Its function was to raise funds, with the support of EU governments, which it would then lend to countries in difficulty.[50]

The issue of moral hazard can be seen to be a dominant theme of the Greek sovereign debt crisis. In many cases, market participants, investors who had had invested millions in Greek debts, were loudest in their demand for government support. Often these investors were people who, under ordinary circumstances, were openly hostile to government inter-vention. They were red-blooded capitalists who saw themselves as bucca-neers of the free market. As other crises took hold of many markets in the years after 2008, a sanguine observer could be forgiven for agreeing with John Gutfreund, a veteran Salomon Brothers trader. Gutfreund, perhaps crudely, observed to a former employee, the American financial journalist Michael Lewis: 'It's laissez-faire until you get in deep shit.'[51]

More generally, the Greek crisis brought focus to a debate in the United States, which had raged between liberals and conservatives, about the nature of the wider financial crisis. Once again, Alan Greenspan can be held up as the star witness for fiscal conservatives, for whom Greece's reck-less expenditure proffered a stark warning to the United States. As against Greenspan's gloomy forebodings, Paul Krugman, with fresh laurels bestowed upon him by the Nobel Prize committee in 2008, was the liber-als' champion. Greenspan wrote an article in the *Wall Street Journal* in June 2010 with the explicit title 'US Debt and the Greece Analogy'. In his jargon-heavy but precise prose, Greenspan described how the 'financial crisis, triggered by the unexpected default of Lehman Brothers in September 2008, created a collapse in global demand that engendered a high degree of deflationary slack in our economy'. This was just a way of saying that falling demand led to an environment in which prices were likely to fall.

Greenspan, well into his eighties at the time he wrote the article, could remember the 1950s when 'U.S. federal budget deficits were no more politically acceptable than households spending beyond their means.' This 'quaint notion gave way over the decades' to such an extent that 'today it is the rare politician who doesn't run on seemingly costless spending increases or tax cuts with borrowed money'. Greenspan's attitude had always been what was the orthodox conservative position from at least the first part of the nineteenth century in Britain, if not before. Tax cuts had to be matched by spending cuts. Increases in spending would be matched, in the same way Truman and Eisenhower had tried to pay for the Korean War, by increases in taxation. In the current environment, however, it was clear to Greenspan that spending, and not unfunded cuts in taxation, was the chronic problem. 'The current federal debt explosion is being driven by an inability to stem new spending initiatives,' he argued. 'Having appropriated hundreds of billions of dollars on new programs in the last year and a half, it is very difficult for Congress to deny an additional one or two billion dollars for programs that significant constituencies perceive as urgent.'

The result of all this spending was a potential fiscal crisis. The United States could not 'grow out of these fiscal pressures'. Demography meant that 'The modest-sized post-baby-boom labor force, if history is any guide, will not be able to consistently increase output per hour by more than 3% annually.' The prognosis was therefore a bleak one: 'The product of a slowly growing labor force and limited productivity growth will not provide the real resources necessary to meet existing commitments.' On the question of reliance upon foreigners, presumably the Chinese, to continue financing 'our current account deficit', Greenspan was cautious: 'We must avoid persistent borrowing from abroad.' He was sounding an alarmist note, which contrasted with his relative buoyancy and optimism at the beginning of the century. In conclusion, he maintained that the 'very severity of the pending crisis and growing analogies to Greece' required 'a serious response'. Nothing less than 'a tectonic shift in fiscal policy' on the part of the 'United States, and most of the rest of the developed world', would do.

Greenspan ruled out 'large tax increases' as these would 'sap economic growth'. As we have noted, he did not believe that the US economy, at any rate, could grow itself out of the debt, as it had done in the past. He believed that 'fears of budget contraction inducing a renewed decline of economic activity' were 'misplaced'. It was clear to him that spending cuts were the only available way to deal with the chronic and structural problem of government deficits. The US government, of course, could create 'dollars at will to meet any obligation'. It would, in Greenspan's view, 'doubtless continue to do so'. But this would risk increasing interest rates (an instance of the old intuitive and observable fact that the more you borrow, the more you have to pay in interest for this privilege). From the point of view of currencies, printing more money could have adverse effects. 'It is little comfort that the dollar is still the least worst of the major fiat currencies.' But the gold market suggested a widespread distrust of even the US dollar among international investors. The 'inexorable rise in the price of gold indicates a large number of investors are seeking a safe haven beyond fiat [paper] currencies'.[52] This was palpably true. The average price of gold was $1,227 an ounce during 2010, the year in which he wrote the article, more than four times the average price of $279 in 2000.[53] There were undoubtedly other issues driving the gold price, but one of the significant factors had been a loss of confidence in paper money as a store of value.

Paul Krugman and other liberal commentators took a more optimistic view of the prospects of American indebtedness. To Krugman, the 'deficit obsession' was even more dangerous than the deficit itself.[54] In an article in the *New York Times* on New Year's Day 2012 entitled 'Nobody Understands Debt', the American economist spoke of the 'allegedly urgent issue of reducing the budget deficit'. He regarded this as a 'misplaced focus'. He pointed out, correctly as it happens, that the economic experts 'on whom much of Congress relies' had been 'repeatedly utterly wrong about the short-run effects of budget deficits'. These experts had believed that interest rates would soar. While they had been waiting, Krugman triumphantly pointed out, 'those rates have dropped to historical lows'. He confidently dismissed the concerns of the 'deficit worriers' who had portrayed, in his words, a 'future in which we're impoverished by the need to pay back money we've been borrowing'. His view was that, just as had been the case after the Second World War, the debt would 'become increasingly irrelevant as the U.S. economy grew, and with it the income subject to taxation'.[55]

Krugman blithely pointed to the experience of Britain, which had laboured at times with far higher levels of national debt than had America in 2010. That is why 'nations with stable, responsible governments have historically been able to live with much higher levels of debt than today's conventional wisdom would lead you to believe'. He continued, 'Britain, in particular, has had debt exceeding 100 percent of G.D.P. for 81 of the last 170 years.' A conservative disputant might have added that for much of that time the British Treasury had managed to balance the budget on an annual basis, thereby not adding much, if anything, to the net debt position. To be fair to Krugman, he was not suggesting that debt did not matter. 'So yes, debt matters,' he conceded. His point was that 'right now, other things matter more'. His prescription was simple: 'We need more, not less, government spending to get us out of our unemployment trap. And the wrongheaded, ill-informed obsession with debt is standing in the way.'

The differing views of Alan Greenspan and Paul Krugman on the debt position of the United States in the 2010s summed up, in an abbreviated form, the debate not just in America but throughout the developed nations. Governments across the world, notably the United States, Great Britain, Japan and France, faced large deficits, but many were unwilling to countenance the 'tectonic shift' in fiscal policy which Greenspan had suggested was inevitable. The global debate became crudely stereotyped as one between 'austerity' – favouring spending cuts – and 'growth' – adopting a more relaxed approach to spending. Extreme 'growthers' advocated even more spending to generate the growth which would make the debt 'irrelevant'. But what of currencies, the dollar and the euro?

It was clear that currencies had played an important role in the development of the crisis and in the ability of governments to withstand the squalls of the financial storm. The ease with which credit could be issued with paper money has already been observed. More paradoxically, the paper money which had been responsible in large part for the explosive increase in credit was now seen to provide the solution. It was in this period that the phrase 'quantitative easing' first entered into everyday speech, at least in the newspapers. If anything symbolized the power of the government to conjure money out of thin air it was quantitative easing. Quantitative easing (QE) was said to be 'an ugly name for a simple idea'. Central banks 'buy long-term government bonds with newly printed money'.[56] The theory was that this purchase of government debt, by which the central bank was effectively printing money and lending it to its own government, would keep bond prices high. High bond prices meant lower interest rates, which would help boost growth. Between November 2010, a full two years after the collapse of Lehman Brothers, and March 2011, the US Treasury issued $589 billion of debt, of which the Federal Reserve bought $514 billion, or 87 per cent. In Britain, from 'early 2009 through to March 2010' Her Majesty's Treasury issued '£247 billion ($396 billion) of extra long-term gilts [UK government bonds], of which the Bank of England bought £199 billion', or 80 per cent.[57]

In the United States, it was significant that Ben Bernanke, an academic economist who specialized in the history of the Great Depression, had taken over the chairmanship of the Federal Reserve from Alan Greenspan. Bernanke had been named *Time* magazine's 'Man of the Year' in 2009. He was determined not to be the Fed Chairman who presided over 'Depression 2.0'. Accordingly, as the US housing bubble burst, he 'conjured up trillions of new dollars and blasted them into the economy'. His style was one of fervent, almost hyperactive intervention. As a scholar of the Great Depression, he had 'embraced the Keynesian view that aggressive government action backed by government money is needed to reverse death spirals by restoring confidence and reviving demand'. As a consequence of this understanding of economic history and Keynesian theory, Bernanke 'engineered massive public rescues of failing private companies; ratcheted down interest rates to zero . . . blew up the Fed's balance sheet to three times its previous size'. His detractors called him 'Bailout Ben' or 'the unelected czar of a fourth branch of government'.[58]

Bernanke's instincts to intervene aggressively chimed with the mood of the Obama administration. Tim Geithner was Obama's Treasury Secretary, and coincidentally an alumnus of the same small elite New England university attended by Hank Paulson, Dartmouth College. A slick and committed public servant, he had earned plaudits from Britain's Alistair Darling, who found him 'unpretentious and easy going', with a 'quiet style' which 'belied a steely determination'.[59] He and most of the other leading figures in both the United States and the West generally were committed to printing and spending large sums of money to avert recession. Such policies as quantitative easing and the running of enormous budget deficits could be applied only in a world which had been totally removed from the constraints imposed by a gold standard.

Central bankers like Bernanke remained committed to providing liquidity and supporting bond prices by means of printing more money. Some drastic spending cuts did occur in some countries in Europe such as Greece, Ireland and Portugal. They had to experience this form of austerity because they were tied into a currency, the euro, over which they had no

control. Larger countries, by contrast, were masters of their own currencies. They did not have to embark on anything as severe. Paper money,
preferably in the form of a national currency over which a country had
exclusive control, allowed governments to print ever-greater quantities of
cash. It was paper money which had so far shielded some of the most
developed countries on earth from the consequences of their excessive
spending. This was an outcome of which John Law would have been
proud.

Epilogue

In June 2012, the people of Greece went to the polls in a general election. The election campaign was particularly tense, since one of the principal parties, Syriza, was an avowedly left-wing party which stood on a platform of rejecting the austerity imposed upon Greece as a condition for receiving a bailout. Syriza's thirty-seven-year-old leader, Alexis Tsipras, was young and charismatic. The first Greek elections of 2012, which had taken place in May, had produced inconclusive results. The centre-right party, New Democracy, had won just under 19 per cent of the vote. After a month during which Tsipras and Antonis Samaras, the leader of New Democracy, had attempted to form a government, new elections were called. Tsipras was an engineer by training, but had spent most of his adult life as a political activist, first as a Communist and eventually as head of Syriza, a motley collection of smaller parties on the Greek left.

Like many successful politicians, Tsipras focused on a very simple message. He resolutely opposed austerity in all its forms. He would reject any bailout agreements, as these had been, in his view, imposed from abroad. Similarly to other political demagogues, he spoke loftily of the 'Greek people', and had a burning sense of mission. He said the Greek people had asked him to 'cancel the memorandum of barbarity' represented by any bailout agreement. He used high-sounding phrases such as 'the people of Europe can no longer be reconciled with the bailouts of barbarism'. He denounced the privatizations, spending cuts, structural reform and austerity which had been prescribed by the other eurozone countries as a condition of helping Greece. A canny political operator and campaigner, Tsipras openly attacked Mrs Merkel, the German Chancellor.[1]

The June elections in Greece gave a narrow victory to Samaras's New Democracy Party, and thus averted the potential hazards of a Syriza government. Greece's choice, reported the *New York Times*, was very much 'welcomed by the finance ministers of the euro zone countries'. They breathed a collective sigh of relief, content that the result 'should allow for the formation of a government that will carry the support of the electorate to bring Greece back on a path of sustainable growth'. As a reward for having voted the right way the eurozone ministers pledged to help Greece in its hour of economic need. Greece's 22 per cent unemployment rate was a matter of concern to the New Democracy Party, which, despite being the 'most pro-Europe of Greece's political parties', was also alarmed by some of the plans for more fiscal austerity demanded by Greece's creditors. The eurozone ministers added that the country's so-called troika of foreign creditors – the European Commission, the European Central Bank and the International Monetary Fund – would discuss emergency loans 'as soon as a government was in place'. As Syriza lost ground, with little prospect of forming a government, there was also widespread relief in the world's markets. One London-based economist remarked, 'It looks like we've avoided the worst-case scenario.' Despite the result, many people on the street in Athens remained defiant. A forty-eight-year-old Athens taxi driver who supported Syriza believed that his vote had sent a message. Syriza's support effectively told Europe, he said, that 'you are not the boss – Mrs. Merkel, or anybody'. He stressed, 'We want somebody from our country to oversee our economic system.'[2]

There had been a genuine fear that, if Tsipras became Prime Minister, Greece would 'crash out of the euro and Europe's ambitious experiment with a common currency could collapse'.[3] Such fears seemed to be fantastic to many people at the time, but the victory of New Democracy in the June 2012 elections did turn out to be a buying signal for Greek assets. The coming to power of an overtly pro-European party of the centre-right was exactly the reassurance that Greece's international investors wanted. As if to demonstrate how closely international capital movements were now tied to politics, money started to flow into Greece; new deals were forged; the atmosphere of panic and collapse experienced at the beginning of 2012, when many observers feared Greece might actually abandon the euro, was slowly dissipated. By the end of November 2012, it seemed that much of the storm surrounding Greece had passed away.

A deal struck by Greece's creditors at that time included measures which would reduce interest rates on Greece's bailout loans, thereby releasing 'a long-delayed €34.4bn aid payment'. There were still finer points to be discussed. The IMF had set a target to reduce Greece's debt levels to 120 per cent of GDP by 2020. This target was controversial as it would mean that many of Greece's international creditors, such as Germany and the Netherlands, would have to take losses on some of the money they had given the stricken country as part of a bailout. In exchange for allowing a loosening of the target to 124 per cent, the IMF managed to win a commitment to get debt levels to 'substantially below' 110 per cent in 2022. According to the *Financial Times*, meeting this pledge would probably force eurozone governments to 'provide even more debt relief in the future'.[4]

As a result of this and other similar deals, Greek bonds began to rally. At the end of November 2012, the ten-year Greek government bond was yielding 16.1 per cent, extremely high when compared to the 2 per cent levels achieved by Germany and Great Britain, but lower than the all-time high of 48.6 per cent reached in March 2012. This sharp reduction in interest rates represented a steep increase in the price of the bond. This in itself showed that many investors had made millions of euros from the effective bailout of Greece. Indeed in December 2012 it was reported that one hedge fund was 'sitting on a $500m profit after making a bet that Greece would not be forced to leave the eurozone'. The US billionaire investor Dan Loeb was head of the firm Third Point which was reported to have been the largest hedge-fund holder of Greek bonds. The Greek government had 'swapped holdings of its own debt for notes issued by one of the eurozone's rescue facilities at a value of 34 cents on the euro'. Third Point, it was revealed, had 'scooped up holdings of Greek debt' earlier in 2012 for 'just 17 cents on the euro'.[5] The firm had doubled its money.

In January 2013, Tsipras embarked on a tour of Europe and America, where he attempted to play the part of a moderate statesman in order to assuage concerns about his suitability for office. The tour was openly described as an exercise in public relations. 'The trip is part of a campaign intended to bolster his [Tsipras's] credibility as a politician.' It was designed to counter what Tsipras's aides called the 'fictional portrayals of him as a financial bomb-thrower in Greece's mainstream news media'.

Tsipras himself revealed a certain impish humour. 'They say I am the most dangerous man in Europe,' he said to the editorial board of the *New York Times*. 'What I feel is dangerous is the policy of austerity in Europe. The Greek people have paid a heavy price.'[6] He went on to Washington, where he met officials from the International Monetary Fund and the US Treasury, the very institutions which had been frightened of his potential electoral success in the early summer of 2012. In a busy month of travel, Tsipras also respectfully visited Germany. His grand language had lost none of its intensity. 'After six year of recession in Greece,' he intoned, 'we are witnessing a humanitarian crisis.'[7]

If Greece remained the most powerful example of government indebtedness, it was the United States whose fiscal problems attracted the attention of the world at the close of 2012. The phrase 'fiscal cliff' was repeated over and over again, as a newly re-elected President Obama wrangled with Republican lawmakers over details of a new budget settlement. The fiscal cliff had materialized suddenly since a number of tax cuts originally made under the presidency of George W. Bush would automatically expire at the beginning of 2013 at the same time as some Obama spending cuts were due to take effect. One somewhat alarmist website explained that the measures, if nothing was done to avert the tumble over the cliff, were expected to 'slash the federal budget deficit by $503 billion' between the financial years 2012 and 2013. This would, it was thought, have potentially ruinous consequences for the United States' economic condition in 2013. The resulting contraction for that year would be 'close to 4 percent of GDP'.

The received opinion was very much that any drop over the fiscal cliff would lead to a new recession. 'The abrupt onset of such significant budget austerity in the midst of a still-fragile economic recovery has led most economists to warn of a double-dip recession and rising unemployment in 2013 if Washington fails to intervene in a timely fashion.'[8] The centrepiece of the tax increases was the unwinding of the Bush-era tax cuts. These cuts were due to expire on 31 December 2012, after which all income tax rates would go up to what they had been in the Clinton era. Significantly for some, on both sides of the political divide, the highest rate of tax would increase from 35 to 39.6 per cent.[9] It was easy to see how such a sharp tax increase for the highest earners could be used as a political stick with which to beat opponents. The Democrats portrayed their Republican opponents as friends of the very rich, the proverbial 'one percent', at the very top of society, who had been made the objects of rancour by such groups as the Occupy the Streets Movement. The Republicans, voicing a small-state philosophy which they had seldom acted upon while in government, were reluctant to countenance any tax increases for anyone. On the spending side, the most notable feature of the fiscal cliff was a restriction in the eligibility to receive federal unemployment benefits.

Debates surrounding the fiscal cliff, its likely consequences and serious-ness became increasingly partisan during the last few weeks of 2012. The newly re-elected President, Barack Obama, faced off a somewhat divided Republican Party under the leadership of House Speaker John Boehner, an Ohio Congressman. After weeks of disputes and broken negotiations, a deal was finally reached. The 'fiscal-cliff deal' was passed in the House of Representatives by 257 votes to 167. Only 217 votes (out of 435) were needed, so the victory had been decisive. The Republican Congressmen were split 151–85 against the Bill, while the Democratic Party in the House voted overwhelmingly (172–16) in favour.[10] Fears of tipping the US back into recession clearly prompted many moderate Republicans to support Obama. 'While the agreement is not perfect,' wrote the moderate Pennsylvania Republican Congressman Glenn Thompson, 'its passage prevented the possibility of relapsing into recession.'

It was notable that the leadership of the Republican Party in the House of Representatives was split. Speaker Boehner voted for the deal, while his deputy, the Republican House Majority Leader Eric Cantor, from Virginia, voted against. It remained unclear during the 2010s to what extent the latent problems of US indebtedness had been addressed by the Bill. As the United States entered Obama's second administration, debt was still very much on the minds of Congressmen and their electorate. Writing in his local Pennsylvania newspaper, the *Meadville Tribune*, Glenn Thompson articulated in straightforward language his understanding of the United States' fiscal problem:

Deficits have grown due to the costs associated with two wars [Iraq and Afghanistan], increased spending on health care and programs such as Medicare and Social Security, and government responses to the 2008 recession ... Even as our economy shows signs of strengthening, our revenues simply cannot keep pace with spending. In the coming decade, health care spending is projected to soar at the same time as more and more Americans will retire and live longer. This will increase the cost of our social safety net programs, which already consume close to two-thirds of the federal budget.

The outcome of the historic spending was a national debt which, 'as an accumulation of yearly deficits', stood at $17 trillion. 'Without spending reforms, by 2020, the interest alone paid by American taxpayers will cost $1 trillion per year.'[11] The President, in his generally optimistic State of the Union address in February 2013, also stressed the need for more fiscal restraint. This was a slight but notable deviation from the orthodox ultra-liberal line, espoused by many on the left, that growth was all that mattered, and that budgetary consolidation should occur at a later date. 'Over the last few years, both parties have worked together to reduce the deficit by more than $2.5 trillion – mostly through spending cuts, but also by raising tax rates on the wealthiest 1% of Americans.' 'As a result,' Obama continued hopefully, 'we are more than halfway towards the goal of $4 trillion in deficit reduction that economists say we need to stabilise our finances.' The President, in seeming agreement with moderate Republicans, believed that 'the biggest driver of our long-term debt is the rising cost of healthcare for an aging population'. While stressing that 'deficit reduction alone is not an economic plan', the President struck a conciliatory note by acknowledging that the US deficit was a problem.[12]

One of the striking features of the crisis which started in 2008 was the way in which international co-operation was sought from the very beginning. As early as November 2008, members of the G20, a group of twenty of the leading industrial and developing nations, gathered at the White House to inaugurate a 'two-day emergency summit' on the global financial crisis. It was significant that emerging economies such as Brazil and South

Africa were given a place at the highest level of international economic diplomacy. According to the left-wing British newspaper the *Guardian*, the summit had been widened at the request of Britain's Labour Prime Minister, Gordon Brown. The conference had been expanded 'beyond the usual parameters of the G8 to include a much wider spectrum in recognition of the global nature of the economic crisis'.[13]

Such international gatherings were to be welcomed, although it was difficult to measure what they had actually achieved beyond a broad commitment to provide liquidity to markets – in other words to print more money. There were various attempts at banking reform, but this was done more on a national basis. While America sought to adopt the Dodd–Frank Act, which aimed to regulate Wall Street and curb the potential for financial recklessness, Britain launched its own Vickers Report on banking regulation. In Europe, plans were afoot to create a banking union. As usual, a 'financial services action plan' was devised by bureaucrats, but at the time of writing it was difficult to see what the eventual structure of such a banking union, or the shape of such new regulations, might be. For those who remembered Bretton Woods, the lack of any decisive and co-ordinated plan was remarkable. Bretton Woods, after some years of preparatory negotiation, had been finalized in three weeks from 1 to 22 July 1944. Such combined and purposeful action seemed to elude international policymakers in the years after 2008.

Bretton Woods not only set up the IMF and World Bank. It also inaugurated a new currency regime. As far as currencies were concerned in the period following the 2008 crisis, there remained little co-ordination between the major countries. America still believed China to be manipulating its currency. As late as March 2010, the historian Niall Ferguson declared, in a paper presented to the US House of Representatives Committee on Ways and Means, that the 'world economy's most glaring structural imbalance' was that the 'second biggest economy' had pegged its currency to that of the largest economy 'at a strongly undervalued rate'. There was no use pretending, argued Ferguson, that this was not 'currency manipulation'. He concluded rather gloomily that 'the longer-term trend has been for the dollar to depreciate relative to other currencies'.[14]

China remained strangely aloof from much of the crisis that afflicted the developed economies of the West. It initially announced a 4 trillion yuan ($585 billion) stimulus plan in November 2008 and took measures to boost its export sector, reversing cuts in export value-added tax (VAT) rebates made in summer 2007.[15] Given the enormous size of its reserves, which had been built up by its successful export policy, many in Europe thought that somehow China could be persuaded to prop up the ailing economies of the EU. In October 2011, London's *Independent* newspaper reported that 'Eurozone leaders were left sweating' after China 'played down expectations that it would quickly make a much-needed cash injection to the EU bailout fund'. Li Dao Kui, a monetary policy adviser to China's central bank, said, 'The chief concern of the Chinese government [would be] how to explain this decision to our own people,' who, despite impressive improvements, still enjoyed a standard of living well below the European average. It was unrealistic to expect China to pay for much of Europe's bloated state spending.

Even by early 2014 the Western world had not fully overcome the events of 2008, though there were signs of recovery in some countries, notably Britain and the United States. Britain had, between 2008 and 2013, experienced its worst downturn ever, longer, when measured in terms of GDP growth, than its depression in the 1930s. In nearly all Western countries, the appetite for what Alan Greenspan called 'politically toxic cuts' remained muted as centre-left governments won power in France in 2012 and in Italy in 2013.[16] President Obama, a Democrat whom many saw as being on the left of his party, won an easy re-election battle for the US presidency in 2012. Although the problem of debts, in particular, was widely acknowledged, there remained little consensus or sense of purpose about how to deal with it. The IMF's *World Economic Outlook* survey, written in April 2012, projected rising debt ratios to GDP, with a steep increase in the G7 economies (US, UK, France, Germany, Italy, Canada and Japan) to an average of '130 percent by 2017'.[17]

To fight this trend, the developed world had clearly taken a view that it should adopt some of the rhetoric of fiscal tightening (spending cuts and tax rises) while at the same time adopting very loose monetary policy (quantitative easing and near-zero interest rates). The success or otherwise of these measures has yet to be fully evaluated. Many countries, particularly those which controlled their own currencies, had not cut spending as aggressively as some of their own domestic politicians and economists would have liked. Others felt that aggressive cuts of this kind would simply exacerbate the problem, and preferred to rely on growth strategies, sketchily defined, to lift economies out of debt, as had been done in the past, most notably after the end of the Second World War.

Conclusion

Money and currency have always, in the modern era, been deeply connected to public finance, to taxation and government spending. The end of the link with gold led directly to a world in which it became easier for governments, banks, other institutions and private individuals to borrow money. There has been an explosion of credit which has been responsible for the enormous asset bubble before 2008, and then the subsequent crash. 'Our civilization has been built on $50 trillion of credit and is now teetering on the brink of bankruptcy because too much of that credit has been misallocated and cannot be repaid,' wrote Richard Duncan in his 2012 book *The New Depression: The Breakdown of the Paper Money Economy*.[1] Philip Coggan, the British financial journalist, was equally pessimistic in 2011, suggesting that debtors, 'from speculative homebuyers to leading governments, have made promises to pay that they are unlikely to meet in full. Creditors who are counting on those debts to be repaid will be disappointed.'[2]

The significant increase in indebtedness of the governments of the advanced economies is well known. This is rather paradoxical, as it had been thought that developing countries typically incurred higher debt burdens, since they would be expected to borrow heavily to finance their growth. At the beginning of the 2010s, by contrast, it was the rich democracies whose debt burdens seemed vast. 'In 1980,' wrote Fareed Zakaria, 'the United States' gross government debt was 42 percent of its total GDP; it is now 107 percent.' 'During the same period', he continued, 'the comparable figure for the United Kingdom moved from 46 percent to 88 percent. Most European governments (including notoriously frugal Germany) now have debt-to-GDP levels that hover around 80 percent, and some, such as Greece and Italy, have ones that are much higher.' Most striking was the development of Japan's national debt: in 1980, it was 50 per cent of GDP; in 2013 it was, according to most sources, in the region of 250 per cent. The world, in Zakaria's view, had 'turned upside down'.[3]

Many advocates of 'big government' had often justified their propensity towards greater spending by invoking the name of John Maynard Keynes, arguably the most influential economist of the twentieth century. Keynes, however, had never advocated deficit finance in times of economic prosperity. His theory was a 'countercyclical' one, in as much as government spending could be used to revitalize a national economy during a downturn. He anticipated that, as prosperity returned, spending would be curtailed. Paul Krugman is fond of quoting, although he has not given an attribution, Keynes's 'central dictum: The boom, not the slump, is the time for austerity'.[4] This, however, has simply not been the practice of Western governments in recent decades. 'They have run deficits during busts and booms, as well.' Crucially, it was not only governments which embarked upon an orgy of spending. In the United States, household debt 'rose from $665 billion in 1974 to $13 trillion' in 2013, an increase of nearly twenty times in nominal terms. Consumption, during that period, 'fuelled by cheap credit, went up and stayed up'.[5]

It is from governments, however, that many of the problems facing the world's economy ultimately originate. Governments are also expected to help come up with solutions. As Reinhart and Rogoff have stated in the preface of their empirical study into financial crises, *This Time is Different*, 'Although private debt certainly plays a key role in many crises, government debt is far more often the unifying problem across the wide range of financial crises we examine.'[6] Government debts, of course, are connected with the stability, or otherwise, of currencies. This is what the Greek crisis taught the world. It is notable that the biggest sovereign debt crisis occurred in the eurozone, given that European monetary union itself was an attempt to restore stability to Europe's currency in the aftermath of the collapse of Bretton Woods in the early 1970s.

Richard Nixon's closing of the 'gold window' therefore had profound consequences. Paper money indisputably contributed to an excess of credit creation and directly to the crisis of 2008, as the mountain of credit turned into an avalanche of bankruptcy. The conclusion is that many participants in the global financial system have dug 'a debt hole far larger than they can reasonably expect to escape from'.[7] This may be an unduly pessimistic judgement. If it is, the question presents itself: what possible means of escape exist?

There are three ways by which debts can be reduced. The first of these involves an outright repudiation. This has happened many times, as Reinhart and Rogoff recount exhaustively. A government may simply refuse to pay debts. This has never happened in the history of the United States at the level of the federal government. The last time Great Britain repudiated a portion of its debt was in the Stop of the Exchequer of 1672, when Charles II's government refused to pay the interest on its outstanding debts to goldsmiths in the City of London. It is unlikely that either of these governments, or those of any of the other leading economies, will embark on this course. The second way in which debts can be alleviated is by means of inflation. Governments can inflate their currencies to such a degree that debts incurred in those currencies become negligible. It is uncertain to what extent this course of action would be opposed by citizens whose hard-earned savings would thus be diminished in value. Such a course of inflation would be embarked upon surreptitiously, of course. No government could retain any credibility if it openly admitted to pursuing such a line of policy. As Keynes memorably wrote, 'By a continuing process of inflation, Governments can confiscate, secretly or unobserved, an important part of the wealth of their citizens.'[8] The important point is that such action would be 'secret or unobserved'. The third way to fight debt is to grow out of it. This was the way which Great Britain and the United States followed – after the Napoleonic Wars of 1792–1815, in Britain's case, and after the Second World War, in the case of both these English-speaking nations. In the early 2010s, the prospects for significant economic growth in the advanced economies look less likely than was the case after 1945. But still the hope of economic expansion persists.

A subtle variation of the first way, the open-repudiation method, may well be practised. Economists call 'fiscal repression' a state of affairs where the government forces creditors to accept lower interest rates than they might normally expect. Indeed, one recent paper has suggested that fiscal repression during the eighteenth century 'allowed the United Kingdom to borrow at below-market rates, thereby outspending its continental rivals'.[9] I have argued that, despite incurring large debts in wartime, British governments were particularly anxious to balance the budget in peacetime. This introduces a further observation. In order to tackle a debt problem, it helps not to keep increasing that debt. This was the lesson that British public finance in the century after 1815 taught the world.

What of gold? Does it still have a role to play? Much to the disappointment of 'goldbugs' and other deprecators of paper money, any return to a gold standard is highly unlikely in the near future. The one country that could take a lead in this respect is China. As the leading creditor nation of the world, China is in a strong position to set the terms of a new monetary order. 'If Britain set the terms of the gold standard, and America set the terms of Bretton Woods, then the terms of the next financial system are likely to be set by the world's biggest creditor – China,' one observer has suggested. This, of course, does not strictly follow. China, despite being suitably placed, may have no wish to play such a hegemonic role. Certainly, nothing in China's history would imply that it would assume such authority to lead a global monetary settlement. Yet the point still stands that China could play such a role. Chinese foreign reserves, at the end of 2011, stood at $3.2 trillion.[10] China clearly has enough reserves unilaterally to peg its currency to gold, much as Britain did when it resumed the gold standard in 1821. The proportion of its foreign reserves which China holds in gold is unknown. But a gold standard based on a fixed exchange rate of yuan to a prescribed quantity of gold is conceivable. Of course, such a development is highly unlikely given China's recent history. A fixed gold-to-yuan rate would make the yuan the strongest currency in the world, which would probably appreciate considerably over time against other currencies, most notably the US dollar. This would totally undermine the export-growth model of economic development which China has pursued for more than two decades.

Gold itself, however, remains embedded in the public's consciousness as a monetary metal. It is held most commonly by central banks and there remains an almost mysterious fixation with it. Its value equally mysteriously can be reflected in the growth of the world economy. A simple thought experiment can be seen to illustrate the relationship between the value of the world's gold stock and global GDP since the end of the First World War. If the entire GDP of the world is assumed to be the balance sheet of a single bank, and the value of the entire gold stock was assumed to be the reserve of that bank, the 2010 proportion, at a dollar price of $1,250 an ounce, is about 12 per cent, a rather high reserve, but not egregiously so. The value of the world gold stock in 2010 at the price just quoted was $7.5 trillion, while global GDP was $65 trillion. This ratio has fluctuated considerably since 1900, but the ratio of the value of the gold stock to GDP returned to around the 10 per cent of world GDP level in the early 1920s, the 1950s and mid-1980s. This ratio hit a century low of 3 per cent in 1970, just before the suspension of Bretton Woods. It hit century highs of 20 and 19 per cent respectively in 1940 and 1980 (see Appendix).

The relationship between the value of the world's gold and global GDP intuitively, but on an infinitely larger scale, matches the advised reserve held by the goldsmiths of seventeenth-century London who, as a rule of thumb, would keep a gold reserve of 10 per cent of their outstanding loans. This is a playful point, but it may well be a truism to suggest that as the global economy expands in nominal dollar terms, even when fuelled by vast quantities of credit, the value of gold, better than perhaps any currency, reflects this process most accurately. The gold standard will never formally return, but movements in the price of gold may well suggest that investors, in their lack of faith in paper money, have informally adopted one.

Appendix: Value of Gold Stock to World GDP

	Average Gold Market Price (2011 $ per fine ounce)	Total World Gold Stock (tonnes)	Total Dollar Value World Gold Stock (2011 $bn)	World GDP (2011 $bn)	Ratio of total value of World Gold Stock to World GDP (%)
1920	182	40,100	258	2,570	10
1925	219	42,800	331	3,120	11
1930	229	45,900	371	3,340	11
1940	456	55,800	898	4,450	20
1950	271	64,700	618	6,050	10
1955	239	69,200	584	8,050	7
1960	213	74,600	562	10,200	6
1965	199	81,400	572	13,500	4
1970	170	88,700	531	18,000	3
1975	545	95,400	1,840	22,500	8
1980	1,450	102,000	5,220	27,900	19
1985	585	109,000	2,250	33,300	7
1990	604	119,000	2,530	34,800	7
1995	536	130,000	2,460	41,400	6
2000	358	143,000	1,800	41,300	4
2005	505	156,000	2,780	51,700	5
2010	1,250	168,000	7,450	64,500	12

Sources:

World GDP:

1900–90 data derived from: J. Bradford De Long, 'Estimates of World GDP, One Million B.C.–Present, 1998', http://delong.typepad.com/print/20061012_LRWGDP.pdf

1990–2010 data derived from: IMF, *World Economic Outlook*, October 2012

US GDP deflator data taken from: Louis Johnston and Samuel H. Williamson, 'What Was the U.S. GDP Then?', MeasuringWorth, 2013, http://www.measuringworth.com/usgdp

Average gold price:

New York market price from: Lawrence H. Officer and Samuel H. Williamson, 'The Price of Gold, 1257–2011', MeasuringWorth, 2012, http://www.measuringworth.com/gold

Total world gold stock:

'Thomson Reuters GFMS Historic Gold Stock', in James Turk, *The Aboveground Gold Stock: Its Importance and Its Size*, GoldMoney Foundation, http://www.goldmoney.com/documents/goldmoney-gold-stock.xls

Notes

Introduction

1 John Maynard Keynes, 'Economic Possibilities for our Grandchildren', in *Essays in Persuasion*, London, 1972 (1st edn 1931), p. 323.
2 Joseph Schumpeter, *The Crisis of the Tax State*, Vienna, 1919.
3 F. W. Maitland, *Domesday Book and Beyond*, Cambridge, 1907, p. 9.
4 Ian Fleming, *Goldfinger*, London, 1959.
5 Philip Coggan, *Paper Promises: Money, Debt and the New World Order*, London, 2011, p. 3.
6 Carmen M. Reinhart and Kenneth S. Rogoff, *This Time is Different: Eight Centuries of Financial Folly*, Princeton, 2009.
7 B. R. Mitchell, *British Historical Statistics*, Cambridge, 1988, pp. 601–3.
8 Niall Ferguson, *The Cash Nexus*, London, 2001, p. 126.
9 A. J. P. Taylor, *The Origins of the Second World War*, London, 1961, p. 25.
10 John Maynard Keynes, *General Theory of Employment, Interest and Money*, London, 2007 (1st edn 1936), p. 383.
11 Peer Vries, *Public Finance in China and Britain in the Long Eighteenth Century*, London School of Economics, Working Papers no. 167/12, London, August 2012, p. 17.
12 John Kenneth Galbraith, *Money: Whence It Came, Where It Went*, 2nd edn, London, 1995 (1st edn 1975), pp. 3–4.

Chapter 1: 'Sweat of the Sun'

1 A. W. Lovett, *Early Habsburg Spain, 1517–1598*, Oxford, 1986, p. 59.
2 Jonathan Williams (ed.), *Money: A History*, London, 1997, p. 80.
3 Geoffrey Parker, *The Military Revolution: Military Innovation and the Rise of the West, 1500–1800*, Cambridge, 1988, p. 62.
4 J. H. Elliott, *Imperial Spain, 1469–1716*, London, 1963, p. 202.
5 Ibid., p. 257.
6 Quoted in Elvira Vilches, *New World Gold: Cultural Anxiety and Monetary Disorder in Early Modern Spain*, Chicago, 2010, p. 26.
7 Michael Wood, *Conquistadors*, London, 2000, p. 267/
8 Ibid., pp. 16–17.

9 W. H. Prescott, *History of the Conquest of Peru*, London, 2002 (1st edn 1847), p. 91.

10 Wood, *Conquistadors*, p. 17.

11 Hugh Thomas, *Rivers of Gold*, London, 2010 (1st edn 2003), pp. 540–2, 550.

12 Stephen Clissold, *Conquistador: The Life of Don Pedro Sarmiento de Gamboa*, London, 1954, p. 10.

13 Hugh Thomas, *The Golden Age: The Spanish Empire of Charles V*, London, 2010, p. 121.

14 John Hemming, *The Conquest of the Incas*, London, 1970, pp. 36, 154.

15 J. H. Elliott, *Empires of the Atlantic World: Britain and Spain in America, 1492–1830*, New Haven, 2006, p. 154.

16 Thomas, *The Golden Age*, pp. 129–30.

17 Ibid., p. 218.

18 Peter Shaffer, *The Royal Hunt of the Sun: A Play Concerning the Conquest of Peru*, London, 1981 (1st edn 1964), p. 53.

19 Hemming, *The Conquest of the Incas*, p. 45.

20 Ibid., p. 47.

21 Ibid., p. 49.

22 Thomas, *The Golden Age*, pp. 250–1; Titu Cusi Yupanqui, *History of How the Spaniards Arrived in Peru*, trans. with an introduction by Catherine Julien, Indianapolis, 2006, p. 29.

23 Pierre Vilar, *A History of Gold and Money, 1450 to 1920*, London 1976 (1st edn, 1960), p. 119

24 Hemming, *Conquest of the Incas*, p. 369.

25 Ibid., p. 119.

26 Glyn Davies, *A History of Money*, Cardiff, 2002 (1st edn 1994), pp. 188–9.

27 Hemming, *The Conquest of the Incas*, p. 408.

28 Elliott, *Imperial Spain*, p. 174.

29 James D. Tracy (ed.), *The Political Economy of Merchant Empires*, Cambridge, 1991, p. 348.

30 Earl Hamilton, *American Treasure and the Price Revolution in Spain, 1501–1650*, Cambridge, MA, 1934, p. 44.

31 Lovett, *Early Habsburg Spain*, p. 84.

32 Vilches, *New World Gold*, pp. 37–8.

33 Paul Kennedy, *The Rise and Fall of the Great Powers*, London, 1988, p. 45.

34 Lovett, *Habsburg Spain*, p. 219.

35 Ibid., p. 222.

36 Ibid., p. 223.

37 Fernand Braudel, *The Mediterranean and the Mediterranean World in the Age of Philip II*, 2 vols, trans. Sian Reynolds, London, 1972 (1st French edn 1949), vol. 1, p. 481.

38 Hamilton, *American Treasure*, p. 207.

39 Quoted in Vilches, *New World Gold*, pp. 41–2.

40 Hamilton, *American Treasure*, p. 293.

41 Denis P. O'Brien, *The Development of Monetary Economics*, Cheltenham, 2007, p. 34.

42 John Black, Nigar Hashimzade and Gareth Miles (eds), *Oxford Dictionary of Economics*, Oxford, 2009 (1st edn 1997), p. 371.

43 Milton Friedman, Wincott Memorial Lecture, given in London on 16 September

1970, quoted in Terry J. Fitzgerald, *Money Growth and Inflation: How Long is the Long-Run?*, Federal Reserve Bank of Cleveland, Cleveland, OH, 1999, p. 1.

44 Jean Bodin, *Response to the Paradoxes of Malestroit*, trans. and ed. Henry Tudor and R. W. Dyson, Bristol, 1997 (1st edn 1568), pp. 59–60.

45 Adam Smith, *An Inquiry into the Nature and Causes of the Wealth of Nations*, London, 2007 (1st edn 1776), p. 124.

46 John Maynard Keynes, 'Economic Possibilities for our Grandchildren', in *Essays in Persuasion*, London, 1972 (1st edn 1931), p. 323.

47 John Maynard Keynes, *A Treatise on Money*, 2 vols, London, 1930, vol. 2, pp. 155, 163.

48 Ibid., pp. 153, 161.

49 John Maynard Keynes, 'Social Consequences of Changes in the Value of Money' (1923), in *Essays in Persuasion*, pp. 67–8.

Chapter 2: Rival Nations: Britain and France

1   P. G. M. Dickson, *The Financial Revolution in England: A Study in the Development of Public Credit*, London, 1967, p. 7.

2   C. D. Chandaman, *The English Public Revenue, 1660–1688*, Oxford, 1975, p. 265.

3   R. D. Richards, *The First Fifty Years of the Bank of England*, The Hague, 1934, p. 7.

4   Sir John Clapham, *The Bank of England*, 2 vols, Cambridge, 2008 (1st edn 1944), vol. 1, p. 24.

5   Richards, *The First Fifty Years of the Bank of England*, pp. 2, 8.

6   *Dictionary of National Biography* (hereafter *DNB*), 'Solomon de Medina'; Oskar K. Rabinowicz, *Sir Solomon de Medina*, London, 1974, pp. 20, lx.

7   *DNB*, 'Solomon de Medina'.

8   John Francis, *Chronicles and Characters of the Stock Exchange*, London, 2001 (reprint of the 1850 US edn; 1st edn 1849), p. 11.

9   *DNB*, 'Sir Henry Furnese'.

10 Francis, *Chronicles and Characters*, p. 8.

11 *DNB*, 'John Law'; John Philip Wood, *Memoirs of the life of John Law of Lauriston, including a detailed account of the rise, progress, and termination of the Mississippi System*, Edinburgh, 1824, pp. 2–5.

12 John Law, *Money and Trade Considered, with a Proposal for Supplying the Nation with Money*, Edinburgh, 1705, p. 94.

13 Ibid., pp. 20, 13.

14 Wood, *Memoirs of the life of John Law*, p. 17; *DNB*, 'John Law'.

15 Wood, *Memoirs of the life of John Law*, p. 22.

16 Ibid., p. 24.

17 Antoin E. Murphy, *John Law: Economic Theorist and Policy-Maker*, Oxford, 1997, p. 331.

18 Wood, *Memoirs of the life of John Law*, p. 40.

19 Ibid., pp. 58, 62–8.

20 *DNB*, 'John Law'.

21 Wood, *Memoirs of the life of John Law*, p. 81.

22 Ibid., pp. 118, 133.

23 Murphy, *John Law*, p. 327.

24 Ibid., p. 125; *DNB*, 'John Law'.

25 Antoin E. Murphy, *Richard Cantillon: Entrepreneur and Economist*, Oxford, 1986, p. 67.

26 John Carswell, *The South Sea Bubble*, Dover, NH, 1993 (1st edn, London, 1960), p. 35.

27 Murphy, *Cantillon*, pp. 67–8; Edward Chancellor, *Devil Take the Hindmost: A History of Financial Speculation*, London, 1999, p. 93.

28 Carswell, *The South Sea Bubble*, p. 79.

29 Ibid., p. 83.

30 William Coxe, *Memoirs of the Life and Administration of Sir Robert Walpole, Earl of Orford*, 3 vols, London, 1798, vol. 1, pp. 131–3; Chancellor, *Devil Take the Hindmost*, pp. 63–4.

31 Coxe, *Memoirs of Sir Robert Walpole*, vol. 1, p. 135.

32 Chancellor, *Devil Take the Hindmost*, pp. 73, 88.

33 Malcolm Balen, *A Very English Deceit: The Secret History of the South Sea Bubble and the First Great Financial Scandal*, London, 2002, p. 119.

34 Ibid., p. 92.

35 Chancellor, *Devil Take the Hindmost*, p. 88.

36 Ibid., p. 93.

37 Dickson, *The Financial Revolution in England*, pp. 11–12.

Chapter 3: Revolutions

1 G. S. Callender, *Selections from the Economic History of the United States, 1765–1860*, Boston, 1909, p. 63.

2 Ibid., p. 64.

3 *DNB*, 'George Grenville'.

4 Albert S. Bolles, *The Financial History of the United States, from 1774 to 1789*, 3 vols, New York, 1969 (1st edn 1879), vol. 1, p. 7.

5 Ibid., p. 30.

6 Charles J. Bullock, *Essays on the Monetary History of the United States*, New York, 1900, p. 65.

7 Bolles, *The Financial History*, vol. 1, pp. 124–5.

8 Ibid., p. 177.

9 Norman Angell, *The Story of Money*, London, 1930, p. 245.

10 Farley Grubb, *The Continental Dollar: How Much Was Issued and What Happened to It?*, Cambridge, MA, 2007, pp. 1, 11.

11 Davis Rich Dewey, *Financial History of the United States*, New York, 1903, p. 41; Bolles, *The Financial History*, vol. 1, p. 3.

12 Milton Friedman, *Money Mischief: Episodes in Monetary History*, New York, 1992, p. 53.

13 William Doyle, *Origins of the French Revolution*, 3rd edn, Oxford, 1999 (1st edn 1980), pp. 45, 50.

14 Robert Lacour-Gayet, *Calonne: Financier, réformateur, contre-révolutionnaire, 1734–1802*, Paris, 1963, pp. 67, 73, 160.

15 Thomas J. Sargent and Francois R. Velde, 'Macroeconomic Features of the

French Revolution', *Journal of Political Economy*, vol. 103, no. 3 (June 1995), pp. 474–518, at pp. 477, 478, 485.

16 Ibid., pp. 491–2.

17 Edmund Burke, *Reflections on the Revolution in France*, New York, 2006 (1st edn, London, 1790), pp. 196, 237.

18 Ibid., p. 240.

19 Charles Alexandre de Calonne, *Considerations on the Present and Future State of France*, trans. from the original French, London, 1791, pp. 87, 96.

20 Florin Aftalion, *L'Economie de la Révolution Française*, Paris, 2007, p. 108.

21 S. E. Harris, *The Assignats*, Cambridge, MA, 1930, p. 186.

22 François Crouzet, *La Grande Inflation: La Monnaie en France de Louis XVI à Napoléon*, Paris, 1993, p. 579.

23 Sargent and Velde, 'Macroeconomic Features', p. 509. The broad outline of the story of the assignat presented in this book is largely based on this excellent article.

24 Ibid., p. 510.

25 Michael D. Bordo and Eugene N. White, 'A Tale of Two Currencies: British and French Finance during the Napoleonic Wars', *Journal of Economic History*, vol. 51, no. 2 (June 1991), pp. 303–16, at p. 304.

26 Sir Albert Feavearyear, *The Pound Sterling: A History of English Money*, Oxford, 1931, p. 167.

27 Francis Baring, *Observations on the Establishment of the Bank of England and Paper Circulation of the Country*, London, 1797, p. 3.

28 *DNB*, 'Francis Baring'.

29 Baring, *Observations*, p. 42.

30 Ibid., p. 44.

31 Ibid., pp. 22, 20.

32 Ibid., p. 81.

33 *New York Times*, 'War Finance in England', 27 January 1862.

34 Elisa Newby, *The Suspension of Cash Payments as a Monetary Regime*, Centre for Dynamic Macroeconomic Analysis, Working Paper Series, University of St Andrews, February 2007, revised June 2007, p. 55.

Chapter 4: Pillars of Order

1 Quoted in Nicholas Mayhew, *Sterling: The History of a Currency*, London, 1999, p. 149.

2 *DNB*, 'Robert Peel'.

3 Norman Gash, *Mr Secretary Peel: The Life of Sir Robert Peel to 1830*, London, 1961, pp. 241–2.

4 Charles Stuart Parker (ed.), *Sir Robert Peel from his Private Correspondence*, 3 vols, London, 1891, vol. 1, p. 293, letter to Rev. C. Lloyd, undated, *c.* March to May 1819.

5 Douglas Hurd, *Robert Peel*, London, 2007, p. 307.

6 E. H. Phelps Brown and Sheila V. Hopkins, 'Seven Centuries of the Prices of Consumables, Compared with Builders' Wage-Rates', *Economica*, New Series, vol. 23, no. 92 (November 1956), pp. 296–314, at pp. 313–14.

7 Percy Bysshe Shelley, *Poetical Works*, ed. Thomas Hutchinson, London, 1905, p. 341 (lines 176–9 of *The Mask of Anarchy*).

8 Mayhew, *Sterling*, p. 152.

9 *Report from the Committee of Secrecy on the Bank of England Charter, with the minutes of evidence*, London, 1832, p. 394.

10 John Francis, *History of the Bank of England*, 2 vols, London, 1848, vol. 2, p. 34.

11 *Report from the Committee of Secrecy*, p. 385.

12 Edward Chancellor, *Devil Take the Hindmost: A History of Financial Speculation*, London, 1999, p. 107.

13 Francis, *History of the Bank of England*, vol. 2, p. 28.

14 Frank Whitson Fetter, *The Development of British Monetary Orthodoxy: 1797–1875*, Cambridge, MA, 1965, p. 113.

15 Mayhew, *Sterling*, p. 155; Chancellor, *Devil Take the Hindmost*, p. 111.

16 Robert Blake, *Disraeli*, London, 1966, pp. 24–6.

17 Eltis, *Lord Overstone*, p. 4.

18 D. P. O'Brien (ed.), *The Correspondence of Lord Overstone*, 3 vols, Cambridge, 1971, vol. 1, p. 391, Lord Overstone to C. Wood, 21 August 1847; p. 392, Charles Wood to Lord Overstone, 22 August 1847.

19 Sir John H. Clapham, *The Bank of England*, 2 vols, Cambridge, 2008 (1st edn 1944), vol. 2, pp. 198–9.

20 Karl Marx, *Capital*, 3 vols, London, 1974 (1st German edn 1867), vol. 3, pp. 389–90.

21 O'Brien (ed.), *Correspondence*, Introduction, p. 14.

22 *DNB*, 'Samuel Jones Loyd'.

23 O'Brien (ed.), *Correspondence*, Introduction, p. 46.

24 *DNB*, 'Samuel Jones Loyd'.

25 Ibid.

26 Parker, *Sir Robert Peel*, vol. 3, p. 143.

27 Sir Robert Peel, *Speeches on the Renewal of the Bank Charter and the Laws of Currency and Banking*, London, 1844, pp. 7–32, speeches in the House of Commons on 6 and 20 May 1844.

28 John Maynard Keynes, *Essays in Persuasion*, London, 1931, p. 162.

29 Lord Overstone, *Tracts and Other Publications on Metallic and Paper Currency*, London, 1857, pp. 313–15, letter to *The Times*, 30 November 1855; pp. 317–18, letter to *The Times*, 14 December 1855.

30 Brooks Adams, *The Gold Standard: An Historical Study*, Washington, DC, 1895, pp. 18, 17.

31 Quoted in O'Brien (ed.), *Correspondence*, p. 7.

32 Frank W. Fetter, *Business History Review*, vol. 46, no. 3 (Autumn 1972), pp. 393–5, at p. 394 (review of D. P. O'Brien (ed.), *The Correspondence of Lord Overstone*).

33 Walter Bagehot, *Lombard Street: A Description of the Money Market*, London, 1873, p. 9.

34 W. F. Finlayson, *A Report on the Case of the Queen v Gurney and others in the court of Queen's Bench*, London, 1870, pp. 36–7.

35 Bagehot, *Lombard Street*, pp. 3–5.

36 Ibid., p. 50.

37 Ibid., pp. 17, 45.

38 Ibid., p. 103.

39 C. H. Sisson, *The Case of Walter Bagehot*, London, 1972, p. 85.

Chapter 5: Great Republic

1   Bray Hammond, *Banks and Politics in America: From the Revolution to the Civil War*, Princeton, 1957, p. 100.

2   Jacob E. Cooke, *The Reports of Alexander Hamilton*, New York, 1964, p. xv.

3   Ibid., p. 47.

4   Davis Rich Dewey, *Financial History of the United States*, New York, 1903, p. 100.

5   Bray Hammond, 'Jackson, Biddle, and the Bank of the United States', *Journal of Economic History*, vol. 7, no. 1 (May 1947), pp. 1–23, at p. 1.

6   Bray, *Banks and Politics*, p. 287.

7   Arthur M. Schlesinger Jr, *The Age of Jackson*, London, 1946, p. 91.

8   Vera C. Smith, *The Rationale of Central Banking*, London, 1936, p. 128.

9   John Steel Gordon, *The Great Game: A History of Wall Street*, New York, 1999, p. 68.

10 Douglas A. Irwin, *The Aftermath of Hamilton's 'Report on Manufactures'*, NBER Working Paper Series, no. 9943, Cambridge, MA, August 2003, p. 2.

11 Alexander Hamilton, *Report on the Subject of Manufactures, made in his capacity of Secretary of the Treasury on Fifth of December, 1791*, 6th edn, Philadelphia, 1827 (1st edn 1791), p. 46.

12 Ibid., pp. 50–1.

13 Dewey, *Financial History*, pp. 193–4.

14 Hamilton, *Report on the Subject of Manufactures*, p. 47.

15 Dewey, *Financial History*, p. 179.

16 Abraham Lincoln, *Collected Works of Abraham Lincoln*, vol. 3, Ann Arbor, MI, 1953, quoted in www.umich.edu (a University of Michigan website), letter to Edward Wallace, 11 October 1859.

17 Bray Hammond, *Sovereignty and an Empty Purse: Banks and Politics in the Civil War*, Princeton, 1970, p. 24.

18 Richard Franklin Bensel, *Yankee Leviathan: The Origins of Central State Authority in America, 1859–1877*, Cambridge, 1990, p. 152.

19 Heather Cox Richardson, *The Greatest Nation of the Earth: Republican Economic Policies during the Civil War*, Cambridge, MA, 1997, pp. 51, 56.

20 Ibid., p. 66.

21 Hammond, *Sovereignty and an Empty Purse*, p. 359.

22 F. W. Taussig, *The Tariff History of the United States*, 6th edn, New York, 1914 (1st edn 1888), pp. 162–6.

23 Ibid., pp. 155, 164.

24 Dewey, *Financial History*, p. 305.

25 Ibid., p. 307.

26 Bensel, *Yankee Leviathan*, p. 251.

27 Frederick C. Hicks, *High Finance in the Sixties*, New Haven, 1929, p. 1.

28 Bensel, *Yankee Leviathan*, p. 249.

29 Taussig, *The Tariff History*, p. 174.

30 Bensel, *Yankee Leviathan*, p. 66; Taussig, *The Tariff History*, p. 175.

31 Malcolm Gladwell, *Outliers: The Story of Success*, New York, 2008, pp. 56–62.

32 Ron Chernow, *Titan: The Life of John D. Rockefeller Sr*, New York, 1998, p. 148.
33 Hicks, *High Finance*, p. 120.
34 Ibid., p. 124.
35 Dewey, *Financial History*, p. 369.
36 Milton Friedman, *Money Mischief: Episodes in Monetary History*, New York, 1992, p. 53.
37 Ibid., p. 61.
38 Ibid., p. 104.
39 Peter Krass, *Carnegie*, Hoboken, NJ, 2002, p. 254.
40 Ellis W. Tallman, *The Panic of 1907*, Working Paper 12.28, Federal Reserve Bank of Cleveland, Cleveland, OH, November 2012, p. 6 n.1.
41 Robert F. Bruner, *The Panic of 1907*, Hoboken, NJ, 2007, p. 7.
42 Ibid., p. 15.
43 Milton Friedman and Anna Jacobson Schwartz, *A Monetary History of the United States, 1867–1960*, Princeton, 1963, p. 159.
44 Oliver Sprague, 'The American Crisis of 1907', *Economic Journal*, vol. 18, no. 71 (September 1908), pp. 353–72, at pp. 357, 360.
45 Ron Chernow, *The House of Morgan: An American Banking Dynasty and the Rise of Modern Finance*, New York, 1990, pp. 124–5.
46 Ibid., p. 125.
47 Ibid., p. 127.

Chapter 6: London 1914

1 John Maynard Keynes, *The Economic Consequences of the Peace*, London, 1919, pp. 9–10.
2 Ibid.
3 John Galsworthy, *The Forsyte Saga*, Oxford, 1995 (1st edn 1906–21), p. 55.
4 John Maynard Keynes, *A Treatise on Money*, 2 vols, London, 1930, vol. 1, pp. 186–7.
5 Ibid., p. 187.
6 Keynes, *The Economic Consequences*, pp. 9–10.
7 Robert Skidelsky, *John Maynard Keynes: Hopes Betrayed, 1883–1920*, London, 1983, p. 271.
8 Ibid., p. 289.
9 *DNB*, 'Francis Hirst'.
10 Herbert Feis, *Europe: The World's Banker, 1870–1914*, New York, 1930, p. 5.
11 Francis W. Hirst, *The Stock Exchange: A Short Study of Investment and Speculation*, London, 1911, pp. 83–4, 98–101.
12 Ibid., pp. 85–6.
13 A. Andreades, *History of the Bank of England, 1640 to 1903*, trans. Christabel Meredith, London, 1909, p. 363.
14 Juan-Huitzi Flores, *Lending Booms, Underwriting and Competition: The Barings Crisis Revisited*, Working Papers in Economic History, Universidad Carlos III de Madrid, January 2007, p. 1.
15 Andreades, *History*, p. 367.
16 *DNB*, 'William Lidderdale'.

17 David Kynaston, *The City of London: Golden Years, 1890–1914*, London, 1995, p. 40.
18 Andreades, *History*, p. 369.
19 Dudley Bahlman (ed.), *The Diary of Sir Edward Walter Hamilton*, Hull, 1993, p. 128, entry for Monday 17 November 1890.
20 Sir Frederick Leith-Ross, *Money Talks: Fifty Years of International Finance*, London, 1968, p. 21.
21 Jamie Camplin, *The Rise of the Plutocrats: Wealth and Power in Edwardian England*, London, 1978, p. 63.
22 Youssef Cassis, *City Bankers, 1890–1914*, trans. Margaret Rocques, Cambridge, 1994, p. 4.
23 Youssef Cassis, 'Merchant Bankers and City Aristocracy', *British Journal of Sociology*, vol. 39, no. 1 (March 1988), pp. 114–20, at pp. 117–18.
24 Nicholas A. H. Stacey, *English Accountancy: A Study in Social and Economic History, 1800–1954*, London, 1954, p. 37.
25 Kynaston, *The City of London: Golden Years*, p. 21.
26 Ibid., p. 319.
27 Ibid., p. 26.
28 Camplin, *The Rise of the Plutocrats*, p. 60.
29 Saemy Japhet, *Recollections from my Business Life*, London, 1931, p. 114.
30 *DNB*, 'Ernest Cassel'.
31 Cassis, *City Bankers*, p. 7.
32 Niall Ferguson, 'Political Risk and the International Bond Market between the 1848 Revolution and the Outbreak of the First World War', *Economic History Review*, vol. 59, no. 1 (2006), pp. 70–112, at pp. 72, 91, 98.
33 Alexander D. Noyes, *The War Period of American Finance, 1908–1925*, New York, 1926, p. 51.
34 Ibid., p. 54.
35 W. R. Lawson, *British War Finance, 1914–1915*, London, 1915, p. 6.
36 Skidelsky, *John Maynard Keynes: Hopes Betrayed*, p. 284.
37 Hartley Withers, *War and Lombard Street*, London, 1915, p. 1.
38 Noyes, *The War Period*, p. 57.
39 Ronald Knox, *Patrick Shaw Stewart*, London, 1920, pp. 99–100.
40 Skidelsky, *John Maynard Keynes: Hopes Betrayed*, p. 290.
41 Ibid.
42 Knox, *Shaw Stewart*, p. 100.
43 B. R. Mitchell, *British Historical Statistics*, Cambridge, 1988, pp. 601–3.
44 Bernard Mallet, *British Budgets, 1887–88 to 1912–13*, London, 1913, p. vii.

Chapter 7: Guns and Shells

1 John Maynard Keynes, *Collected Writings*, 30 vols, London and Cambridge, 1971–89, vol. 16, p. 3.
2 Ibid., p. 20, from the *Morning Post*, 11 August 1914.
3 Ibid., p. 37, from the *Morning Post*, 16 October 1914.
4 Ibid., p. 46, notes on French Finance, finished 6 January 1915.
5 Ibid.
6 Hartley Withers, *War and Lombard Street*, London, 1915, p. 100.

7 Winston Churchill, *The Speeches of Winston Churchill*, ed. David Cannadine, London, 1990, p. 70.

8 Quoted in A. J. P. Taylor, *From the Boer War to the Cold War: Essays on Twentieth-Century Europe*, London, 1995, p. 196.

9 Fred Rogers Fairchild, 'German War Finance – A Review', *American Economic Review*, vol. 12, no. 2 (June 1922), pp. 246–61, at p. 247.

10 Ibid., pp. 248–9.

11 Ibid., pp. 256, 249–50.

12 Ibid., p. 257.

13 Karl Helfferich, *Der Weltkrieg*, 2 vols, Berlin, 1919, vol. 2, p. 154. Author's translation.

14 Ibid., pp. 155–6.

15 Fairchild, 'German War Finance', p. 258.

16 R. R. Kuczynski, 'German Taxation Policy in the World War', *Journal of Political Economy*, vol. 31, no. 6 (December 1923), pp. 763–89, at p. 770.

17 Fairchild, 'German War Finance', pp. 257–8.

18 W. R. Lawson, *British War Finance, 1914–1915*, London, 1915, p. 274.

19 Stephen Broadberry and Peter Howlett, *The United Kingdom during World War I: Business as Usual?*, University of Warwick, 2003, p. 11.

20 Ibid., pp. 12–13.

21 Ibid.

22 Ibid., pp. 16–19.

23 Alexander D. Noyes, *The War Period of American Finance, 1908–1925*, New York, 1926, p. 88.

24 Ibid., p. 97.

25 Ibid., p. 116.

26 Ibid., p. 118.

27 John Douglas Forbes, *J. P. Morgan Jr*, Charlottesville, 1981, pp. 90, 93.

28 John Douglas Forbes, *Stettinius Sr: Portrait of a Morgan Partner*, Charlottesville, 1974, p. 47.

29 Kathleen Burk, *Britain, America and the Sinews of War, 1914–1918*, London, 1985, p. 25.

30 Forbes, *Morgan Jr*, p. 88.

31 John Maynard Keynes, 'New Taxation in the United States', *Economic Journal*, vol. 27, no. 108 (December 1917), pp. 561–5, at pp. 561–2.

32 Noyes, *American Finance*, pp. 106–7.

33 Ron Chernow, *The House of Morgan: An American Banking Dynasty and the Rise of Modern Finance*, New York, 1990, p. 130.

34 Henry F. Grady, *British War Finance, 1914–1919*, New York, 1927, p. 75.

35 Broadberry and Howlett, 'The United Kingdom during World War I', p. 23.

36 R. H. Brand, 'The Financial and Economic Future' (December 1918), in *War and National Finance*, London, 1921, p. 170.

37 Ibid., pp. 173, 180.

38 John Maynard Keynes, *The Economic Consequences of the Peace*, London, 1919, pp. 223, 226–8.

39 A. J. P. Taylor, *The Origins of the Second World War*, London, 1961, p. 25.

40 Keynes, *The Economic Consequences*, p. 2.

41 Niall Ferguson, *The Pity of War*, London, 1998, p. 113.

Chapter 8: Victors and Vanquished

1 *DNB*, 'Ralph Hawtrey'.
2 Ralph Hawtrey, 'The Gold Standard', *Economic Journal*, vol. 29, no. 116 (December 1919), pp. 428–42. I have quoted liberally from the entire article.
3 W. T. Layton, 'British Opinion on the Gold Standard', *Quarterly Journal for Economics*, vol. 39, no. 2 (February 1925), pp. 184–95, at p. 189.
4 Ibid., p. 195.
5 George Bernard Shaw, *The Intelligent Woman's Guide to Socialism and Capitalism*, London, 1929 (1st edn 1928), p. 263.
6 Gustav Cassel, 'The Restoration of the Gold Standard', *Economica*, no. 9 (November 1923), lecture delivered at the London School of Economics, 18 June 1923, pp. 171–85, at pp. 171, 173, 184.
7 Ibid., p. 172.
8 Ibid.
9 Albert Ross Eckler, 'Recent Expansion of Bank Credit', *Review of Economics and Statistics*, vol. 11, no. 1 (February 1929), pp. 46–51, at p. 50.
10 E. A. Goldenweiser, 'Effects of Further Gold Imports on our Banking Situation', *American Economic Review*, vol. 13, no. 1 (March 1923), pp. 84–91, at pp. 84–5, 91.
11 O. M. W. Sprague, 'The Discount Policy of the Federal Reserve Banks', *American Economic Review*, vol. 11, no. 1 (March 1921), pp. 16–29, at p. 19.
12 C. Reinold Noyes, 'The Gold Inflation in the United States, 1921–1929', *American Economic Review*, vol. 20, no. 2 (January 1930), pp. 181–98, at pp. 181–2, 187.
13 Charles E. Persons, 'Credit Expansion, 1920 to 1929, and its Lessons', *Quarterly Journal of Economics*, vol. 45, no. 1 (November 1930), pp. 94–130. Much of the following description of the 1920s credit bubble in the United States is derived from this article.
14 Ibid., p. 100.
15 Ibid., p. 101.
16 Ibid., pp. 114–15.
17 Lawrence H. Sloan, 'The Business Prospect in the United States', *Economic Journal*, vol. 38, no. 150 (June 1928), pp. 175–92, at pp. 186, 178.
18 John F. Sinclair, 'America and the Debts of Europe', *Annals of the American Academy of Political and Social Science*, vol. 102, America and the Rehabilitation of Europe (July 1922), pp. 85–100, at pp. 85–6.
19 Quoted in Andrew Boyle, *Montagu Norman: A Biography*, London, 1967, p. 189.
20 Ibid., p. 196.
21 John Maynard Keynes, 'The Economic Consequences of Mr Churchill', in *Essays in Persuasion*, London, 1931, pp. 207–30, at p. 208.
22 Joseph Schumpeter, 'The Instability of Capitalism', *Economic Journal*, vol. 38, no. 151 (September 1928), pp. 361–86, at p. 362.
23 Sir George Paish, 'The Rehabilitation of Europe Dependent on America', *Annals of the American Academy of Political and Social Science*, vol. 102, America and the Rehabilitation of Europe (July 1922), pp. 147–51, at p. 148.

24 Quoted in Jack Beatty, 'President Coolidge's Burden', *Atlantic Magazine*, December 2003 (review of Robert E. Gilbert's *The Tormented President: Calvin Coolidge, Death, and Clinical Depression*), found on http://www.theatlantic. com/magazine/archive/2003/12/president-coolidges-burden/303175/.

25 Paish, 'Rehabilitation of Europe', pp. 149, 151.

26 John Maynard Keynes, *The Economic Consequences of the Peace*, London, 1919, pp. 148, 198.

27 Theo Balderston, *Economics and Politics in the Weimar Republic*, London, 2002, p. 11.

28 For a discussion of the causes of the hyperinflation, see David E. Laidler and George W. Stadler, 'Monetary Explanations of the Weimar Republic's Hyperinflation: Some Neglected Contributions in Contemporary German Literature', *Journal of Money, Credit and Banking*, vol. 30, no. 4 (November 1998), pp. 816–31.

29 Harold James, *The German Slump: Politics and Economics, 1924–1936*, Oxford, 1986, p. 138.

30 Clyde William Phelps, *The Foreign Expansion of American Banks: American Branch Banking Abroad*, New York, 1927, pp. 3, 125.

31 William C. McNeil, *American Money and the Weimar Republic: Economics and Politics on the Eve of the Great Depression*, New York, 1986, p. 82.

32 John Maynard Keynes, 'The Progress of the Dawes Scheme', *Nation and Athenaeum*, 11 September 1926, in *Collected Writings*, vol. 18, London, 1978, p. 281.

33 Gerald D. Feldman, 'Industrialists, Bankers and the Problem of Unemployment in the Weimar Republic', *Central European History*, vol. 25, no. 1 (1992), pp. 76–91.

34 Hans Luther, *Politiker ohne Partei*, Stuttgart, 1960, p. 276. Author's translation.

35 John Maynard Keynes, 'Professor Fisher Discusses Reparations Problems with John M. Keynes', New York *Evening World*, 25 March 1929, in *Collected Writings*, vol. 18, p. 313.

36 *Time*, 'Germany: Reparations Report', 26 December 1927.

37 Balderson, *Economics and Politics*, p. 82.

38 McNeil, *American Money*, p. 137.

39 Ibid., p. 183.

40 Ibid., p. 177.

41 Persons, 'Credit Expansion', p. 120.

42 Silvano A. Wueschner, *Charting Twentieth-Century Monetary Policy: Herbert Hoover and Benjamin Strong, 1917–1927*, Westport, CT, 1999, p. 161.

43 James D. Hamilton, 'Monetary Factors in the Great Depression', *Journal of Monetary Economics*, vol. 19 (1987), pp. 145–69, at p. 154.

44 Milton Friedman and Anna Jacobson Schwartz, *A Monetary History of the United States, 1867–1960*, Princeton, 1963, p. 264.

45 Persons, 'Credit Expansion', p. 95.

Chapter 9: World Crisis

1 John Kenneth Galbraith, *The Great Crash of 1929*, New York, 1954, p. 25.
2 Lionel Robbins, *The Great Depression*, London, 1934, p. 51.
3 Wesley Mitchell, 'Review of Lionel Robbins, *The Great Depression*', *Quarterly Journal of Economics*, vol. 49, no. 3 (May 1935), pp. 503–7, at p. 503.
4 Ibid.
5 Robbins, *The Great Depression*, p. 11.
6 Ben Bernanke, Remarks on Milton Friedman's 90th Birthday, University of Chicago conference, 8 November 2002, quoted in Milton Friedman and Anna Jacobson Schwartz, *The Great Contraction, 1929–1933*, Princeton, 2007, p. 247.
7 Ibid., p. 231.
8 Ibid., Preface by Anna Jacobson Schwartz, p. ix.
9 Bernanke, Remarks on Milton Friedman's 90th Birthday, p. 232.
10 Milton Friedman and Anna Jacobson Schwartz, *A Monetary History of the United States, 1867–1960*, Princeton, 1963, p. 391.
11 Ibid., p. 407.
12 Ben S. Bernanke, *Essays on the Great Depression*, Princeton, 2000, pp. 41, 44–5.
13 Ibid., p. 46.
14 Robbins, *The Great Depression*, p. 11.
15 John Maynard Keynes, letter to Walter Case, dated 4 December 1931, in *Collected Writings*, vol. 21, London, 1978, p. 29.
16 John Maynard Keynes, lecture to the International Economic Society of Hamburg under the title 'The Economic Prospects', 8 January 1932, in *Collected Writings*, vol. 21, pp. 39–40.
17 John Maynard Keynes, 'The Future of the World', *Sunday Express*, 27 September 1931, in *Essays in Persuasion*, London, 1931, pp. 245, 248.
18 Charles Maddison, *French Inter-War Monetary Policy: Understanding the Gold Bloc*, San Domenico, 1994, p. 602.
19 Keynes, *Essays in Persuasion*, p. 249.
20 Friedman and Schwartz, *A Monetary History*, pp. 462–3.
21 Milton Friedman, *Money Mischief: Episodes in Monetary History*, New York, 1992, p. 157.
22 David Kennedy, *Freedom from Fear: The American People in Depression and War, 1929–1945*, Oxford, 1999, p. 197.
23 Friedman and Schwartz, *A Monetary History*, pp. 469–71.
24 Bernanke, *Essays on the Great Depression*, p. 77.
25 Barry Eichengreen, *Golden Fetters: The Gold Standard and the Great Depression, 1919–1939*, Oxford, 1992, p. 317.
26 Ibid., p. 350.
27 Ibid., p. 377. The phrase 'golden fetters', coined by Keynes, provides the title of Barry Eichengreen's pioneering study of international finance in the inter-war period.
28 Harold James, *The German Slump: Politics and Economics, 1924–1936*, Oxford, 1986, p. 372.

29 Adam Tooze, *Wages of Destruction: The Making and Breaking of the Nazi Economy*, London, 2006, p. 45.
30 Quoted in ibid., p. 220.
31 Arthur Schweitzer, 'Schacht's Regulation of Money and the Capital Markets', *Journal of Finance*, vol. 3, no. 2 (June 1948), pp. 1–18, at p. 16.
32 Tooze, *Wages of Destruction*, p. 230.
33 www.usgovernmentspending.com.
34 Hjalmar Schacht, *76 Jahre meines Lebens*, Bad Wörishofen, 1953, pp. 390–1.
35 Peter Clarke, *Keynes: The Twentieth Century's Most Influential Economist*, London, 2009, p. 81.
36 Paul Einzig, *Bankers, Statesmen and Economists*, London, 1935, p. 147.
37 Ibid., pp. 135, 226–7.
38 Clarke, *Keynes*, p. 76.
39 Ibid., p. 168.
40 John Maynard Keynes, *A Treatise on Money*, 2 vols, London, 1930, vol. 2, p. 149.

Chapter 10: Bretton Woods

1 Peter Clarke, *Keynes: The Twentieth Century's Most Influential Economist*, London, 2009, p. 81.
2 Lionel Robbins quoted in Roy Harrod, *The Life of John Maynard Keynes*, London, 1951, p. 576.
3 Sir Frederick Leith-Ross, *Money Talks: Fifty Years of International Finance*, London, 1968, p. 316.
4 Harrod, *John Maynard Keynes*, p. 536.
5 Stanley W. Black, *A Levite among the Priests: Edward M. Bernstein and the Origins of the Bretton Woods System*, Boulder, CO, 1991, pp. 39, 44. Bernstein's comments were derived from a series of interviews he gave in Washington in November 1983.
6 David Rees, *Henry Dexter White: A Study in Paradox*, London, 1973, p. 137.
7 Barry Eichengreen, *Globalizing Capital: A History of the International Monetary System*, Princeton, 1996, p. 93.
8 Clarke, *Keynes*, pp. 88–9.
9 Paul Davidson, *John Maynard Keynes*, Basingstoke, 2007, p. 149.
10 Philip Coggan, *Paper Promises: Money, Debt and the New World Order*, London, 2011, p. 100.
11 Clarke, *Keynes*, p. 88.
12 Barry Eichengreen, *Exorbitant Privilege: The Rise and Fall of the Dollar*, Oxford, 2011, p. 47.
13 *DNB*, 'Robert Boothby'.
14 Robert Boothby, *Goods or Gold? The Meaning of the Bretton Woods Agreement*, London, 1944, pp. 4–5.
15 Ibid., p. 7.
16 John Maynard Keynes, letter to the *Economist*, 29 July 1944, in *Collected Writings*, vol. 26, London, 1980, p. 85.
17 John Maynard Keynes, speech given in the House of Lords, 23 May 1944, in ibid., pp. 17–18.

18 Ibid., p. 19.
19 John Maynard Keynes, letter to H. D. White, 24 May 1944, in ibid., p. 27.
20 Shirras G. Findlay, 'The Position and Prospects of Gold', *Economic Journal*, vol. 50, no. 198–9 (June– September 1940), pp. 207–23, at pp. 207–8.
21 R. G. Hawtrey, *Bretton Woods for Better or Worse*, London, 1946, p. 25.
22 Robert Skidelsky, *John Maynard Keynes: Fighting for Britain, 1937–1946*, London, 2000, p. xx.
23 Ibid., p. xxi.
24 John Maynard Keynes, letter to R. F. Kahn, 13 March 1946, in *Collected Writings*, vol. 26, p. 217.
25 John Maynard Keynes, letter to Hugh Dalton, 29 March 1946, in ibid., p. 221.
26 Ibid., p. 227.
27 *New York Times*, obituary for Fred M. Vinson, 9 September 1953.
28 Keynes, *The Economic Consequences*, p. 2.
29 www.cbo.gov (website of the Congressional Budget Office).
30 Hawtrey, *Bretton Woods*, p. v.
31 Ibid., pp. 12, v.
32 Ibid., p. 91.
33 Ibid., p. 47.
34 Anthony M. Endres, *Great Architects of International Finance: The Bretton Woods Era*, Abingdon, 2005, p. 23.
35 John Maynard Keynes, letter to Lord Addison, 16 May 1944, in *Collected Writings*, vol. 26, p. 6.
36 Camille Gutt, 'Les Accords de Bretton Woods et les institutions qui en sont issues', *Recueil de Cours*, Académie de Droit International, The Hague, 1948, p. 75.

Chapter 11: Pax Americana

1 Alfred Sloan, *My Life with General Motors*, London, 1986 (1st edn 1963), p. 204.
2 Alan Taylor III, *Sixty to Zero: An Inside Look at the Collapse of General Motors – and the Detroit Auto Industry*, New Haven, 2010, p. ix.
3 Ibid., p. 17.
4 *Time*, 1 November 1954.
5 Robert P. Bremner, *Chairman of the Fed: William McChesney Martin Jr and the Creation of the Modern American Financial System*, New Haven, 2004, p. 2.
6 Remarks by William McChesney Martin Jr at the International Finance Session of the 33rd National Foreign Trade Convention, New York City, 12 November 1946, Martin Papers, St Louis Federal Reserve.
7 Ibid.
8 Hugh Gaitskell, 'The Sterling Area', *International Affairs*, vol. 28, no. 2 (April 1952), pp. 170–6, at p. 176.
9 Remarks by William McChesney Martin Jr before the House Banking and Currency Committee, 28 May 1946, Martin Papers, St Louis Federal Reserve.

10 Oral History Interview with John W. Snyder, Washington, DC, 15 January 1969, by Jerry N. Hess, Harry S. Truman Library and Museum, Independence, MO.

11 Remarks by William McChesney Martin Jr, 12 November 1946.

12 Remarks by William McChesney Martin Jr, 28 May 1946.

13 Robert Skidelsky, *John Maynard Keynes: Fighting for Britain, 1937–1946*, London, 2000, pp. 453–4, 451.

14 Edward Cray, *General of the Army: George C. Marshall, Soldier and Statesman*, New York, 1990, pp. 607, 624–6.

15 John Lewis Gaddis, *The Cold War*, London, 2005, p. 31.

16 Barry Eichengreen, *Exorbitant Privilege: The Rise and Fall of the Dollar*, Oxford, 2011, pp. 47–8.

17 Ibid., p. 50.

18 Lawrence H. Seltzer, 'The Changed Environment of Monetary-Banking Policy', *American Economic Review*, vol. 36, no. 2 (May 1946), pp. 65–79, at pp. 65–6.

19 Ibid., p. 67.

20 Ibid., pp. 67, 70.

21 Ibid., p. 76.

22 Jacob Viner, 'International Finance in the Postwar World', *Journal of Political Economy*, vol. 55, no. 2 (April 1947), pp. 99–107, at p. 97.

23 Ibid., p. 130.

24 Ralph H. Blodgett, 'The Impact of Total War', *American Economic Review*, vol. 36, no. 2 (May 1946), pp. 126–38, at pp. 129–30.

25 Benjamin Graham and David L. Dodd, *Security Analysis: Principles and Technique*, 3rd edn, New York, 1951 (1st edn 1934), p. 10.

26 John H. Williams, *Post-War Monetary Plans and Other Essays*, Oxford, 1949, pp. 218–20, 235.

27 Harry S. Truman, 'State of the Union, 1950', delivered on 4 January 1950, retrieved from the University of Groningen website, www.let.rug.nl/usa.

28 Robert L. Hetzel and Ralph F. Leach, 'The Treasury–Fed Accord: A New Narrative Account', Federal Reserve Bank of Richmond, *Economic Quarterly*, vol. 87, no. 1 (Winter 2001), pp. 33–55, at pp. 33, 40.

29 Ibid., p. 47.

30 Ibid., p. 33.

31 Gavyn Davies, 'How the Fed defeated President Truman to win its independence', *Financial Times*, 20 January 2012.

32 Allan H. Meltzer, *A History of the Federal Reserve*, vol. 1: *1913–1951*, Chicago, 2003, p. 726.

33 Remarks by William McChesney Martin Jr before the 77th Annual Convention of the American Bankers Association, Chicago, Illinois, 2 October 1951, Martin Papers, St Louis Federal Reserve.

34 Remarks by William McChesney Martin Jr, address before the New York Group of the Investment Bankers Association of America, New York City, 19 October 1955, Martin Papers, St Louis Federal Reserve, pp. 4, 9.

35 Ibid., p. 11.

36 Ibid., p.12.

37 Remarks by William McChesney Martin Jr, address to the Economic Club of New York, 12 March 1957, 'Our American Economy: Strength of the Republic', Martin Papers, St Louis Federal Reserve, pp. 5–6.

38 Internal Memo to Katz with questions about the Gold Standard, with attached response from Katz to Senator Robertson, 26 July 1957, Martin Papers, St Louis Federal Reserve, pp. 2–3.

39 George M. Humphrey, *The Basic Papers of George M. Humphrey as Secretary of the Treasury, 1953–1957*, Cleveland, OH, 1965, pp. 15, 29, 43.

40 Ibid., pp. 111, 119.

41 Ibid., pp. 122–3.

42 Christina D. Romer, 'Macroeconomic Policy in the 1960s: The Causes and Consequences of a Mistaken Revolution', Presented at Plenary Session A of the Economic History Association Annual Meeting, Lyndon B. Johnson Presidential Library, Austin, TX, 7 September 2007.

Chapter 12: Weary Titans

1   C. C. S. Newton, 'The Sterling Crisis of 1947 and the British Response to the Marshall Plan', *Economic History Review*, New Series, vol. 37, no. 3 (August 1984), pp. 391–408, at p. 392.

2   David Kynaston, *The City of London: A Club No More, 1945–2000*, London, 2001, p. 2.

3   Ibid., p. 11.

4   *DNB*, 'Hugh Dalton'.

5   Ben Pimlott, *Hugh Dalton*, London, 1985, p. 445.

6   Ibid., p. 455.

7   Correlli Barnett, *The Lost Victory: British Dreams, British Realities, 1945–1950*, London, 1995, p. 182.

8   Kynaston, *The City of London: A Club No More*, p. 9.

9   Ibid., p. 41.

10 Ibid., pp. 108–9.

11 Ibid., p. 110.

12 Newton, 'The Sterling Crisis', p. 400.

13 TNA, T236/1669, 'Overseas Payments Problems, Draft of 8th September, 1947'.

14 TNA, T236/1756, 'Note from Hugh Dalton to Sir Edward Bridges, dated 2nd November, 1947'; ibid., 'Note: the Dollar Drain, Sir Edward Bridges to Hugh Dalton, 11th November, 1947'.

15 Ibid., 'Outward Telegram to Treasury, 3rd December 1947'.

16 *DNB*, 'Stafford Cripps'.

17 Kynaston, *The City of London: A Club No More*, p. 33.

18 TNA, T269/1, Robert Hall, 'Caliban: The Future of Sterling', memorandum dated 16 June 1949.

19 Ibid., Douglas Jay, 'Dollar Situation', dated 6 July 1949.

20 Kynaston, *The City of London: A Club No More*, p. 23.

21 TNA, T269/1, note from Cameron Cobbold to the Chancellor of the Exchequer, dated 18 June 1949; note from Sir Edward Bridges to the Chancellor of the Exchequer, dated 18 June 1949.

22 TNA, T236/1758, note dated 14 July 1949.
23 TNA, T269/1, Robert Hall, 'Caliban: The Future of Sterling', memorandum dated 16 June 1949.
24 Kynaston, *The City of London: A Club No More*, p. 33.
25 Alec Cairncross and Barry Eichengreen, *Sterling in Decline: The Devaluations of 1931, 1949 and 1967*, Oxford, 1983, p. 121.
26 Robert Hall, *The Robert Hall Diaries*, ed. Alec Cairncross, London, 1989, p. 83.
27 *Daily Mail*, 19 September 1949.
28 www.fhwa.dot.gov.
29 Fred H. Klopstock, 'Monetary Reform in Western Germany', *Journal of Political Economy*, vol. 57, no. 4 (August 1949), pp. 277–92, at p. 278.
30 Pol O'Dochartaigh, *Germany since 1945*, Basingstoke, 2004, p. 28.
31 Konrad Adenauer, *Memoirs, 1945–1953*, trans. Beate Ruhm von Oppen, London, 1966, p. 146, speech in Berne, 23 March 1949.
32 Lucius D. Clay, *Decision in Germany*, London, 1950, pp. 209–11.
33 Ibid., pp. 63, 208.
34 Lucius D. Clay, *The Papers of General Lucius D. Clay: Germany, 1945–1949*, ed. Jane Edward Smith, 2 vols, Bloomington, 1974, vol. 2, p. 593.
35 O'Dochartaigh, *Germany since 1945*, p. 31.
36 Clay, *Decision in Germany*, p. 214.
37 O'Dochartaigh, *Germany since 1945*, p. 31.
38 Ibid., p. 32.
39 Clay, *Decision in Germany*, pp. 364–5.
40 O'Dochartaigh, *Germany since 1945*, pp. 32–3.
41 Adenauer, *Memoirs*, p. 146.
42 Walter W. Heller, 'The Role of Fiscal-Monetary Policy in German Economic Recovery', *American Economic Review*, vol. 40, no. 2 (May 1950), pp. 531–47, at pp. 540, 542, 544.
43 Otmar Emminger, *The D-Mark in the Conflict between Internal and External Equilibrium, 1948–1975*, Essays in International Finance, no. 122, Princeton, June 1977, p. 3.

Chapter 13: Japan Incorporated

1 William Manchester, *American Caesar: Douglas MacArthur, 1880–1964*, London, 1979, p. 15.
2 Ibid., pp. 16–17.
3 Ibid., pp. 424–5.
4 G. C. Allen, *Japan's Economic Expansion*, London, 1965, p. 4.
5 Jerome B. Cohen, 'Fiscal Policy in Japan', *Journal of Finance*, vol. 5, no. 1 (March 1950), pp. 110–25, at p. 110.
6 Allen, *Japan's Economic Expansion*, p. 2.
7 Ibid., p. 4.
8 Chalmers Johnson, *MITI and the Japanese Miracle: The Growth of Industrial Policy, 1925–1975*, Stanford, 1982, p. 6.
9 Ibid., p. 15.

10 Kenneth K. Kusihara, 'Postwar Inflation and Fiscal-Monetary Policy in Japan', *American Economic Review*, vol. 36, no. 5 (December 1946), pp. 843–54, at pp. 844–5.

11 Ibid., p. 846.

12 Ibid., p. 17.

13 Allen, *Japan's Economic Expansion*, pp. 17–18.

14 *American National Biography*, 'Joseph Morrell Dodge'.

15 Shigeto Tsuru, 'Toward Economic Stability in Japan', *Public Affairs*, vol. 22, no. 4 (December 1949), pp. 357–66, at pp. 361–2.

16 Cohen, 'Fiscal Policy in Japan', p. 110.

17 Allen, *Japan's Economic Expansion*, p. 19.

18 Shigeto Tsuru, *Japan's Capitalism: Creative Defeat and Beyond*, Cambridge, 1993, p. 47.

19 Cohen, 'Fiscal Policy in Japan', p. 111.

20 Ibid., p. 114.

21 Tsuru, *Japan's Capitalism*, p. 48.

22 Cohen, 'Fiscal Policy in Japan', p. 114.

23 Mark Metzler, *Lever of Empire: The International Gold Standard and the Crisis of Liberalism in Prewar Japan*, Berkeley, 2006, pp. 267–8.

24 Kazuo Tatewaki, *Banking and Finance in Japan: An Introduction to the Tokyo Market*, London, 1991, p. 11.

25 Hugh T. Patrick, 'The Bank of Japan: A Case Study in the Effectiveness of Central Bank Techniques of Monetary Control', *Journal of Finance*, vol. 15, no. 4 (December 1960), pp. 573–4, at p. 574.

26 Allen, *Japan's Economic Expansion*, p. 69.

27 Shigeto Tsuru, 'Growth and Stability of the Postwar Japanese Economy', *American Economic Review*, vol. 51, no. 2 (May 1961), pp. 400–11, at p. 410.

28 Johnson, *MITI and the Japanese Miracle*, pp. 209, 211.

29 Ibid., p. 21.

30 Ibid., p. 211.

31 Richard Werner, *Princes of the Yen: Japan's Central Bankers and the Transformation of the Economy*, Armonk, NY, 2003, p. 5.

32 Albert Ando, Hidekazu Eguchi, Roger Farmer and Yoshio Suzuki (eds), *Monetary Policy in our Times*, Proceedings of the First International Conference Held by the Institute for Monetary and Economic Studies of the Bank of Japan, Cambridge, MA, 1985, p. 86.

33 Thomas F. Cargill, Michael M. Hutchinson and Ito Takatoshi, *The Political Economy of Japanese Monetary Policy*, Cambridge, MA, 1997, p. 30.

34 Kenneth K. Kusihara, 'Japan's Trade Position in a Changing World Market', *Review of Economics and Statistics*, vol. 37, no. 4 (November 1955), pp. 412–17, at p. 412.

35 Johnson, *MITI and the Japanese Miracle*, p. 200.

36 Allen, *Japan's Economic Expansion*, p. 18.

37 Shigeto Tsuru, *The Selected Essays of Shigeto Tsuru*, vol. 2: *The Economic Development of Modern Japan*, Aldershot, 1995, p. 310 (from 'The Economic Problems of Japan: Present and Future', lecture delivered in Australia, October 1964).

38 Tsuru, *Japan's Capitalism*, p. 1.

39 Johnson, *MITI and the Japanese Miracle*, p. 3.
40 Correspondents of the *Economist, Consider Japan*, London, 1963, pp. 31, 39.
41 Werner, *Princes of the Yen*, p. 3.
42 Correspondents of the *Economist, Consider Japan*, pp. 39–40.
43 Tsuru, *The Selected Essays*, vol. 2, p. 322.
44 Cargill, Hutchinson and Takatoshi, *The Political Economy*, p. 31.
45 Johnson, *MITI and the Japanese Miracle*, p. 15.
46 Tsuru, *The Selected Essays*, vol. 2, p. 320.
47 Johnson, *MITI and the Japanese Miracle*, p. 15.

Chapter 14: Imperial Retreat

1   Christina D. Romer, 'Macroeconomic Policy in the 1960s: The Causes and Consequences of a Mistaken Revolution', Presented at Plenary Session A of the Economic History Association Annual Meeting, Lyndon B. Johnson Presidential Library, Austin, TX, 7 September 2007, pp. 1, 5.
2   Ibid., p. 7.
3   Ibid., pp. 4, 7.
4   Ibid., p. 9.
5   Ibid.
6   Ibid., p. 11.
7   For 'compensatory finance' see www.thefreedictionary.com; for definition of 'deficit financing' see Graham Bannock and R. E. Baxter, *The Penguin Dictionary of Economics*, 8th edn, London, 2011 (1st edn 1972), p. 89.
8   Herbert Stein, *The Fiscal Revolution in America*, Chicago, 1969, p. 454.
9   Ibid., p. 459.
10 Robert Sobel, *The Last Bull Market: Wall Street in the 1960s*, New York, 1980, p. 160.
11 Robert Dallek, *Lyndon B. Johnson: Portrait of a President*, New York, 2004, p. 232.
12 Ibid., p. 233.
13 Ibid., p. 234.
14 Sobel, *The Last Bull Market*, pp. 161–2.
15 Ibid., p. 171.
16 Remarks by William McChesney Martin Jr, 'Reminiscences and Reflections', speech in Hot Springs, Virginia, 17 October 1969, Martin Papers, St Louis Federal Reserve, p. 6.
17 Ibid., pp. 7–8.
18 Ibid., pp. 10–11.
19 Remarks by William McChesney Martin Jr, 'Good Money is Coined Freedom', speech given before the Economic Club of Detroit, 18 March 1968, Martin Papers, St Louis Federal Reserve, pp. 3, 7.
20 Ibid., pp. 7-8, 11.
21 Ibid., pp. 11–12.
22 Ibid., p. 13.
23 Barry Eichengreen, *Exorbitant Privilege: The Rise and Fall of the Dollar*, Oxford, 2011, p. 4.

24 Remarks by William McChesney Martin Jr, speech before the Rotary Club of Toledo, Ohio, 26 June 1967, Martin Papers, St Louis Federal Reserve, p. 4.
25 Ibid., p. 4.
26 Ibid., pp. 3–5.
27 Allan H. Meltzer, *A History of the Federal Reserve*, vol. 2, Book 1: *1951–1969*, Chicago, 2009, p. 472.
28 *Time*, 'Money: De Gaulle v The Dollar', 12 February 1965.
29 Ibid.
30 Transcription of General de Gaulle's 'Conférence de presse du 4 février 1965', found on www.ina.fr.
31 Malcolm Craig, *How to Invest in Gold*, Cambridge, 1991, pp. ix–x.
32 Harry Johnson, 'The Gold Rush of 1968 in Retrospect and Prospect', *American Economic Review*, vol. 59, no. 2 (May 1969), pp. 344–8, at p. 344.
33 Meltzer, *History of the Federal Reserve*, vol. 2, Book 1, pp. 270, 267, 35.
34 Ibid., pp. 269–70.
35 Henry Brandon, *The Retreat of American Power*, New York, 1972, p. 213.
36 Allen J. Matusow, *Nixon's Economy: Booms, Busts, Dollars, and Votes*, Lawrence, KS, 1998, p. 124.
37 Daniel Yergin and Joseph Stanislaw, *The Commanding Heights: The Battle between Government and the Marketplace That is Remaking the Modern World*, New York, 1998, p. 61.
38 Stephen Ambrose, *Nixon: The Triumph of a Politician, 1962–1972*, London, 1989, pp. 225–6.
39 Yergin and Stanislaw, *The Commanding Heights*, p. 60.
40 Matusow, *Nixon's Economy*, p. 126.
41 William McChesney Martin Jr, 'Toward a World Central Bank?', Basle, Switzerland, Per Jacobsson Foundation Lecture, given 14 September 1970, pp. 9–10.
42 Arthur Burns, *Inside the Nixon Administration: The Secret Diary of Arthur Burns, 1969–1974*, ed. Robert H. Ferrell, Lawrence, KS, 2010, p. viii.
43 Robert Sobel, *The Worldly Economists*, New York, 1980, p. 39.
44 Charles Ashman, *Connally: The Adventures of Big Bad John*, New York, 1974, p. 197.
45 Ibid., pp. 199, 201.
46 Henry Kissinger, *The White House Years*, New York, 1979, p. 951.
47 Ambrose, *Nixon: The Triumph of a Politician*, p. 457.
48 Brandon, *The Retreat of American Power*, p. 229.
49 Matusow, *Nixon's Economy*, p. 131.
50 Yergin and Stanislaw, *The Commanding Heights*, p. 62.
51 Matusow, *Nixon's Economy*, pp. 144–5.
52 William H. Branson, 'The Trade Effects of the 1971 Currency Realignments', *Brookings Papers on Economic Activity*, vol. 3, no. 1 (1972), pp. 15–69, at p. 15.
53 Brandon, *The Retreat of American Power*, p. 224; Yergin and Stanislaw, *The Commanding Heights*, p. 62.
54 H. R. Haldeman, *The Haldeman Diaries*, New York, 1994, p. 340.
55 Yergin and Stanislaw, *The Commanding Heights*, p. 62.
56 Ibid.
57 Brandon, *The Retreat of American Power*, p. 223.

58 Richard Nixon, 'Address to the Nation Outlining a New Economic Policy: "The Challenge of Peace"', 15 August 1971, found on www.presidency.ucsb.edu.
59 *Time*, 'The Economy: Nixon's Grand Design for Recovery', 30 August 1971.
60 Ibid.
61 Joel Kurtzman, *The Death of Money: How the Electronic Economy Has Destabilized the World's Markets and Created Financial Chaos*, New York, 1993, p. 51.
62 Brandon, *The Retreat of American Power*, pp. 219–20.

Chapter 15: The Impact of Oil

1 Daniel Yergin, *The Prize: The Epic Quest for Oil, Money, and Power*, New York, 1991, p. 588.
2 Paul A. Volcker and Toyoo Gyohten, *Changing Fortunes: The World's Money and the Threat to American Leadership*, New York, 1992, p. 88.
3 Ibid., p. 90.
4 Ibid., p. 101.
5 Yergin, *The Prize*, p. 591.
6 Ibid., p. 592.
7 *Time*, 'The Arab World: Oil, Power, Violence', 2 April 1973.
8 Ibid.
9 Henry Kissinger, *Years of Upheaval*, London, 1982, pp. 872–3.
10 *Economist*, 'An Uncertain Weapon', 20 October 1973.
11 *Economist*, 'Living in a Dollar World Again', 17 November 1973; *Economist*, 'Gold: The Great Freeze', 15 December 1973.
12 *Economist*, 'Gold Shares', 8 December 1973.
13 *Financial Times*, 'Nine to Seek US Backing for Gold Price Plan', 24 April 1974.
14 *Financial Times*, 'Gold at Record Levels', 9 January 1974.
15 Malcolm Craig, *How to Invest in Gold*, Cambridge, 1991, p. x.
16 *Financial Times*, 'Nine to Seek US Backing for Gold Price Plan'.
17 Otto Eckstein, *The Great Recession with a Postscript on Stagflation*, Amsterdam, 1978, pp. 112–13.
18 Robert Z. Aliber, *The International Money Game*, 2nd edn, London, 1977 (1st edn 1973), p. 229.
19 Eckstein, *The Great Recession*, pp. 120, 124.
20 *Economist*, 'Living in a Dollar World Again'.
21 *Economist*, 'The Return of the Dollar', 12 January 1974.
22 Yergin, *The Prize*, p. 595.
23 *Time*, Man of the Year, 'A Desert King Faces the Modern World', 6 January 1975.
24 *Economist*, 'When an Era Trembles', 29 March 1975.
25 Jeffrey Robinson, *Yamani: The Inside Story*, London, 1988, pp. 15, 129.
26 Ibid., p. 130.
27 Volcker and Gyohten, *Changing Fortunes*, p. 140.
28 David Rockefeller, *Memoirs*, New York, 2002, pp. 284–5.

29 Ibid., p. 285; Charles Tripp, *A History of Iraq*, 3rd edn, Cambridge, 2007 (1st edn 2000), p. 206.
30 Rockefeller, *Memoirs*, p. 285.
31 Volcker and Gyohten, *Changing Fortunes*, pp. 136, 140–1.
32 William E. Simon, *A Time for Truth*, New York, 1978, pp. 4–5, 10.
33 Ibid., p. 101.
34 Ibid., p. 102.
35 Ibid., p. 110.
36 *New York Times*, 'Milton Friedman, Free Markets Theorist, Dies at 94', 16 November 2006.
37 *Economist*, 'A Heavyweight Chap, at Five Foot Two', 23 November 2006.
38 Simon, *A Time for Truth*, p. xi.
39 Allan H. Meltzer, *A History of the Federal Reserve*, vol. 2, Book 2: *1970–1986*, Chicago, 2009, p. 901.
40 Ibid., p. 904.
41 Volcker and Gyohten, *Changing Fortunes*, pp. 145–6.
42 Meltzer, *A History of the Federal Reserve*, vol. 2, Book 2, p. 960.
43 Paul A. Volcker, *The Rediscovery of the Business Cycle*, The Charles C. Moskowitz Memorial Lectures, no. 19, New York, 1978, p. 28.
44 Ibid., p. 55.
45 James E. Carter, 'Crisis of Confidence Speech', 15 July 1979, Miller Center Archive, Charlottesville.
46 *Time*, 'Ripples from Iran', 5 February 1979.
47 Ronald W. Klein, 'Japan 1979: The Second Oil Crisis', *Asian Survey*, vol. 20, no. 1 (January 1980), pp. 42–52, at p. 49.
48 *Time*, 'The Squeeze of '79', 22 October 1979.
49 Malcolm Craig, *How to Invest in Gold*, Cambridge, 1991, p. x; see also charts on www.kitco.com.
50 *Time*, 'The Squeeze of '79'.
51 Ibid.
52 Arthur F. Burns, 'The Anguish of Central Banking', The 1979 Per Jacobsson Lecture, delivered in Belgrade, Yugoslavia, 30 September 1979, pp. 5–7.
53 Ibid., p. 7.
54 Ibid., pp. 13–14.
55 James Callaghan, speech delivered to the Labour Party conference, 28 September 1976, found on www.britishpoliticalspeech.org.

Chapter 16: Thatcher and Reagan

1 Margaret Thatcher, *The Downing Street Years*, London, 1993, p. 7.
2 Ibid., pp. 41–2.
3 Ian Gilmour, *Dancing with Dogma*, London, 1993, p. 20.
4 Geoffrey Howe, *Conflict of Loyalty*, London, 1994, p. 143.
5 Nigel Lawson, *The View from No. 11*, London, 1992, p. 39.
6 Ibid., pp. 41–2.
7 Thatcher, *The Downing Street Years*, pp. 50–1.
8 Ibid., p. 52

9 Ibid., p. 53.

10 Gilmour, *Dancing with Dogma*, p. 9.

11 John Bright, speech delivered in Edinburgh, 5 November 1868, found on www.libertyfund.org.

12 John Campbell, *Margaret Thatcher*, vol. 1: *The Grocer's Daughter*, London, 2000, p. 10.

13 Thatcher, *The Downing Street Years*, p. 123.

14 Gilmour, *Dancing with Dogma*, p. 15.

15 Thatcher, *The Downing Street Years*, p. 123.

16 *Parliamentary Debates*, 5th Series, vol. 979, col. 1596, 28 February 1980, found on www.margaretthacher.org.

17 Margaret Thatcher, speech to Conservative Party conference ('the lady's not for turning'), delivered 10 October 1980, found on www.margaretthatcher.org.

18 Milton Friedman, *Free to Choose*, London, 1980, pp. 298, 316.

19 John Campbell, *Margaret Thatcher*, vol. 2: *The Iron Lady*, London, 2003, pp. 80–1.

20 David Stockman, *The Triumph of Politics: Why the Reagan Revolution Failed*, Boston, 1987, pp. 123–4.

21 Lou Cannon, *President Reagan: The Role of a Lifetime*, New York, 1991, p. 41.

22 Ronald Reagan, 'A Time for Choosing', speech delivered in Los Angeles, 27 October 1964, found on www.reagan.utexas.edu.

23 *Time*, 'Defender of the Dollar', 22 October 1979.

24 Cannon, *President Reagan*, p. 270.

25 Ibid., p. 271.

26 Paul A. Volcker and Toyoo Gyohten, *Changing Fortunes: The World's Money and the Threat to American Leadership*, New York, 1992, pp. 166–7.

27 Cannon, *President Reagan*, p. 271.

28 Edward Chancellor, *Devil Take the Hindmost: A History of Financial Speculation*, London, 1999, p. 255.

29 William R. Neikirk, *Volcker: Portrait of the Money Man*, New York, 1987, pp. xi, 29.

30 Alan Greenspan, *The Age of Turbulence: Adventures in a New World*, New York, 2007, p. 84.

31 Ron Paul and Lewis Lehrman, *The Case for Gold*, Washington, DC, 1982, p. ix.

32 *Report to the Congress of the Commission on the Role of Gold in the Domestic and International Monetary Systems, March 1982*, Washington, DC, 1982, p. 1.

33 Paul and Lehrman, *The Case for Gold*, pp. 197, x.

34 Cannon, *President Reagan*, p. 493.

35 Ibid., p. 516.

36 Herbert Stein, *Presidential Economics: The Making of Economic Policy from Roosevelt to Reagan and Beyond*, 2nd edn, Washington, DC, 1988 (1st edn 1986), p. 239.

37 Stockman, *The Triumph of Politics*, p. 9.

38 Ibid., p. 14.

39 Ibid., pp. 426, 429.

40 George Soros, *The Alchemy of Finance*, New York, 1994 (1st edn 1987), p. 110.

41 Volcker and Gyohten, *Changing Fortunes*, p. 228.

42 Otmar Emminger, 'The International Role of the Dollar', Federal Reserve Bank of Kansas City, *Economic Review*, September–October 1985, pp. 17–24, at pp. 17–19.

43 Soros, *The Alchemy of Finance*, p. 112.

44 Emminger, 'The International Role of the Dollar', p. 21.

45 Barry Eichengreen, *Globalizing Capital: A History of the International Monetary System*, Princeton, 1996, p. 146.

46 *New York Times*, 'Now Harley Davidson is All Over the Road', 17 April 1988.

47 Lawson, *The View from No. 11*, p. 197.

48 Ibid.

49 Philip Augar, *The Death of Gentlemanly Capitalism: The Rise and Fall of London's Investment Banks*, London, 2000, p. 33.

50 Ibid., p. 103.

51 Ibid., p. 4.

52 Hugo Young, *One of Us: A Biography of Margaret Thatcher*, London, 1989, p. 149.

53 Greenspan, *The Age of Turbulence*, p. 53.

54 Ibid.

55 Ibid., pp. 105–6.

56 Ibid., p. 109.

57 Ibid., p. 105.

58 Ibid., p. 110.

59 Ibid., p. 102.

60 Lawson, *The View from No. 11*, p. 645.

61 Thatcher, *The Downing Street Years*, p. 674.

Chapter 17: The Creation of the Euro

1 Jacques Delors, *Mémoires*, Paris, 2004, p. 336.

2 Ibid.

3 Otmar Issing, *The Birth of the Euro*, trans. from the original German by Nigel Hulbert, Cambridge, 2008, p. 229.

4 Delors, *Mémoires*, p. 336.

5 Philip Coggan, *Paper Promises: Money, Debt and the New World Order*, London, 2011, p. 129.

6 Ken Endo, *The Presidency of the European Commission under Jacques Delors: The Politics of Shared Leadership*, Basingstoke, 1999, p. 152.

7 Delors, *Mémoires*, p. 365.

8 Margaret Thatcher, *The Downing Street Years*, London, 1993, p. 696.

9 Nigel Lawson, *The View from No. 11*, London, 1992, pp. 501–4.

10 Ibid., p. 843.

11 Thatcher, *The Downing Street Years*, p. 137.

12 *Daily Telegraph*, obituary for Sir Alan Walters, 5 January 2009.

13 Lawson, *The View from No. 11*, p. 961.

14 Ibid., p. 958.

15 Thatcher, *The Downing Street Years*, pp. 714–15.

16 Lawson, *The View from No. 11*, p. 961.

17 Thatcher, *The Downing Street Years*, p. 717,

18 John Major, *The Autobiography*, London, 2000, pp. 133–4.

19 Ibid., p. 157.

20 Ibid., p. 159.

21 Ibid., pp. 162–3.

22 Delors, *Mémoires*, pp. 409, 477.

23 Norman Lamont, *In Office*, London, 1999, p. 211.

24 Ibid., p. 216.

25 Ibid., p. 245.

26 Ibid., p. 231.

27 Major, *The Autobiography*, p. 312.

28 Ibid., p. 314.

29 Ibid., p. 329.

30 Ibid., p. 334.

31 George Soros, with Byron Wien and Krisztina Koenen, *Soros on Soros: Staying Ahead of the Curve*, New York, 1995, pp. 81–5.

32 *Financial Times*, 'Sterling is Suspended within ERM', 17 September 1992.

33 Robert Solomon, 'The Birth of the Euro and its Effects', *Brown Journal of World Affairs*, vol. 6, no. 2 (Summer/Fall 1999), pp. 142–8.

34 Tommaso Padoa-Schioppa, 'The Euro: Significance for Europe and Beyond', speech delivered to the House of Councillors Committee of Financial Affairs, Tokyo, 9 March 1999.

35 Issing, *The Birth of the Euro*, pp. 9, 13.

36 Matt Marshall, *The Bank: The Birth of Europe's Central Bank and the Rebirth of Europe's Power*, London, 1999, p. 159.

37 Issing, *The Birth of the Euro*, p. 7.

38 Ibid., p. 15.

39 Graham Bannock and R. E. Baxter, *The Penguin Dictionary of Economics*, 8th edn, London, 2011 (1st edn 1972), p. 264.

40 Issing, *The Birth of the Euro*, p. 193.

41 Marshall, *The Bank*, p. 89.

42 Ibid., pp. 89–90.

43 *Der Spiegel*, 'Es gibt kein Zurück', 9 December 1991.

44 *Le Monde*, 'Réunion des ministres des finances à la Haye: Les Douze ont progressé vers l'union monétaire', 1 December 1991.

45 *Der Spiegel*, 'Es gibt kein Zurück'.

46 *Independent*, 'Kohl acts to quash revolt over the euro', 2 July 1997.

47 www.businessweek.com, from 20 June 1997.

48 Issing, *The Birth of the Euro*, p. 229.

49 Ibid., p. 232.

50 Ibid., p. 21.

51 Otmar Issing, speech delivered at the Danish Society of Financial Analysts' 25th Jubilee, Copenhagen, 7 May 1999.

52 Francesco Giordano and Sharda Persaud, *The Political Economy of Monetary Union: Towards the Euro*, London, 1998, p. 37.

53 Ibid., p. 53.

54 Issing, *The Birth of the Euro*, p. 193.

55 *Der Spiegel*, 'Aufbruch ins Ungewisse', 29 December 2001.

56 Matthew Lynn, *Bust: Greece, the Euro and the Sovereign Debt Crisis*, London, 2011, p. 34.

Chapter 18: The Rise of China

1 *New York Times*, 'Deng Xiaoping: A Political Wizard Who Put China on the Capitalist Road', 20 February 1997.
2 Ezra F. Vogel, *Deng Xiaoping and the Transformation of China*, Cambridge, MA, 2011, p. 49.
3 Ibid., pp. 217–18.
4 Ibid., pp. 218, 220.
5 Eli Heckscher, *Mercantilism*, 2 vols, 1st English edn, London, 1935, vol. 2, p. 46.
6 Paul Krugman, from 'The Conscience of a Liberal', a blog appearing in the *New York Times*, 31 December 2009.
7 Patrick Buchanan, 'Yankee Utopians in a Chinese Century', 2 July 2010, found on http://buchanan.org/blog/yankee-utopians-in-a-chinese-century-4227.
8 Ibid.
9 Lawrence J. Braham, *Zhu Rongji and the Transformation of Modern China*, Singapore, 2002, pp. 6–7.
10 Kui-yin Cheung, 'The Impact of Renminbi Devaluation on Hong Kong and China Trade', in Y. Y. Kueh (ed.), *The Political Economy of Sino-American Relations: A Greater China Perspective*, Hong Kong, 1997, pp. 163–80, at pp. 163, 166.
11 Braham, *Zhu Rongji*, p. 24.
12 *New York Times*, 'Devaluation by China', 16 December 1989.
13 Nicholas R. Lardy, 'Chinese Foreign Trade', *China Quarterly*, no. 131 (September 1992), pp. 691–720, at p. 717.
14 Ibid.
15 Zhiang Jialin, *The Debate on China's Exchange Rate – Should or Will It be Devalued?*, Hoover Institute Essays in Public Policy, No. 112, Stanford, 2004, p. 2.
16 *Time*, 'Zhu Rongji's Year of Living Dangerously', 12 April 1999.
17 Braham, *Zhu Rongji*, p. xxix.
18 Ibid., p. xxx.
19 Paul Krugman, *The Return of Depression Economics*, London, 1999, pp. 84–6.
20 Ibid., p. 69.
21 Fumio Hayashi and Edward C. Prescott, *The 1990s in Japan: A Lost Decade*, Working Papers 607, Federal Reserve Bank of Minneapolis, Minneapolis, MN, 2000, p. 1.
22 Krugman, *Depression Economics*, pp. 94–6.
23 Ibid., pp. 94–5.
24 Matthew Bishop, *Economics: An A–Z Guide*, London, 2009, p. 67.
25 Philip Coggan, *Paper Promises: Money, Debt and the New World Order*, London, 2011, p. 125.
26 Krugman, *Depression Economics*, pp. 144, 141.
27 Xiao-Ming Li, 'China's Macroeconomic Stabilization Policies Following the Asian Financial Crisis: Success or Failure?', *Asian Survey*, vol. 40, no. 6 (November–December 2000), pp. 938–57, at p. 938.

28 *Economist*, 'East Asia's Whirlwind Hits the Middle Kingdom', 14 February 1998.
29 *Economist*, 'China's Currency', 12 August 1999.
30 *Business China*, 'Devaluing the renminbi', 2 February 1998.
31 *New York Times*, 'China Won't Reduce Value of Currency, Official Says', 1 December 1997.
32 James Kynge, *China Shakes the World: The Rise of a Hungry Nation*, London, 2006, pp. 27–8.
33 *Economist*, 'China Pedals Harder', 11 June 1998.
34 Zhu Rongji, *Zhu Rongji Meets the Press*, Hong Kong, 2011, p. 172.
35 Ibid., p. 241.
36 Ibid., p. 259.
37 Ibid., p. 262.
38 *New York Times*, 'U.S. Calls Revaluation a Good Start for Beijing', 22 July 2005.
39 Ibid.
40 www.chinadaily.com.cn, 'Greenspan: Yuan revamp unlikely to help US', 14 July 2005.
41 Wayne M. Morrison and Marc Labonte, *China's Currency Policy: An Analysis of the Economic Issues*, CRS Report for Congress, Washington, DC, 19 December 2011, p. 1.
42 www.bbc.co.uk, 27 November 2012.
43 www.xinhua.net, 18 March 2010.
44 www.bbc.co.uk, 13 January 2012.

Chapter 19: Delusions of Debt

1 *Economist*, Lexington, 'Alan Greenspan, Fiscal Fiddler', 1 February 2001.
2 Ibid.
3 Alan Greenspan, *The Age of Turbulence: Adventures in a New World*, New York, 2007, p. 183.
4 *New York Times*, 'The Doctrine was Not to Have One', 25 August 2005.
5 *Time*, '25 People to Blame for the Financial Crisis', 12 February 2009, found on http://content.time.com/time/specials/packages/completelist/0,29569,1877351,00.html.
6 *New York Times*, 25 August 2005.
7 Greenspan, *The Age of Turbulence*, p. 27.
8 *New York Times*, 25 August 2005.
9 *Time*, 'Who Swiped the Surplus?', 3 September 2001.
10 *Time*, 'Dissecting Bush's Tax-Cut Plan', 27 February 2001.
11 Paul Weyrich, 'Bush's Legacy Not Yet Written', www.frontpagemag.com, 16 January 2009.
12 Greenspan, *The Age of Turbulence*, p. 235.
13 Remarks by R. Glenn Hubbard, *Tax Notes*, 30th Anniversary, 10 December 2002.
14 Stephen Slivinski, *Buck Wild: How Republicans Broke the Bank and Became the Party of Big Government*, Nashville, 2006, pp. 119–21.

15 Ibid., p. 123.
16 Ibid., pp. 126, 3.
17 Ibid., p. 149.
18 *Wall Street Journal*, 'Bush Finds Party Faithful in an Ugly Mood', 9 February 2004.
19 James Bovard, *The Bush Betrayal*, New York, 2004, pp. 2–3.
20 *Wall Street Journal*, 'Big Government Conservatism', 15 August 2003.
21 Greenspan, *The Age of Turbulence*, pp. 238–9.
22 Advertisement in the *New York Times*, 11 February 2003.
23 Greenspan, *The Age of Turbulence*, p. 241.
24 *Los Angeles Times*, 'Fears of Dot-Com Crash, Version 2.0', 16 July 2006.
25 www.cnn.com, 29 October 2001.
26 Mark M. Zandi, 'Assessing President Bush's Fiscal Policies', July 2004, p. 3, www.pbs.org.
27 Ibid.
28 Richard Duncan, *The Dollar Crisis: Causes, Consequences, Cures*, Singapore, 2005 (1st edn 2003), pp. 78–9.
29 Ibid., pp. 81, 87.
30 Ibid., p. 113.
31 Peter Warburton, *Debt and Delusion: Central Bank Follies That Threaten Economic Disaster*, London, 2000, p. 1.
32 Ibid., p. 3.
33 Ibid., p. 11.
34 Ibid., pp. 18–19.
35 Ibid., p. 236.
36 Ibid., p. 251.
37 Niall Ferguson and Moritz Schularick, '"Chimerica" and the Global Asset Market Boom', *International Finance*, vol. 10, no. 3 (2007), pp. 215–39, abstract; ibid., p. 230.
38 John Francis, *History of the Bank of England*, 2 vols, London, 1848, vol. 2, p. 34.
39 Warburton, *Debt and Delusion*, p. 49.
40 www.lbma.org.uk.
41 Philip Coggan, *Paper Promises: Money, Debt and the New World Order*, London, 2011, p. 3.
42 James Rickards, *Currency Wars: The Making of the Next Global Crisis*, New York, 2011, p. xii.
43 Detlev S. Schlichter, *Paper Money Collapse: The Folly of Elastic Money and the Coming Monetary Breakdown*, Hoboken, NJ, 2011, pp. 1, 1–2, 5.

Chapter 20: Crises and 'Bailouts'

1 *Time*, '25 People to Blame for the Financial Crisis', quoted in *New York Daily News*, 13 February 2009.
2 *Economist*, 'Accounting for Angelo', 5 June 2009; *New York Times*, 15 October 2010.
3 *Economist*, 'Accounting for Angelo'.
4 *New York Times*, 'The Original Subprime Crisis', 26 December 2007.

5 Louis Hyman, *Debtor Nation: The History of America in Red Ink*, Princeton, 2011, pp. 283–4.

6 Ibid., p. 285.

7 Paul Krugman, *The Return of Depression Economics and the Crisis of 2008*, London, 2008, p. 148.

8 Matthew Bishop, *Economics: An A–Z Guide*, London, 2009, p. 287.

9 *Wall Street Journal*, 'Bankers Hope for a Reprise of "Bowie Bonds"', 23 August 2005.

10 Philip Coggan, *Paper Promises: Money, Debt and the New World Order*, London, 2011, p. 179.

11 Robin Blackburn, 'The Subprime Crisis', *New Left Review*, March–April 2008, pp. 63–106, at pp. 64–5.

12 Ibid., p. 72.

13 Michael Lewis, *The Big Short: Inside the Doomsday Machine*, London, 2010, p. 209.

14 Krugman, *The Return of Depression Economics and the Crisis of 2008*, pp. 168–9.

15 www.newyorkfed.org.

16 *New York Times*, 'Why a US Subprime Mortgage Crisis is Felt around the World', 31 August 2007.

17 Alan Greenspan, Economists' Forum, www.blogs.ft.com/economists, 6 April 2008.

18 *New York Times*, 'Lehman Files for Bankruptcy; Merrill is Sold', 15 September 2008.

19 *Washington Post*, review of Vicky Ward, *The Devil's Casino*, 18 April 2010.

20 *Financial Times*, 'The High Stakes Games, Backstabbing and Greed behind Lehman's Demise', 8 April 2010.

21 *New York Times*, 'Lehman Files for Bankruptcy'.

22 Coggan, *Paper Promises*, p. 181.

23 William Shakespeare, *Titus Andronicus*, ed. Jonathan Bate, London, 1995, p. 186. (This quotation is from Act II.)

24 Andrew Ross Sorkin, *Too Big to Fail: Inside the Battle to Save Wall Street*, London, 2009, p. 449.

25 Ibid., p. 456.

26 Hank Paulson, *On the Brink: Inside the Race to Stop the Collapse of the Global Financial System*, New York, 2010, pp. 266–7.

27 Ibid., pp. 279–80.

28 Ibid., p. 290.

29 Ibid., p. 335.

30 Sorkin, *Too Big to Fail*, p. 513.

31 Paulson, *On the Brink*, p. 369.

32 Sorkin, *Too Big to Fail*, p. 513.

33 Gordon Brown, *Beyond the Crisis: Overcoming the First Crisis of Globalization*, London, 2010, p. 65.

34 Sorkin, *Too Big to Fail*, p. 514.

35 Alistair Darling, *Back from the Brink*, London, 2011, pp. 140–1.

36 www.treasurydirect.gov.

37 *Time*, 'The US Deficit', 25 August 2009.

38 www.treasurydirect.gov.

39 www.usgovernmentspending.com.

40 Quoted in Matthew Lynn, *Bust: Greece, the Euro and the Sovereign Debt Crisis*, London, 2011, p. 37.
41 Michael Lewis, *Boomerang*, London, 2011, p. 47.
42 Lynn, *Bust*, p. 115.
43 Ibid., pp. 115, 46.
44 Ibid., p. 120.
45 Ibid., pp. 121,123.
46 *New York Times*, 'Greek Leader Offers Plan to Tackle Debt Crisis', 15 December 2009.
47 *New York Times*, 'Greece's Stumble Follows a Headlong Rush into the Euro', 5 May 2010.
48 *Economist*, 'A Very European Crisis', 4 February 2010.
49 Evangelos Venizelos, 'The Greek Debt Crisis: Prospects and Opportunities', remarks delivered at the Peterson Institute for International Economics, Washington, DC, 25 July 2011.
50 Coggan, *Paper Promises*, p. 206.
51 Lewis, *The Big Short*, p. 264.
52 *Wall Street Journal*, 'US Debt and the Greece Analogy', 18 June 2010 (article written by Alan Greenspan).
53 www.lbma.org.uk.
54 Paul Krugman, *End This Depression Now!*, London, 2011, p. 149.
55 *New York Times*, 'Nobody Understands Debt', 1 January 2012 (article written by Paul Krugman).
56 *Economist*, 'Twisted Thinking', 31 March 2011.
57 Ibid.
58 *Time*, Person of the Year 2009, 'Ben Bernanke', 16 December 2009.
59 Darling, *Back from the Brink*, p. 198.

Epilogue

1 www.forbes.com, 'Bailout-Hater Tsipras Now Trying to Form Government in Greece', 7 May 2012.
2 *New York Times*, 'Supporters of Bailout Claim Victory in Greek Election', 17 June 2012.
3 www.cnn.com, 'Greek New Democracy Leader Hails "Victory for All Europe"', 18 June 2012.
4 *Financial Times*, 'Eurozone Agrees Greek Aid Deal', 27 November 2012.
5 *Financial Times*, 'Greek Bond Bet Pays Off for Hedge Fund', 18 December 2012.
6 *New York Times*, 'Greek Opposition Leader Seeks Conference on Debt', 25 January 2013.
7 Ibid.
8 Council on Foreign Relations, *What is the Fiscal Cliff?*, 12 December 2012, found on http://www.cfr.org/world/fiscal-cliff/p28757.
9 Ibid.
10 *Washington Post*, 'The Fiscal Cliff: How the House Voted', 2 January 2013.
11 *Meadville Tribune*, 'Averting the Real Fiscal Cliff', 31 January 2013 (article

written by Glenn Thompson, Republican US Representative for Pennsylvania's 5th District).

12 www.bbc.co.uk, 'State of the Union: Obama Pledges to Reignite Economy', 13 February 2013.

13 *Guardian*, 'G20 Summit Marks Largest Such Gathering in a Decade', 14 November 2008.

14 Niall Ferguson, 'The End of Chimerica: Amicable Divorce or Currency War?', before the Committee on Ways and Means, US House of Representatives, 24 March 2010.

15 *China Business Review*, 'China Tackles Economic Crisis with Fiscal Stimulus', vol. 36, no. 2 (March 2009), found on http://www.chinabusinessreview.com/.

16 *Wall Street Journal*, 'US Debt and the Greece Analogy', 18 June 2010 (article written by Alan Greenspan).

17 IMF, *World Economic Outlook*, April 2012, p. 9.

Conclusion

1 Richard Duncan, *The New Depression: The Breakdown of the Paper Money Economy*, Singapore, 2012, p. 169.

2 Philip Coggan, *Paper Promises: Money, Debt and the New World Order*, London, 2011, p. 267.

3 Fareed Zakaria, 'Can America be Fixed?: The New Crisis of Democracy', *Foreign Affairs*, vol. 92, no. 1 (January–February 2013), pp. 22–33, at p. 26.

4 Paul Krugman, *End This Depression Now!*, London, 2011, p. xi.

5 Zakaria, 'Can America Be Fixed?', p. 26.

6 Carmen M. Reinhart and Kenneth S. Rogoff, *This Time is Different: Eight Centuries of Financial Folly*, Princeton, 2009, p. xxxiii.

7 Ibid.

8 John Maynard Keynes, *The Economic Consequences of the Peace*, London, 1919, p. 220.

9 Mauricio Drelichman and Hans-Joachim Voth, 'Debt Sustainability in Historical Perspective: The Role of Fiscal Repression', *Journal of the European Economic Association*, vol. 6, no. 2–3 (April–May 2008), pp. 657–67, abstract.

10 www.forbes.com, 'China's Cash Position Swells to Record High', 15 October 2011.

Bibliography

Manuscripts

The National Archives (TNA), Kew, London
T236/1669.
T236/1756.
T236/1758.
T269/1.

Other Archives
Harry S. Truman Library and Museum, Independence, MO.
William McChesney Martin Jr Papers, St Louis Federal Reserve, Missouri History Museum, St Louis, MO, found at http://collections.mohistory.org/archive/ARC:A0990.

Published Sources

Articles, Papers etc
Beatty, Jack, 'President Coolidge's Burden', *Atlantic Magazine*, December 2003 (review of Robert E. Gilbert's *The Tormented President: Calvin Coolidge, Death, and Clinical Depression*), found on www.theatlantic.com/magazine/archive/2003/12/president-coolidges-burden/303175/.
Blackburn, Robin, 'The Subprime Crisis', *New Left Review*, March–April 2008, pp. 63–106.
Blodgett, Ralph H., 'The Impact of Total War', *American Economic Review*, vol. 36, no. 2 (May 1946), pp.126–38.
Bordo, Michael D. and White, Eugene N., 'A Tale of Two Currencies: British and French Finance during the Napoleonic Wars', *Journal of Economic History*, vol. 51, no. 2 (June 1991), pp. 303–16.
Branson, William H., 'The Trade Effects of the 1971 Currency Realignments', *Brookings Papers on Economic Activity*, vol. 3, no. 1 (1972), pp. 15–69.
Bright, John, speech delivered in Edinburgh, 5 November 1868, found on www.libertyfund.org.

Broadberry, Stephen and Howlett, Peter, *The United Kingdom during World War I: Business as Usual?*, University of Warwick, 2003.

Buchanan, Patrick, 'Yankee Utopians in a Chinese Century', 2 July 2010.

Burns, Arthur F., 'The Anguish of Central Banking', The 1979 Per Jacobsson Lecture, delivered in Belgrade, Yugoslavia, 30 September 1979.

Business China, 'Devaluing the renminbi', 2 February 1998.

Callaghan, James, Speech delivered to the Labour Party Conference, 28 September 1976, found on www.britishpoliticalspeech.org.

Carter, James E., 'Crisis of Confidence Speech', 15 July 1979, Miller Center Archive, Charlottesville.

Cassel, Gustav, 'The Restoration of the Gold Standard', *Economica*, no. 9 (November 1923), lecture delivered at the London School of Economics, 18 June 1923, pp. 171–85.

Cassis, Youssef, 'Merchant Bankers and City Aristocracy', *British Journal of Sociology*, vol. 39, no. 1 (March 1988), pp. 114–20.

China Business Review, 'China Tackles Economic Crisis with Fiscal Stimulus', vol. 36, no. 2 (March 2009).

Cohen, Jerome B., 'Fiscal Policy in Japan', *Journal of Finance*, vol. 5, no. 1 (March 1950), pp. 110–25.

Council on Foreign Relations, *What is the Fiscal Cliff?*, 12 December 2012.

Daily Mail, 19 September 1949.

Daily Telegraph, obituary for Sir Alan Walters, 5 January 2009.

Davies, Gavyn, 'How the Fed defeated President Truman to win its independence', *Financial Times*, 20 January 2012.

de Gaulle, Charles, 'Conférence de presse du 4 février, 1965', found on www.ina.fr.

Der Spiegel, 'Es gibt kein Zurück', 9 December 1991.

Der Spiegel, 'Aufbruch ins Ungewisse', 29 December 2001.

Drelichman, Mauricio and Voth, Hans-Joachim, 'Debt Sustainability in Historical Perspective: The Role of Fiscal Repression', *Journal of the European Economic Association*, vol. 6, no. 2–3 (April–May 2008), pp. 657–67.

Economist, 'Accounting for Angelo', 5 June 2009.

Economist, 'China Pedals Harder', 11 June 1998.

Economist, 'China's Currency', 12 August 1999.

Economist, 'East Asia's Whirlwind Hits the Middle Kingdom', 14 February 1998.

Economist, 'Gold: The Great Freeze', 15 December 1973.

Economist, 'Gold Shares', 8 December 1973.

Economist, 'A Heavyweight Chap, at Five Foot Two', 23 November 2006.

Economist, Lexington, 'Alan Greenspan, Fiscal Fiddler', 1 February 2001.

Economist, 'Living in a Dollar World Again', 17 November 1973.

Economist, 'The Return of the Dollar', 12 January 1974.

Economist, 'Twisted Thinking', 31 March 2011.

Economist, 'An Uncertain Weapon', 20 October 1973.

Economist, 'A Very European Crisis', 4 February 2010.

Economist, 'When an Era Trembles', 29 March 1975.

Eltis, Walter, *Lord Overstone and the Establishment of British Nineteenth-Century Monetary Orthodoxy*, Discussion Papers in Economic and Social History, no. 42, Oxford, December 2001.

Emminger, Otmar, *The D-Mark in the Conflict between Internal and External Equilibrium, 1948–1975*, Essays in International Finance, no. 122, Princeton, June 1977.

Emminger, Otmar, 'The International Role of the Dollar', Federal Reserve Bank of Kansas City, *Economic Review*, September–October 1985, pp. 17–24.

Fairchild, Fred Rogers, 'German War Finance – A Review', *American Economic Review*, vol. 12, no. 2 (June 1922), pp. 246–61.

Feldman, Gerald D., 'Industrialists, Bankers and the Problem of Unemployment in the Weimar Republic', *Central European History*, vol. 25, no. 1 (1992), pp. 76–91.

Ferguson, Niall, 'The End of Chimerica: Amicable Divorce or Currency War?', before the Committee on Ways and Means, US House of Representatives, 24 March 2010.

Ferguson, Niall, 'Political Risk and the International Bond Market between the 1848 Revolution and the Outbreak of the First World War', *Economic History Review*, vol. 59, no. 1 (2006), pp. 70–112.

Ferguson, Niall and Schularick, Moritz, '"Chimerica" and the Global Asset Market Boom', *International Finance*, vol. 10, no. 3 (2007), pp. 215–39.

Fetter, Frank W., *Business History Review*, vol. 46, no. 3 (Autumn 1972), pp. 393–5 (review of D. P. O'Brien (ed.), *The Correspondence of Lord Overstone*).

Financial Times, 'Eurozone Agrees Greek Aid Deal', 27 November 2012.

Financial Times, 'Gold at Record Levels', 9 January 1974.

Financial Times, 'Greek Bond Bet Pays Off for Hedge Fund', 18 December 2012.

Financial Times, 'The High Stakes Games, Backstabbing and Greed behind Lehman's Demise', 8 April 2010.

Financial Times, 'Nine to Seek US Backing for Gold Price Plan', 24 April 1974.

Financial Times, 'Sterling is Suspended within ERM', 17 September 1992.

Findlay, Shirras G., 'The Position and Prospects of Gold', *Economic Journal*, vol. 50, no. 198–9 (June–September 1940), pp. 207–23.

Flores, Juan-Huitzi, *Lending Booms, Underwriting and Competition: The Barings Crisis Revisited*, Working Papers in Economic History, Universidad Carlos III de Madrid, January 2007.

Gaitskell, Hugh, 'The Sterling Area', *International Affairs*, vol. 28, no. 2 (April 1952), pp. 170–6.

Goldenweiser, E. A., 'Effects of Further Gold Imports on our Banking Situation', *American Economic Review*, vol. 13, no. 1 (March 1923), pp. 84–91.

Greenspan, Alan, Economists' Forum, www.blogs.ft.com/economists, 6 April 2008.

Guardian, 'G20 Summit Marks Largest Such Gathering in a Decade', 14 November 2008.

Gutt, Camille, 'Les Accords de Bretton Woods et les institutions qui en sont issues', *Recueil de Cours*, Académie de Droit International, The Hague, 1948.

Hamilton, James D., 'Monetary Factors in the Great Depression', *Journal of Monetary Economics*, vol. 19 (1987), pp. 145–69.

Hammond, Bray, 'Jackson, Biddle, and the Bank of the United States', *Journal of Economic History*, vol. 7, no. 1 (May 1947), pp. 1–23.

Hawtrey, Ralph, 'The Gold Standard', *Economic Journal*, vol. 29, no. 116 (December 1919), pp. 428–42.

Hayashi, Fumio and Prescott, Edward C., *The 1990s in Japan: A Lost Decade*, Working Papers 607, Federal Reserve Bank of Minneapolis, Minneapolis, MN, 2000.

Heller, Walter W., 'The Role of Fiscal-Monetary Policy in German Economic Recovery', *American Economic Review*, vol. 40, no. 2 (May 1950), pp. 531–47.

Hetzel, Robert L. and Leach, Ralph F., 'The Treasury–Fed Accord: A New Narrative Account', Federal Reserve Bank of Richmond, *Economic Quarterly*, vol. 87, no. 1 (Winter 2001), pp. 33–55.

Hubbard, R. Glenn, Remarks by, *Tax Notes*, 30th Anniversary, 10 December 2002.

Independent, 'Kohl acts to quash revolt over the euro', 2 July 1997.

Irwin, Douglas A., *The Aftermath of Hamilton's 'Report on Manufactures'*, NBER Working Paper Series, no. 9943, Cambridge, MA, August 2003.

Issing, Otmar, speech delivered at the Danish Society of Financial Analysts' 25th Jubilee Copenhagen, 7 May 1999.

Johnson, Harry, 'The Gold Rush of 1968 in Retrospect and Prospect', *American Economic Review*, vol. 59, no. 2 (May 1969), pp. 344–8.

Keynes, John Maynard, 'New Taxation in the United States', *Economic Journal*, vol. 27, no. 108 (December 1917), pp. 561–5.

Klein, Ronald W., 'Japan 1979: The Second Oil Crisis', *Asian Survey*, vol. 20, no. 1 (January 1980), pp. 42–52.

Klopstock, Fred H., 'Monetary Reform in Western Germany', *Journal of Political Economy*, vol. 57, no. 4 (August 1949), pp. 277–92.

Krugman, Paul, 'The Conscience of a Liberal', a blog appearing in the *New York Times*, 31 December 2009.

Kuczynski, R. R., 'German Taxation Policy in the World War', *Journal of Political Economy*, vol. 31, no. 6 (December 1923), pp. 763–89.

Kui-yin Cheung, 'The Impact of Renminbi Devaluation on Hong Kong and China Trade', in Y. Y. Kueh (ed.), *The Political Economy of Sino-American Relations: A Greater China Perspective*, Hong Kong, 1997, pp. 163–80.

Kusihara, Kenneth K., 'Japan's Trade Position in a Changing World Market', *Review of Economics and Statistics*, vol. 37, no. 4 (November 1955), pp. 412–17.

Kusihara, Kenneth K., 'Postwar Inflation and Fiscal-Monetary Policy in Japan', *American Economic Review*, vol. 36, no. 5 (December 1946), pp. 843–54.

Laidler, David E. and Stadler, George W., 'Monetary Explanations of the Weimar Republic's Hyperinflation: Some Neglected Contributions in Contemporary German Literature', *Journal of Money, Credit and Banking*, vol. 30, no. 4 (November 1998), pp. 816–31.

Lardy, Nicholas R., 'Chinese Foreign Trade', *China Quarterly*, no. 131 (September 1992), pp. 691–720.

Layton, W. T., 'British Opinion on the Gold Standard', *Quarterly Journal for Economics*, vol. 39, no. 2 (February 1925), pp. 184–95.

Le Monde, 'Réunion des ministres des finances à la Haye: Les Douze ont progressé vers l'union monétaire', 1 December 1991.

Li, Xiao-Ming, 'China's Macroeconomic Stabilization Policies Following the Asian Financial Crisis: Success or Failure?', *Asian Survey*, vol. 40, no. 6 (November–December 2000), pp. 938–57.

Los Angeles Times, 'Fears of Dot-Com Crash, Version 2.0', 16 July 2006.

Martin Jr, William McChesney, 'Toward a World Central Bank?', Basle, Switzerland, Per Jacobsson Foundation Lecture, given 14 September 1970.

Meadville Tribune, 'Averting the Real Fiscal Cliff', 31 January 2013 (article written by Glenn Thompson, Republican US Representative for Pennsylvania's 5th District).

Mitchell, Wesley, 'Review of Lionel Robbins, *The Great Depression*', *Quarterly Journal of Economics*, vol. 49, no. 3 (May 1935), pp. 503–7.

Morrison, Wayne M. and Labonte, Marc, *China's Currency Policy: An Analysis of the Economic Issues*, CRS Report for Congress, Washington, DC, 19 December 2011.

New York Times, advertisement, 11 February 2003.

New York Times, 'China Won't Reduce Value of Currency, Official Says', 1 December 1997.

New York Times, 'Deng Xiaoping: A Political Wizard Who Put China on the Capitalist Road', 20 February 1997.

New York Times, 'Devaluation by China', 16 December 1989.

New York Times, 'The Doctrine was Not to Have One', 25 August 2005.

New York Times, 'Greece's Stumble Follows a Headlong Rush into the Euro', 5 May 2010.

New York Times, 'Greek Leader Offers Plan to Tackle Debt Crisis', 15 December 2009.

New York Times, 'Greek Opposition Leader Seeks Conference on Debt', 25 January 2013.

New York Times, 'Lehman Files for Bankruptcy; Merrill is Sold', 15 September 2008.

New York Times, 'Milton Friedman, Free Markets Theorist, Dies at 94', 16 November 2006.

New York Times, 'Nobody Understands Debt', 1 January 2012 (article written by Paul Krugman).

New York Times, 'Now Harley-Davidson is All Over the Road', 17 April 1988.

New York Times, obituary for Fred M. Vinson, 9 September 1953.

New York Times, 'The Original Subprime Crisis', 26 December 2007.

New York Times, 'Supporters of Bailout Claim Victory in Greek Election', 17 June 2012.

New York Times, 'U.S. Calls Revaluation a Good Start for Beijing', 22 July 2005.

New York Times, 'War Finance in England', 27 January 1862.

New York Times, 'Why a US Subprime Mortgage Crisis is Felt around the World', 31 August 2007.

New York Times, 25 August 2005.

New York Times, 15 October 2010.

Newby, Elisa, *The Suspension of Cash Payments as a Monetary Regime*, Centre for Dynamic Macroeconomic Analysis, Working Paper Series, University of St Andrews, February 2007, revised June 2007.

Newton, C. C. S., 'The Sterling Crisis of 1947 and the British Response to the Marshall Plan', *Economic History Review*, New Series, vol. 37, no. 3 (August 1984), pp. 391–408.

Nixon, Richard, 'Address to the Nation Outlining a New Economic Policy: "The Challenge of Peace"', 15 August 1971, found on www.presidency.ucsb.edu.

Noyes, C. Reinold, 'The Gold Inflation in the United States, 1921–1929', *American Economic Review*, vol. 20, no. 2 (January 1930), pp. 181–98.

Padoa-Schioppa, Tommaso, 'The Euro: Significance for Europe and Beyond', speech delivered to the House of Councillors Committee of Financial Affairs, Tokyo, 9 March 1999.

Paish, Sir George, 'The Rehabilitation of Europe Dependent on America', *Annals of the American Academy of Political and Social Science*, vol. 102, America and the Rehabilitation of Europe (July 1922), pp. 147–51.

Patrick, Hugh T., 'The Bank of Japan: A Case Study in the Effectiveness of Central Bank Techniques of Monetary Control', *Journal of Finance*, vol. 15, no. 4 (December 1960), pp. 573–4.

Persons, Charles E., 'Credit Expansion, 1920 to 1929, and its Lessons', *Quarterly Journal of Economics*, vol. 45, no. 1 (November 1930), pp. 94–130.

Phelps Brown, E. H. and Hopkins, Sheila V., 'Seven Centuries of the Prices of Consumables, Compared with Builders' Wage-Rates', *Economica*, New Series, vol. 23, no. 92 (November 1956), pp. 296–314.

Reagan, Ronald, 'A Time for Choosing', speech delivered in Los Angeles, 27 October 1964.

Romer, Christina D., 'Macroeconomic Policy in the 1960s: The Causes and Consequences of a Mistaken Revolution', Presented at Plenary Session A of the Economic History Association Annual Meeting, Lyndon B. Johnson Presidential Library, Austin, TX, 7 September 2007.

Ross Eckler, Albert, 'Recent Expansion of Bank Credit', *Review of Economics and Statistics*, vol. 11, no. 1 (February 1929), pp. 46–51.

Sargent, Thomas J. and Velde, François R., 'Macroeconomic Features of the French Revolution', *Journal of Political Economy*, vol. 103, no. 3 (June 1995), pp. 474–518.

Schumpeter, Joseph, *The Crisis of the Tax State*, Vienna, 1919.

Schumpeter, Joseph, 'The Instability of Capitalism', *Economic Journal*, vol. 38, no. 151 (September 1928), pp. 361–86.

Schweitzer, Arthur, 'Schacht's Regulation of Money and the Capital Markets', *Journal of Finance*, vol. 3, no. 2 (June 1948), pp. 1–18.

Seltzer, Lawrence H., 'The Changed Environment of Monetary-Banking Policy', *American Economic Review*, vol. 36, no. 2 (May 1946), pp. 65–79.

Sinclair, John F., 'America and the Debts of Europe', *Annals of the American Academy of Political and Social Science*, vol. 102, America and the Rehabilitation of Europe (July 1922), pp. 85–100.

Sloan, Lawrence H., 'The Business Prospect in the United States', *Economic Journal*, vol. 38, no. 150 (June 1928), pp. 175–92.

Solomon, Robert, 'The Birth of the Euro and its Effects', *Brown Journal of World Affairs*, vol. 6, no. 2 (Summer/Fall 1999), pp. 142–8.

Sprague, Oliver, 'The American Crisis of 1907', *Economic Journal*, vol. 18, no. 71 (September 1908), pp. 353–72.

Sprague, O. M. W., 'The Discount Policy of the Federal Reserve Banks', *American Economic Review*, vol. 11, no. 1 (March 1921), pp. 16–29.

Tallman, Ellis W., *The Panic of 1907*, Working Paper 12.28, Federal Reserve Bank of Cleveland, Cleveland, OH, November 2012.

Thatcher, Margaret, speech to Conservative Party Conference ('the lady's not for turning'), delivered 10 October 1980.

Time, '25 People to Blame for the Financial Crisis', quoted in *New York Daily News*, 13 February 2009.

Time, 'The Arab World: Oil, Power, Violence', 2 April 1973.

Time, 'Defender of the Dollar', 22 October 1979.

Time, 'Dissecting Bush's Tax-Cut Plan', 27 February 2001.

Time, 'The Economy: Nixon's Grand Design for Recovery', 30 August 1971.

Time, 'Germany: Reparations Report', 26 December 1927.

Time, Man of the Year, 'A Desert King Faces the Modern World', 6 January 1975.

Time, 'Money: De Gaulle v The Dollar', 12 February 1965.

Time, Person of the Year 2009, 'Ben Bernanke', 16 December 2009.

Time, 'Ripples from Iran', 5 February 1979.

Time, 'The Squeeze of '79', 22 October 1979.

Time, 'The US Deficit', 25 August 2009.

Time, 'Who Swiped the Surplus?', 3 September 2001.

Time, 'Zhu Rongji's Year of Living Dangerously', 12 April 1999.

Time, 1 November 1954.

Truman, Harry S., 'State of the Union, 1950', delivered on 4 January 1950, retrieved from University of Groningen website, www.let.rug.nl/usa.

Tsuru, Shigeto, 'Growth and Stability of the Postwar Japanese Economy', *American Economic Review*, vol. 51, no. 2 (May 1961), pp. 400–11.

Tsuru, Shigeto, 'Toward Economic Stability in Japan', *Public Affairs*, vol. 22, no. 4 (December 1949), pp. 357–66.

Venizelos, Evangelos, 'The Greek Debt Crisis: Prospects and Opportunities', remarks delivered at the Peterson Institute for International Economics, Washington, DC, 25 July 2011.

Viner, Jacob, 'International Finance in the Postwar World', *Journal of Political Economy*, vol. 55, no. 2 (April 1947), pp. 99–107.

Volcker, Paul A., *The Rediscovery of the Business Cycle*, The Charles C. Moskowitz Memorial Lectures, no. 19, New York, 1978.

Vries, Peer, *Public Finance in China and Britain in the Long Eighteenth Century*, London School of Economics, Working Papers no. 167/12, London, August 2012.

Wall Street Journal, 'Bankers Hope for a Reprise of "Bowie Bonds"', 23 August 2005.

Wall Street Journal, 'Big Government Conservatism', 15 August 2003.

Wall Street Journal, 'Bush Finds Party Faithful in an Ugly Mood', 9 February 2004.

Wall Street Journal, 'US Debt and the Greece Analogy', 18 June 2010 (article written by Alan Greenspan).

Washington Post, 'The Fiscal Cliff: How the House Voted', 2 January 2013.

Washington Post, review of Vicky Ward, *The Devil's Casino*, 18 April 2010.

Weyrich, Paul, 'Bush's Legacy Not Yet Written', www.frontpagemag.com, 16 January 2009.

Zakaria, Fareed, 'Can America be Fixed?: The New Crisis of Democracy', *Foreign Affairs*, vol. 92, no. 1 (January–February 2013), pp. 22–33.

Zandi, Mark M., 'Assessing President Bush's Fiscal Policies', July 2004, www.pbs.org.

Zhiang Jialin, *The Debate on China's Exchange Rate – Should or Will It be Devalued?*, Hoover Institute Essays in Public Policy, no. 112, Stanford, 2004.

Books

Adams, Brooks, *The Gold Standard: An Historical Study*, Washington, DC, 1895.

Adenauer, Konrad, *Memoirs, 1945–1953*, trans. Beate Ruhm von Oppen, London, 1966.

Aftalion, Florin, *L'Economie de la Révolution Française*, Paris, 2007.

Aliber, Robert Z., *The International Money Game*, 2nd edn, London, 1977 (1st edn 1973).

Allen, G. C., *Japan's Economic Expansion*, London, 1965.

Ambrose, Stephen, *Nixon: The Triumph of a Politician, 1962–1972*, London, 1989.

Ando, Albert, Eguchi, Hidekazu, Farmer, Roger and Suzuki, Yoshio (eds), *Monetary Policy in Our Times*, Proceedings of the First International Conference Held by the Institute for Monetary and Economic Studies of the Bank of Japan, Cambridge, MA, 1985.

Andreades, A., *History of the Bank of England, 1640 to 1903*, trans. Christabel Meredith, London, 1909.

Angell, Norman, *The Story of Money*, London, 1930.

Ashman, Charles, *Connally: The Adventures of Big Bad John*, New York, 1974.

Augar, Philip, *The Death of Gentlemanly Capitalism: The Rise and Fall of London's Investment Banks*, London, 2000.

Bagehot, Walter, *Lombard Street: A Description of the Money Market*, London, 1873.

Bahlman, Dudley (ed.), *The Diary of Sir Edward Walter Hamilton*, Hull, 1993.

Balderston, Theo, *Economics and Politics in the Weimar Republic*, London, 2002.

Balen, Malcolm, *A Very English Deceit: The Secret History of the South Sea Bubble and the First Great Financial Scandal*, London, 2002.

Bannock, Graham and Baxter, R. E., *The Penguin Dictionary of Economics*, 8th edn, London, 2011 (1st edn 1972).

Baring, Francis, *Observations on the Establishment of the Bank of England and Paper Circulation of the Country*, London, 1797.

Barnett, Correlli, *The Lost Victory: British Dreams, British Realities, 1945–1950*, London, 1995.

Bensel, Richard Franklin, *Yankee Leviathan: The Origins of Central State Authority in America, 1859–1877*, Cambridge, 1990.

Bernanke, Ben S., *Essays on the Great Depression*, Princeton, 2000.

Bishop, Matthew, *Economics: An A–Z Guide*, London, 2009.

Black, John, Hashimzade, Nigar and Miles, Gareth (eds), *Oxford Dictionary of Economics*, Oxford, 2009 (1st edn 1997).

Black, Stanley W., *A Levite among the Priests: Edward M. Bernstein and the Origins of the Bretton Woods System*, Boulder, CO, 1991.

Blake, Robert, *Disraeli*, London, 1966.

Bodin, Jean, *Response to the Paradoxes of Malestroit*, trans. and ed. Henry Tudor and R. W. Dyson, Bristol, 1997 (1st edn 1568).

Bolles, Albert S., *The Financial History of the United States, from 1774 to 1789*, 3 vols, New York, 1969 (1st edn 1879).

Boothby, Robert, *Goods or Gold? The Meaning of the Bretton Woods Agreement*, London, 1944.

Bovard, James, *The Bush Betrayal*, New York, 2004.

Boyle, Andrew, *Montagu Norman: A Biography*, London, 1967.

Braham, Lawrence J., *Zhu Rongji and the Transformation of Modern China*, Singapore, 2002.

Brand, R. H., *War and National Finance*, London, 1921.

Brandon, Henry, *The Retreat of American Power*, New York, 1972.

Braudel, Fernand, *The Mediterranean and the Mediterranean World in the Age of Philip II*, 2 vols, trans. Sian Reynolds, London, 1972 (1st French edn 1949).

Bremner, Robert P., *Chairman of the Fed: William McChesney Martin Jr and the Creation of the Modern American Financial System*, New Haven, 2004.

Brown, Gordon, *Beyond the Crisis: Overcoming the First Crisis of Globalization*, London, 2010.

Bruner, Robert F., *The Panic of 1907*, Hoboken, NJ, 2007.

Bullock, Charles J., *Essays on the Monetary History of the United States*, New York, 1900.

Burk, Kathleen, *Britain, America and the Sinews of War, 1914–1918*, London, 1985.

Burke, Edmund, *Reflections on the Revolution in France*, New York, 2006 (1st edn, London, 1790).

Burns, Arthur, *Inside the Nixon Administration: The Secret Diary of Arthur Burns, 1969–1974*, ed. Robert Ferrell, Lawrence, KS, 2010.

Cairncross, Alec and Eichengreen, Barry, *Sterling in Decline: The Devaluations of 1931, 1949 and 1967*, Oxford, 1983.

Callender, G. S., *Selections from the Economic History of the United States, 1765–1860*, Boston, 1909.

Campbell, John, *Margaret Thatcher*, vol. 1: *The Grocer's Daughter*, London, 2000.

Campbell, John, *Margaret Thatcher*, vol. 2: *The Iron Lady*, London, 2003.

Camplin, Jamie, *The Rise of the Plutocrats: Wealth and Power in Edwardian England*, London, 1978.

Cannon, Lou, *President Reagan: The Role of a Lifetime*, New York, 1991.

Cargill, Thomas F., Hutchinson, Michael M. and Takatoshi, Ito, *The Political Economy of Japanese Monetary Policy*, Cambridge, MA, 1997.

Carswell, John, *The South Sea Bubble*, Dover, NH, 1993 (1st edn, London, 1960).

Cassis, Youssef, *City Bankers, 1890–1914*, trans. Margaret Rocques, Cambridge, 1994.

Chancellor, Edward, *Devil Take the Hindmost: A History of Financial Speculation*, London, 1999.

Chandaman, C. D., *The English Public Revenue, 1660–1688*, Oxford, 1975.

Chernow, Ron, *The House of Morgan: An American Banking Dynasty and the Rise of Modern Finance*, New York, 1990.

Chernow, Ron, *Titan: The Life of John D. Rockefeller Sr*, New York, 1998.

Churchill, Winston, *The Speeches of Winston Churchill*, ed. David Cannadine, London, 1990.

Clapham, Sir John, *The Bank of England*, 2 vols, Cambridge, 2008 (1st edn 1944).

Clarke, Peter, *Keynes: The Twentieth Century's Most Influential Economist*, London, 2009.

Clay, Lucius D., *Decision in Germany*, London, 1950.

Clay, Lucius D., *The Papers of General Lucius D. Clay: Germany, 1945–1949*, ed. Jane Edward Smith, 2 vols, Bloomington, 1974.

Clissold, Stephen, *Conquistador: The Life of Don Pedro Sarmiento de Gamboa*, London, 1954.

Coggan, Philip, *Paper Promises: Money, Debt and the New World Order*, London, 2011.

Cooke, Jacob E., *The Reports of Alexander Hamilton*, New York, 1964.

Correspondents of the *Economist*, *Consider Japan*, London, 1963.

Coxe, William, *Memoirs of the Life and Administration of Sir Robert Walpole, Earl of Orford*, 3 vols, London, 1798.

Craig, Malcolm, *How to Invest in Gold*, Cambridge, 1991.

Cray, Edward, *General of the Army: George C. Marshall, Soldier and Statesman*, New York, 1990.

Crouzet, François, *La Grande Inflation: La Monnaie en France de Louis XVI à Napoléon*, Paris, 1993.

Dallek, Robert, *Lyndon B. Johnson: Portrait of a President*, New York, 2004.

Darling, Alistair, *Back from the Brink*, London, 2011.

Davidson, Paul, *John Maynard Keynes*, Basingstoke, 2007.

Davies, Glyn, *A History of Money*, Cardiff, 2002 (1st edn 1994).

de Calonne, Charles Alexandre, *Considerations on the Present and Future State of France*, trans. from the original French, London, 1791.

Delors, Jacques, *Mémoires*, Paris, 2004.

Dewey, Davis Rich, *Financial History of the United States*, New York, 1903.

Dickson, P. G. M., *The Financial Revolution in England: A Study in the Development of Public Credit*, London, 1967.

Doyle, William, *Origins of the French Revolution*, 3rd edn, Oxford, 1999 (1st edn 1980).

Duncan, Richard, *The Dollar Crisis: Causes, Consequences, Cures*, Singapore, 2005 (1st edn 2003).

Duncan, Richard, *The New Depression: The Breakdown of the Paper Money Economy*, Singapore, 2012.

Eckstein, Otto, *The Great Recession with a Postscript on Stagflation*, Amsterdam, 1978.

Eichengreen, Barry, *Exorbitant Privilege: The Rise and Fall of the Dollar*, Oxford, 2011.

Eichengreen, Barry, *Globalizing Capital: A History of the International Monetary System*, Princeton, 1996.

Eichengreen, Barry, *Golden Fetters: The Gold Standard and the Great Depression, 1919–1939*, Oxford, 1992.

Einzig, Paul, *Bankers, Statesmen and Economists*, London, 1935.

Elliott, J. H., *Empires of the Atlantic World: Britain and Spain in America, 1492–1830*, New Haven, 2006.

Elliott, J. H., *Imperial Spain, 1469–1716*, London, 1963.

Endo, Ken, *The Presidency of the European Commission under Jacques Delors: The Politics of Shared Leadership*, Basingstoke, 1999.

Endres, Anthony M., *Great Architects of International Finance: The Bretton Woods Era*, Abingdon, 2005.

Feavearyear, Sir Albert, *The Pound Sterling: A History of English Money*, Oxford, 1931.

Feis, Herbert, *Europe: The World's Banker, 1870–1914*, New York, 1930.

Ferguson, Niall, *The Cash Nexus*, London, 2001.

Ferguson, Niall, *The Pity of War*, London, 1998.

Fetter, Frank Whitson, *The Development of British Monetary Orthodoxy: 1797–1875*, Cambridge, MA, 1965.

Finlayson, W. F., *A Report on the Case of the Queen v Gurney and others in the court of Queen's Bench*, London, 1870.

Fitzgerald, Terry J., *Money Growth and Inflation: How Long is the Long-Run?*, Federal Reserve Bank of Cleveland, Cleveland, OH, 1999.

Fleming, Ian, *Goldfinger*, London, 1959.

Forbes, John Douglas, *J. P. Morgan Jr*, Charlottesville, 1981.

Forbes, John Douglas, *Stettinius Sr: Portrait of a Morgan Partner*, Charlottesville, 1974.

Francis, John, *Chronicles and Characters of the Stock Exchange*, London, 2001 (reprint of the 1850 US edn; 1st edn 1849).

Francis, John, *History of the Bank of England*, 2 vols, London, 1848.

Friedman, Milton, *Free to Choose*, London, 1980.

Friedman, Milton, *Money Mischief: Episodes in Monetary History*, New York, 1992.

Friedman, Milton and Schwartz, Anna Jacobson, *The Great Contraction, 1929–1933*, Princeton, 2007.

Friedman, Milton and Schwartz, Anna Jacobson, *A Monetary History of the United States, 1867–1960*, Princeton, 1963.

Gaddis, John Lewis, *The Cold War*, London, 2005.

Galbraith, John Kenneth, *The Great Crash of 1929*, New York, 1954.

Galbraith, John Kenneth, *Money: Whence It Came, Where It Went*, 2nd edn, London, 1995 (1st edn 1975).

Galsworthy, John, *The Forsyte Saga*, Oxford, 1995 (1st edn 1906–21).

Gash, Norman, *Mr Secretary Peel: The Life of Sir Robert Peel to 1830*, London, 1961.

Gilmour, Ian, *Dancing with Dogma*, London, 1993.

Giordano, Francesco and Persaud, Sharda, *The Political Economy of Monetary Union: Towards the Euro*, London, 1998.

Gladwell, Malcolm, *Outliers: The Story of Success*, New York, 2008.

Gordon, John Steel, *The Great Game: A History of Wall Street*, New York, 1999.

Grady, Henry F., *British War Finance, 1914–1919*, New York, 1927.

Graham, Benjamin and Dodd, David L., *Security Analysis: Principles and Technique*, 3rd edn, New York, 1951 (1st edn 1934).

Greenspan, Alan, *The Age of Turbulence: Adventures in a New World*, New York, 2007.

Grubb, Farley, *The Continental Dollar: How Much was Issued and What Happened to It?*, Cambridge, MA, 2007.

Haldeman, H. R., *The Haldeman Diaries*, New York, 1994.

Hall, Robert, *The Robert Hall Diaries*, ed. Alec Cairncross, London, 1989.

Hamilton, Alexander, *Report on the Subject of Manufactures, made in his capacity of Secretary of the Treasury on Fifth of December, 1791*, 6th edn, Philadelphia, 1827.

Hamilton, Earl, *American Treasure and the Price Revolution in Spain, 1501–1650*, Cambridge, MA, 1934.

Hammond, Bray, *Banks and Politics in America: From the Revolution to the Civil War*, Princeton, 1957.

Hammond, Bray, *Sovereignty and an Empty Purse: Banks and Politics in the Civil War*, Princeton, 1970.

Harris, S. E., *The Assignats*, Cambridge, MA, 1930.

Harrod, Roy, *The Life of John Maynard Keynes*, London, 1951.

Hawtrey, R. G., *Bretton Woods for Better or Worse*, London, 1946.

Heckscher, Eli, *Mercantilism*, 2 vols, 1st English edn, London, 1935.

Helfferich, Karl, *Der Weltkrieg*, 2 vols, Berlin, 1919.

Hemming, John, *The Conquest of the Incas*, London, 1970.

Hicks, Frederick C., *High Finance in the Sixties*, New Haven, 1929.

Hirst, Francis W., *The Stock Exchange: A Short Study of Investment and Speculation*, London, 1911.

Howe, Geoffrey, *Conflict of Loyalty*, London, 1994.

Humphrey, George M., *The Basic Papers of George M. Humphrey as Secretary of the Treasury, 1953–1957*, Cleveland, OH, 1965.

Hurd, Douglas, *Robert Peel*, London, 2007.

Hyman, Louis, *Debtor Nation: The History of America in Red Ink*, Princeton, 2011.

IMF, *World Economic Outlook*, April 2012.

Issing, Otmar, *The Birth of the Euro*, trans. from the original German by Nigel Hulbert, Cambridge, 2008.

James, Harold, *The German Slump: Politics and Economics, 1924–1936*, Oxford, 1986.

Japhet, Saemy, *Recollections from my Business Life*, London, 1931.

Johnson, Chalmers, *MITI and the Japanese Miracle: The Growth of Industrial Policy, 1925–1975*, Stanford, 1982.

Kennedy, David, *Freedom from Fear: The American People in Depression and War, 1929–1945*, Oxford, 1999.

Kennedy, Paul, *The Rise and Fall of the Great Powers*, London, 1988.

Keynes, John Maynard, *Collected Writings*, 30 vols, London and Cambridge, 1971–89.

Keynes, John Maynard, *The Economic Consequences of the Peace*, London, 1919.

Keynes, John Maynard, *Essays in Persuasion*, London, 1931.

Keynes, John Maynard, *General Theory of Employment, Interest and Money*, London, 2007 (1st edn 1936).

Keynes, John Maynard, *A Treatise on Money*, 2 vols, London, 1930.

Kissinger, Henry, *The White House Years*, New York, 1979.

Kissinger, Henry, *Years of Upheaval*, London, 1982.

Knox, Ronald, *Patrick Shaw Stewart*, London, 1920.

Krass, Peter, *Carnegie*, Hoboken, NJ, 2002.

Krugman, Paul, *End This Depression Now!*, London, 2011.

Krugman, Paul, *The Return of Depression Economics*, London, 1999.

Krugman, Paul, *The Return of Depression Economics and the Crisis of 2008*, London, 2008.

Kurtzman, Joel, *The Death of Money: How the Electronic Economy Has Destabilized the World's Markets and Created Financial Chaos*, New York, 1993.

Kynaston, David, *The City of London: A Club No More, 1945–2000*, London, 2001.

Kynaston, David, *The City of London: Golden Years, 1890–1914*, London, 1995.

Kynge, James, *China Shakes the World: The Rise of a Hungry Nation*, London, 2006.

Lacour-Gayet, Robert, *Calonne: Financier, réformateur, contre-révolutionnaire, 1734–1802*, Paris, 1963.

Lamont, Norman, *In Office*, London, 1999.

Law, John, *Money and Trade Considered, with a Proposal for Supplying the Nation with Money*, Edinburgh, 1705.

Lawson, Nigel, *The View from No. 11*, London, 1992.

Lawson, W. R., *British War Finance, 1914–1915*, London, 1915.

Leith-Ross, Sir Frederick, *Money Talks: Fifty Years of International Finance*, London, 1968.

Lewis, Michael, *The Big Short: Inside the Doomsday Machine*, London, 2010.

Lewis, Michael, *Boomerang*, London, 2011.

Lincoln, Abraham, *Collected Works of Abraham Lincoln*, vol. 3, Ann Arbor, MI, 1953, found on www.umich.edu.

Lovett, A. W., *Early Habsburg Spain, 1517–1598*, Oxford, 1986.

Luther, Hans, *Politiker ohne Partei*, Stuttgart, 1960.

Lynn, Matthew, *Bust: Greece, the Euro and the Sovereign Debt Crisis*, London, 2011.

McNeil, William C., *American Money and the Weimar Republic: Economics and Politics on the Eve of the Great Depression*, New York, 1986.

Maddison, Charles, *French Inter-War Monetary Policy: Understanding the Gold Bloc*, San Domenico, 1994.

Maitland, F. W., *Domesday Book and Beyond*, Cambridge, 1907.

Major, John, *The Autobiography*, London, 2000.

Mallet, Bernard, *British Budgets, 1887–88 to 1912–13*, London, 1913.

Manchester, William, *American Caesar: Douglas MacArthur, 1880–1964*, London, 1979.

Marshall, Matt, *The Bank: The Birth of Europe's Central Bank and the Rebirth of Europe's Power*, London, 1999.

Marx, Karl, *Capital*, 3 vols, London, 1974 (1st German edn 1867).

Matusow, Allen J., *Nixon's Economy: Booms, Busts, Dollars, and Votes*, Lawrence, KS, 1998.

Mayhew, Nicholas, *Sterling: The History of a Currency*, London, 1999.

Meltzer, Allan H., *A History of the Federal Reserve*, vol. 1: *1913–1951*, Chicago, 2003.

Meltzer, Allan H., *A History of the Federal Reserve*, vol. 2, Book 1: *1951–1969*, Chicago, 2009.

Meltzer, Allan H., *A History of the Federal Reserve*, vol. 2, Book 2: *1970–1986*, Chicago, 2009.

Metzler, Mark, *Lever of Empire: The International Gold Standard and the Crisis of Liberalism in Prewar Japan*, Berkeley, 2006.

Mitchell, B. R., *British Historical Statistics*, Cambridge, 1988.

Moggridge, D. E., *Keynes*, London, 1976.

Murphy, Antoin E., *John Law: Economic Theorist and Policy-Maker*, Oxford, 1997.

Murphy, Antoin E., *Richard Cantillon: Entrepreneur and Economist*, Oxford, 1986.

Neikirk, William R., *Volcker: Portrait of the Money Man*, New York, 1987.

Noyes, Alexander D., *The War Period of American Finance, 1908–1925*, New York, 1926.

O'Brien, D. P. (ed.), *The Correspondence of Lord Overstone*, 3 vols, Cambridge, 1971.

O'Brien, Denis P., *The Development of Monetary Economics*, Cheltenham, 2007.

O'Dochartaigh, Pol, *Germany since 1945*, Basingstoke, 2004.

Overstone, Lord, *Tracts and Other Publications on Metallic and Paper Currency*, London, 1857.

Parker, Charles Stuart (ed.), *Sir Robert Peel from his Private Correspondence*, 3 vols, London, 1891.

Parker, Geoffrey, *The Military Revolution: Military Innovation and the Rise of the West, 1500–1800*, Cambridge, 1988.

Paul, Ron and Lehrman, Lewis, *The Case for Gold*, Washington, DC, 1982.

Paulson, Hank, *On the Brink: Inside the Race to Stop the Collapse of the Global Financial System*, New York, 2010.

Peel, Sir Robert, *Speeches on the Renewal of the Bank Charter and the Laws of Currency and Banking*, London, 1844.

Phelps, Clyde William, *The Foreign Expansion of American Banks: American Branch Banking Abroad*, New York, 1927.

Pimlott, Ben, *Hugh Dalton*, London, 1985.

Prescott, W. H., *History of the Conquest of Peru*, London, 2002 (1st edn 1847).

Rabinowicz, Oskar K., *Sir Solomon de Medina*, London, 1974.

Rees, David, *Henry Dexter White: A Study in Paradox*, London, 1973.

Reinhart, Carmen M. and Rogoff, Kenneth S., *This Time is Different: Eight Centuries of Financial Folly*, Princeton, 2009.

Report from the Committee of Secrecy on the Bank of England Charter, with the minutes of evidence, London, 1832.

Report to the Congress of the Commission on the Role of Gold in the Domestic and International Monetary Systems, March 1982, Washington, DC, 1982.

Richards, R. D., *The First Fifty Years of the Bank of England*, The Hague, 1934.

Richardson, Heather Cox, *The Greatest Nation of the Earth: Republican Economic Policies during the Civil War*, Cambridge, MA, 1997.

Rickards, James, *Currency Wars: The Making of the Next Global Crisis*, New York, 2011.

Robbins, Lionel, *The Great Depression*, London, 1934.

Robinson, Jeffrey, *Yamani: The Inside Story*, London, 1988.

Rockefeller, David, *Memoirs*, New York, 2002.

Schacht, Hjalmar, *76 Jahre meines Lebens*, Bad Wörishofen, 1953.

Schlesinger Jr, Arthur M., *The Age of Jackson*, London, 1946.

Schlichter, Detlev S., *Paper Money Collapse: The Folly of Elastic Money and the Coming Monetary Breakdown*, London, 2011.

Shaffer, Peter, *The Royal Hunt of the Sun: A Play Concerning the Conquest of Peru*, London, 1981 (1st edn 1964).

Shakespeare, William, *Titus Andronicus*, ed. Jonathan Bate, London, 1995.

Shaw, George Bernard, *The Intelligent Woman's Guide to Socialism and Capitalism*, London, 1929 (1st edn 1928).

Shelley, Percy Bysshe, *Poetical Works*, ed. Thomas Hutchinson, London, 1905.

Simon, William E., *A Time for Truth*, New York, 1978.

Sisson, C. H., *The Case of Walter Bagehot*, London, 1972.

Skidelsky, Robert, *John Maynard Keynes: Fighting for Britain, 1937–1946*, London, 2000.

Skidelsky, Robert, *John Maynard Keynes: Hopes Betrayed, 1883–1920*, London, 1983.

Slivinski, Stephen, *Buck Wild: How Republicans Broke the Bank and Became the Party of Big Government*, Nashville, 2006.

Sloan, Alfred, *My Life with General Motors*, London, 1986 (1st edn 1963).

Smith, Adam, *An Inquiry into the Nature and Causes of the Wealth of Nations*, London, 2007 (1st edn 1776).

Smith, Vera C., *The Rationale of Central Banking*, London, 1936.

Sobel, Robert, *The Last Bull Market: Wall Street in the 1960s*, New York, 1980.

Sobel, Robert, *The Worldly Economists*, New York, 1980.

Sorkin, Andrew Ross, *Too Big to Fail: Inside the Battle to Save Wall Street*, London, 2009.

Soros, George, *The Alchemy of Finance*, New York, 1994 (1st edn 1987).

Soros, George, with Wien, Byron and Koenen, Krisztina, *Soros on Soros: Staying Ahead of the Curve*, New York, 1995.

Stacey, Nicholas A. H., *English Accountancy: A Study in Social and Economic History, 1800–1954*, London, 1954.

Stein, Herbert, *The Fiscal Revolution in America*, Chicago, 1969.

Stein, Herbert, *Presidential Economics: The Making of Economic Policy from Roosevelt to Reagan and Beyond*, 2nd edn, Washington, DC, 1988 (1st edn 1986).

Stockman, David, *The Triumph of Politics: Why the Reagan Revolution Failed*, Boston, 1987.

Tatewaki, Kazuo, *Banking and Finance in Japan: An Introduction to the Tokyo Market*, London, 1991.

Taussig, F. W., *The Tariff History of the United States*, 6th edn, New York, 1914 (1st edn 1888).

Taylor III, Alan, *Sixty to Zero: An Inside Look at the Collapse of General Motors – and the Detroit Auto Industry*, New Haven, 2010.

Taylor, A. J. P., *The Origins of the Second World War*, London, 1961.

Taylor, A. J. P., *From the Boer War to the Cold War: Essays on Twentieth-Century Europe*, London, 1995.

Thatcher, Margaret, *The Downing Street Years*, London, 1993.

Thomas, Hugh, *The Golden Age: The Spanish Empire of Charles V*, London, 2010.

Thomas, Hugh, *Rivers of Gold*, London, 2010 (1st edn 2003).

Tooze, Adam, *Wages of Destruction: The Making and Breaking of the Nazi Economy*, London, 2006.

Tracy, James D., *The Founding of the Dutch Republic: War, Finance, Politics in Holland, 1572–1588*, Oxford, 2008.

Tracy, James D. (ed.), *The Political Economy of Merchant Empires*, Cambridge, 1991.

Tripp, Charles, *A History of Iraq*, 3rd edn, Cambridge, 2007 (1st edn 2000).

Tsuru, Shigeto, *The Economic Development of Modern Japan: The Selected Essays of Shigeto Tsuru*, Aldershot, 1995.

Tsuru, Shigeto, *Japan's Capitalism: Creative Defeat and Beyond*, Cambridge, 1993.

Vilar, Pierre, *A History of Gold and Money, 1450 to 1920*, London 1976 (1st edn 1960).

Vilches, Elvira, *New World Gold: Cultural Anxiety and Monetary Disorder in Early Modern Spain*, Chicago, 2010.

Vogel, Ezra F., *Deng Xiaoping and the Transformation of China*, Cambridge, MA, 2011.

Volcker, Paul A. and Gyohten, Toyoo, *Changing Fortunes: The World's Money and the Threat to American Leadership*, New York, 1992.

Warburton, Peter, *Debt and Delusion: Central Bank Follies That Threaten Economic Disaster*, London, 2000.

Werner, Richard, *Princes of the Yen: Japan's Central Bankers and the Transformation of the Economy*, Armonk, NY, 2003.

Williams, John H., *Post-War Monetary Plans and Other Essays*, Oxford, 1949.

Williams, Jonathan (ed.), *Money: A History*, London, 1997.

Withers, Hartley, *War and Lombard Street*, London, 1915.

Wood, John Philip, *Memoirs of the life of John Law of Lauriston, including a detailed account of the rise, progress, and termination of the Mississippi System*, Edinburgh, 1824.

Wood, Michael, *Conquistadors*, London, 2000.

Wueschner, Silvano A., *Charting Twentieth-Century Monetary Policy: Herbert Hoover and Benjamin Strong, 1917–1927*, Westport, CT, 1999.

Yergin, Daniel, *The Prize: The Epic Quest for Oil, Money, and Power*, New York, 1991.

Yergin, Daniel and Stanislaw, Joseph, *The Commanding Heights: The Battle between Government and the Marketplace That is Remaking the Modern World*, New York, 1998.

Young, Hugo, *One of Us: A Biography of Margaret Thatcher*, London, 1989.

Yupanqui, Titu Cusi, *History of How the Spaniards Arrived in Peru*, trans. with an introduction by Catherine Julien, Indianapolis, 2006.

Zhu Rongji, *Zhu Rongji Meets the Press*, Hong Kong, 2011.

Websites

www.bbc.co.uk.
www.blogs.ft.com/economists.
www.britishpoliticalspeech.org.
www.businessweek.com.
www.cbo.gov (website of the Congressional Budget Office).
www.chinadaily.com.cn.
www.cnn.com.
www.fhwa.dot.gov.
www.forbes.com.
www.frontpagemag.com.
www.ina.fr.
www.kitco.com.
www.lbma.org.uk.
www.let.rug.nl/usa.
www.newyorkfed.org.
www.pbs.org.
www.presidency.ucsb.edu.
www.reagan.utexas.edu.
www.treasurydirect.gov.
www.usgovernmentspending.com.
www.xinhua.net.

Acknowledgements

As is to be expected, while writing this book I have incurred many debts of gratitude. I would especially like to thank, in no particular order, the staff at the British Library, the National Archives and the House of Commons library, who all behaved in a thoroughly efficient and professional manner in providing me assistance. I would also like to thank Anna Simpson and Michael Fishwick at Bloomsbury, as well as Peter James, my excellent copy editor. I am also immensely grateful to my agent, Georgina Capel, for her unstinting help and support over the many years that it took to conceive, research and write this book.

Index

A NOTE ON THE AUTHOR

Kwasi Kwarteng was born in London to Ghanaian parents. He
has a PhD in History from Cambridge University and was
elected as the Member of Parliament for Spelthorne in Surrey.
His first book, *Ghosts of Empire*, was published to critical
acclaim in 2011.

The text of this book is set in Adobe Garamond. It is one of several versions of Garamond based on the designs of Claude Garamond. It is thought that Garamond based his font on Bembo, cut in 1495 by Francesco Griffo in collaboration with the Italian printer Aldus Manutius. Garamond types were first used in books printed in Paris around 1532. Many of the present-day versions of this type are based on the *Typi Academiae* of Jean Jannon cut in Sedan in 1615.

Claude Garamond was born in Paris in 1480. He learned how to cut type from his father and by the age of fifteen he was able to fashion steel punches the size of a pica with great precision. At the age of sixty he was commissioned by King Francis I to design a Greek alphabet; for this he was given the honourable title of royal type founder. He died in 1561.